Petals Plucked from Sunny Climes

LIBRARY PRESS@UF

AN IMPRINT OF UF PRESS AND
GEORGE A. SMATHERS LIBRARIES

Petals Plucked from Sunny Climes

SILVIA SUNSHINE

LibraryPress@UF
GAINESVILLE, FLORIDA

Cover: Map of the West Indies, published in Philadelphia, 1806. From the Caribbean Maps collection in the University of Florida Digital Collections at the George A. Smathers Libraries.

Reissued 2017 by LibraryPress@UF on behalf of the University of Florida
This work is licensed under a Creative Commons Attribution-Noncommercial-No Derivative Works 4.0 Unported License. To view a copy of this license, visit https://creativecommons.org/licenses/by-nc-nd/4.0/. You are free to electronically copy, distribute, and transmit this work if you attribute authorship. Please contact the University Press of Florida (http://upress.ufl.edu) to purchase print editions of the work. You must attribute the work in the manner specified by the author or licensor (but not in any way that suggests that they endorse you or your use of the work). For any reuse or distribution, you must make clear to others the license terms of this work. Any of the above conditions can be waived if you receive permission from the University Press of Florida. Nothing in this license impairs or restricts the author's moral rights.

ISBN 978-1-947372-50-4 (pbk.)
ISBN 978-1-947372-51-1 (ePub)

LibraryPress@UF is an imprint of the University of Florida Press.

LIBRARY PRESS@UF

**AN IMPRINT OF UF PRESS AND
GEORGE A. SMATHERS LIBRARIES**

University of Florida Press
15 Northwest 15th Street
Gainesville, FL 32611-2079
http://upress.ufl.edu

The Florida and the Caribbean Open Books Series

In 2016, the University Press of Florida, in collaboration with the George A. Smathers Libraries of the University of Florida, received a grant from the National Endowment for the Humanities and the Andrew W. Mellon Foundation, under the Humanities Open Books program, to republish books related to Florida and the Caribbean and to make them freely available through an open access platform. The resulting list of books is the Florida and the Caribbean Open Books Series published by the LibraryPress@UF in collaboration with the University of Florida Press, an imprint of the University Press of Florida. A panel of distinguished scholars has selected the series titles from the UPF list, identified as essential reading for scholars and students.

The series is composed of titles that showcase a long, distinguished history of publishing works of Latin American and Caribbean scholarship that connect through generations and places. The breadth and depth of the list demonstrates Florida's commitment to transnational history and regional studies. Selected reprints include Daniel Brinton's *A Guide-Book of Florida and the South* (1869), Cornelis Goslinga's *The Dutch in the Caribbean and on the Wild Coast, 1580–1680* (1971), and Nelson Blake's *Land into Water—Water into Land* (1980). Also of note are titles from the Bicentennial Floridiana Facsimile Series. The series, published in 1976 in commemoration of America's bicentenary, comprises twenty-five books regarded as "classics," out-of-print works that needed to be in more libraries and readers' bookcases, including Sidney Lanier's *Florida: Its Scenery, Climate, and History* (1876) and Silvia Sunshine's *Petals Plucked from Sunny Climes* (1880).

Today's readers will benefit from having free and open access to these works, as they provide unique perspectives on the historical scholarship on Florida and the Caribbean and serve as a foundation upon which today's researchers can build.

Visit LibraryPress@UF and the Florida and the Caribbean Open Books Series at http://ufdc.ufl.edu/librarypress.

Florida and the Caribbean Open Books Series Project Members

LIBRARYPRESS@UF

Judith C. Russell
Laurie N. Taylor
Brian W. Keith
Chelsea Dinsmore
Haven Hawley

EDITORIAL ADVISORY BOARD

Gary R. Mormino
David R. Colburn
Patrick J. Reakes

UNIVERSITY OF FLORIDA PRESS

Meredith M. Babb
Linda Bathgate
Michele Fiyak-Burkley
Romi Gutierrez
Larry Leshan
Anja Jimenez
Marisol Amador
Valerie Melina
Jane Pollack
Danny Duffy
Nichole Manosh
Erika Stevens

This book is reissued as part of the Humanities Open Books program, funded by a grant from the National Endowment for the Humanities and the Andrew W. Mellon Foundation.

BICENTENNIAL COMMISSION OF FLORIDA.

Governor Reubin O'D. Askew, *Honorary Chairman*
Lieutenant Governor J. H. Williams, *Chairman*
Harold W. Stayman, Jr., *Vice Chairman*
William R. Adams, *Executive Director*

Dick J. Batchelor, Orlando
Johnnie Ruth Clarke, St. Petersburg
A. H. "Gus" Craig, St. Augustine
James J. Gardener, Fort Lauderdale
Jim Glisson, Tavares
Mattox Hair, Jacksonville
Thomas L. Hazouri, Jacksonville
Ney C. Landrum, Tallahassee
Mrs. Raymond Mason, Jacksonville
Carl C. Mertins, Jr., Pensacola
Charles E. Perry, Miami
W. E. Potter, Orlando
F. Blair Reeves, Gainesville
Richard R. Renick, Coral Gables
Jane W. Robinson, Cocoa
Mrs. Robert L. Shevin, Tallahassee
Don Shoemaker, Miami
Mary L. Singleton, Jacksonville
Bruce A. Smathers, Tallahassee
Alan Trask, Fort Meade

Bicentennial Commission.

Edward J. Trombetta, Tallahassee
Ralph D. Turlington, Tallahassee
William S. Turnbull, Orlando
Robert Williams, Tallahassee
Lori Wilson, Merritt Island

GENERAL EDITOR'S PREFACE.

ANONYMITY seems to have been almost a fetish with Abbie M. Brooks, alias Silvia Sunshine, authoress of *Petals Plucked from Sunny Climes*, which is being published as one of the volumes in the Bicentennial Floridiana Facsimile Series. So complete is the mystery of her background and the incidents of her life, that Richard A. Martin, who has written the introduction to this facsimile edition, after much diligent research was able to find almost nothing at all about Abbie M. Brooks. It is not known whether she was a professional writer or a journalist, where she was born, or anything about her education or her personal life. The wall of mystery which she built in the nineteenth century remains intact to the present time. That she was something of a traveler is suggested by her writing; she obviously spent time both in Cuba and in Spain. She worked in the Archives of the Indies in Seville, Spain, where she studied original documents covering Florida history from the 1500s to the beginning of the nineteenth century. Assisted by an archives employee, she translated many of these documents, and later published some of these in a book entitled *The Unwritten History of Old St. Augustine*. Many of Miss Brooks' original transcripts are in the Library of Congress.

Obviously Abbie Brooks lived and worked in Florida, and traveled throughout the state. How else could she have written a travel book as comprehensive as *Petals Plucked from Sunny Climes* without having visited the scenes which she describes? She could not have written so personally about people without observation. *Petals* conducts the reader on a tour of Florida, from Fernandina south to Key West, and then along the Gulf Coast into the Florida Panhandle and on to Pensacola. Miss Brooks obviously had charted this route herself. How she traveled or when is not known. Whether it was one continuous trip, or whether she had visited different places at different times is not revealed. There is no mystery about the fact that Miss Brooks saw the places which she describes, and she observed the people whom she writes about. She had an eye for the colorful and the unusual; she visited out-of-the-way places like cracker cabins and a cigar factory in Key West; she obviously had sailed on an Oklawaha River steamboat. Miss Brooks lived for a time in St. Augustine; her book is filled with many descriptive passages of that ancient city.

If we do not know very much of Miss Brooks as a person, we do know her as a writer. In his introduction, Richard Martin notes, "though she does not always wield an incisive pen, she frequently demonstrates a journalist's mastery for observing detail and communicating the sense of it with a minimum of words." According to him, *Petals* has "enduring value"; Martin ranks it "among the classics of its kind in Florida literature." It was one of the many travel books about Florida published during the second half of the nineteenth century, particularly in the years after the Civil War. The New South had come into being during the postwar era. This was also the time when Florida was "rediscovered." The new discoverers were for the most part wealthy northerners who looked upon Florida as a new kind of Eden—sunshiny days, blue skies, tropical fruits and flowers, white sand beaches, and lush scenery. Even before the Civil War, at a time when tuberculosis and consumption claimed many lives, affluent northerners came to Florida, hoping to regain their health and prolong their lives. Jacksonville and St. Augustine were the Meccas for these visitors.

Celebrities like Robert E. Lee, Ulysses S. Grant, Mary Todd Lincoln, and Presidents Chester Arthur and Grover Cleveland toured Florida. Harriet Beecher Stowe lived with her family in Mandarin on the St. Johns River, not far from Jacksonville, and she described the years in Florida as among the happiest of her life. Later, millionaires like Henry Morrison Flagler, using both wealth and creative genius, built great resorts like Palm Beach, with lavish hotels and private residences for visitors. Travel and guide books were in demand. Some, such as *Florida: Its Scenery, Climate, and History*, by Sidney Lanier, were commissioned by a railroad. Others, like Rufus King Sewall's *Sketches of St. Augustine*, were subsidized by owners of popular tourist hotels. Besides the railroad companies, promoters, and developers, who sent out printed matter designed to sell land to prospective settlers, many books, such as *Petals Plucked from Sunny Climes*, appeared under private auspices. Interest in Florida was widespread and growing, and the sales of these books, pamphlets, and descriptive articles were good. Americans had expressed a curiosity about Florida; writers like Abbie Brooks helped to fulfill that need.

Petals Plucked from Sunny Climes is one of the twenty-five, rare, out-of-print volumes being republished by the Florida Bicentennial Commission. This series of facsimiles, covering all periods of Florida's long and rich history, is part of the Commission's research and publications program. Each of the facsimile volumes includes an introduction written by a well-known authority in Florida history. These facsimiles, published by the University Presses of Florida, Gainesville, are available at moderate prices for libraries, scholars, researchers, and all those interested in Florida's past.

The twenty-seven-member Florida Bicentennial Commission was created by the state legislature in 1970 to plan Florida's participation in the celebration of the two hundredth anniversary of the American Revolution. Governor Reubin O'D. Askew serves as honorary chairman of the Commission. Members of the legislature, representatives of state agencies, and ten public members appointed by the governor make up the Commission. Executive offices are in Tallahassee.

Richard A. Martin, a native of New York, was a graduate of the University of Florida and a former teacher in Marion County public schools. He has written several books on Jacksonville and Florida. These include *The City Makers; St. Luke's Hospital: A Century of Service; Eternal Spring: Man's 10,000 Years of History at Florida's Silver Springs;* and *Consolidation: Jacksonville–Duval County: The Dynamics of Urban Political Reform.* He edited the University of Florida's quadricentennial edition of T. Frederick Davis' *History of Jacksonville*. He recently completed a history of Jacksonville in the antebellum and Civil War period. Mr. Martin's articles have appeared in newspapers, magazines, and professional and scholarly journals. He was the recipient, in 1974, of the Arthur W. Thompson Memorial Prize in Florida history for an article on Jacksonville during the Civil War, published that year in the *Florida Historical Quarterly*.

SAMUEL PROCTOR.
General Editor of the
BICENTENNIAL FLORIDIANA
FACSIMILE SERIES.

University of Florida.

INTRODUCTION.

AMONG the many travel books written about Florida in the decades immediately following the Civil War, *Petals Plucked from Sunny Climes* is perhaps one of the most unusual, both for its own sake and for what it tells us about its mysterious author, Miss Abbie M. Brooks, who attempted to conceal her identity behind the pseudonym of Silvia Sunshine. This clearly tongue-in-cheek pen name might seem appropriate for a book of this kind, but it also is likely that Miss Brooks used it for serious reasons of her own related to a love of anonymity that continues to protect her privacy even to this day. Consequently, although this volume should be regarded on its own merit as a delightful and informative reading experience, let it be noted at the outset that one of its most intriguing aspects relates to the author and her later writing career. For *Petals Plucked from Sunny Climes* was to have far more impact on its author than on the readers of her day, who carried it by demand only as far as a second edition. In preparing this volume, Miss Brooks passed over a personal threshold that changed the course of her life and led her into the production of her greatest work as a pioneer of notable achievement in the field of Florida historiography. But more about these things later. For the moment, let us consider the book at hand.

In the pages of her book Miss Brooks conducts the reader on an itinerary that begins at Fernandina on Amelia Island and makes a circuit of the peninsula and the Panhandle, touching most of the important cities and towns before moving overseas to Cuba. Although this is an itinerary she may have taken several years to cover on her own, she presents it as a single journey for the reader, and her entertaining prose makes the trip seem all too short in retrospect. One comes to enjoy vicariously, through her gifted pen, that fascinating Florida of a century ago in the colorful period immediately following the Reconstruction Era when the state was entering what might be called its Golden Age of Tourism. Most interesting of all, perhaps, is the manner in which Miss Brooks leads one on to adventure—for she was a traveler in time as well as space; and as he relaxes and gives himself up to the pleasant tour she conducts, he soon realizes that she is guiding him through two dimensions: Florida past and Florida present—Florida from the time of its discovery to the Florida she explored more than 350 years later during the 1870s.

Although this was not a journey without pitfalls for Miss Brooks—she made the same errors of fact and oversight common to authors of similar books written during the period—her "ramble into the Early History of Florida" emerges as better than most attempts, and is redeemed by an obvious infatuation for the subject which expresses itself in passages that are both colorful and inspired.[1] Best of all, Abbie Brooks is a good storyteller.

Introduction.

She has the gift of helping one see and hear the sights and sounds she experienced; and she has a flair for blending with her facts an occasionally humorous and always interesting mixture of local lore and legend. As the reader will discover, the "petals" Silvia Sunshine plucks are from a garden of Florida anecdotes—some honeyed with humor, others colored with drama, most still sparkling with the nectar of life.

Is there anything in Florida literature to compare with the story of Matt Driggers and what might be called "The Great Mastodon Hunt," as told by Abbie Brooks (84-86)? And what about the Indian legend of Silver Springs Miss Brooks culls from another publication but uses so effectively to embellish her own? Here are all the elements of romantic tragedy in the tale of the handsome young Indian chief, Chuleotah, and the beautiful Indian princess, Weenonah, who died tragically for their love and whose spirits not only haunt Silver Springs, but, in the best tradition of Indian legends, account for their present beauty: " 'Now, mark those long, green filaments of moss . . . swaying to and fro to the motion of the waves; these are the loosened braids of Weenonah's hair, whose coronet gives us such beautiful coruscations, sparkling and luminous, like diamonds of the deep. . . . These relics of the devoted Indian girl are the charm of Silver Springs' " (72-75).

When Miss Brooks describes the places she visits and the people she encounters, her pages often come to life with the clarity of photographic impressions. Though she does not always wield an incisive pen, she frequently demonstrates a journalist's mastery for observing detail and communicating the sense of it with a minimum of words. In fact, it is the journalist in Abbie Brooks, and not the storyteller or historian—no matter how inspired—which lends this volume its enduring value and ranks it among classics of its kind in Florida literature.

For example, the steamboat wharf at Jacksonville springs into being as Miss Brooks describes her experience in stepping ashore: "We are importuned and jostled on every side by black boys, dray and carriage-drivers, who worry us for our baggage, raising their whips with the imperious movement of a major-general, and suddenly lowering them at half-mast when we say, No! Then the officious hotel-runners, who scream in our ears to patronize the houses that employ them, until we are on the verge of desperation, and feel as though the plagues of Egypt could not have been worse" (36). Again, Miss Brooks manages to convey an unmistakable and colorful impression of the cosmopolitan city Jacksonville had become, using just a few sentences and phrases applied like brush strokes by a master artist: "No costumes, however peculiar, appear out of style. . . . Celebrities or millionaires walk the streets without creating any sensation. The Mormon, with his four or fourteen wives, can come from Salt Lake City, take rooms at the St. James, enter all the frequented resorts with the same fear from molestation that a genuine Floridian feels of being Ku-Kluxed. Any strong-minded market-woman can don the Bloomer costume . . . and peddle vegetables verdant as the idea which prompted her to forsake the flowing robes of her fair sisters, and assume the half masculine attire of the sterner sex, without attracting any more attention than the lazy loungers in the market-

Introduction. xvii

house. The citizens are so accustomed to sight-seeing that nothing would astonish them but an honest politician" (42-43).

In a happily lengthy passage comparing northern and southern varieties of poor folk, Miss Brooks opts for the southern cracker because he "has a hearty welcome for the stranger, which puts the blush of contempt upon those claiming a much higher degree of civilization. Everything the house contains is free to visitors. . . . Chickens are always killed for company, without counting the number of Christmas holidays they have seen. Your plate is piled with sweet potatoes and corn-dodger bread, or ash-cake, to be washed down with strong coffee. . . . The old folks are very attentive; but where are the children? Run away like wild rabbits. They are out taking a view of the company. Watch, and you will soon see curious little eyes looking through the cracks, or slipping around the corners" (64-65).

Visiting a cigar factory in Key West, Miss Brooks can speak volumes in a few sentences: "Upon the first floor are seated eighty females, engaged in stripping tobacco from the stems. Here mother and daughter work side by side, the daughter earning five dollars per week on account of her more nimble fingers, and the mother three. The daughter puffs a delicate cigarette, while the mother smokes a huge cigar, it being considered a disgrace for the young ladies to use—only cigarettes. Two hundred and fifty men are occupied in one room upon the second floor, all forming those cylindrical tubes through which is to be drawn so much enjoyment in the present, while a perfect *abandon* of all anxiety for the future is felt. These operatives employ a reader, who reads aloud from newspapers printed in Spanish, while they are working, for which luxury each one bears his proportion of the expense. When any news favoring the cause of the [Cuban] insurgents is read, the house echoes with shouting and stamping of feet" (321).

One walks the sands of North Beach outside St. Augustine, the streets of Pensacola and Havana; he is jostled by the same tourists who crowd with her at the rails of an Oklawaha River steamer, staring at Negro deckhands leaping through the forest along the shore carrying burning brands to light the way for the vessel through the pitch-black night. He bumps over rutted trails in a stage coach, gets a first-hand view of seamen at work hauling lines and canvas aboard a schooner bound for Cuba, pokes through churches and cathedrals from Jacksonville and St. Augustine to Cienfuegos and Havana.

Miss Brooks provides her readers with a glimpse of the celebrated Harriet Beecher Stowe nodding off to sleep in a Jacksonville church, while her husband, Dr. Calvin Stowe, preaches a sermon. One shares her amusement at the false fire alarm raised by a visiting Catholic bishop at St. Augustine, who, on rising early one Sabbath and finding no one present at the cathedral to attend mass, rang mightly on the bell with the result that the streets were soon filled with people in various stages of dress and undress. The reader tours a marmalade factory, witnesses a cockfight, digs through ancient Indian mounds, explores mighty forts, visits aging cemeteries, looks into schools and classrooms of a century ago—and all along the way hears stories dredged from local lore embellished by the tidbits of early Florida history which so fascinate this guide.

Introduction.   xix

Although she has an occasional word of advice for tourists who might follow in her footsteps, Miss Brooks makes few concessions in this direction. In fact, she does not seem to be very much in sympathy with the travelers she meets along her way. At St. Augustine, for example, she admires "what is left of the city gates, the most interesting relic that remains from a walled city," describes the architecture of the now gateless pillars as "arabesque surmounted by a carved pomegranate," and observes that "if a protection is not built around these pillars, the hand of vandalism will soon have them destroyed, as so many careless visitors are constantly chipping off fragments" (198–99).

Her occasional description of tourists shows how little human nature and the style of this particularly distinctive class of travelers has changed, and at one point Miss Brooks pauses to classify them as "the defiant, the enthusiastic, and the indifferent." Elaborating on these definitions, Miss Brooks reserves her scorn for the latter: "The indifferent tourist is an anomaly to everybody. Why he ever thought of leaving home to travel, when with his undemonstrative nature he appears so oblivious to all scenes and sights around him, is an unsolved problem. He maintains an unbroken reticence on every occasion, the mantle of silence being thrown about all his movements, while his general appearance evinces the same amount of refinement as a polar bear, his perceptive powers the acuteness of an oyster, his stupidity greater than Balaam's saddle-animal" (209).

It becomes obvious, as one travels with Miss Brooks, that her interest in the Florida of the tourist comes into early conflict with the Florida of history. Not far into

Introduction.

her text Miss Brooks observes that "The early history of Florida Territory ... being written in characters of blood for years, it is considered both appropriate and interesting to intersperse a sprinkling of historical facts in this work, to the authenticity of which some now living can testify" (90). But later she notes that "Many writers who come to Florida [merely] copy an abstract of the most interesting portions contained in the guide-books, besides what they can hear, afterward filling up the interstices from their imaginations" (154). As for herself, she pauses while in St. Augustine to wonder at those who inquire, "How do you kill time in that ancient city?" Her answer: "To the historian, there is no spot so well adapted to meditation on the past. ..." (208). Somewhere amidst these statements the reader senses a growing interest in Florida history that seems to be developing beyond the ordinary, and is not surprised to see her delving beneath the superficial and bringing forth source documents as her infatuation with the past begins to assume a perhaps greater importance than she originally intended. "We look to the old Spaniards for information, but alas! they are like the swamp cypress which the gray moss has gathered over until its vitality has been absorbed—age has taken away their vigor," she reports at one point (154). And, as one will see from what is known of her work after the publication of *Petals,* she was to do more than merely complain about the "lacuna of a century and a half" which she discovered in the Spanish source documents relating to early Florida history.[2]

Two periods of this history appealed most to Miss Brooks. The first was the period of exploration and early development and the events surrounding the founding

Introduction. xxi

of Spanish St. Augustine and French Fort Caroline. The second was the Seminole War. In treating the former, Miss Brooks pauses frequently on her journey to highlight relevant developments from earliest times and relate them meaningfully to the places she is visiting. This use of the remote past to illustrate Florida present, as she saw it a century ago, tended to invest the state with an antiquity most of her contemporaries were scarcely familiar with, since Florida was then still largely a wilderness. Her final "Ramble into the Early History of Florida" summarized all she had learned of this early period and was as good an introduction to the subject as any then available. This interest is reflected in Miss Brooks' treatment of St. Augustine, to which she devotes more effort and space than any other single subject or place. In fact, her concentration on so many aspects of St. Augustine as she observed it during the late 1870s accounts in large part for this book's enduring value and interest. There can be no doubt that it was the early Spanish influence in the ancient city as she saw it—its Spanish-speaking natives and traditions and its Old World architecture—that inspired her abiding interest in the larger history of Florida.

Also developing as a major theme in this volume is the Seminole War and the character of the Indians who fought it. The author's fascination for Florida's Indians is obvious throughout, and may relate to the fact that she saw some western Indians at Fort Marion. Apparently she was also present at an Indian festival at St. Augustine in 1876. Describing her own thoughts on the latter occasion, Miss Brooks says that during "the grand war-dance of the season [which] came off after dark, when prisoners were captured and treated with sham hostilities ... the mind of the imaginative could portray what would be done in reality to a helpless captive in their power" (192). Unfortunately, it is this darker side of the Indian character Miss Brooks concentrates on most, sprinkling her text with accounts of Seminole War murders, massacres, and atrocities (see 49–50, 99–100, 141–43, 241–43, 334–38).

Equally as intriguing to Miss Brooks was the sometimes enigmatic character of Indian leaders like Osceola and Coacoochee or Wild Cat, whose eloquence seemed to transcend and contradict their reputed savagery. Though she repeats the usual stories concerning these celebrated Seminole chieftains, she succeeds in presenting them favorably as individuals, using their own words to achieve a sympathetic effect. She quotes Osceola reacting to the Treaty of Payne's Landing: "There is little more to be said. The people have agreed in council . . . it is truth, and must not be broken. I speak; what I say I will do; there remains nothing worthy of words. If the hail rattles, let the flowers be crushed" (96). Again, when Osceola is arrested, Miss Brooks savors his "native eloquence," sharing with her readers the Indian's defiance: "The sun is overhead, I shall remember the hour; the [Indian] Agent has his day, I will have mine" (97). As for Coacoochee, the Wild Cat, she excuses his sins against the white man with the observation that "war to him was only a source of recreation" (151). But she also gives his eloquence free rein, allowing him to speak at length, as if pleading for all of his kind while he recounts his bewilderment over the white man's duplicity and the relentlessness of his encroachments (291–93). Finally,

Introduction.   xxiii

Miss Brooks reveals her admiration for the audacity and courage of the Indians, even in the midst of one of their bloodiest excursions, the one against Indian Key, which she rates as "among the boldest feats of the [Seminole] war" (243).

As has been noted, despite her preoccupation with such subjects, it was the personalities and events surrounding the founding and development of St. Augustine which appealed most to Miss Brooks, and which claimed her primary attention. The reasons for this seem to relate to an almost mystical empathy she developed for St. Augustine and its blend of Old World and New, as well as the frustrations she experienced on discovering that "lacuna of a century and a half in its early history" which obscured much that she wanted to know.[8] In her introductory chapter on St. Augustine Miss Brooks observes: "This point appears to be a favored place for the stimulus of thought . . . [and] inspiration. . . . Daily we are more impressed with the fact how treacherous are the links which connect the chain of tradition in a country where its earliest history is mingled with a record wonderful as the champions of knight-errantry who figured in the pages of romance" (154). Warming to her subject she conveys most clearly the mingled awe and frustration she experienced in her enjoyment of the ancient city and her initial exploration of its past:

We feel as though, in trying to describe this place, we were hovering on the brink of uncertainty, and drifting along its shores, not knowing where to land, that we might find the stand-point to commence our task. It is here we realize a kind of traditional flickering between the forgotten and neglected past, shrouded in awful obscurity. . . . Before the forest-trees which covered the grounds upon which New York City now stands were felled, St. Augustine was the seat of power.... It is here, as in no other place, that two forms of civilization find a foothold.... This city is like ancient Rome, with which many found fault while there, but, from some kind of fascination, they always returned again.... During the Spanish rule, it was a place of importance as a military post, being the Government head-quarters.... What a strange sensation steals over us to be awakened just before the old cathedral bells have chimed twelve by the sound of musical instruments, accompanied with singing, in a foreign tongue, a song which has echoed through the same town for more than three centuries!... The language spoken by ... [some of the oldest inhabitants] is supposed to have been identical with that used in the Court of Spain before the days of Ferdinand and Isabella. It has the terseness of the French, without the grandiloquence of the Spanish, being derived directly from the Latin.... The religion here is that which sprang into existence during the Middle Ages.... What a host of past memories rise before us on every side as we walk its narrow streets, overshadowed by mid-air balconies (159-66)!

It was that "brink of uncertainty," that "neglected past, shrouded in awful obscurity," which led Abbie Brooks into her most important work following publication of *Petals Plucked from Sunny Climes*. And this brings us, at last, to one of the most intriguing aspects of this book—the mystery surrounding Miss Brooks herself.

Who was Abbie M. Brooks? Where was she born and educated? What kind of background did she come from? What happened to her later in life? Unfortunately, some of the answers to these and other questions still evade the researcher. But one has learned enough about Miss Brooks to place her life and work in some kind of perspective for the reader—enough to hope that republica-

Introduction. xxv

tion of this volume will stimulate a new interest in her, possibly promoting the continuation of this tentative research toward a more satisfactory conclusion. For, as will be seen, the life and labors of Miss Brooks, particularly in the field of Florida historiography, deserve at least a definitive monograph.

The reader gets his first clue to the author's background in the preface to this volume, which suggests that she may have been a professional writer, quite possibly a journalist. Indeed, certain elements of her style strongly suggest the latter. The preface shows also that Miss Brooks probably came to Florida for reasons of health, and that during the course of writing *Petals Plucked from Sunny Climes* she was interrupted by occasional lapses of illness. The text itself provides additional information—for example, the fact that Miss Brooks launched her journey into Florida from Atlanta, although whether she was living and working there, or merely passing through from some other point of origin, cannot be ascertained (17). It cannot be judged with any certainty when Miss Brooks made her journey to Florida, or, for that matter, whether *Petals* was the product of one or several journeys. Nor can one say when she may have first visited the state or when she became interested in its history, although she suggests herself that it was an interest which developed in the course of her work on this book. The book itself provides some leads for answering these questions in the way Miss Brooks used occasional contemporary dates. Some are presented like entries from a diary and the text following them is not enclosed in quotation marks, whereas datelines from articles Miss Brooks uses are set in quotations. This suggests that the diary-like entries are from her own notes, and because they are dated between 1876 and 1878, it is assumed this was the period when Miss Brooks first visited Florida and did most of the work on her book (see 209, 228). The final manuscript probably was submitted to her printer in 1879, the year of her copyright, and this, of course, was followed by publication of the first edition in 1880 (3, 4). A second and final edition followed in 1885.[4]

When this investigation of Miss Brooks's background first began there was reason to believe that some of her papers were located either in the North Carolina Collection or in the Southern Historical Collection in the University of North Carolina Library at Chapel Hill. But an examination of these facilities yielded "no trace of Ms. Brooks" and not even a copy of her book, save on microcards.[5] Investigation of standard sources, including the Library of Congress, revealed only one source mentioning Miss Brooks, and that simply a brief identification of her as "an American writer, of the South."[6]

One other question occurred: did Miss Brooks have any connection with Nashville or Tennessee? Was she born or raised there; had she lived or worked in Nashville where many periodicals and publishing houses were located? Surely she had some link with that city, since she chose to have her book privately printed there at the Southern Methodist Publishing House. But neither the records nor a history of that institution yielded any evidence, and the Tennessee State Library and Archives could offer no information either.[7]

Miss Brook's extensive travels in Florida, combined with her voyage to Cuba and leisurely exploration of that island, leads one to wonder whether she might have been independently wealthy—a question which occurs also in respect to her later travels and apparently lengthy visits in Spain. It appears that by the time Miss Brooks completed the manuscript for this volume her interest in early Florida history had transcended the ordinary. What the volume at hand does not reveal, however, is how this interest came to dominate her life, so much so that she became a pioneer in Florida historiography and "the first person since Buckingham Smith[8] to reproduce from the originals in Spain documents especially pertinent to the history of Florida."[9]

It was an impressive accomplishment, but like her work in Florida for *Petals Plucked from Sunny Climes*, it is not known when she began her research into the original documents, how long she labored at it, or when she finished. It is known that she did go to the Archives of the Indies at Seville, Spain, and remained there long enough to make a study of original documents comprehensive enough to produce a substantial body of material covering Florida history from 1500 to 1810. In this formidable and time-consuming undertaking she was assisted by Sr. Don Antonio Suárez, an employee of the archives, who was "especially familiar with the documentary history of Florida."[10] Additional research may also have been conducted in the archives at Madrid.[11] According to Woodbury Lowery, a later scholar in the field who discussed the project with both Miss Brooks and Suárez, the latter told him that the work in Seville was carried out with Miss Brooks making transcriptions of the original documents in her own hand "at the dictation of Sr. Suárez, who read from the originals."[12]

xxviii *Introduction.*

These transcriptions were of documents which dealt exclusively with Florida affairs, and, according to Lowery —who examined them— were "entirely trustworthy, and . . . accurate transcription of the originals."[13]

As finally compiled, the collection of transcripts consisted of five volumes, covering the following periods: I, 1500–1580; II, 1581–1620; III, 1621–1689; IV, 1690–1740; and V, 1741–1810.[14] On completion of this remarkable work, Miss Brooks returned to the United States and, in 1899, she was living in St. Augustine and preparing to publish a book based on the documents she had unearthed.[15] What she did was to select representative documents from the period 1565 to 1784, and with the assistance of a Mrs. Annie Averette as translator, organize these into a volume which was privately printed under the title of *The Unwritten History of Old St. Augustine.* But once again, as was the case with *Petals Plucked from Sunny Climes,* Miss Brooks's penchant for personal anonymity makes it difficult to learn much about the circumstances surrounding the later publication. *The Unwritten History* carries neither the imprint of the printer nor the place and date of publication! Miss Brooks merely allows her readers the information on the title page that *The Unwritten History* is based on documents "Copied from the Spanish Archives in Seville, by Miss A. M. Brooks and Translated by Mrs. Annie Averette." The only evidence for a publication date is through a presentation copy given to the Library of Congress by the St. Augustine Institute of Science and Historical Society, on February 20, 1909, which bears the legend, "Presented by the Author Miss A. M. Brooks," presumably written in her own hand.[16] However, several years earlier,

Introduction. xxix

April 4, 1901, Miss Brooks sold her original transcripts to the Library of Congress for three hundred dollars, under accession number 134,[17] although as early as 1893 advanced sheets of the books were published as columns in the *Florida Times-Union*.[18] There is still another clue in the files of the Library of Congress Manuscript Division, "a reference to 'a scrapbook of the 1900's' which contained a translation sent from Spain by Miss Amanda [*sic*] Brooks and printed in the [St. Augustine] *News* of January 1902."[19] This scanty and often conflicting evidence suggests that *The Unwritten History* was in preparation from 1899, and that it was published sometime after 1901, when Miss Brooks sold her collection of transcriptions, and prior to 1909, when the autographed copy of the book was presented to the Library of Congress.

Unlike *Petals Plucked from Sunny Climes*, which provided at least a few leads concerning the author, *The Unwritten History* yields absolutely nothing about her, save what is stated in a brief preface:

We [Abbie Brooks and Annie Averette] take pleasure in presenting to our readers information connected with St. Augustine never before published. It is comprised largely of reports and letters to the King of Spain, much of it written by Pedro Menendez himself, and contains decrees and letters from the King to the Governor, Generals, and Officers having charge of the Florida Provinces. It has been buried for over three centuries in Seville, Spain. It is reliable, having been written in old Spanish and guarded with care. It contains facts for which many have sought in vain. The style in which it is written is clear and comprehensive, without being diffuse or overdrawn. It is the true history of our country.

Unfortunately, *The Unwritten History* contains no supplementary commentary to bridge the various selections and place them in some kind of historical perspective. Annotations citing the location of the selections in the Spanish archives are also omitted, as are the original Spanish texts, thereby limiting the value of the work to scholars.[20] But Miss Brooks apparently intended the volume for general readership, made no claim to scholarship, and sought no special recognition for her work.

The Unwritten History opens with a royal decree of King Philip II of Spain, authorizing certain expenditures and procedures for the further settlement of Florida, and is signed from "Bosque de Segovia, August 15, 1565." A letter follows to the king from Pedro Menéndez de Avilés, dated October 15, 1565, which describes the march against Fort Caroline and the massacre of the French garrison. The letter is especially interesting for the details Menéndez includes concerning his personal leadership and the part he played in the assault upon the fort.[21] The final documents include correspondence between the king at Madrid, written to the bishop of Cuba, Santiago José, dated August 4, 1773; and letters to the king posted in 1784 from the governor of St. Augustine and Nicholas Grenier, a commander of troops in Florida. The two latter letters relate to military operations in northeast Florida, between Fernandina and Jacksonville, against outlaw bands who were reported to consist of "men who have neither God nor law ... who are capable of the greatest atrocities."[22]

Despite the reservations among scholars initially, Miss Brooks's original transcripts and her published selections in *The Unwritten History* achieved their purpose. They bridged that lacuna of a century and a half which she had found when she first explored Florida history in the late 1870s, and they shed light at last on that "neglected past, shrouded in awful obscurity" which had frustrated her so during the preparation of *Petals Plucked from Sunny Climes* (159). As one authority in the field observed: "In a day when few such materials had been transcribed, hers was a notable achievement, although her work did not begin to compare either in quantity or in quality with [Buckingham] Smith's. . . . Miss Brooks did succeed, however, in giving a suggestion of the continuity of the Spanish colony [in Florida] by making public this series of papers covering the years from the founding to the late eighteenth century. In the absence of any substantial, scholarly printed materials on the Spanish regime as a whole, this questionable collection served as a noteworthy addition to the historical literature of Florida."[23] It was this kind of academic reservation which led Woodbury Lowery to examine the transcripts and translations and to authenticate their accuracy and reliability "in justice to Miss Brooks' work and in order to remove any suspicions which their appearance might at first awaken."[24]

In the sources the given name of Miss Brooks is given variously as Abbie M., Amanda M., and Mary A.[25] She moved to St. Augustine in the late 1890s, she purchased property at number 84 or 85 Charlotte Street, she lived there until 1903 or 1904 and possibly longer.[26] But even this brief information concludes on a note of uncertainty, and after that all traces of her vanish. Whatever her beginning or her end, this much is certain. Florida made a lasting impression on Abbie M. Brooks when she visited the state to write *Petals Plucked from Sunny Climes*, and she in turn has made an impact on the literature of Florida and on its history. As the custodians of her original transcripts at the Library of Congress noted in reference to her work, she was, indeed, "the remarkable Miss Brooks."[27] Now one may hope that her own neglected past, shrouded in obscurity, will one day be illuminated by a scholar who will be as equal to the challenge she left behind as she was to the one she accepted and triumphed over in her own time.

RICHARD A. MARTIN.

Jacksonville, Florida.

NOTES.

1. Silvia Sunshine (Abbie M. Brooks), *Petals Plucked from Sunny Climes*, p. 16. Future citations to this facsimile will be by page numbers inside parentheses within the text.

2. Woodbury Lowery, "The Spanish Settlements within the Present Limits of the United States" (original MS), vol. 1, 1513–1561, introduction (microfilm no. 141-A, P. K. Yonge Library of Florida History, University of Florida, Gainesville.)

3. Lowery quotes Miss Brooks on this point in "The Spanish Settlements."

4. This edition was also published privately, using the same printer, Southern Methodist Publishing House, Nashville, Tenn.

5. H. G. Jones to Richard A. Martin, August 7, 1974. Mrs. R. Royall Rice of Durham, N.C., also attempted to find some trace of Miss Brooks in the Carolinas, without success.

6. Robert H. Land, chief, Reference Department, General Reference and Bibliography Division, Library of Congress, to Richard A. Martin, October 3, 1974. The reference is from William Cushing, *Initials and Pseudonyms: A Dictionary of Literary Disguises* (New York, Crowell, 1885), p. 366.

Introduction.   xxxiii

7. Mrs. Maxine Carnahan, assistant reference librarian, Tennessee State Library and Archives, to Richard A. Martin, March 25, 1975; *Since 1789: The Story of the Methodist Publishing House* (Nashville, Abingdon Press, 1964); Charles Allen Madison, *Book Publishing in America* (New York, McGraw-Hill, 1966). The Methodist Publishing House conducted a search of its records, but found no mention of Miss Brooks.

8. Buckingham Smith, born in 1810 on Cumberland Island, reared at St. Augustine, educated at Harvard, was a Florida legislater who held diplomatic posts in Mexico and Spain during the 1850s, which enabled him to devote himself to "the passion of his life, the study of archeology and Indian philology," and to conduct important research into the colonial history of Louisiana and Florida. Among his published works, most of them privately printed in limited editions, were translations of de Vaca and de Soto, as well as numerous monographs bearing on Indian philology and the history of the early Spanish periods in Mexico and Florida. See the biographical sketch in Rowland H. Merrick, *Memoirs of Florida* (Atlanta, 1902), p. 683.

9. Ray E. Held, "Spanish Florida in American Historiography, 1821–1921" (Ph.D. dissertation, University of Florida, 1955), p. 218.

10. Lowery, "The Spanish Settlements."

11. Jacqueline Bearden, St. Augustine Historical Society, to Richard A. Martin, September 20, 1974. Miss Bearden reports several clippings from the *Florida Times-Union* in the Society's possession, which reproduce some of these transcriptions in translation, with the editorial note that they are "as copied from the 'Spanish archives of San Augustin' at Seville *and Madrid* [italics added] by Miss A. M. Brooks and furnished from her compilations for the *Times-Union*." This is the only mention of Madrid in the sources. Unfortunately, only one of the clippings reported had a date penned on it—January 8, 1893. This appears to be an error, however, since a careful search of the paper on that and surrounding dates, and other years, failed to locate any of the columns. As for the amount of time Miss Brooks may have spent on her researches in Spain, the sources are silent. We do not learn whether she conducted the research continuously, possibly while living temporarily in Spain, or whether the work was accomplished over a period of many years during any number of visits abroad. This much is certain: merely searching through the archives at Seville and Madrid for documents related exclusively to Florida in the period 1500–1810 would have consumed a great deal of time, to say nothing of the work of transcribing these documents by the tedious method described by Lowery.

12. Lowery, "The Spanish Settlements."

13. Ibid.

14. Held, "Spanish Florida in American Historiography," p. 219.

15. Bearden to Martin, September 20, 1974.

16. John G. Broderick, assistant chief, Library of Congress Manuscript Division, to Richard A. Martin, September 24, 1974.

17. Ibid. The original transcripts are now housed "unbound, in two manuscript containers," at the Library of Congress, according to Broderick.

18. Bearden to Martin, September 20, 1974. As reported in note 11, 1893 may not be the correct date.

19. Broderick to Martin, September 24, 1974. It was not possible to trace this article, and the whereabouts of the scrapbook, if it still exists, is not known.

20. The original Brooks transcripts, now in the Library of Congress, are chronologically arranged with a transcript of each document filed with its translation.

21. *Unwritten History*, pp. 1–15.

22. Ibid., pp. 226–31.

23. Held, "Spanish Florida in American Historiography," pp. 219–20.

24. Lowery, "The Spanish Settlements."

25. Abbie is the most commonly used. The Library of Congress reports Amanda once, and Lowery refers to the "Mary A. Brooks Collection" of transcripts.

26. Bearden to Martin, September 20, 1974, states: "In the 1899 St. Augustine Directory, Miss A. Brooks is listed as living at 85 Charlotte Street. . . . Miss Brooks once owned the property where our Library now stands at 271 Charlotte Street. She bought it from a Dr. C. P. Carver. We are not sure of the date but Dr. Carver bought it in 1884. Miss Brooks probably bought it sometime after 1899. In 1903 Miss Brooks sold the property to William Murray. In the 1904 Directory Miss A. Brooks is listed as living at 84 Charlotte Street . . . [but] the address may be in error also since it is [listed as number] 85 [in the 1899 Directory]. . . . These listings may not be Abbie M. "Although all this seems rather uncertain, the Society reports definitely that "we have a photograph of Miss Brooks circa 1900."

27. Broderick to Martin, September 24, 1974.

Founding of St. Augustine by Pedro Melendez, September 8, 1565.

Petals Plucked

FROM

Sunny Climes.

BY SILVIA SUNSHINE.

With Illustrations.

Nashville, Tenn.:
SOUTHERN METHODIST PUBLISHING HOUSE.
PRINTED FOR THE AUTHOR.
1880.

Entered, according to Act of Congress, in the year 1879, by

THE AUTHOR,

in the Office of the Librarian of Congress, at Washington.

TO

ALL THE FLORIDA SETTLERS,

AND

THOSE WHO WISH IT

A BRIGHT AND PROSPEROUS FUTURE,

THIS VOLUME IS RESPECTFULLY

DEDICATED.

NEW MAP OF FLORIDA, 1879.

Published by the Bureau of Immigration.   *Red Lines denote Chartered Railroads.*

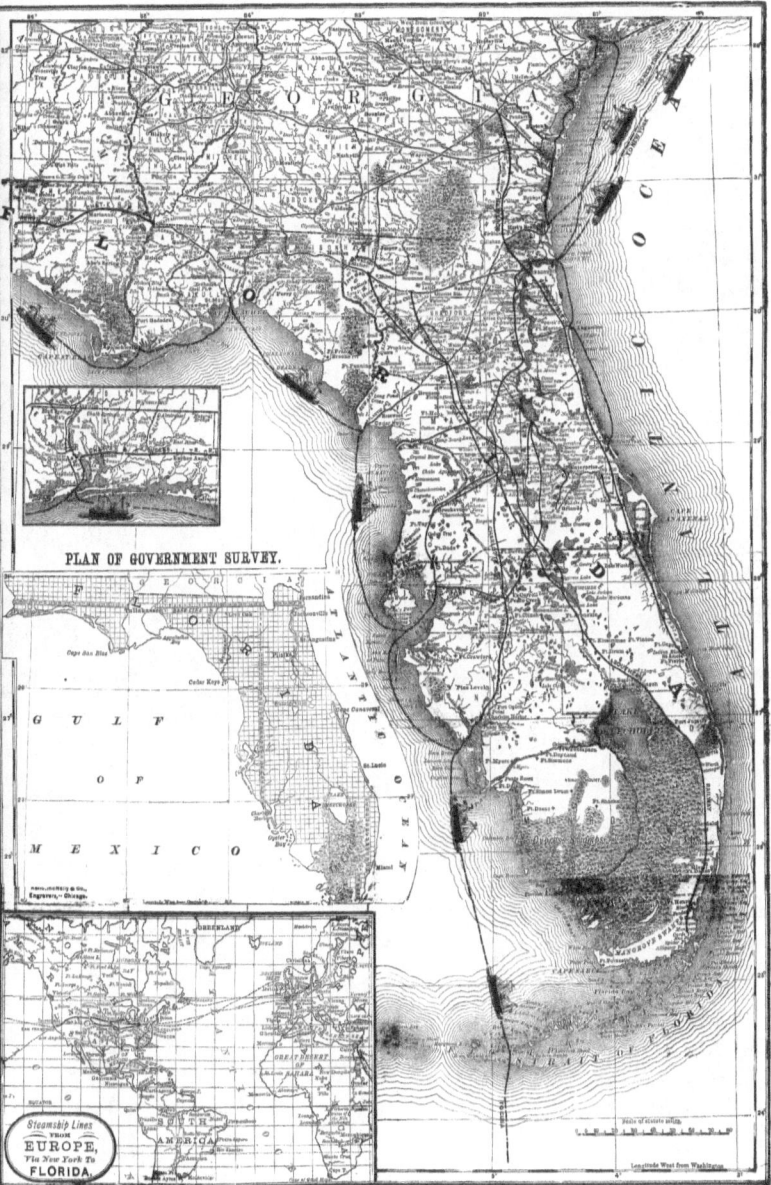

INTRODUCTORY NOTE.

THIS book contains a brief account of the early settlement of Florida, and some of its Indian conflicts, together with many amusing incidents connected with its present history; also a new illustration, prepared expressly for this work—the whole being a collection of travels, and what is to be seen in various portions of Florida, Key West, and Cuba; with a Gazetteer and Florida Guide-book attached, designed for the use of tourists and settlers.

PREFACE.

WRITING, like other employments, furnishes a reward to those who are fond of it—elevates the mind to a higher and happier state of enjoyment than merely grasping for earthly treasure, a desire to discover something beautiful in our surroundings, a nobility of character in mankind, a grandeur in all God's works.

My travels, both in Florida and Cuba, when not suffering from sickness, were an uninterrupted source of pleasure and entertainment, made thus by the smiles of friendship, intercourse among kind-hearted people, combined with the luscious fruits and delightful scenery by which I was almost constantly surrounded.

In arranging the historical portion of this work, I have endeavored to sift conflicting events, at all times retaining those which were the most tangible, and rejecting many which have been received by superficial observers as consistent truths.

I shall feel amply rewarded if any sad, sensitive heart, wounded in life's struggles, is cheered even for awhile in perusing these pages, or the consumptive invalid entertained with a pleasanter potion than his cod-liver and gloomy forebodings of future ill.

Contents.

Chapter I..17

Adieu to Atlanta and arrival in Macon—Early settlement of Savannah by General Oglethorpe—Met by the Yamacraw Indians with presents—Death of Count Pulaski—Bonaventure Cemetery—The inland route to Florida—Pass St. Simon's Island—Wesley visits Frederica to establish his faith — Cumberland Island, the home of Nathanael Greene — Olives — The scuppernong vine — Dungenness, the burial-place of Light-Horse Harry Lee — General Robert E. Lee visits the grave of his father—Amelia Island—Taken by filibusters—Their surrender — Fine beach and light-house — The turtle — Sea-shells— God's treasures—A resting-place for the weary.

Chapter II..28

Fate of the Spanish galleons—St. John's Bar and River—General remarks on Florida—Lumber-mills—Jacksonville—Grumblers—The invalid—Churches—Dr. Stowe preaches in the Methodist church—Mrs. Harriet Stowe goes to sleep—Sermon by a colored brudder—Journalism—Moncrief Springs—The invincibility of boarding-house keepers— The cemetery—Too much delay with invalids before coming to Florida.

Chapter III..46

Jacksonville Agricultural Association, and its advantages—Exhibits of wine, perfume, and fruits—Industries of the ladies—Yachts—General Spinner—Steamer Dictator—Nimbus on the river—Mandarin— Employment of its inhabitants—Murder of Mr. Hartley by Indians— Weariness of war by the settlers—Fanciful names given to towns— Hibernia and Magnolia—Green Cove Springs—Fort at Picolata—Pilatka—Putnam House—The *Herald*, edited by Alligator Pratt—Colonel Harte's orange-grove—The Catholic Bishop as sexton—Ocklawaha River.

Chapter IV..55

No fossilized Spaniards on the Ocklawaha—Scenery on its banks— Thick growth of timber—Passengers amuse themselves killing alligators—Climbing asters—Air-plants—Water-lily—An affectionate meeting at Orange Springs—The deaf lady—Pleasure-riding in a cracker-cart—Northern and Southern crackers—March of improvement—Make fast!—Wooding up—Passengers take a walk—Night on the water— Surrounded by thickets—Our flame-lit craft moves on with its pillar of fire—Who!—Plutonic regions—Pyrotechnic displays.

Chapter V..69

Incident as we enter Silver Springs—A gentleman loses his grinders —The Mirror of Diana—Sunset—A beautiful legend of the Princess

10   *Contents.*

Weenonah—A scientific description by Prof. J. Le Conte—Vicinity of the springs—Improvements—Description of Ocala—Impressions of De Soto—Public Square—Contented, hospitable people—Marion county the back-bone of the State—Matt. Driggers and his neighbors go on a mastodon hunt—Lakes and long prairie-grass above Silver Springs— The man who wanted a sheriff to marry him—Leesburg and its improvements—A dredging-boat mistaken for a cook-stove—Indian trails —Historic relics—Lake Dunham—Okahumkee—The Ocklawaha historic ground.

CHAPTER VI...90

Florida during the Indian war—Cumbersome movements of the troops —Cause of the war—Treaty of Payne's Landing—Birthplace of Osceola—Lives with his mother in Okefinokee Swamp—Afterward in the Big Swamp—Osceola expresses opposition to the "treaty"—Jumper unwilling to go West—Charlie Emaltha—Plea for remaining—Indian poetry—Appearance of Osceola—Hostility toward the survey force— Does not favor immigrating—Decision of Micanopy—Osceola in irons at Fort King—Sullen, then penitent—First hostile demonstration from the Indians—Murder of Private Dalton—Killing of Charlie Emaltha—Osceola seeks revenge in the assassination of General Thompson—Dade Massacre—Micanopy fires the first gun—More than one hundred whites killed—Depredations of daily occurrence—Battle of Withlacoochee—Captain Ellis, of Gainesville—Capture of Osceola by General Jessup—Imprisoned first in Fort Marion, afterward sent to Fort Moultrie—His death—Chechotar, his wife—Poetry by a friend —Sisters of Osceola now living in the West.

CHAPTER VII..105

Shores of the upper St. John's, where various kinds of timber grow, and bony stock range—Mounds and their contents—Their obscure origin—The chasm not yet bridged—Belief in the immortality of the soul—The mounds a shrine—Conduct of the Spanish invaders—Ancestral veneration—Articles for use deposited with the body—Unanswered questions—History of mound-building in its infancy—Found in Europe—Uses of mounds—Monumental mounds—The mystery shrouding their structure—Intrusive burial—The growth on Florida mounds, and the distinguishable feature of mound-builders—Mound near New Smyrna—Mounds in South Florida—The large one at Cedar Keys—Mounds for sacrifice—Description of a victim—Pyramid of Cholula—Mexican teocalli—Pyramids for kings—Mounts of ordinance—Sacred fires—Indians worshiped "high places"—The temple at Espiritu Santo—Residence of King Philip—Lake Jessup mound— Copper weapons—Indians worship the sun and moon—Burial urns— Pearls a heavenly product—The Indian empress a prisoner—Manufacture of beads from conch-shells—Pearls of no value found on the coast of Florida—Who were these architects?—A veil obscures our vision in trying to discover the engineers of these mounds—The key never found—*Tumuli*, mounds, and plateaus, all objects of interest.

CHAPTER VIII...121

A description of the animals and birds seen on the St. John's a century since—Lovely landscape—The happy family—Lake George—Enterprise—Mellonville—Sulphur Springs—Lake Harney and Salt Lake

Contents. 11

—Indian River—Settlers discouraged on account of the Indians—An order for blood-hounds—Battle of Caloosahatchee—Famished soldiers, and fidelity of the dog—Big Cypress Swamp—Locality of the chiefs—What the Indians cultivate—Their babies never cry—The Prophet, and his influence as a medicine man—Wild Cat in command of Fort Mellon—Speech of Sam Jones—Hanging of Chekika—Major Belknap takes his command into the Big Cypress—Country developed by war—Indian River after the war the sportsman's heaven—Game, oysters, and fish—Scientific theory on the formation of coquina—Fine products of the Indian River country—A resort for consumptives—Camp-cooking—Soothing influences from the surroundings—Coming down the St. John's—The sick man—Stewardess and "'gaitors"—Curious people with curious things—The chameleon—The fawn—The crane—The bug-hunter and his treasures—The many old people in Florida—The sportsman.

CHAPTER IX..139

Stop at Tocoi for St. Augustine—Scenery along the route—Stage-contractor's notice—Murder of Dr. Weedman—Cloth houses—Two mail-carriers murdered—The blood-hounds—Mr. Francis Medicis and four others shot—Remarks by a resident on witnessing the scene—Wild Cat the leader of this atrocity—The theatricals fill their engagement—Coacoochee admires himself in the glass, also one of General Hernandez's beautiful daughters—His capture and escape—His twin sister and her pearls—Returns, dressed in theatricals, for a parley with the whites—Starts West, and dies on the way.

CHAPTER X...154

St. Augustine described in rhyme—The old Spaniards—A place for stimulus of thought—Treachery of legends—Early settlers lured by tales of wealth—Historical antiquity—Astonished Seloes—Capture by Sir Francis Drake—St. Augustine, 1764—French privateers—Rory McIntosh the Don Quixote of the times—American flag raised in 1821—Freedom to worship God—St. Augustine archives—Dr. McWhir the founder of Presbyterianism in Florida—Appearance in 1834—The frost—Every thing shrouded in a kind of tradition—Fromajardis, or Garden Feast—Matanzas River—Nuns—Escribanio, or St. Mary's Convent—The ancient city sleeps all summer—The dear old folks from their Northern homes, and the young ones too—Curiosities—Crafts of all kinds—Gayety of the winter—Remarkable memory of the natives—Peaceful days—No welcome for adventurers—St. Augustine supposed to have been the residence of the Peri—Expressing an unfavorable opinion about Florida not popular here.

CHAPTER XI..173

The cathedral—Regular attendance of its worshipers—Harsh tones of the church chime—Early mass—Cathedral finished in 1793—Material employed—Moorish belfry—Irreverent visitors—Religion of the natives a part of their existence—The bishop regarded as a vicegerent—Mistaken conclusions of outsiders—Peculiar frescoes representing death—Christmas Eve—Ceremonial conducted by Bishop Verot—Administration of the sacrament—Tolemato Cemetery—Its custodian—Murder of Father Corpa by the Indians—Chapel dedicated to Father Varela—Tablet-inscriptions erased by time—A medallion supposed to have been worn by Father Corpa, which was brought from Rome.

12   Contents.

Chapter XII 183

Castle San Marco—Indestructibility of the material employed—Commenced in 1565—Completed by Montiano, 1756, with the aid of Mexican convicts—Attacked by Oglethorpe—Appearance in 1740—Improper change of names—Description of Fort Marion—Its resemblance to Scott's Garde Douloreuse—The chapel and its holy mysteries—Iron cages—Caving in of the bastion—No cages sent to the Smithsonian Institute—The wooden machine—The old sergeant—Human bones not unusual in other ruins—Spaniards branded with the cruelties of the Inquisition—True version of the iron cages from Señor B. Oliveros—No nation exempt from cruelties during some period of their history—The Western Indians retained as hostages in the fort.

Chapter XIII 198

The sea-wall—when commenced—Material employed—Boulevard of the city—City gates and vandal visitors—Tapoquoi village—Murder of Father Rodriguez—La Sylphide rose—Fine pulpit talent—Sabbath in January—The Presbyterian Church—Flowers from the gardens of Messrs. Alexander and Atwood—Gushing young men—Dr. Daniel F. March and his words of comfort—A description of the Episcopal church—A curious question about disputed grounds—Dr. Root, the clergyman—A peculiar man and his dog, that walked into the church from habit—St. Augustine a restorer to both health and reason—Public reading-room—Circulating library—What shall we eat?—Ships constantly coming in with supplies—Fresh vegetables—Oranges—Hotels and fine boarding-houses—Growlers—Gratuitous hospitality now obsolete—The most eligible houses—Summer resort—Pleasant people found by the sea.

Chapter XIV 214

How they spend their time in the ancient city—A slight departure into history—Different kinds of visitors—Grand opening of the Lunch-basket on the North Beach—Music and moonlight on the water—The Indian buffalo-hunt near the old fort—Dancing inside by the Indian prisoners—Preparation for a gala day, March, 1877—Post-band—Yacht-race—A jockey-race—The hurdle—A foot-race by the Indians—Wheelbarrow contest—Victor and greenbacks—Ham and money—The cat a musical animal—St. Augustine Hotel, where music is made from their sinews.

Chapter XV 224

Longevity in St. Augustine—Manufacture of orange marmalade and wine—"El Pavo Real"—Genovar & Brother, wine-makers—Visitors leaving—A page from unwritten history—Tolling the bells for the pope—Grand illumination by the Yacht Club—The *ignes-fatui* boats—String-band and dancing—Capricious weather a comfort to growlers—A change to balmy air and waving palms—The Indians leave—They have no use for Government clothes on the plains—Mrs. Black Horse and Mochi dressed in hats and plumes—The Indians leave their Moody & Sankey song-books—A picture-written letter from the squaw of Minimic—These Indians differ from novel-writer characters—The strain of civilization during their stay being too great they mutiny, headed by White Horse—A squad of soldiers from the barracks search

Contents. 13

and iron four of them—Fort closed to visitors—They pine for home, the aristocracy of their nature scorning restraint—Money made by polishing sea-beans, etc.—Description of St. Anastasia Island—Ponies feeding on marsh-grass—Attack of General Oglethorpe in 1740—The old light-house built by the Spanish, and used as a fortress—Fresh water in mid-ocean caused from lime-sinks—Treaty of Fort Moultrie —Origin of the Seminoles.

CHAPTER XVI......................................235

Burning of the Spanish Governor's son by the Indians over a century since—The Great Spirit as arbiter—Fort Matanzas—Its age, use, present appearance—Entered by an escalade—New Smyrna settled by Dr. Turnbull with his Greek colony—They at first engage in the culture of indigo, which soon fails—Great dissatisfaction among the colonists, who are finally released, and retire to St. Augustine—The Douglass Dummit Plantation—Indian Key Massacre, August 15, 1840—Murmurings of the citizens.

CHAPTER XVII......................................245

The Everglades Expedition, under Colonel Harney, 1841—Preparations—Spanish Indians—Leave Fort Dallas, arriving at Chitto's Island —The bird flown—Sam Jones's Island, containing villages and pleasure-grounds—The soldiers greatly annoyed by roaches and musquitoes —Prophet's Island—Discovery by Indians—Sergeant Searles mortally wounded—Arrival at New River—Fort Dallas—General appearance and extent of the Everglades—Manilla hemp and the cotton-plant indigenous—Return of Colonel Harney—Grand ovation in St. Augustine—Sorrowful reflection on the situation—Present inhabitants of the Everglades—Old Tiger Tail—Intrenches himself in Mexico as brigand, afterward makes his way to Florida, and becomes chief of the Seminoles—Father Dufau goes to the Everglades as a missionary —"Two squaws no good"—Dress of the Indians—Everglade alligators and moccasins no respecters of persons—Primeval condition of the country, with its trees, birds, and native growth.

CHAPTER XVIII......................................260

From Jacksonville to Cedar Keys—The Florida Central—Baldwin— Alligators and moccasins—West India Transfer Railroad—Piney Woods —Trail Ridge—Lawtey—Starke—Turpentine distillery—Serenades— Waldo—Alachua county—Hummock-lands and phosphates—The indignant Boston lady—Alachua settled in 1750 by an Indian named Secoffe—Juggs or sinks—Approach to Gainesville—This town named for General E. P. Gaines—Accommodations for visitors—Tillandsia and its uses—Orange Lake the natural home of the orange—Budded trees—Eucalyptus-tree for malarial districts—Information on the subject of lands—Orange City, Arredondo, Albion, and other prospective cities—Bronson—Its good settlers—Otter Creek—"Great Gulf Hummock"—Its tropical growth.

CHAPTER XIX......................................270

Cedar Keys, the terminus of the West India Transit Railway—Extortion—Dr. McIlvaine's Hotel—Fourth of July toasts, 1843—Steamers from Cedar Keys to Manatee—Early settlement of Clear Water Harbor—The unfortunate Narvaez—Inaccessibility of South Florida—

Contents.

Manatee—Its dwellings embowered among orange-trees—Tenacity of contesting Indians—Their independence subdued by association—The cactus pear eaten by Indians—Present population—Church privileges for worship—Schools—Good physicians—Sowing before reaping—Boarding-houses kept as sanitariums—Pantry supplies—Fine fish—An Elysium for rheumatics—No starving—The grape-culture suggested—Also wine-making—A variety of crops—Sugar-cane ratooning for six years—Old-fashioned bees in gums—This locality a fine resort for those who wish to avoid cold—The sunny-side of nature turned out in February—Oleander and orange-buds bursting their pink and white petals—The banana—Spring flowers, etc.—Zephyr breezes—The rose—"A child of summer"—Historic records—Hon. Judah P. Benjamin—Remains of the mastodon and megatherium.

Chapter XX.................................285

Tampa—Undisturbed slumbers—First settlement by Narvaez—Poor Juan Ortiz!—His vigils among the dead—Espiritu Santo Bay—De Soto and his festive soldiers—Billy Bowlegs—Cedar and pine lumber-mills in Tampa—A school and its teacher—Old Tampa—Uses of the cabbage palm—Fort Brooke—Appeal of General Worth to the vanity of Coacoochee, which finally results in his band being sent West—An invocation to the Great Spirit during a storm.

Chapter XXI.................................296

Marooning from Tampa to Key West—Drum-fish—Loons—Acrobat fleas—Roaches—Bilge-water—The Methodist preacher and his children—Sailor's fare—Landing lady-passengers—Terrasilla Island and its products—Madam Joe—The romantic young couple—Sarasota Bay—Stock-raising—Health—Mangrove thickets—Perpetual verdure—Palmetto houses—Striking for fish—Varied amusements for visitors—Hunting deer—Bugs and butterflies—Egmont Key—Rare shells and a rarer Spiritualist, with his toothless wife—Professor Agassiz—Buccaneers—Jean Lafitte—Sunset at sea—Isles of the sea—Boca Grande—Felippe the Spaniard, and his Indian concubines—Polly goes West for money—Punta Rassa, the terminus of the International Telegraph.

Chapter XXII.................................313

Alone with God and the stars—Phosphorescent waves—Reefs and coral formation—Key West—Cocoa-trees—Chief of the Everglades—Dwellings—Inhabitants—Early settlers—Conchs—Their origin and occupation—Court of Admiralty—Wrecking—The International Telegraph Survey—Public schools—The sisters—Cigar-makers—Reading while working—Monkey-jugs and their use—Cochineal—Sponge and spongers—Fort Taylor and other fortifications—Curiosity-shop—Captain Dixon its Greek keeper.

Chapter XXIII.................................327

Middle Florida and South Georgia—Jealousy between Middle and East Florida—Good landed titles in Middle Florida—Disappointment the result of overestimation—No spot with every thing desirable—Diseased people tinctured with a sullen melancholy—Lake City—Derivation of the name—The citizens—Style of architecture adapted to the climate—Products—Atmosphere for asthmatics—Monticello—Its peo-

Contents. 15

ple—Former wealth evidenced by the numerous freedmen—Good hotel here—The festive frogs: great variety, some with loud-sounding voices—The "pretty frog" that went to England—The singing-wasp—Tallahassee, where De Soto spends his first winter, 1539—The Spanish soldiers and their armor—Town incorporated, 1825—Corner-stone of the capitol laid, 1826—Situation of Tallahassee—Governor Reed's message, 1840—Blood-hounds and leash-men from Cuba—Two Indians caught by them—Bounties on heads—Indian scare—Only a goat—Indians attack wagons, relieving negroes of their clothing—Former wealth and culture in Tallahassee—Colonel Murat and his mother come to America—Visit the Catholic Bishop, but not in regal style—The neighbors are disappointed in a king's son—Birthplace, home, and early associations of the gifted authoress, Mrs. Mary E. Bryan—Wakulla Spring, with a beautiful description by Bartram—Chattahoochee—State penitentiary—Montgomery and Eufaula route to Florida—Town of Quincy—Mountain-streams with a musical cadence—Cuban tobacco and scuppernong grapes grown here—Stage communication between Quincy and Bainbridge—Cherokee rose-hedges—Bainbridge—Its decline on account of railway communication—Thomasville—Mitchell House—Gulf House—Embowered dwellings—Brisk trade—Newspapers—Female college—Churches—Former wealth of Thomas county—Colored politicians prefer speaking by proxy—No water communication from Thomasville—Wire-grass country—Quitman—Home-like hotels—Cotton factory—Valdosta—Pine-trees—Plenty to eat—Valdosta editor—Crowds on public days—Trip on the Gulf road—The light-wood fires an epitome of the Arabian Nights' Entertainment.

CHAPTER XXIV..................................355

Pensacola musings—Its early settlement and capacious harbor—Origin of the name—The soil contains clay for brick and pottery—Casa Blanca—The city conquered by the Spaniards—Causes for its not competing with other Gulf cities—Description of Fort Barrancas—It is supposed to contain a dungeon—Fort Pickens—Fort St. Michael and Fort St. Bernard—Ten dollars offered for the scalps of colonists—General movements of General Andrew Jackson—Governor Callavea in the calaboose—Description of the old plaza—Present appearance of Pensacola—It contains no fabled fountains—A plank walk on which sailors reel like drunken elephants—Prosperity of the place dependent on the demand for lumber—Commotion on the arrival of a ship—Resinous wood and its light accompaniments—The Indians hated to leave it—Ferdinand Park and its rural scenery—The market-house—The singing fishermen—The proud fishermen with their big fish—An ox-horn announces the sales—Fresh-water wells—Drawers of water lose their vocation—Porpoises—Tropical fruit-culture not very successful here—The washing bayou and its water-nymphs—Florida hunters—The fleet-footed fawn a past record—The yellow-fever visitor—Perdido, or Lost Bay—Escambia Bay—The alligator: her nest, and her young—Churches—Free schools—Catholic schools—Episcopal school, and its founder, Mrs. Dr. Scott.

CHAPTER XXV..................................378

Leaving Pensacola—Contentment in our moving habitation—A calm—*Physalia utriculus*—A genuine nor'-wester and its accompaniments—A moment of terror—Morning at last—Isle of Pines and its products

16   Contents.

—Pirates—Water-spouts—Early history of Cuba—The Spaniards burn an Indian—Cienfuegos—The fort on the bay—Cuban houses—Clothing of the children—Cruelty to northern seamen—Mother Carey and her unlucky chickens—The fate of the insurgents, and their numerical strength—" La Purisima Conception "—Neglect of ceremonial duties—The church inside—Its lady-attendants furnish their seats—The slave receives a gentle admonition—The largest plaza on the island—The beautiful señoritas and the band-music.

CHAPTER XXVI.................................399

Distances from Cienfuegos to Havana—Railroads—Three classes of passenger-cars—Smoking—Rain-drops—Harvest—Lo! the poor ox—Goads—Sugar-cane in bloom—Cattle-herders—The war—Arabian stock of horses—Devastations by the insurgents—Vegetation and variety—Depots and drinking—Flowers—Fences from vegetation—Royal palm and its uses—Slaves gathering palm-fruit—Great variety of growth—Cactus family—Sugar and sugar-makers—Negro slaves and coolies—Their miserable quarters—Chicken-fighting—Inhuman treatment of the poor fowls—Matanzas—A Pentecostal illustration—"English and French spoken"—Dinner and its condiments—Matanzas Bay at night—The tough old tars—Their families on shore—The phosphorescent lights on the water—The plaza and hotel—Our French *valet de chambre*—*Siesta*—My *café*—*El volante*—Up the mountain-side—*El Cueva de Bellamar*, being a remarkable subterranean temple—Stalactites and stalagmites—Names given to the different formations inside the cave—Return to Matanzas.

CHAPTER XXVII.................................424

From Matanzas to Havana—Buzzards—Description of El Moro Castle, A.D. 1519—Captured, 1619, by Sir George Pocock—El Moro like the Venetian "Bridge of Sighs"—Havana a century since—Its harbor and fleet of ships—Architecture of the houses—Narrow streets—A view from El San Carlos Hotel—Beautiful moonlight on the bay—El Paseo—French coaches—Residence of the Captain-general—Ladies shopping in *volantes*—Market-house—Mules, panniers, etc.—Working-class receive an early supply of grace—No Sabbath here—"Lottera"—Beggars—Description of the cathedral—Bishop—Acolytes—Organ—Tomb of Columbus—Santo Christobal—His life and mission as Christ-bearer—Cemetario de Espeda—Its walls, vaults, tablets, inscriptions—Three bodies for sepulture—The poor without coffins—The Protestant dead not admitted in Catholic grounds—Fragility of promises in Cuba.

A Ramble into the Early History of Florida........439

Florida Gazetteer, etc......................................481

Petals Plucked from Sunny Climes.

CHAPTER I.

A TRIP to Florida during the winter season is now the popular move for everybody, whether invalid or not, which those living in so close proximity as Atlanta find difficult to resist.

Atlanta is a delightful summer resort, situated a thousand feet above sea-level, visited by healthful mountain breezes in summer, besides being blessed with the purest of freestone and chalybeate water in the world. The night passenger train leaves at 10 P.M. for Macon, one hundred and five miles distant.

We arrive in Macon about 7 A.M., where, after being fortified with a good breakfast at the Brown House, the train departs for Savannah—Macon being the commencement of the mountain-slope which continues to the sea-shore. Many pleasant little towns are passed through on the route, most of which have never recovered from the devastating effects of the war.

Savannah is at last reached, one hundred and ninety-two miles from Macon. To say that Savannah is a pleasant place conveys an indefinite idea of its attractiveness. Many persons stop to remain only a night, but are so much pleased they tarry a month before proceeding farther South.

The present site of Savannah is where General Oglethorpe was met, in 1733, by the Yamacraw Indians, who, after he had landed, presented him with a buffalo-skin, on the inside of which was painted the plumage of an eagle, accompanied with the following address: "The feathers of the eagle," said the chief, "are soft, and signify love; the buffalo-skin is warm, the emblem of protection; therefore love and protect our families." Oglethorpe, in coming to America, was stimulated with the desire of finding a home for the oppressed Protestants and bankrupt gentlemen of England. Upon the adjustment of terms with the Indians he proceeded to lay out the city of Savannah with the greatest regularity. It then contained ten public squares of two acres each, in which were trees, walks, and a pump. The number of squares has now been increased to twenty-four—the walks all being paved with granite, and swept daily. Forsyth Park is on a more extended plan than these small squares, containing a large fountain, fine flowers, magnolia grandiflora trees, a small zoölogical collection—all objects of interest, displaying the taste and refinement of a well-cultured people. Pulaski Square is named for Count Pulaski, who was mortally wounded during the American Revolution while in an engagement on the ground where the Central Depot now stands. He died on board the brig Wasp as she was leaving

A SCENE IN FORSYTH PARK, SAVANNAH.

Tybee for Charleston, when his body was consigned to the sea. The citizens of Georgia, through their munificent bequests, have erected in Monterey Square a monument to Count Pulaski, the cornerstone of which was laid when General La Fayette visited America for the last time.

Savannah has made another fine exhibit of her discriminating powers in selecting a retired and lovely spot, made sacred to them by depositing all that remains of the loved ones who have crossed the river a little before. They have christened it Bonaventure, derived from the Spanish, signifying, *Coming good*. Here rest, in the unyielding embrace of death, those whose warfare in life has ended, where the huge live-oaks, with overlapping limbs, entwine with their companions, forming natural triumphal archways, while the somber-hanging gray moss clings lovingly to its outstretched arms, waving in the winds like some weird fancy that lingers only on the brink of uncertainty. These beautiful grounds were once the home of the Tatnall family, but have now been purchased and devoted to the dwelling of the dead, whither the living can come and contemplate the change which awaits them all.

Travelers, in leaving Savannah for Florida, can go outside by sea, or the inland route, many preferring the latter on account of avoiding sea-sickness, the passage being made between sounds, inlets, and islands, before Fernandina is reached. The inland steamers are first-class in every respect, and the long marsh-grass contains many of those colossal lizards called alligators. They crawl about fearlessly in their hiding-places, while the swamp blackbird whistles very sweetly for us as we pass along so quietly most of the time that we are not exactly certain of any movement, but ten miles an hour is the *pro rata* of speed.

We are now close to St. Simon's Island, where General Oglethorpe commenced another settlement in 1736, called Frederica. On this equable-tempered island they laid out a town, built a fort with four bastions to protect their palmetto cabins, which, as the historian describes them, appeared like a camp with bowers, "being covered with leaves of a pleasing color." Natural paths and arbors were found here by the English, as if formed by the hand of art, with the ripe grapes hanging in festoons of a royal purple hue. The settlements made by Oglethorpe in this portion of the country were the first formed in the true spirit of improvement and colonization.

With him came the great founder of Methodism in America, Wesley, who planted his standard on this island, and mentions their object in the following manner: "It is not to gain riches and honor, but to live wholly to the glory of God, as we have come in the serene hour of peace, when the floods of controversy have subsided, to sow the gospel seeds."

John Bartram visited St. Simon's Island in 1744, and makes the following record of his repast with a friend: "Our rural table was spread under the shadow of oaks, palms, and sweet-bays, fanned by the lively, salubrious breezes, wafted from the spicy groves. Our music was the responsive love-lays of the painted nonpareil and the alert, gay mocking-bird, while the brilliant humming-bird darted through the flowery groves, suspended in air, drinking nectar from the blooms of the yellow jasmine, lonicera, andromeda, and azalea."

As we approach Fernandina we are nearing historic ground—Dungenness, once a most charming and attractive place, located near the southern extremity of Cumberland Island, the former home of Nathanael Greene, of revolutionary fame, where his last days were spent peacefully, of which pleasant period he thus speaks: "The mocking-birds that sing around me morning and evening, the mild and balmy atmosphere, with the exercise which I find in my garden culture." This locality seemed to have constituted a happy close to his eventful career.

The English planted an olive-grove on this island that succeeded well, as though the trees were indigenous. They used the fruit in making pickles, which were considered very fine. Is it not the olive-tree which the Christian should love and venerate, even to the "hoary dimness of its delicate foliage, subdued and faint of hue, as though the ashes of the Gethsemane agony had been cast upon it forever?" It was at the foot of the Mount of Olives, beneath the shadow of the trees from which it derives its name, that was selected for the most mournful of scenes— "The Saviour's Passion." The good and the wild olive-tree will flourish in this climate. It was these trees which furnished the Apostle Paul with one of his most powerful allegories. The wild olive blooms in March, producing a profusion of pink-tinted, white, star-shaped flowers, while its polished, evergreen verdure, remains all the year, affording a compact and beautiful shade.

On this island, before the late war, was seen a scuppernong grape-vine, nearly three hundred years old, supposed to have been planted by the Spanish missionaries. It was then pronounced a prolific bearer, producing two thousand pounds of fruit per annum, and covering nearly three acres of ground. Here rests all that remains of Light-Horse Harry Lee, the gifted and honored dead. "Here his lamp of life flickered before being extinguished." He died March 25, 1818. The decaying marks of time, and the more ruthless destruction of war, have fearfully invaded and devastated this once revered retreat. "Silent though it be, there are memories lingering still vocal amid the mutations of fortune and the desolations of war—memories which carry the heart back to happy days and peculiar excellences which come not again."

When General R. E. Lee last visited Savannah the burial-place of his illustrious parent was not forgotten. It was the only tribute of respect which his great feeling heart could bestow, the last mission of love he was able to perform. Did he think before spring should return again, decked in her gay robes, flinging ten thousand odors upon its balmy breath, that his grave would then be visited by weeping friends, and that loving hands should twine fresh flowers for his remains?

> How sleep the brave who sink to rest,
> By all their country's honors blest!

We next pass the mouth of St. Mary's River, the source of which is a vast lake, where dwelt the far-famed beautiful women, or Daughters of the Sun. These were the last of the Yemassee tribe, who had intrenched themselves here for protection, all efforts to pursue them being like the enchanted lands, which receded as they were approached.

Fernandina is situated on Amelia Island, which is eighteen miles in length and two in width. Vessels can approach the harbor any time without fear from shoals, as the water on the bar will always furnish an average of nineteen feet. Its first settlers, as of many other places in Florida, were Spaniards, a few of whom are remaining. During the movements of the Embargo War, together with the privateers and slavers, three hundred square-rigged vessels have been seen in this harbor at one time. Another settler mentions the mounds when the country was first explored by the Spaniards.

General Oglethorpe, like other explorers in America, was impressed with the coast of Florida, and thus speaks of Amelia Island: "The sea-shore, covered with myrtle and peach-trees, orange-trees and vines in the wild woods, where echoed the sound of melody from the turtle-doves, nonpareils, red-birds, and mocking-birds." Different nationalities looked upon Amelia Island with longing eyes for many years, coveting it for their possession.

In 1817, Gregor McGregor, a Scottish baronet—an enthusiast on the subject of contest—came, with only fifty followers, making proclamations and issuing edicts, of more magnitude than plans for their execution, but soon retired to the quieter quarters of his Highland home.

Afterward came Commodore Aury, with one hundred and fifty men, on a filibustering expedition, and overpowered the Spanish troops. At this time it would have been a difficult task to find a more motley, medley crowd of residents in any country than upon Amelia Island, composed of English adventurers, Irish and French refugees, Scotch, Mexicans, Spaniards, privateers, natives, and negroes. Factions of such varied dispositions and inclinations were not designed to promote harmony in any community; consequently, riots and disturbances were of frequent occurrence.

Previous to this movement by Aury, negotiations had been pending between the United States and the Spanish Government for Florida; consequently, President Monroe and his Cabinet looked upon the disputed property, in a manner, as their own possessions. These Spaniards, being unable to expel the privateering adventurers, President Monroe sent United States troops, which took possession of Fernandina without resistance, in the name of His Catholic Majesty of Spain. This event happened in the spring of 1818.

On Amelia Island is situated a light-house, which exhibits a flash-light, one hundred feet above the level of the sea, visible sixteen miles. The tower is built upon a promontory which overlooks the surrounding country and the Atlantic as far as the eye can extend.

At Fernandina the Atlantic Gulf and West India

Transit Railroad commences, where the gentlemanly officers connected with and in charge of the road reside. The obliging superintendent is always in readiness here to give information upon the peculiar facilities resulting from living on this route, as a health-location, besides being so closely connected by steam-ships with all parts of the world. It now contains a population of about three thousand inhabitants, and, on account of the fine sea air, has been a resort for many years during the summer season by persons from the interior of the State.

The misfortunes of our late war fell heavily on Fernandina, crippling its energies and crushing its present prospects for a time. The real estate of its residents was confiscated and sold for taxes. Some of it has been redeemed, and the remainder is passing through a series of lengthy litigations, which, when settled, are designed to decide the validity of tax-sales generally throughout the entire State. The present condition of affairs places the inhabitants in rather a Micawber-like condition, waiting for something to turn up in the future.

As a resort far away from the busy, bustling cares of life, this place seems peculiarly fine. The island being entirely surrounded by salt-water, a delightful breeze visits the inhabitants at all seasons of the year—in summer, zephyry as the vale of Cashmere, or the soft winds which bore the silver-oared barge of Cleopatra through the Cydnus. The most attractive feature of all in this locality is the beautiful beach, connected with the town by a good shell-road two miles in length, bordering the island for twenty-one miles, and over two hundred yards in width. It is this unsurpassed drive about which the inhabitants love to entertain you at all times, until you can see it in your dreams. A good livery-stable is kept here, well filled with fine, fast horses, trained to trot, or wade in the surf, allowing visitors to admire the wonderful vastness of the most beautiful expanse of waters which wash the Atlantic shores. At ebb-tide the imagination cannot conceive of a finer place, the beach being so firm that a pair of horses and carriage scarcely make an indentation on the surface in passing over it. The pavement is God's own workmanship, being composed of white sand, occasionally interspersed with shells, many of them the tiniest in existence. Here the happy sea-birds ride on the silvery foam, or flit across the breezy water; the seagulls and pelicans luxuriate and flap their wings in peaceful quietude, while the sand-crab takes his walks, standing upright like a pigmy of the human species, presenting arms in a soldier-like manner, and never turning his back, however hotly pursued. These are in reality very curious little creatures, reminding us of the Lilliputians in Gulliver's Travels. Here the turtle comes to deposit her eggs beyond high-water mark, and when they are hatched returns to escort a family of one hundred and fifty babies to her home in the sea. Here the bright moonbeams dance upon the surface of the water, in silence and solitude, until it resembles the surface of a silver mirror. Many pretty shells are found on this beach, of various sizes and designs, with occasionally desirable cabinet specimens, which are thrown out when the waters become much agitated. This is the spot for the jilted lover to forget his idol, and the disconsolate lady her imaginary devotee; for those fretted by the rough edges of corroding care to retire and find a respite from their struggles; the bankrupt who has been conquered in the battles of brokerage, to visit and be reminded God has given us more treasures to delight us than the dross which passes from our grasp like a shadow, but which all are struggling and striving to win; the store-house of the fathomless deep, where we can contemplate that great image of eternity, "the invisible, boundless, endless, and sublime."

CHAPTER II.

IN leaving Fernandina we come out Amelia River, which is formed by the tide-water from the Atlantic. We pass Old Town, one mile from Fernandina, which has a look-out for pilots who take vessels across the bar, besides a few houses, the residence of Spaniards. Fort Clinch is the last noticeable point before we reach the St. John's River bar.

It is the month of January—a bland breeze greets us, when our thoughts revert to the early settlement of this country, when the Spanish galleons—a strange-looking craft—navigated these waters; also ponderous old ships, with sailing figures of various devices carved on their prows, and high-peaked sterns, the timber used being mahogany and cedar, many of which were driven to pieces in a most merciless manner among the breakers, thus scattering their treasures of silver and gold on the strand, to tempt and satisfy the cupidity of those who found them. Vessels dread this bar, as those drawing only six feet of water are oftentimes detained when going and returning with their cargoes of lumber. The white caps wave their snowy plumes, as a warning, when the wind blows, which sends terror to the hearts of the timid, but the more daring exclaim, It looks grand!

As we cross the bar we are in sight of two resorts
—Mayport and Fort George Island—both places arranged for the accommodation of summer and winter visitors. Fishermen also live in these diminutive towns, and are engaged, like the apostles when their Saviour called them, in mending their nets. Shad-fishing is very profitable here during the season. Shad abounds in this river, and being a delicious fish, it is much sought after.

The various descriptions published from the pens of those who visit Florida now are read by persons looking to this locality as a winter-resort, or in search of new homes and health, as items of unsurpassed interest. For this reason writers should be reliable in their statements. In many tourists the emotional current is created so far from the surface that it is a difficult matter for them to be impressed with external objects. For this cause we meet with a multitude of fault-finders.

Settlers living in remote localities from the St. John's River complain because visitors resort there in preference to all other parts of the State. If the facilities and inducements were the same elsewhere, the desire to go would be equal; but it requires the fortitude of a Livingstone to commence a trip into many of the most attractive parts of Florida, with the indistinct prospect how they are to get away when inclined to make a change. The Americans are a restless, roving people, fond of varied scenery, and when confined where they cannot get away, manifest very much the disposition of caged captives.

Laudonnière thus speaks of the St. John's River:

"The place is so pleasant that those who are melancholy would be forced to change their humor." This stream, with its tributaries, is the great artery of the State, where the savage roamed at will for nearly three hundred years after its settlement by the Spaniards, who came in search of hidden treasures, its former history being a page in the past. Here this river glides before us, with its dark, coffee-colored waters, and no perceptible current except where the tide comes in, it being a remarkable stream, unlike any other in North America. The coloring matter it contains is not precipitated by standing, and for this reason is attributed to a colored earth through which it passes from the upper lakes, together with the different kinds of vegetation that environ it. It varies in width from one to three miles, and is thought by many to be an estuary. From the mouth of the St. John's to Pilatka there are numerous bluffs, some of them ten or twelve feet in height, with an under-stratum of shells, on which elevations the pine-tree flourishes. The cypress, ash, and cabbage-palmetto grow on the banks above Pilatka. The weeping cypress, with its leafless, conical excrescences, called knees, and dropsical feet, loves to be alone. It gives a friendly greeting to the gray moss, which lives and swings from its tallest limbs to the lowest twigs, furnishing a complete mantle of grace to the naked-appearing trees. This moss has no affinity for the pine or palm, which thrives in close proximity, colonizing and fraternizing in groups, oftentimes solitary, sighing or rustling as the sea-breeze comes to meet and kiss its feathery crowns and perennial foliage. A few of the trees are deciduous, as the swamp-oak, ash, and poplar; most of the others are persistent, the change of foliage occurring so quietly it is scarcely observed. The mistletoe, with its green, tufted foliage, fastens on the oak, and is a regular parasite—a thief—for it deprives the tree of vitality. The mistletoe seeds are used as an article of food by the birds, and, being thus transported to the forest-trees, adhere by means of a gluten until germination commences.

The change of flags in 1821 produced a change with many of the citizens, when much local information connected with the history of Florida was lost. This province, when ceded to the United States, was divided in two parts, called East and West Florida. Petitions were then frequently forwarded to Washington, with a request to have it remain divided, as it was inconveniently large. During the war which soon followed, many new explorations were made in the hidden hummocks and intricate recesses of the State.

The drinking-water used in Florida does not come from mountain-streams or arctic regions, but in summer, mixed with sugar and lemon-juice, or sour orange, forms a most palatable and healthful mixture.

Land-snakes are not plentiful, as many have supposed, there being very few but water-snakes, which can be easily accounted for, as the intense heat from the fires which sweep through the long grass every year destroy them; then there are no rocks for their hiding-places, where they could rear patriarchal families.

Musquitoes abound in some places on the coast, and to the dwellers in tents the impression has, no doubt, been received that the air was made of these insects. There is a due proportion of fleas in portions of Florida, but not more than in the sandy soil of other countries.

The climate is constantly tempered by the Gulf Stream, that conducts away the tropical heat, returning in a submarine current, the cooler waters from the North thus producing an atmosphere of salubrious influences and life-renewing properties.

No month is without its fresh products and fruits, while every warm day the mocking-bird sings above our heads on some airy perch.

Many theories have been advanced in regard to the formation of *terra firma* on our continent, the one most generally received being that it was all once submerged under water—as a proof of which shells and other marine fossils have been found in elevated positions, which only could have been placed there by the sea overflowing the land, and afterward receding. When this conclusion is attained, Florida cannot be included, as every year the land augments from the combined efforts of the coral insect, *limulus*, and barnacles, together with the *débris* which is deposited upon them afterward. If the disturbing influences along the shores were less, the increase of land would be much greater, as winds and waves are as destructive to the prosperity of these subterranean architects as tornadoes and cyclones to the growth of fine forest-trees. The coral insect is constantly working in his briny bed, making masonry which resists the action of the element in which it is placed, thus laying the foundation for islands and continents. It is the work of these madrepores and polyps that form reefs which wreck so many vessels on its coast, thus making fortunes for those who follow salvage entirely for a support.

The fact of Florida as a health-resort has long been established, the proof being furnished by the length of time consumptives who come for the purpose of lingering a little longer than they otherwise could North, and living in the enjoyment of sufficiently good health to pursue any lucrative vocation their tastes may decide, is sufficient evidence of the efficacy of the climate for pulmonic complaints. Exposure in Florida, as in other places, has its penalties affixed. Near bodies of water a chilliness pervades the air as soon as the sun sets, which is plainly perceptible to all delicate persons. No barometer was ever more sensitive to atmospheric variations than the feelings of a sick person; no magnet was ever attracted to steel more suddenly than their nervous sensibilities to an agreeable or disagreeable object. This prescribing invariable rules for every disease is all a humbug; the patient is usually the best judge. The resort for invalids, when the dew and shades of night are falling on the face of nature, is before a pleasant light-wood fire, surrounded by cheerful companions—remembering that an interview of the internal emotions frequently for the sick is not beneficial. Try and keep from thinking how badly off you really are, as much as practicable. Many have lived for years with only one lung. All sudden changes from heat to cold should be avoided: when you are cold, get warm as soon as possible, and when you are tired, stop—your life depends upon it. All invalids should select a locality which best suits their malady; then settle down, with the determination to extract all the sweets of contentment in store for them which the world contains, keeping their bodies comfortable in every respect, their minds free from all exciting or unpleasant thoughts, their hearts purified while living, and, if death comes, prepared to meet their Maker.

About ten miles from the mouth of the St. John's Laudonnière established his Huguenot colony, building his fortification on a hill of "mean height," naming it Caroline, from their sovereign, Charles IX., of France, now known as St. John's Bluff. The former site of Fort Caroline can be traced with some degree of accuracy, from the fact of this being the first point on the river above its mouth where its banks are approached by the stream, besides being the only elevated spot where a fort could be built between the St. John's Bluff and the mouth of the river. As Fort Caroline was constructed more than three hundred years ago, from materials of so perishable a nature—being pine-logs and sand—none of it remains to be seen at the present day.

The first lumber-mills on the St. John's are located near the estate of Marquis de Talleyrand, eight miles from Jacksonville. The busy hum of industry now echoes from the shores, where pine-logs are being sawed into material for making houses, not only in Florida, but in Boston and other Northern cities. Mr. Clark's mill, in East Jacksonville, received an order, after the big Boston fire, for a million feet at one time. These mills, besides being a source of revenue to the owners, furnish work for the poor, and the refuse pieces fuel, while in cold weather the big fires that consume the slabs afford a free lodging for benighted travelers; also for those who have no good houses, and would be unwelcome visitors in almost any place.

Twenty-five miles from the sea, on the banks of the St. John's, once stood an insignificant place, known as Cow Ford, but now the fine, thriving city of Jacksonville, named in honor of General Andrew Jackson. This city is the head-center of Florida, where visitors can come, and stay, with no prospect of starving, and from which place they can migrate when and where they please, with ample facilities furnished them at all times for the furtherance of their plans.

A combination of singular emotions here seizes the Northern visitor, after being transported in midwinter from his frozen home to a clime where every thing is fresh and blooming, where the market is furnished with cabbages, sweet potatoes, lettuce, turnips, green peas, and radishes, just gathered, besides strawberries red as the blush of morn, with bouquets of rose-buds, upon which still lingers the morning dew-drop.

Many persons come here with unhappy temperaments, to whom peace and contentment in any place, or under all circumstances, has been deficient, but always vainly expecting to find happiness hanging on every new object they meet, waiting for them to pluck; but, unfortunately, it hangs so high they can never reach it—when they commence abusing every thing with which they come in contact. We hear them constantly exclaiming, "Too much sand! too little to eat! too high prices for things!" Nothing can please them. Their faces are drawn up in disgust, and their tongues ready to strike with the venom of contempt, at every person who has a good word to say in favor of Florida.

The unbroken quiet which has been with us since we left Savannah is interrupted as soon as the steamer touches the Jacksonville wharf. We are importuned and jostled on every side by black boys, dray and carriage-drivers, who worry us for our baggage, raising their whips with the imperious movement of a major-general, and suddenly lowering them at half-mast when we say, No! Then the officious hotel-runners, who scream in our ears to patronize the houses that employ them, until we are on the verge of desperation, and feel as though the plagues of Egypt could not have been worse. Most of these public criers are dirty, ragged, and lazy, having no legitimate vocation, except what they can make from visitors, or in drumming for boarding-houses. This city has fine accommodations, and for that reason receives more envy than admiration from other Florida towns. It can furnish more than one hundred good places of entertainment, among which may be found several colossal hotels, capable of containing two or three hundred guests, also boarding-houses of less pretentious dimensions, where, no doubt, a nearer approximation to the acknowledgment for value received is oftener realized. Selections can be made where money may be expended rapidly or slowly, according to the inclination of the visitor. Here, as in other places, we meet with boarding-house complainers. This class of grumblers must remember that hotel-keepers stand fault-finding as quietly as a delinquent schoolboy his deserved punishment; they are used to it; they expect it, and would be disappointed if they did not get it.

The influx of visitors commences sooner some seasons than others. The first cold blast from the North sends the feeble invalid South to bask in the summer sunshine of a milder atmosphere, and when spring comes he returns home like the migratory birds.

Jacksonville and its adjacent towns number a population of over twelve thousand inhabitants, the whole area being three miles long and about two wide. The different names given to this small space of country looks larger on the map than in reality. These corporations are distinguished from each other by the names of Jacksonville, East Jacksonville, Brooklyn, La Villa, Riverside, Springfield, Hansom Town, etc.—each town containing from fifty to fifteen hundred houses. The inhabitants say they were laid out into lots and named, with the expectation of a large increase of persons; consequently there are desirable building-spots in these surveyed sites for growing cities, for sale at all times upon moderate terms.

Jacksonville makes a display of architectural skill, in which are seen the improvements of the nineteenth century. Yards and lawns are laid out fronting many of the residences, where the beauties of landscape gardening may be found blending in harmony with the artistically-arranged walks and pleasure promenades. The sidewalks are made of plank and brick, shaded and overhung with liveoaks, forming archways of inviting appearance, from which swings pendant moss, presenting a perennial, picturesque scene of nature's grandeur. There are over twenty church-edifices in and around the city, where both white and colored people come to worship in crowds. We are happy to state these statistics find the inhabitants in a much better spiritual condition than has been represented. However, we have no partiality for many of the doctrines preached by itinerant reformers who come here. We prefer our old orthodox faith, which made us contented while we lived, and carried us to heaven when we died. But these new isms, such as Spiritualism, Liberalism, Free-loveism, and every other species of modernized infidelity that is now gaining ground and receiving accessions from our Sunny South, are designed only to delude and drown the souls of their followers in eternal misery. The Churches here are representatives of various creeds and beliefs — Methodist, Presbyterian, Protestant Episcopalian, and Roman Catholic.

Petals Plucked from Sunny Climes.

The Sabbath dawns in Florida with its recreations and steam-boat excursions, well patronized by Northern visitors, as very few appear to bring their religion when they come South.

Mrs. Harriet Beecher Stowe is here to-day from her home in Mandarin, for the purpose of attending church. Dr. Stowe, her husband, accompanies her as he preaches. When they both entered the Southern Methodist church a slight rustle was heard in the congregation, and a few persons left the house. Mr. and Mrs. Uncle Tom were more than a Sabbath dose for some of the Jacksonville community. Harriet B. has no resemblance to a perpetrator of discord or scandal, or one who has swayed the divining-rod of Abolitionism with sufficient potency to immortalize herself for many coming generations, or probed the private life of a man who, during the period of his checkered existence, never carved out virtue for his shrine. The three snowy curls on each side of her face give her a matronly look, and her stout-built frame, well covered with flesh, a substantial appearance.

The service was opened by a very long prayer from Dr. Stowe, after which he preached a purely orthodox sermon on the subject of godliness. Mrs. Harriet had confidence in the ability of her husband; she knew the discourse would be right without her vigilant eye, and she went to sleep. Like other sleepers, she nodded naturally; her digits were concealed beneath kid covers, and thrusting at no one. She looked the picture of content, and was no doubt dreaming of that far-off, beautiful country, where those who create dissensions and stir up strife can never enter.

Places of worship have had an existence for both colors throughout the entire South since the country was settled, the negroes being naturally inclined to religion more than the whites. The African Church has always been a full-developed institution, attended with its peculiarities and noisy accompaniments, where the colored zealots could always give vent to their religious enthusiasm by howling their emotional feelings among others equally excited. The preacher usually leads the singing with his loud, soul-stirring strains, manifesting much fervor, sometimes improvising a strain or two with his own invention, if the rhyme and tune do not measure equal.

The following is a correct copy of an original sermon delivered by a very black Baptist brother to a Jacksonville colored congregation a short time previous to the Freedmen's Bank explosion, which appears prophetic in regard to that swindling institution. The text was, "Lay up for yourselves treasure in heaven":

"MY DEAR BREDREN:—De Lord is here to-day, goin' from de African to de white folks church, ridin' on a milk-white steed in de air. He knows all yer hearts, and what you're thinkin' about. Ef yer hearts are not right, dey must all undergo a radical change until dey are made good. De Lord taught his disciples on de lake of Genesis, and I'm now telling you all de way do do. I 'spec you all cum to de house of de Lord just kase yer friends are here. While yer preacher is tryin' to permulgate de gospel, you is lookin' down de street to see what is comin', and den you're thinkin' about what you will wear to-night when you come to preachin', payin' no attention to me, who is tryin' to save yer souls.

"O my bredren, dis is a fine new meetin'-house, but we should all seek a house whose builder and maker is de great Lord! Labor not for de perishin', spilin' meat!

"Last night was Saturday, and you have spent most of yer week's wages and earnin's, dun put de rest in de Freedmen Savin' Bank, and you don't know as you'll ever see it any more in dis world! Somebody may git it, or you may die, and den you will leave it. How much did you bring here for de Lord? O my bredren, when dem jerudic angels come you will be sorry you haven't done more for de Lord! When dey come, ef you hasn't dun nothin' for yer blessed Jesus, den dey will not say, 'Come, ye blessed, home!'

"You must do nothin' wrong ef yer want ter git up by dat great white throne among dem snow-white angels, and be one yerselves. You must never cuss or drink any whisky. Paul told Timothy his son to drink some wine when he had de stumak-ake. My bredren, don't think yer sufferin' when yer not, jest for an excuse to git a dram. Old Master in heaven knows when yer sure enuff sick! Can't fool him about nothin'!"

Journalism in Jacksonville is commencing to rest on a firmer basis than heretofore. The present pop-

ulation demand more knowledge on the subject of
the country, consequently papers and periodicals
published in the interest of the State are much
sought after. The *Semi-tropical*, a monthly established here, will be found to contain both readable
and reliable articles on the climate and various products of Florida. The *Sun and Press* is a daily democratic paper, unswerving in its efforts to inculcate
correct principles among those in power. There
were other organs whose politics was gauged for the
season, and since the war until now have been on
the winning side, the Republicans being in the majority. The ephemeral existence of newspapers has
passed away here, and the morning news, fresh and
well printed, containing the latest telegrams, are
found lying on the breakfast-table, furnishing a potent auxiliary to the peace and happiness of the
household.

The privilege of doing as one pleases is not to
be overlooked in Jacksonville. No costumes, however peculiar, appear out of style, or the wearers,
as in some other places, obliged to seek protection
from the police. Celebrities or millionaires walk
the streets without creating any sensation. The
Mormon, with his four or fourteen wives, can come
from Salt Lake City, take rooms at the St. James,
enter all the frequented resorts with the same fear
from molestation that a genuine Floridian feels of
being Ku-Kluxed. Any strong-minded marketwoman can don the Bloomer costume, make and
sell sugar, brown as her own bun-colored face, and
peddle vegetables verdant as the idea which prompt-

ed her to forsake the flowing robes of her fair sisters, and assume the half masculine attire of the sterner sex, without attracting any more attention than the lazy loungers in the market-house. The citizens are so accustomed to sight-seeing that nothing would astonish them but an honest politician.

Unfortunately for all parties concerned, this winter there is a large influx of men in search of employment, fifty looking for situations with only one vacancy. It is well to come prepared for all exigencies, and bring a tent to stop in, provided nothing better presents itself. The woods, waters, and oyster-bars are free to all; but boarding-house keepers, from the pressure of surrounding circumstances, have a peculiarly persistent way of watching strangers closely and *interviewing* them frequently, particularly if there is a suspicion that funds are running low with them. Camping in the open air in this genial clime is pleasanter than would be imagined by persons not accustomed to it, and is accompanied with more peace of mind than being dunned for board-bills without money to pay them.

Pleasant places of resort are springing up in the vicinity of Jacksonville, which furnish lovely drives behind some of the teams kept in the city. Moncrief Springs, four miles distant, now appears to be the most popular resort. Here the orange marmalade factory may be visited—a recently-developed branch of industry — making use of the wild oranges which flourish so abundantly throughout the State without culture. Many other improvements have been made at this place—bath-houses,

bowling-alley, dancing-saloon, and restaurant—all
of which contribute much to the diversion of
strangers.

Visitors always form an idea of the cultivation or
ignorance of a locality by the manner in which the
dead are cared for, together with the various styles
of monuments, inscriptions upon the tablets, neatness and taste displayed in the surroundings. Upon
this hypothesis a favorable conclusion would be
formed in regard to the Jacksonville cemetery,
which last resting-place of its citizens is pleasantly
located on a slightly elevated piece of ground beyond the city. It was on the Sabbath we visited it,
when all kinds of people were present. Some of
them were much stricken with grief, while others
came for recreation. It is really very surprising
why so many persons of exceedingly low morals resort to grave-yards for the sole purpose of enjoyment, and the indulgence of obscene conduct and
conversation. Certainly rude sounds must jar very
inharmoniously upon the feelings of those who come
to visit and weep over the remains of their departed
friends.

Too many invalids, before coming to Florida, wait
until they have already felt the downy flappings
from the wings of the unrelenting destroyer, and
heard the voices from a spirit-land calling them, but
come too late to be benefited and take a new lease
on life. The climate should not be blamed because
the sick will stay away until death claims them.
Those who do not wait derive the same benefit in
remaining that flowers receive from gentle rains in

spring-time—the atmosphere being a tranquillizer, the pure sea-breeze on the coast a lotion and tonic to the lungs. God grant that the genial air which visits this peninsula may restore the health-seeking invalids to vigor, strength, and usefulness, that their presence may again gladden the hearts of those left at home, now saddened by their absence!

CHAPTER III.

EVERY year, during the month of February, Jacksonville has an exhibit of industries, from all portions of the State, thus furnishing visitors an opportunity for seeing specimens of the best Florida products for themselves, before purchasing. Another advantage is the exchange of experience in growing the same things, besides receiving new suggestions in regard to those which may have failed, and, finally, it keeps up a friendly intercourse with old acquaintances, also enabling new immigrants to form pleasant associations, in the absence of those whom they have left behind — thus promoting harmony, not only in a community, but throughout the entire State.

The weather—that important auxiliary—this year was unpropitious a greater portion of the week. Nature put on a wild, damp face, which chilled the ardor of many who had intended coming. However, the exhibit was very good, in every department. All kinds of semi-tropical fruits, from the most perfect pine-apple that has flourished in any clime, to the sweetest orange, whose cheek had been kissed by a golden sunbeam. Pure wines were not wanting to complete the conviviality of the occasion, or perfumes distilled from Florida leaves and flowers, to waft odors around us, sweet as the memory of a first love. The industrious ladies sent their needle-work, some of which looked as if wrought by fairy fingers, more than real flesh and blood.

Each succeeding year this organization gathers strength as the State becomes more populous, and the necessity of comparing the products from different latitudes is made a criterion for those who wish to examine the local products of a country. In addition to what has already been done, there is much room for improvement, which will be accomplished as the necessities demand, until the Agricultural Florida Fair shall be numbered among the permanent institutions, where the ingathering harvest of tropical fruits every year will be a fixed fact, where immense crowds shall come to look, wondering at its magnitude, and silent with admiration before the grandeur of its extensive proportions. The future of the Fair, like that of the State, has not been attained.

Another source of entertainment with many who come here is yachting. The white-winged little crafts are constantly flitting about the Jacksonville wharves, like summer songsters in a clear sky. The boats, in reality, have become quite indispensable to the excitement of visitors. Those that draw the least water, and make the best time, or with a fair wind can sail on a heavy dew, are the class of craft most in demand. General Spinner, formerly of the United States Treasury, has a fine little yacht, in which he takes pleasure-excursions, looking much happier than when the responsibility of a nation's finances rested on his movements.

Our stay in Jacksonville has been very pleasant; but its surroundings furnish a poor criterion for the fertile lands lying in other parts of the State.

The ocean steamer Dictator is waiting at the wharf for passengers, and we will be among the happy number to embark on this reliable-running craft. Her former efficient commander, Captain Coxetter, has gone where bars or rough waters never imperil his safety. However, his place has been supplied by a skillful seaman, thus placing the Dictator at the head of the list for palatial accommodations and attentive officers.

The St. John's to-day appears overspread with a kind of semi-transparent mist, through which the sun shines with a nimbus of golden sheen, that fills the air and sky. Imagination could not paint the River of Life more beautiful. How smoothly we glide on its peaceful bosom, while fleecy clouds of unrivaled purity float over us like airy forms, which leave an indefinable idea of an invisible presence hovering near.

The first noticeable landing, after we leave Jacksonville, is Mandarin, fifteen miles distant—the winter residence of Harriet Beecher Stowe—at which point many stop, as though she was expected to furnish a gratuitous exhibition of herself, designed for the benefit of those who walk her domains. Visitors come here thinking they are at the same liberty to inspect her person as though she were connected with a menagerie, and obligated to present herself for their entertainment. Very curious ones open her window-blinds if they cannot see her in any other way. These impudent violations of etiquette do not meet with her approval, while those indulging in them must take the consequences, remembering that although patience is a virtue, it is not always exercised.

Mandarin is quite unpretentious in its general appearance. The inhabitants raise fine sweet oranges and other produce, which they bring down in little boats to market; this is the most perceptible stir made by any of its residents. Like many other localities in the State, historic records of tragic events, extending back to the Indian wars, are yet remembered by some of its old citizens. The following is dated December 25, 1841:

"For some time the settlers in this section of the country had been lulled into apparent security, under the belief that there was no danger to be apprehended, since the notorious Wild Cat and his party were shipped to the West.

"On Monday a band of twenty-one Indians approached the settlement of Mandarin, when, after capturing an old negro belonging to Mr. William Hartley, lay by until night, when they attacked the house of Mr. H., who was absent hunting. They murdered his wife and child, also Messrs. Domingo Acosta and William Molpus. These savages, after committing this foul deed, plundered the house and applied the torch. They then proceeded to the plantations of Nathan and George Hartley, and as the inmates had fled, they destroyed their homes. The Indians camped near until morning, when they released the old negro, and fled. Captain Hurry, of

Mandarin, and a few other citizens, followed their trail the next day for some distance, but finally lost it."

The settlers then gave expression to their feelings:

"We, the citizens of Mandarin, cannot too strongly urge upon Col. Worth the propriety of keeping in this vicinity a force sufficiently strong to render to our citizens that protection to which they are justly entitled. Many of them had returned to their abandoned places, others making preparations for that purpose; but their plans are now frustrated, as there can be no possible security until the last Indian is hunted out of Florida; while our troops are operating in the South, they are murdering in our unprotected settlements. This is the seventh Christmas-day we have witnessed since the Indian war has been raging in our territory, it being now our painful duty to record it is far from being ended. The blood of our citizens is still warm upon the hillocks and turfs of Florida, and the wily savage roams undismayed, with his thirst for the blood of fresh victims unquenched."

One noticeable feature in traveling through Florida is the fanciful names we hear given to unimportant places—the name being the most prominent point, the towns so diminutive that it is difficult to locate them with any degree of certainty. The first high-sounding ones, after Mandarin, are Hibernia and Magnolia, both little stopping-places, considered quite exclusive in their associations with the world in general and themselves in particular, where guests are so well contented they think the fabled land for which the Spaniards searched so long is at last reached.

Green Cove Mineral Springs, thirty miles above Jacksonville, is a noted resort for those afflicted with rheumatism—the temperature of the water always being warm enough in winter to stimulate the system and give relief to pain. Many other diseases are also greatly mitigated. Very happy faces come down here to look at us, which is, no doubt, attributable to the exhilarating influences of the water and fine fare at the hotels.

Picolata, forty-five miles above Jacksonville, on the east bank of the river, is more famous for what it has been than for what it is now, its former greatness having departed, leaving scarcely a shadow to guide us. This was formerly the stage terminus from St. Augustine, eighteen miles distant, and of some importance as a commercial point, with a weekly stage running to Tallahassee and St. Mark's. During Spanish times this place was called Fort Picolata, where once stood a very ancient fortress. The following is a description of its dimensions, written over one hundred years since: "It was constructed with a high wall, without bastions, about breast-high on the inside, with loop-holes, and surrounded by a deep ditch. The upper story was open on each side, with battlements supporting a cupola, or roof. These parapets were formerly mounted with eight four-pounders—two on each side. The works were built with hewn stone, cemented in lime. The shell-rock from which it was constructed was cut out of quarries on St. Anastasia Island, opposite St. Augustine." The object of this fort was to guard the passage of the river, and preserve communication with St. Mark's and Pensacola.

As we propose describing Tocoi on our return, we will now proceed to Pilatka, the county-seat of Putnam, with a population of fifteen hundred inhabitants. The land on which the town stands is high, the soil being mixed with shells. The accommodations here for visitors are fine, where many come to stay all winter, in preference to any other place. The Putnam House is well kept, being refreshingly neat, and the whole premises in perfect order. It is now February, and the garden is producing peas, lettuce, radishes, Irish potatoes, and many other vegetables, from which the house is supplied. The tables groan with good things, while the proprietor tries to make everybody welcome. The politeness of the servants reminds us of the palmy days of the past, when they were trained for use, and not permitted to roam, as many do now, like untamed beasts, seeking something which they can kill and eat, or steal, and trade for money. The citizens are very industrious and law-abiding—the town having been settled thirty years—and never had a county jail until recently; but, in keeping with the improvements of the age, they have one now which is equal to any emergency. Among the various other buildings, we notice a court-house, several churches, and many boarding-houses. The principal industries are a moss-factory, sea-island cotton-gin, a steam grist-mill and saw-mill, also a guano fish-oil factory. Shad-fishing is profitable here in March, when large quantities are shipped. One paper—the *Pilatka Herald*—publishes all the news. The editor is called "Alligator" Pratt—he having obtained his title by giving descriptions of the immense numbers of alligators which frequented the streams, as recorded by the early settlers, but bringing it down to the present time, as a visible fact, which is not true, nor ever will be again, while so many are being killed every year. When we visited the *Herald* office, two lads, sons of the proprietor, were working like busy bees, the youngest being thirteen, and the oldest seventeen, years of age. They said their father was in Tallahassee, and they were "getting out the paper." Such enterprise is commendable.

Many of the tropical fruits are cultivated here, some of which grow to perfection, while others are experimental, but at present very flourishing. Ripe strawberries, luscious and sweet, are now ready for market, on Col. Hart's place—the fertilizer used being river-muck, which is inexhaustible. The weather is milder here than in other localities of the same latitude, not on the river, which is accounted for by the waters of the St. John's flowing from a milder clime, thus checking any proposed invasion from Jack Frost.

A very amusing circumstance happened here this morning. The Catholic bishop from St. Augustine being in town, according to his usual custom, proposed to have early morning mass. On repairing to the church, and finding none of his members in attendance, and not being inclined to say mass for the repose of their souls and bodies while in bed, as a gentle reminder of their duties he commenced pulling vigorously at the bell-rope. The jingling at so early an hour caused a consternation among the inhabitants, who supposed it to be a fire-alarm, and, thinking the safety of their dwellings in danger, rushed from every street in hasty-made toilets, looking for the conflagration. However, on quiet being restored, the affair was considered a good joke.

Pilatka is the head of navigation for ocean steamers, the river narrowing so rapidly soon after leaving here that they cannot run any farther. Parties going up the Ocklawaha must always stop at this point, as steamers made for no other purpose leave here daily. No Florida tour would be complete without a trip up this narrow, tortuous stream, which turns its course so often the wonder is that it does not forget which way it was going to run.

The name of our boat is Okahumkee, which bears a slight resemblance to the pictures designed to represent Noah's ark, but only in shape, not in size or age. On account of the obstacles she has to meet in navigation, there can be no surplus work or embellishment on her; but she is clean and comfortable, the fare good as on any river-craft. The propelling power is at the stern, and sends the steamer ahead at the rate of eight miles an hour. The owner, Col. Hart, is a man of undaunted energies, whose pioneer movements in navigating this river will ever remain a monument worthy of emulation.

Twenty-five miles above Pilatka the Ocklawaha comes in, which name signifies boggy river, or turgid water, so called by the Indians.

CHAPTER IV.

WHILE in Florida, if tourists wish for a variety, let them travel up the meandering course of that peculiar stream, the Ocklawaha. There is no signaling here, as at other rivers in the State, for fossilized Spaniards to take us over the bars. After describing a triangle, we enter its dark waters without obstacle or interruption, when our steamer glides along easily, if not quickly, as a Florida sun behind the horizon.

The Ocklawaha is the largest tributary of the much-admired St. John's River. It is only from fifty to seventy-five feet in width at any point, and navigable all seasons of the year. Its banks are lined with "forests primeval," while its crooked course can only be traced by a seat upon the decks of its steamers. The banks are low, with an occasional bluff, accompanied by a wildness of scenery not so unvaried as to become monotonous. The river runs through heavily-timbered lands, consisting of sweet-gum, sweet-bay, and live-oak, from which hangs a drapery of long moss so dense it is only visited by zephyr breezes. The swaying of this pendant growth appears like the movements of magic, preparing a revelation from the secret abodes of wood-nymphs, or a *début* from the weird form of some dark-eyed Indian maid.

The cypress-trees grow here to the height of two hundred feet, some of them being twenty-four in circumference, and eight feet through at the base. From this kind of timber spars for vessels are made, which excel in durability any other in use.

The trees on the banks are set closely as a cane thicket, thus obscuring all view of the surrounding country as effectually as if it were a thousand miles distant. It is to this point the sportsman resorts to indulge his propensity for killing birds, which sing songs of joy as we pass; but when wounded, their helpless bodies fall into the turbid waters—the last that is seen of them being a fluttering pinion, signaling their sinking condition, with no one to pity or rescue. The click of the rifle is heard on every side from the hands of passengers, with the exciting remark: "O there is another alligator! Sight him quick! Kill him!" Although this seems to be great sport for the huntsman, it is not always death to the game.

As we approach the source of the river the scenery is constantly changing, like a kaleidoscopic view, and although it is mid-winter the river-banks are lined with flowers in full bloom, as though Jack Frost was not abroad with his withering breath, and had killed many of their companions far away, and buried them under his white covering, bound with icy fetters.

Among the most conspicuous plants which we see now is the aster, climbing twenty or thirty feet, forming bowers filled with blooms, supported by woody stems, sending forth their fragrance to gladden the senses of those who love perfumery made in nature's laboratory.

The water-lily, enthroned on her emerald seat, sits like a queen, spreading a snowy crown in every quiet corner of the stream; while the air-plants, with a more ambitious turn, are clinging to the trees, with their pink petals bursting into bloom, as the wild oranges and scarlet berries combined form a panorama which creates new-born emotions of happiness in the minds of all who look on their beauties and retain in imagination their charms.

Captain Rice, who has charge of the steamer Okahumkee, is the alpha and omega of the inhabitants on this river. He supplies all their wants, makes all their contracts, and sells all their produce. The men expect him to furnish them with whatever they need, from a sugar-mill to a plug of tobacco. From this portion of the country are shipped sea-island cotton, moss, oranges, vanilla, chickens, and eggs. These are sold in Jacksonville to obtain their family supplies. The Captain goes shopping for the young ladies, buys their pin-backs, tilters, face-powder, and sometimes snuff—for their mothers only! For these numerous services he rarely ever receives any thing but a smile! No wonder the man looks thin, fed on such intangible substance!

Orange Springs, thirty-five miles from the mouth of the river, is our first landing-place. This was formerly a resort for invalids, on account of the mineral properties contained in the water. Here we witnessed an affectionate meeting between a husband and wife. The lady had just returned from

Jacksonville on the steamer. When she stepped on shore, and saw her husband waiting for her, she threw her arms around his neck and cried. Some of the experienced passengers said she wept because she thought of all that old fat bacon she would have to eat after feasting so high in Jacksonville.

A log is something which our boat appears to understand. It leaps over at a single bound, then goes crashing against the large limbs, which sounds like the rattling of musketry, or crashing of a cyclone.

We met a lady on board who, since her last visit up the Ocklawaha, has been deprived of her hearing. Not aware of the great change through which she had passed, she quietly inquired if the obstructions had not all been removed from the river. The sound, then, of big limbs rasping across the boat, which had been crushed by coming in contact with it, resembled thunder. The Captain changed his seat very suddenly to go forward, while the passengers were all busy looking after birds and alligators; but no one asserted that navigation was without impediments, so far as last heard from. "Where ignorance is bliss, 't is folly to be wise."

On this river is the home of the genuine crackers. You can see them come to the steamer when it lands; and clever people they are, too. They appear to come from nowhere, their first appearance being on a *bateau*, or little platform, by the riverbanks, where are seen standing specimens of humanity so thin a musquito would be doing a bad business in trying to obtain sustenance from their bloodless bodies.

Hoping that the mind of the public may be relieved of the impression that a kind of hybrid bipeds circulate through the South entirely unknown in other localities, called crackers, I herewith append

PLEASURE-RIDING IN A CRACKER CART.

a description of the Northern crackers, in connection with our Southern product, taken from my own observation.

From the Alleghany Mountains of Pennsylvania

to the sands of Florida there exists a certain class of the *genus homo*, defined by different names, but possessing traits of character nearly allied, called in the North "the lower class," in the South "crackers." In the Northern States these poor, uneducated creatures ruminate without restraint. The localities they prefer are removed from the principal towns and cities. During the summer they spend a portion of the season in raising a little corn and potatoes, together with other "garden sass," which is consumed by their numerous families to sustain them during the cold winter weather. The little attention this crop receives is when they are not working out as the hired help, in assisting their neighbors through "hayin' and harvestin', or diggin' taters." Many of them never "hire out," but subsist entirely by hunting, fishing, or gathering berries, for which pursuits their wild natures and unsettled habits well adapt them. They excel in the piscatorial profession, studying the habits of the finny tribe during their various stages, together with their times of ascending and descending the streams. Sometimes the city folks come out to spend a few days with tent and reels, which movement these self-constituted sovereigns of the soil regard as a direct innovation of their rights; and if the supposed intruders escape without their tent being burned, or their clothes stolen, during the day when they are absent, it may be regarded as a fortunate circumstance. Many of these "lower class" specimens of humanity cannot read or write, while those who can do not often imbibe orthodox opinions in their religious belief, but embrace theories mapped out by New England fanatics, upon which they try to make an improvement during the cold winter days when they cannot be "stirrin' out doors." If a thaw comes they hunt deer and other wild game, which is bartered for groceries. Hogs with them, as most other people, are an important item for winter food. These animals manage to live tolerably well during the summer on grass, besides occasionally breaking into a neighbor's field of corn or potatoes, and fattening in the autumn on wild mast, which is plentiful.

This "lower class" have never been credited with being strictly honest, and frequently a stray sheep, calf, or turkey, makes an important addition to the family larder, which is eaten by all without any scruples, no questions being asked. Generosity cannot be classed among their virtues. If a benevolent impulse ever forces its way into their stingy souls, it is soon frozen out for want of sustenance. Never a weary wanderer rests upon their beds, or is fed from their table, unless pay is expected for it, nor a drop of milk given to pleasure-excursionists without collection on delivery. Their clothes are made mostly of wool, it being a home product, and the winters so severe they are obliged to be protected. The "wimmen folks" weave the cloth, then color it blue or red, and when the garments are made they are worn through all seasons—in winter to keep out the cold, and in summer the heat. There is no changing of raiment, nor any record kept of the time each garment is worn, it being only removed when patching becomes necessary, and a Joseph's coat among them is not an uncommon sight. They are not remarkable for their powers of articulation, but communicate with a peculiar twang through their noses, as though that was the design of the organ. Cow is pronounced as though it was spelled "keow;" how, "heow." "Awful" is their principal adjective, upon which they ring changes at all times: "Awful mean!" "Awful good!" Conversation through the nose for the old women is a difficult experiment, as they deposit large quantities of snuff in that organ, whether for disease, or to fill a vacuum in their *crania*, has never been determined, but it is really a most disgusting and filthy practice to witness.

The above is a correct description of the Northern crackers, of which some scribblers seem to have lost sight in their unfeeling efforts to abuse the South, and impress the world with the idea that crackers and poor whites are entirely of Southern origin, and only found in that locality, they being the outgrowth of a slave oligarchy.

That indigenous class of persons called Southern crackers receive names according to their locality. In South Carolina and South Georgia they are called "Poor Buckra," and in Florida "Sand Lappers," or "Crackers." The Florida crackers are supposed to be named from the facility with which they eat corn, it being their chief article of diet, while some few contract the habit of dirt-eating, and have been named "Sand Lappers."

The true derivation of cracker, notwithstanding

all the evidence given before on the subject, is the original word for Quaker, which in Spanish is *cuacero*, first changed into *cuaker* by the English, and again into cracker. From this we may learn that neither cattle-whips nor corn-cracking had any thing to do with the naming of these people.

These crackers have few local attachments; moving twice in a year does not inconvenience them; indeed, no earthly state of existence can be imagined freer from care and less fraught with toil than the one they lead. When settled, they are not fastidious about their habitations, as the mild climate does not require close quarters; a good shelter will subserve their purpose. Like birds of the air, they only want a roosting-place when night overtakes them. Their houses are mostly made of logs, notched to fit at the corners, the floors being oftentimes of earth, but usually boards sawed by hand. These tenements are scoured once a week, when the beds are sunned, and every thing turned out. The men are not always dressed in "store-clothes," with a corresponding outfit, but usually country-made cotton home-spun. The genuine cracker wears a broad-brimmed hat, braided from palmetto, a brown-jean coat and breeches, a deer-skin vest with the fur left on, and a pair of stout, useful cow-skin boots, or shoes. He supports a very unkempt mustache and whiskers, before which a Broadway dandy would shrink with the most intense disgust. This natural growth obscures a mouth well filled with teeth, which were nature's gift, and the handiwork of no dentist—from whence is kept a constant ejecting of tobacco-juice. He always has a body-guard of dogs whenever and wherever you find him, the number varying according to his condition in life — the poorer the man, the larger the number of canines. These animals are very thin, whether from a deficiency in their master's larder, or the constant rambling life they lead, has not been exactly determined. Around his master's neck is suspended a flask of shot and powder-horn, while in his hands is a rifle named "Sure-fire," which he says was never known to flicker, warranted to bring down any game within a range of two hundred yards, running or flying. These people, like the patriarchs of old, have large families, which require about the same attention as puppies or kittens. When night comes the children curl up in almost any corner to sleep, and at dawn of day, when the early songsters dash the dew-drops from the grass and flowers, they are out hunting for berries, or watching the birds building their nests, that they may know where to find the eggs, in which enterprise they are experts.

The cracker has a hearty welcome for the stranger, which puts the blush of contempt upon those claiming a much higher degree of civilization. Every thing the house contains is free to visitors. Although the bill of fare bears no resemblance to the St. James Hotel or Carleton House in Jacksonville, yet quantity will make up for quality. Chickens are always killed for company, without counting the number of Christmas holidays they have seen. Your plate is piled with sweet potatoes and corndodger bread, or ash-cake, to be washed down with strong coffee, which they always manage to keep on hand for special occasions. The old folks are very attentive; but where are the children? Run away like wild rabbits. They are out taking a view of the company. Watch, and you will soon see curious little eyes looking through the cracks, or slipping around the corners. These crackers are a very communicative class of persons, always full of information pertaining to Florida, and as ready to talk as a freshly-wound, well-regulated Yankee clock to keep time. The father of the family is called "dad," the mother "mam." The husband speaks of his wife as "the old woman," the wife says "old man," while the children are always called girls and boys. Women among no class of people in the South, however poor, are ever called "heifers," as one Northern writer has represented, unless by their conduct they are lost both to virtue and shame. The cracker exercises his prudential care by always keeping hogs. It is the main support of the family; and these razor-backed tourists are constantly going on voyages of discovery, either by land or sea. They often excite the sympathies of visitors on account of their thin bodies, but they possess more self-sustaining qualities than those who are sorry for them, showing what hogs can do as well as people, when thrown on their own resources. The sea-shore swine, which receive sustenance from the beach, can feed twice in twenty-four hours, when the tide recedes, and no depleted stores tell the amount of fish, oysters, and other marine morsels, which are deposited within their bony frames.

The above is a true statement in regard to the Southern crackers, which excites the commiseration of so many people who know nothing about them, and would, no doubt, be greatly benefited by reserving their concern for themselves, remembering, "Where little is given, little is required."

Civilization has commenced making its mark on the Ocklawaha, and the march of improvement, which never tires in its efforts, is leaving its footprints here. These new developments are visible from the various landings which the steamer makes, as it advances through the rapid current. In order to effect a landing, the bow of the craft is run against the shore, when the command is given by the Captain, with as much authority as though a ship from England had arrived on foreign shores, "Make fast!" This order is executed by putting a hawser an inch in circumference around a stake driven in the ground. Here are two cords of wood waiting to be loaded, called in cracker vernacular "light-wood," filled with turpentine, from which the article of commerce is manufactured. The vender of this commodity is on shore, waiting for an opportunity to dispose of his pile when "the charcoal sketches" commence "wooding-up."

Nearly all the passengers improve the time by taking a walk on shore to see the country while the hands on board are working. A countryman is trying to sell a bear-skin to some of the crowd. These Floridians always ask more than they can get, to see what visitors will stand.

The sun has set, and we are now entering upon a

night of darkness, in a wilderness of leaves and blooms, on the water, near thickets where the hungry wolf lurks for his prey, and the bear growls from his covert of security; where the wild deer nips the grass and feasts from herbage green, frequenting haunts where the hounds lose their trail, and the foot of the civilized hunter has never trod. A bright blaze, made from light-wood knots, is placed in a frame on the bow of our craft, and, like the "pillar of fire" which preceded the Israelites through the wilderness, is our guide. Here, encircled by trees whose long limbs overlap each other so thickly that only a glimmer of dawn is seen through the small openings, our flame-lit craft winds up the serpentine stream, and our night-fires send out a glare which illumines the darkness far as the eye can see, while on the boughs above our heads in silence sits the owl, with only an occasional "Who!" to let us know vitality is not entirely extinct in these wilds.

WHO!

The queer, dusky-looking figures, moving about with their pine torches, flashing through the darkness, and yelling at each other in cases of emergency, when our boat appears trying to climb a tree, remind us of the historic plutonian regions. As we glide along, our pathway is marked by volumes of pyrotechnic showers more numerous and brilliant than can be conceived, which burst from the smoke-stacks, and fall on the water before they are extinguished. Phantom-like we move, while weird forms retire before us, but still clinging to our boat as the connecting-link between civilized and savage life, a thoughtless move from it in any direction being a dangerous and hazardous experiment.

Every landing has its name, kept up as a mark of distinction by the boatmen and settlers, but unknown to history.

CHAPTER V.

MANY incidents of travel are related by different *savants*, and those of humbler pretensions, who circulate through the country for various purposes; but the following stands without a parallel as a genuine fact, so far as last heard from, in the wilds of Florida.

As we entered the famous Silver Springs this morning, about 4 o'clock, on the steamer Okahumkee, another boat that had arrived slightly in advance of us was anchored very near our stopping-place. Upon the bows of each were burning large light-wood fires, the reflection on the water being only comparable to the magic movements of enchantment, while the shore, encircled with tall forest-trees, embowered the whole in a sylvan retreat, where Diana herself might repose, and be refreshed for the more exciting amusements of the chase. One of our gentlemen-passengers, upon being suddenly aroused from his sound slumbers, opened his blind for the purpose of taking observations of the outside world. At the same instant a very fresh morning breeze fanned his brow, causing him to make a most convulsive sneeze—which effort being too much for his artificial superstructure, all his upper teeth were ejected from his mouth into the water. Upon the return of his wandering thoughts from the vision of beauty before him, he was again apprised of the stern realities which would have to be met and faced without the valuable accessories for administering to his comfort—particularly in the mastication of Florida beef—teeth. Soon as day dawned, sympathetic friends gathered around him with words of condolence, while the services of all experts in the art of descending into the watery fluid, without being drowned, were called into requisition. They all went down repeatedly, and returned without the lost treasures. Poles were spliced, armed with instruments of various designs, with which they raked and dredged for hours, with toothless success. Large rewards were offered, while hope in the heart of the owner sunk below zero, and expectation stimulated the movements of only one artisan, who finally succeeded in securing the truant grinders by fastening a tin scoop on the end of a forty-foot pole, and bringing them out, amid the congratulations of friends and the great joy of the owner, who gave the persevering negro his proffered reward—ten dollars. The first investment made by the colored individual was two bits for tobacco, which he could chew without the aid of foreign intervention.

The most noticeable point on the Ocklawaha is the Mirror of Diana, or Silver Springs, which is the source of this river, where, from the depths of some invisible cavern, boils up a large body of water, gathered from far away, forming a succession of springs nine miles in length, with an average depth of thirty-five feet. These waters rise from the subterranean depths of the earth, with their crystal streams pure as an angel, clear as the noonday sun, bright and beautiful as the radiance of heavenly light. This spring is to the campers and movers who travel through the country what Jacob's Well was to the land of Samaria. It is entirely surrounded by trees, forming columns unknown to drafts or plans of architectural skill, except the great Architect of the universe. More than thirty years since, the land around this spring was entered as a homestead by a relative of that memorable martyr, John Rogers. Mr. Rogers, with whom we had the pleasure of conversing, said its present appearance was the same as when he first saw it—the water being so clear that looking down in it appeared like the sky above it: he could see no difference in depths, look which way he would, up or down. The basin is lined with a grayish limestone, which lies in ledges on the bottom, from under the crevices of which dart out patriarchal fish of immense size; but no hook, however delicately baited and concealed, can lure them to bite. They are occasionally captured with lines by striking, which custom was practiced by the Indians, "while graceful poised they threw the spear." At midday the sunbeams kiss the placid surface of this crystal fluid, while they are reflected by the transparent waters, which tremble and shimmer with resplendent glories.

A sunset viewed from this Mirror of Diana fills the imagination with emotions of grandeur, to be

remembered as past joys, where descriptive powers
are inadequate to the task. The parting rays of old
Sol shine upon the vast forest of tall trees, draped
with Spanish moss suspended in mid-air, resembling
the fragile texture of some fairy realm more than a
tangible substance; or when twilight deepens, then
the stars raise their eyelids, and peep into the depths
of this land-locked mystery, which reveals nothing
of its past history, age, or origin.

The following legend, which appeared in the *National Repository*, seems so much in keeping with
what might have been a reality, we have copied it
for the benefit of those who are fond of legendary
tales:

"A long time ago, when Okahumkee was king
over the tribes of Indians who roamed and hunted
around the South-western lakes, an event occurred
which filled many hearts with sorrow. The king
had a daughter named Weenonah, whose rare beauty was the pride of the old man's life. Weenonah
was exceedingly graceful and symmetrical in figure.
Her face was of an olive complexion, tinged with
light brown, her skin finely transparent, exquisitely
clear. It was easy to see the red blood beneath the
surface, and often it blushed in response to the impulses of a warm and generous nature. Her eye
was the crystal of the soul — clear and liquid, or
flashing and defiant, according to her mood. But
the hair was the glory of the woman. Dark as the
raven's plume, but shot with gleams of sacred arrows, the large masses, when free, rolled in tresses of
rich abundance. The silken drapery of that splendid

hair fell about her 'like some royal cloak dropped from the cloud-land's rare and radiant loom.' Weenonah was, in truth, a forest-belle—an idol of the braves—and many were the eloquent things said of her by the red men, when they rested at noon, or smoked around the evening fires. She was a coveted prize, while chiefs and warriors vied with each other as to who should present the most valuable gift, when her hand was sought from the king, her father. But the daughter had already seen and loved Chuleotah, the renowned chief of a tribe which dwelt among the wild groves near Silver Springs.

"The personal appearance of Chuleotah, as described by the hieroglyphics of that day, could be no other than prepossessing. He was arrayed in a style suitable to the dignity of a chief. Bold, handsome, well-developed, he was to an Indian maiden the very ideal of manly vigor. But it was a sad truth that between the old chief and the young, and their tribes, there had long been a deadly feud. They were enemies. When Okahumkee learned that Chuleotah had gained the affections of his beloved child, he at once declared his purpose of revenge. A war of passion was soon opened, and carried on without much regard to international amenities; nor had many weeks passed away before the noble Chuleotah was slain—slain, too, by the father of Weenonah.

"Dead! Her lover dead! Poor Weenonah! Will she return to the paternal lodge, and dwell among her people, while her father's hand is stained with the drippings of her lover's scalp? No; she hurries away to the well-known fountain. Her heart is there; for it is a favorite spot, and was a trysting-place, where herself and Chuleotah met. Its associations are all made sacred by the memories of the past, while on the glassy bosom of the spring the pale ghost of Chuleotah stands beckoning her to come. 'Yes, my own, my beloved one, I come. I will follow where thou leadest, to the green and flowery land.' Thus spake the will, if not the lips, of the maiden. It is not a mere common suicide which she now contemplates; it is not despair, nor a broken heart, nor the loss of reason; it is not because she is sick of the world, or tired of life. Her faith is, that by an act of self-immolation she will join her lover on that spirit-plain, whose far-off, strange glory has now for her such an irresistible attraction.

"The red clouds of sunset had passed away from the western skies. Gray mists came stealing on, but they soon melted and disappeared, as the stars shone through the airy blue. The moon came out with more than common brilliancy, and her light silvered the fountain. All was still, save the night-winds, that sighed and moaned through the lofty pines. Then came Weenonah to the side of the spring, where, gazing down, she could see on the bottom the clear, green shelves of limestone, sloping into sharp hollows, opening here and there into still profounder depths. Forty feet below, on the mass of rock, was her bed of death—easy enough for her, as before she could reach it the spirit must have fled. The jagged rocks on the floor could therefore produce no pain in that beautiful form. For a moment she paused on the edge of the spring, then met her palms above her head, and with a wild leap she fell into the whelming waves.

"Down there in the spring are shells, finely polished by the attrition of the waters. They shine with purple and crimson, mingled with white irradiations, as if beams of the Aurora, or clouds of a tropical sunset, had been broken and scattered among them. Now, mark those long, green filaments of moss, or fresh-water algæ, swaying to and fro to the motion of the waves; these are the loosened braids of Weenonah's hair, whose coronet gives us such beautiful coruscations, sparkling and luminous, like diamonds of the deep, when in the phosphorescence of night the ocean waves are tipped with fire. These relics of the devoted Indian girl are the charm of Silver Springs. But as to Weenonah herself—the real woman who could think and feel, with her affections and memory—she has gone to one of those enchanted isles far out in the western sea, where the maiden and her lover are united, and where both have found another Silver Spring, amid the rosy bowers of love eternal."

Thus runs the Indian legend of Silver Springs, in Florida.

The following description of Silver Spring, written by Prof. John Le Conte, although entirely divested of myth and mystery, contains truthful facts that continue to invest it with a charm which stirs the current of our thoughts as no other natural scenery in the State:

"This remarkable spring is situated near the center of Marion county, in the State of Florida, in latitude 29° 15' north, and longitude 82° 20' west. It is about five miles north-east of Ocala, the county-seat, and nearly in the axis of the peninsula, being equally distant from the Atlantic and Gulf coasts. Its waters are discharged by a short stream bearing the same name, which, after running about six miles, unites with the Ocklawaha, a tributary of the St. John's River. The stream takes its origin in a deep pool, or head-basin, which is called the Silver Spring. This basin is nearly circular in shape, about two hundred feet in diameter, and surrounded by hills covered with live-oaks, magnolias, sweet-bays, and other gigantic evergreens. The amount of water discharged is so large that small steamers and barges readily navigate the Silver Spring, up to the pool, or head-spring, where there is a landing for the shipment of cotton, sugar, and other produce. These steamers and barges make regular trips between the Spring and Pilatka, on the St. John's. The boatmen informed me that at its junction with the Ocklawaha more than one-half the water is contributed by the Silver Spring stream. This stream, for about two miles from its source, varies in breadth from forty-five to one hundred feet, and its depth in the shallowest parts from ten to fifteen feet, its average velocity being about two miles per hour. The fluctuations of water-level in this spring seem to be connected with the season of rains, but never varying more than two feet. The commencement of the rainy season changes from the 15th of June to the

15th of July. The waters of the spring begin to rise about the middle of the season of summer rains, and attain their maximum height about its termination. The maximum depth of water in the basin constituting the head of the spring was found to be not more than thirty-six feet in the deepest crevice from which the water boils up; the general depth in the central and deep parts of the basin was found to be about thirty feet. Inasmuch as accurate quantitative determinations, however easily applied, are seldom resorted to by the unscientific, we need not be surprised that its real depth falls very far short of its reputed depth. In South Carolina, the reported depth was variously stated at from one hundred and twenty to one hundred and fifty feet, while the smallest estimate in the vicinity of the spring was forty-five feet! This affords an illustration of the general law, that the accuracy of popular statements bears an inverse proportion to the distance from the point of observation—probably, like all emanations from centers, following the law of inverse squares.

"Doubtless, the greater portion of the water which flows in the Silver Spring River is furnished by this principal or head-spring; but there are several tributary springs of similar character along the course of the stream, which contribute more or less to the volume of water. These usually occur in deep basins, or coves, along the margin of the stream. The depth of one of these coves, situated about two hundred yards below the head-spring, was found to be thirty-two feet in the crevice in the limestone bottom from which the water boiled; in other deep parts of the basin the depth was about twenty-four feet. The 'Bone-yard,' from which several specimens of mastodon bones have been taken, is situated two miles below the head-spring, it being a cove, or basin, measuring twenty-six feet.

"The most remarkable and really interesting phenomenon presented by this spring is the truly extraordinary transparency of the water—in this respect surpassing any thing which can be imagined. All of the intrinsic beauties which invest it, as well as the wonderful optical properties which popular reports have ascribed to its waters, are directly or indirectly referable to their almost perfect diaphaneity. On a clear and calm day, after the sun has attained sufficient altitude, the view from the side of a small boat floating on the surface of the water, near the center of the head-spring, is beautiful beyond description, and well calculated to produce a powerful impression upon the imagination. Every feature and configuration of the bottom of this gigantic basin is as distinctly visible as if the water was removed, and the atmosphere substituted in its place.

"A large portion of the bottom of this pool is covered with a luxuriant growth of water-grass and gigantic moss-like plants, or fresh-water algæ, which attain a height of three or four feet. The latter are found in the deepest parts of the basin. Without doubt, the development of so vigorous a vegetation at such depths is attributable to the large amount of solar light which penetrates these waters. Some parts are devoid of vegetation; these are composed of limestone rock and sand, presenting a white appearance. The water boils up from fissures in the limestone; these crevices being filled with sand and comminuted limestone, indicate the ascending currents of water by the local milk-like appearance produced by the agitation of their contents.

"These observations were made about noon, during the month of December—the sunlight illumining the sides and bottom of this remarkable pool, brilliantly, as if nothing obstructed the light. The shadows of our little boat, of our hanging heads and hats, of projecting crags and logs, of the surrounding forest, and of the vegetation at the bottom, were distinctly and sharply defined; while the constant waving of the slender and delicate moss-like *alga*, by means of the currents created by the boiling up of the water, and the swimming of numerous fish above this miniature subaqueous forest, imparted a living reality to the scene which can never be forgotten. If we add to this picture, already sufficiently striking, that objects beneath the surface of the water, when viewed obliquely, were fringed with the prismatic hues, we shall cease to be surprised at the mysterious phenomena with which vivid imaginations have invested this enchanting spring, besides the inaccuracies which have been perpetuated in relation to the wonderful properties of its waters. On a bright day the beholder seems to be looking down from some lofty air-point on a truly fairy scene in the immense basin beneath him—a scene whose beauty and magical effect is vastly enhanced by the chromatic tints with which it is inclosed.

"Popular opinion has ascribed to these waters remarkable magnifying power. In confirmation of this, it is commonly reported that the *New York Herald* can be read at the deepest parts of the pool. It is almost needless to state that the waters do not possess this magnifying power; that it is only the large capitals constituting the heading of this paper which can be read at the bottom, and that the extraordinary transparency of the water is abundantly sufficient to account for all analogous facts. A variety of careful experiments were made, with a view of testing this point, by securing printed cards to a brick attached to a fathoming-line, and observing at what depth the words could be read when seen vertically. Of course, when looked at obliquely, the letters were distorted and colored by refraction. Numerous comparative experiments were likewise executed in relation to the distances at which the same cards could be read in the air. The results of these experiments may be announced in a few words—namely, that when the letters are of considerable size—say a quarter of an inch or more in length—on a clear, bright day, they could be read at about as great a vertical distance beneath the surface of the water as they could in the atmosphere. In some instances cards were read by those ignorant of the contents at depths varying from six to thirty feet. The comparative experiments in reading the cards in air and water serve to convey a more distinct idea of the wonderful diaphanous properties of the latter than any verbal description.

"Some have thought there was something mysterious in the fact that objects beneath the surface of the water, when viewed obliquely, are fringed with prismatic hues. It is unnecessary to remind the physicist that such a phenomenon is a direct physical consequence of the laws of dispersion of light by refraction. Observation has proved that white objects on a dark ground were fringed with blue at the top, with orange and red at the bottom, while the color of the fringing was reversed for dark objects on a white ground—this being exactly in accordance with recognized optical principles. In the present case, the phenomenon is remarkably striking and conspicuous, probably from two causes: first, because the extraordinary transparency of the water rendered subaqueous objects highly luminous; and secondly, because the gigantic evergreens which fringed the pool cut off most of the surface reflection, which would otherwise have impaired the visual impression produced by the more feeble refracted and dispersed rays proceeding from the objects — the shadow of the surrounding forest forming a dark background, analogous to the black cloud on which a rainbow is projected."

The land improvements near the springs are not particularly fascinating. There are two landings about one-half mile distant from each other, called Upper and Lower. At the Lower Landing is a large turpentine distillery, the property of Messrs. Agnew & Co., where thirty barrels of turpentine and one hundred of rosin are manufactured monthly. The Upper Landing has a large ware-house, usually well filled with goods from steamers, to furnish the back country, together with produce for shipment to New York and many other points.

Mrs. F. A. House has a dry-goods store in the vicinity, and a small orange grove of very promising appearance. A boarding-house is kept open in the winter, but we are unable to state what benefit could be derived in drinking the strong limestone water from the spring, unless the scenery would compensate for the lack of life-giving properties in the transparent fluid. A bar-room is kept here by a man with much-inflamed eyes, which are, no doubt, caused by imbibing his villainous compounds too freely, in the absence of better-paying customers.

Tourists wishing to visit Ocala can be accommodated with a conveyance on reasonable terms. Ocala is a nice little town, six miles distant, nestled among the hummocks, embowered in a growth of grand water-oaks, orange-trees, and ornamental shrubbery. It is the capital of Marion county. A good hotel is kept here by Mr. E. J. Harris, where about forty boarders can be accommodated. In the center of the park stands a very creditable courthouse, while churches of various creeds are located in the suburbs. It is a central business resort for the country people many miles around.

This locality is described by De Soto as being "a fertile region of country where maize is abundant, also acorns, grapes, and plums." Near here the Spaniards entered upon the territory of a chief called Vitachuco, who received them with demonstrations of hostility; "where a bloody battle was fought between two lakes on a level plain, when two hundred warriors plunged into the water, and there remained without touching land for twenty-four hours." Ocala has a population of several hundred inhabitants, which have more the appearance of enjoyment than those of any other town in the State. The climate being so mild, no arrangements are made in the stores and offices for warming; consequently when a cool morning comes, little camp-fires are built around the public square, before which are gathered many happy, contented-looking faces, of all professions, accepting things as they find them, taking a cool breeze with the firmness of a Stoic, knowing it is only of short duration—a kind of Northern aggression, which the warm sunshine will soon waft away. As the fragments of lost fortunes float by them, they do not settle into apathy and despair over the wreck, but all seem resigned to their fate, trying to be as happy as the force of circumstances will permit. They are mostly persons of fine mental culture, besides being the best, most hospitable people in existence; indeed, their society seems like an oasis in the desert of this cold, selfish world.

The lands around are gently undulating, with an abundance of rolling hummock and first-class pine. It was formerly considered the most productive county in the State, containing the best orange groves, and before the war raising the largest amount of sea-island cotton, besides oranges, sugar, and sirup in abundance. Many planters became discouraged during the late war on account of inability to work their large plantations, and abandoned them. These fertile tracts are for sale now in lots to suit colonists, or accommodate single settlers. An average of two thousand pounds of sugar to the acre can be produced here. The soil is dark, alluvial, and porous, containing phosphate of lime and other fertilizers, which possess the power of recuperation when not being cultivated. Lime-rock abounds, covering the earth in the form of bowlders and drifts, indicating a clay soil. Good lands can be purchased at from five to ten dollars per acre.

Marion county is called the back-bone of the State—it being the center from which the waters recede on each side, until what was the ocean's bed is now cultivated land. This theory is confirmed from the fact of numerous fossil remains to be seen on the surface, consisting of fish, birds, alligators'-shells, oysters, together with the bones of an animal unknown to the present generation; but if his voice was proportionate to his body, he must have made the earth tremble with sound. The following amusing story is related in reference to this mammoth animal during the pioneer movements of boats which first navigated the Ocklawaha River:

One morning early, as the gray dawn was stealing through the shades of night, the inhabitants were aroused from their slumbers by an unusual noise. An old hunter named Matt. Driggers, whose ear was ever on the alert for the scream of the wild cat, the howl of the wolf, the yell of the panther, or the growl of the bear, rushed out, exclaiming, "What on airth is that?" The sound was repeated, when

Matt. convulsively grasped his hunting-horn, and blew a blast from his stentorian lungs which echoed through a vast extent of country. His faithful hounds came whining about him, anxious for the hunt. Taking down his rifle "Dead Shot" from the hooks, he mounted his lank steed, and rode with haste to the nearest neighbor, Pat Kennedy. "Hellow, Pat! you in thar asleep, and the devil unchained in the swamp! Hark! now don't you hear him?" "O Matt., that's nothin' but one of those old masterdons! You know we dun seed his bones where he was drowned in the Wakulla Spring." "I dunno, may be so; one thing sartain, he's a mighty big varmint, an' his voice is curoser than any thing I ever hearn afore in my time." "But," says Pat, "one thing sure: there is nothing ranges these parts but what my dogs and 'Kill Quick' can bring down." Summoning all his dogs, he was soon on his way with Matt. Driggers to the house of the next frontiersman. Attracted by the baying of hounds and the blowing of horns, the excitement ran like wild-fire throughout the entire neighborhood, until all the settlers were collected.

After reviewing his comrades and counting his dogs, Matt. Driggers, confident that the full force of the country was mustered, then rode bravely through bushes and swamps, fording creeks and swimming lagoons, in pursuit of the great "varmint." When he imagined they were sufficiently near, he ordered the dogs to be put on the trail. Simultaneous with this movement came another shrill echo from the supposed huge monster, which sent the dogs cowering to their masters, at the same time unnerving the courage of the bravest hunter. A look of superstitious awe was depicted upon every countenance, and none dared advance a step farther except Matt. Driggers, who, bolder than the rest, led the way, saying, "Come, boys; if the dogs are scared, we will follow by the sound!"

Winding their course cautiously through the valley, they followed in the direction of the strange sound, until they reached the basin of Silver Springs, where they found a curious-looking craft discharging cargo. The hunters commenced making inquiries if they had heard that great monster while passing through the valley, at the same time describing, and trying to imitate, its voice to the best of their ability. The Captain, to their great satisfaction, then told and illustrated to them that the great noise about which they were so much excited was only a *steam-boat whistle!*

Sometimes, the water being too low for steamers above Silver Springs, visitors are deprived of a great pleasure in not seeing this portion of the country, barges and slow coaches being the only medium of communication. However, this inconvenience will soon be overcome by a contemplated railroad. Large portions of the country in this locality are yet open to homestead settlers, where all good people will receive a hearty welcome.

As we leave the river and springs, the scenery changes from trees and foliage to fertile prairies and long marsh-grass, which sways in the breeze like troubled waves. Here the huge alligators luxuriate and crawl about in peaceful security, swallowing their light-wood knots before commencing to hibernate in winter, which precaution is said to be necessary, that their diaphragms may not contract during this torpid state.

In these wilds the palmetto rears its crowned head in solitude, and the wild orange matures its golden fruit, kissed by an eternal spring-time. This is the home of the curlew, plume-crane, blue heron, fish-hawk, royal king-fisher, mocking-bird, paroquet, red-bird, blue-peter, water-turkey, limkin, and duck —all of them God's free birds.

Our steamer has now commenced making its pathway through wide, deep lakes, and we are one hundred and fifty miles above Pilatka. In these waters are found a great variety of fish—pike, trout, bream, perch; while in the surrounding country live the black bear, wild cat, deer, gray fox, squirrels of all kinds, and wild hogs.

The first body of water is Lake Griffin, twelve miles long; Lake Eustace, of less dimensions; then Lake Harris, fifteen miles in length, seven miles wide, with an average of water thirty feet in depth. The tide of immigration is concentrating on this lake very rapidly.

The following incident is related as having occurred among the primitive inhabitants in this portion of the country, when priests were not always waiting in the church to administer the rites of matrimony to willing lovers:

A devoted suitor, having made the preliminary arrangements for the celebration of his nuptials, set out in search of an official to perform the ceremony. He, never having been initiated into the mysteries of matrimony before, ignorantly inquired of the first person he met where he could find a sheriff. The man replied there was no sheriff nearer than Pilatka. "Why do you wish for him?" "I'm going to be married, sir." "O you want the squire, or preacher." "Do you know where a preacher lives, then? I thought the sheriff would do as well." "The preacher has gone on the circuit." Knowing a good deacon lived near, he repaired thither as a last resort. Finding the deacon at home, he related to him, in tremulous tones, his disagreeable condition. The deacon informed him that marrying did not come within the pale of his jurisdiction. "But I must be married," replied the intended bridegroom. The deacon replied, "Impossible, sir!" "Well, deacon, can't you marry us just a little till the preacher comes home?"

Leesburg, fronting partly on Lake Harris, is a thriving town; has a post-office, court-house, Masonic hall, hotel, private boarding-houses, church, steam cotton-gin, grist-mill, lumber dressing machine, etc. A sugar-cane mill is in operation, connected with which is a centrifugal sugar-dryer, the only one in the State. This mill can turn out fifteen barrels per day. Every thing produced here finds a ready market, as boats pass almost daily, which enables the settlers to change all their surplus into money, from a bale of cotton or moss to a dozen eggs.

When Colonel Hart's little open boat and engine first came up to dredge out the barnets and swamp-grass, the natives gathered around him, thinking it was a cook-stove.

The Indians traveled through these swamps by wading in the water, and using a cow-hide fastened at the ends to transport their provisions, women, and children, which they drew after them, thus making a trail that lasted several days, which enabled their friends or foes to follow them.

In this vicinity we find historical relics, and approach tragic grounds. A portion of the cypress log mentioned by De Soto in his travels through Florida is still to be seen; also an artificial causeway, several hundred yards in length, made of shells from which the Indians extracted food and pearls, near which yet remains a portion of one of those immense mounds, supposed to be the residence of the Cazique.

Lake Dunham is the last in the chain of these inland waters, upon which is situated Okahumkee, two hundred and twenty-five miles above Pilatka. It is the terminus of navigation.

The Ocklawaha River was the memorable place where the Payne's Treaty Landing was drawn up, and between the terminus of this chain of lakes and the Withlacoochee River are located the tragic grounds of General Thompson's murder and the Dade Massacre.

CHAPTER VI.

THE early history of Florida Territory, soon after it came into the possession of the United States, being written in characters of blood for years, it is considered both appropriate and interesting to intersperse a sprinkling of historical facts in this work, to the authenticity of which some now living can testify.

The Indians were intensely opposed to emigrating West, as that country offered them no such means of idleness as Florida, where they lived with as little solicitude as the buzzards that lazily flew above their heads—while in Arkansas they would have to work They were a race of hunters and fishermen, with no habits of industry, gliding on the surface of lakes and rivers, with as little idea of locating as the watery inhabitants they captured.

The movements of the Indians and American troops, encumbered with their wagons, or a field-piece, compared unfavorably with the agile foe they had to meet in warfare, who could swim the streams and leap over the logs of the wide forest, and vanish, like the whooping crane, that made its nest at night far from the spot where it dashed the dew from the flowers and grass in the morning.

One of the occasions of the Seminole war, like our own late struggle, was on account of the fugitive slaves, which the Indians harbored, instead of returning to their owners, or permitting their masters to come and get them.

The following is a correct copy of an interesting document, to which frequent reference was made during the Florida war, as a compact which had been violated. We have transferred it as an item of interest. As the whites found the Indians becoming troublesome neighbors, this treaty was drawn up in order to rid the country of them—its violation being the true cause of the war:

Treaty of Payne's Landing, concluded May 9, 1832, and ratified April 12, 1834.

ARTICLE I. That the Seminole Indians relinquish to the United States all claim to the lands they at present occupy in the Territory of Florida, and agree to immigrate to the country assigned to the Creeks, west of the Mississippi River—it being understood that an additional extent of territory, proportioned to their numbers, will be added to the Creek country, and that the Seminoles will be received as a constituent part of the Creek Nation, and be reädmitted to all the privileges as a member of the same.

ART. II. For and in consideration of the relinquishment of claim in the first article of this agreement, and in full compensation for all the improvements which may have been made on the lands thereby ceded, the United States stipulate to pay to the Seminole Indians fifteen thousand dollars, to be divided among the chiefs and warriors of the several towns, in a ratio proportioned to their population, the respective portions of each to be paid on their arrival in the country they consent to move to: it being understood their faithful interpreters, Abraham and Cudjo, shall receive two hundred dollars each of the above sum, in full remuneration for the improvements to be abandoned, now cultivated by them.

ART. III. The United States agree to distribute, as they arrive at their homes in the Creek Territory, west of the Mississippi River, a blanket and home-spun frock to each warrior, women and children, of the Seminole tribe of Indians.

ART. IV. The United States agree to extend the annuity for the support of a blacksmith, provided for in the sixth article of the treaty at Camp Moultrie, for ten years beyond the period therein stipulated; and in addition to the other annuities secured under that treaty, the United States agree to pay three thousand dollars a year for fifteen years, commencing after the removal of the whole tribe—these sums to be added to the Creek annuities, and the whole sum to be divided, that the chiefs and warriors of the Seminole Indians may receive their equitable portion of the same, as members of the Creek Confederation.

ART. V. The United States will take the cattle belonging to the Seminoles, at the valuation of some discreet person appointed by the President, and the same shall be paid for in money to the respective owners, after their arrival at their new homes; or other cattle, such as may be desired, will be furnished them, notice being given through their agent of their wishes on this subject, before their removal, that time may be afforded to supply the demand.

ART. VI. The Seminoles being anxious to be relieved from certain vexatious demands for slaves and other property, alleged to have been stolen and destroyed by them, so that they may remove unembarrassed to their new homes, the United States stipulate to have the same property investigated, and to liquidate such as may be satisfactorily established, provided the amount does not exceed seven thousand dollars.

ART. VII. The Seminole Indians will remove in three years after the ratification of this agreement, and the expenses of their removal shall be paid by the United States; and such subsistence shall also be furnished for a term not exceeding twelve months after their arrival at their new residence, as in the opinion of the President their numbers may require, the emigration to commence early as practicable in A.D. 1833, and with those Indians at present occupying the Big Swamp and other parts of the country beyond, as defined in the second article of the treaty concluded at Camp Moultrie Creek, so that the whole of that proportion of Seminoles may be removed within the year aforesaid, and the remainder of the tribe, in about equal proportions, during the subsequent years 1834 and 1835.

Done at Camp at Payne's Landing, on the Ocklawaha River, in the Territory of Florida, May 9, 1832.

JAMES GADSDEN, Commissioner, [L. S.]
and fifteen Chiefs.

Osceola figured very conspicuously during the early history of our Florida troubles; indeed, we consider the following statements connected with his movements as items of unsurpassed interest to those who are more fond of facts without fiction than the wondrous legends of any day-dreamer.

The mother of Osceola belonged to the Red Stick tribe of Indians, a branch of the Creeks. She was married to Powell, who was an English trader among the Indians for twenty years, and for this reason he is sometimes called Powell instead of Osceola. He was born in the State of Georgia, on the Tallapoosa River, about the year 1800. In 1808 a quarrel occurred among the Indians of the Creek tribe, when the mother of Osceola left, taking him with her, and retiring to the Okefinokee Swamp. Powell remained in Georgia, with his two daughters, and emigrated to the West with them.

In 1817 Osceola retreated before General Jackson, with a small party, and settled on Pease Creek. A few years afterward he removed to the Big Swamp, in the neighborhood of Fort King, uniting himself with the Micosukees. The greater portion of his life was spent in disquietude, when there was neither peace nor war, but depredating in various ways. He was opposed to the Payne Treaty, declaring he would fight before signing it, or kill any of his followers who made a move toward its ratification.

When the Indians held a council at Fort King, consisting of thirteen chiefs, only eight of them were willing to leave for the West. Hoithlee Mattee, or Jumper, a sworn enemy of the whites, who was called in their language "The Lawyer," and for whom General Jackson had offered a reward of five hundred dollars, rose in their council, with all the dignity of a Roman orator, after which he announced his intention in thundering tones: "I say there is no good feeling between Jumper and the white man. Every branch he hews from a tree on our soil is a limb lopped from Hoithlee's body. Every drop of water that a white man drinks from our springs is so much blood from Hoithlee's heart."

After the return of Charlie Emaltha from the West, who was the most intelligent of their chiefs, he met with the whites in council, that he might give expression to his opinion: "Remain with us here," said he to the whites, "and be our father; the relation of parent and child to each other is peace—it is gentle as arrow-root and honey. The disorderly among us have committed some depredations, but no blood has been spilled. We have agreed that if we met a brother's blood on the road, or even found his dead body, we should not believe it was by human violence, but that he had snagged his foot, or that a tree had fallen upon him; that if blood was spilled by either, the offender should answer for it."

Previous to this period the Indians were lords of the soil, and considered themselves located in a land of undisputed titles, as entirely their own property, by right of possession, as though they held registered deeds.

The following is an effort at Indian poetry, descriptive of their condition previous to hostile demonstrations:

> We were a happy people then,
> Rejoicing in our hunter mood;
> No footsteps of the pale-faced men
> Had marred our solitude.

Osceola was not tall, but of fine figure and splendid *physique*, his head being always encircled with a blue turban, surmounted by the waving *tafa luste*, or black-eagle plumes, with a red sash around his waist. He was a time-server, a self-constituted agent, and a dangerous enemy when enraged. In 1834 the United States survey corps, while camping at Fort King, was visited by Osceola, Fred L. Ming being the captain. Indians always show their friendship by eating with their friends. On this occasion he refused all solicitations to partake of their hospitality, and sat in silence, the foam of rage resting in the corners of his mouth. Finally he rose to retire, at the same time assuming a menacing manner, and, seizing the surveyor's chain, said: "If you cross my land I will break this chain in as many pieces as there are links in it, and then throw the pins so far you can never get them again." Like most of his race, he was possessed of a native eloquence, the following of which is a speçimen, after the Payne's Landing Treaty was framed and signed by some of the chiefs: "There is little more to be said. The people have agreed in council; by their chiefs they have uttered it; it is well; it is truth, and must not be broken. I speak; what I say I will do; there remains nothing worthy of words. If the hail rattles, let the flowers be crushed; the stately oak of the forest will lift its head to the sky and the storms, towering and unscathed."

The whites continued urging the stipulations of the treaty to be enforced, while the Indians continued opposing it in every way. It is a law of our nature that the weak should suspect the strong; for this reason the Seminoles did not regard the Creeks as their friends, but feared them. Captain Wiley Thompson, the Agent, kept reminding the Indians that they had made a promise to leave for the West. Messages were also sent to Micanopy, who, after much debating, said he would not go. Some time afterward General Thompson ordered Osceola to come up and sign the emigration list, which request moved the indignation of this savage to the highest pitch of desperation, and he replied, "I will not." General Thompson then told him he had talked with the Big Chief, in Washington, who would teach him better. He replied, "I care no more for Jackson than for you," and, rushing up to the emigration treaty, as if to make his mark, stuck his knife through the paper. For this act of contempt he was seized, manacled, and confined in Fort King.

When Col. Fanning arrested him he was heard to mutter, "The sun is overhead, I shall remember the hour; the Agent has his day, I will have mine." After he was first imprisoned he became sullen, but soon manifested signs of penitence, and called the interpreter, promising, if his irons were taken off, to come back when the sun was high overhead, and bring with him one hundred warriors to sign the paper—which promise was fulfilled. The great mistake was made in releasing him from Fort King. If he had then been sent West, much blood and treasure would have been spared. He had one talk for the white man, and another for the red—being a strange compound of duplicity and superiority. After his release he commanded his warriors to have their knives in readiness, their rifles in order, with plenty of powder in their pouches, and commenced collecting a strong force, not eating or sleeping until it was done.

The first direct demonstration of hostility was on June 19, 1835, near what was called the Hogg's Town settlement, at which time one Indian was killed, another fatally injured; also three whites wounded. The fray commenced by some whites whipping a party of five Indians, whom they had caught in the act of stealing. Private Dalton, a dispatch-rider, was killed August 11, 1835, while carrying the mail from Fort Brooke to Fort King. This was an act of revenge for an Indian killed in a former encounter. Dalton was found twenty miles from Fort King with his body cut open and sunk in a pond. The Indians commenced snapping their guns in the face of the Government, at the same time expressing their contempt for the laws, and threatening the country with bloodshed if any force should be used to restrain them. November 30, 1835, the following order was issued by the Agent: "The citizens are warned to consult their safety by guarding against Indian depredations." Hostilities were soon inaugurated in a most shocking manner, with a tragedy of deep import — the killing of Charlie Emaltha, November 26, 1835—which act was only a cold-blooded murder, Osceola heading this band of savages. Charlie Emaltha was shot because he favored immigration, and was preparing to move West.

Osceola afterward selected ten of his boldest warriors, which were to wreak vengeance on General Thompson. The General was then camping at Fort King, little dreaming that the hour of his dissolution was so near, or that Osceola was lying in wait to murder him. Although a messenger was sent to tell Osceola of the Wahoo Swamp engagement being in readiness, no laurels won on other fields had any charms for him until Thompson should be victimized by his revengeful machinations. After lingering about for seven days, the opportune moment presented itself, when Thompson was invited away from the fort. On the afternoon of December 28, 1836, as he and Lieutenant Smith, who had dined out that day, were unguardedly walking toward the sutler's store, about a mile from the post, the savages discovered them. Osceola said, "Leave the Agent for me; I will manage him." They were immediately attacked by these warriors, when they both received the full fire of the enemy, and fell dead. Thompson was perforated with fourteen bullet-holes, and Smith with five. The Indians then proceeded to the store, where they shot Rogers and four others. After the murder they robbed the store and set fire to the building. The smoke gave the alarm, but the garrison at Fort King being small, no assistance could be rendered them.

On the same day (December 28), and nearly the same hour, Major F. L. Dade, when five miles from Wahoo Swamp, was attacked while on his way from Fort Brooke to Fort King. The Indians were headed by Jumper, who had previously warned those who were cowards not to join him. Micanopy, their chief, who was celebrated for his gluttony, like the Trojan heroes, could eat a whole calf or lamb, and then coil up in a snake-like manner for digestion. On a previous occasion, when an appeal was made to him by the argument of bullet-force, he replied, "I will show you," and afterward stationed himself behind a pine-tree, awaiting the arrival of the Fort Brooke force, while his warriors lay concealed in the high grass around him. When Major Dade arrived opposite where the chief and his men were ambushed, Micanopy, in honor of his position as top chief, leveled his rifle and killed him instantly. Major Dade was shot through the heart, and died apparently without a struggle. The savages rushed from their coverts, when Captain Frazier was their next victim, together with more than a hundred of his companions. The suddenness of the attack, the natural situation of the country, with its prairies of tall grass, each palmetto thicket being a fortress of security from which they could hurl their death-dealing weapons, were all formidable foes with which the whites had to contend. Within a few hours' march of Fort King, under the noonday splendor of a Florida sun, were one hundred and seven lifeless bodies, which had been surprised, murdered, and scalped, with no quarter, and far from the sound of human sympathy.

The night after the "Dade Massacre" the Indians returned to Wahoo Swamp with the warm life-current dripping from the scalps of those they had slain. These scalps were given to Hadjo, their Medicine Man, who placed them on a pole ten feet high, around which they all danced, after smearing their faces with the blood of their foes, and drinking freely of "*fire-water.*" One instance is mentioned worthy of remark, in regard to finding Major Dade's men with their personal property untouched. Breastpins of the officers were on their breasts, watches in their places, and silver money in their pockets. They took the military coat of Major Dade, and some clothing from his men, with all the arms and ammunition, which proved they were not fighting for spoils, but their homes. The "Bloody Eight Hundred," after they had committed the murder, left the bodies unburied, and without mutilation, except from scalping. They were buried by the command of Major-general Gaines, who also named this tragic ground "Field of the Dead."

Fights now followed each other in rapid succession. Long-impending hostilities burst upon the white settlers, who in turn sought every opportunity of gratifying their revenge for outrages committed. No person was safe; death lurked in every place, and there was security in none. Acts of fiendish barbarity were of common occurrence; houses burned — the labor of years gone forever — while many of the missing were consumed in the flames of their own dwellings, the savages dancing around the funeral-pile. The Indians appeared seized with a kind of desperation which knew no quarter, and asked for none, constantly posting themselves in the most frequented highways, with the intention of slaying or being slain.

On the 31st of December, same year, the Indians, receiving information that the troops under General Clinch were approaching, and would cross the Withlacoochee, posted themselves at the usual fording-place for the purpose of intercepting them. General Clinch was surprised by them, as they had greatly the advantage, being among the trees, while the troops were in an open space, with only an old leaky canoe to cross in, under constant fire of the enemy, some of them being obliged to swim. The soldiers accustomed to Indian warfare never forded twice in the same place. Captain Ellis, now a worthy citizen of Gainesville, Florida, who commanded a company during the Seminole war, being present when this attack was made, says: "I was so much afraid the war would be over before I had a chance to be in a fight, I was glad when I saw the Indians coming, but I got enough fighting before it was through with." When he saw the savages at the commencement of this engagement, not knowing of the "Massacre," he said, "Boys, the Indians have been killing our men, for they have got on their coats."

Osceola was the prime leader in this first battle of Withlacoochee, and although whole platoons were leveled at him, from behind the tree where he was stationed he brought down his man every fire to the number of forty, while he ordered his warriors not to run from the pale faces, but to fight. The contest was a close one, but General Clinch held his ground. After the Indians retreated the troops buried their dead, and built log-fires over their remains to keep the enemy from digging them up and scalping them.

During September, 1837, Osceola sent in negotiations of peace to General Hernandez through an envoy, accompanied with presents of a bead pipe and white plume, as an assurance that the path of the pale face was peaceful and safe. General Hernandez, with the sanction of General Jessup, returned presents and friendly messages, requesting the presence of Osceola, with the distinct understanding that it was for the purpose of making arrangements for the immigration of his people. The messenger returned in accordance to his previous contract, reporting that Osceola was then on his way to St. Augustine with one hundred warriors. Osceola had never heretofore regarded the sacredness of a flag of truce as binding, besides being engaged in the abduction of Micanopy and others, who would otherwise have complied with the terms of the treaty. General Jessup intended before his arrival to have him detained. General Hernandez, who was the soul of honor, remonstrated with him, when he replied, "I am your superior; it is your duty to obey." General Hernandez met them at Fort Peyton, near Pelicier Creek, about seven miles south-west of St. Augustine. From the inquiries of General Hernandez in regard to the other chiefs and their locality, Osceola soon comprehended the situation; and when asked for replies to the General's questions, he said to the interpreter, "I feel choked; you must speak for me." The place where they were assembled for parley being surrounded by a detachment of dragoons, they closed in on them, capturing the whole band without firing a gun.

This strategy in taking Osceola did not tarnish the laurels of General Jessup in the least; a much greater blunder was committed in turning him loose after his first capture. Those who have condemned him must think of the anxiety by day and horrors at night through which these poor settlers struggled, when time passed like a bewildering dream of terrors, improvement of all kinds languishing with a sickly growth, while the dragon of war sowed the seeds of discord, and desecrated the golden fleece of the harvest with a bloody hand.

When Osceola was first captured he was imprisoned in Fort Marion, but was afterward removed to Sullivan's Island, where his wife and child accompanied him. He was a sad prisoner—never known to laugh during his confinement, but often heard to sigh. During his last illness he had the best medical attention from Charleston, whose skill he refused, believing they intended poisoning him. To one of his wives he was much attached, and his spirit passed away while leaning on her bosom. He died in 1838, from an inflammation of the throat.

> The eagle plumes droop o'er his piercing eyes,
>   The fire of youth was there!

Osceola had always lived among the Seminoles, and regarded their lot as his. The name of his wife was Chécho-ter, or Morning Dew. She was a Creek, and their family consisted of four children. The following lines were composed after his death by one of his friends in Charleston:

> The rich blue sky is o'er,
>   Around are tall green trees,
> And the jasmine's breath from the everglades
>   Is borne on the wand'ring breeze.
>
> On the mingled grass and flowers
>   Is a fierce and threat'ning form,
> That looks like an eagle when pluming his wing
>   To brave the gath'ring storm.

We recently conversed with a missionary from the Creek Nation, who had been preaching among the Indians in that locality, who says Osceola has two sisters living there, both exemplary Christians, upon whom the serpent's trail had evidently rested very lightly.

CHAPTER VII.

S we approach the upper shores of the St. John's River, extensive swamp-lands, overgrown with various kinds of timber, are seen, where very bony-looking stock eke out a spare subsistence during a portion of the year, but commence recruiting as soon as the grass begins to grow, in February. Habitations are not frequent, the only variations being mounds, or bluffs, as they are usually termed. Many of these voiceless monuments of the mute past, around which cluster records of deep import, are found scattered throughout various portions of Florida, as in many other localities, furnishing food for the thoughtful, and conjecture for the inquiring mind. All efforts heretofore made to enlighten the world, or explain these curious structures, are founded upon the diversity of opinion and research of the different writers. Their appearance sheds sufficient light on the subject for us to know they are the cemeteries of an early, though partial, civilization—probably a relic of the Mexican race—from which we may derive illustrations of the habits, manners, and ideas of a people, "on whose graves the firmly-rooted oak has so long kept its dominion that it seems to the Indian supplanters to have been the first occupant of the soil."

Although we have no means left us of determining the cause by which the change was produced, the day dawned on them not less abruptly than that of the Aztecs of Mexico, or the Incas of Peru, when their sacred fires were extinguished, their altars desecrated, and the "primeval forest slowly resumed its sway over the deserted temples and silent cities of the dead," thus leaving glimpses of an unwritten history, full of interest, even in a tantalizing form. The remains of the American mound-builders are replete with surprise for us, which the magnificence of Montezuma's capital throws in the shade; and, while reading with implicit faith the narrative of the conqueror, we cannot but think the age of America's infancy lies buried in these older mounds. The chasm between these monumental mounts and the present time has never been bridged by any historian, however well versed in archæological records, or chronological *data*—except their belief in the resurrection of the body, which may be inferred from the careful manner in which they disposed of their friends after death.

It is within the remembrance of some persons still living that tribes of Indians now extinct have been seen passing through the country on pilgrimages to the graves of their sires, where they regard the earth that entombs the dust of their friends as too sacred for any thing but a shrine. When the Spanish invaders came to conquer Mexico, they disinterred the bones from the mounds, when the Indians entreated them to desist, "as their owners would not find them together when they returned."

"Ancestral veneration was a peculiar trait belonging to the aborigines, which is shadowed with an air of melancholy."

In these *tumuli* were deposited all the implements which the departed were supposed to require on their entrance into the unexplored regions. Here we find the ax upon which months and years had been expended in reducing to useful proportions, attrition being the only means employed; also the mortar and pestle, to pound their maize; the stone spear and arrow-head, to kill game; the bone fish-hook, to seize the astonished finny tribe as they swam though the purling streams of the newly-found paradise; the calumet, to be used while communing face to face with the Great Spirit; the pearl ornaments, to deck their persons in a becoming manner for their new position; the essential wampum, that no reflections could be cast as to their former condition in life, as lacking the important requisite to become a member of the *élite* society in the "long-fancied mild and beautiful hunting-grounds."

Mausoleums reared with many hands, inscriptionless monuments, tombs without epitaphs! Whose ashes rest beneath your storm-beaten, time-scarred surfaces? what prowess could you boast beyond your peers? was it the hand of violence or disease that severed the silver cord, and ushered you into the presence of the Great Spirit? We may continue to question, but the locked secrets of by-gone deeds will be borne on no zephyr, however soft, to gratify the longings of those who try to lift the misty veil of obscurity. When searching for a record of the architects of these pyramidal structures, we find our mind drifting upon the quicksands of instability. That the archæological history of the mound-builders in America is in its infancy cannot be doubted, although some imagine they have probed it to the foundation, as they have stood where a few bones, beads, and pottery were thrown out. Mounds are not limited to America, but are found in Europe and Asia, although dignified by different titles—as barrows, moat-hills, and cairns—all belonging to the same family as our earth-mounds. The Indians say that before the "pale faces" scattered them, they had mounds erected for different purposes—for sepulture, for sacrifice, for signals, for refuge in war, and the residence of the cazique. The first and most frequent of these was for sepulture. Homer and Hesiod both speak of monumental mounds over the graves of heroes.

While surveying these colossal works, reared by hands of clay, a wonder seizes our minds how the almost nude aborigines, with so limited a number of implements, could collect so much material, and fashion it into any form adapted to their necessities. It is true, they had some knowledge of the manner in which stone could be utilized, as chert and flint have both been found in the oldest earth-works, several feet below the surface—from which also can be deduced facts with reference to their roving habits of life, as this formation does not exist naturally in Florida.

The strong argument against Florida not having been the first location of the inhabitants who built these earth-works, is their tendency toward the West, not being found on the Atlantic coast, showing the course of emigration to have been from the West to the South. These structures also indicate strength, and not the hasty work of a nomadic tribe, having once been the site of a vast population.

The Florida mounds, unlike those of the Mexicans, bear no marks of magnificence or grandeur, but are of gigantic proportions, in consideration of the appliances with which they had to work, not having either plow or draft animals. They are the only records left us for determining the habits, occupation, and manner of living, of its former residents, which, if more enduring, are scarcely less satisfactory than a foot-print in the sand, as a guide to the pursuits and inclinations of its owner.

Intrusive burial has, without doubt, been practiced in Florida, as mounds which have been fully excavated furnish evident marks of burial at different periods, the lower strata having hardly a vestige of ossified substance, with only a few shells or stone implements remaining. The forest-growth on these mounds dates farther back than the earliest settlement of America, but anterior to that leaves us sailing upon the sea of conjecture. Whatever may be said in regard to the aborigines manifesting a natural instinctive downward tendency in the erection of earth and shell, they developed a different direction—that of elevating their residences while living, and having their remains above a common level after death. Here may not the question be asked, If the pyramids of the East, erected to the memory of kings, and those of America have not a connection, or common origin? A distinguishable feature has been observed in regard to the ancient mound-builders, different from the other Indians, in having their skulls flattened—only one of which has ever been exhumed whole.

The largest sepulchral mound of which we have any knowledge, on the upper St. John's, is located in the vicinity of New Smyrna, containing the remains of the Yemassees, who were slain by the Creeks—a fierce, warlike tribe—they being driven into a point of land, where they became an easy prey to their enemies. Thirty of these burial-mounds were seen here by Bartram, more than a century since, covering an area of two or three acres. Their form was oblong, being twenty feet in length, and ten or twelve in width, varying from three to four in height, covered with a heavy growth of laurels, red-bays, magnolias, and live-oaks—all composing a dark and solemn shade.

Many burial-mounds, three or four feet in height, can be seen now in South Florida, as we have been present when excavations were made in the vicinity of Tampa and Manatee, where beads, pottery, and well-preserved *tibia* of both sexes, were dug out. These bodies had been buried with their heads all toward a common center, with the greatest regularity. The cranium seems to crumble more than any other ossified portion of the body—the jaw-bones being very perfect, teeth much worn, having belonged to old persons in whose service they had been employed for many years. Firmly-rooted oaks of ancient date were resting on these graves, and spreading a mantle of green for several feet around them.

The large mound at Cedar Keys, about which so much has been said, has trees growing on it of immense size, which the winds and tempests of that boisterous coast have rocked for five centuries; but no one, however shrewd or learned, has ever been able to elicit a single historical event from them, during that lapse of years, their age only being determined from the rings, or exogenous growth, of their trunks. This mound is taller than most of those found in Florida, no doubt produced in part by the action of the tides and waves which have washed the earth away from the base. Solid mounds have been opened which contained no bones, and, on account of their peculiar structure, were no doubt used for sacrifice, where human beings had been offered, their enemies being the victims.

The following is a record taken from an ancient Spanish author in regard to the manner of sacrifice by an extinct tribe of Indians: "They laid him on a great mound of earth, with the sacred fire burning at his head, in a large vessel of baked clay, formed with a nice art by the savages, on the outside of which was painted the mystic figure, with the bloody hand. His garments were removed, and his limbs fastened separately to stakes driven in places about the mound. Thus were his hands and legs, his body, and his very neck, made fast, so that whatever might be the deed done upon him, he was unable to oppose it, even in the smallest measure."

The stupendous sacrificial pyramid of Cholula, bearing a resemblance to the Egyptian structures, but larger, is probably the most remarkable specimen extant. Its form, like that of the other Mexican teocalli, was a truncated cone. The following description, taken from Prescott, will enable us to form an idea of its gigantic proportions: "Its greatest perpendicular is one hundred and seventy-seven feet, the base one thousand four hundred and twenty-three feet — twice the length of the Cheops pyramid — this temple being dedicated to the god of the air." High over all rose this grand structure, with its undying fires, flinging their radiance far and wide around the capital, thus proclaiming to the nations that there was the mystic worship. It covered forty-four acres at its base, and the platform on its summit more than one acre. The effect, when the sun shone on these dazzling splendors with such bright effulgence, was the eclipsing of every other object but the reflection of the grand luminary — which caused a saying among the Indians, that "gold was the tears wept by the sun." On these altars horrid deeds of darkness were perpetrated, inhuman butcheries enacted, to appease the war-god of the Aztecs, who was supposed to delight in offerings of human hearts, torn fresh from the helpless victims, guilty of no crime but self-defense against blood-thirsty persecutors.

The teocalli found in the City of Mexico was unsurpassed in grandeur, but of less dimensions, being three hundred feet square and one hundred in height, on the summit of which was an altar for human sacrifices. They ascended by flights of steps on the outside, each flight extending to a platform, which reached quite around the structure—the exhibition of pageant on State occasions being terribly imposing, conducted by priests and victims, marching around their temple, rising higher on the sides as the place of inhuman sacrifice was reached, amid the shouts of a gazing and excited throng. Before each of these altars burned the undying flame, the vestal lamp, whose pale, constant light boded good while burning, but ill when extinguished.

In other parts of Mexico Cortez found monuments dedicated to the sun and moon, with lesser ones to the stars. For many years it had been supposed all pyramids were hollow, but discoveries have been made of some with only a small opening, which, like the one in Egypt, no doubt contained the bones of a king.

Another class of mounds held in much veneration by the early tribes of Florida Indians were the sacred mounds, or mounts of ordinance, only used on certain occasions, when the Medicine Man, after ablutions similar to those practiced by the Rabbis before entering the temple to offer sacrifices for sin, ascended to commune with the Great Spirit, like Moses, the lawgiver, on Sinai. He was always accompanied by a few of his warriors, whom he took to witness the descent of sacred fire which he invoked and they obtained by vigorous efforts with flint and steel. This ceremony was conducted during the month of July, when the maize, being in

the milk, the heavenly fire was procured for cooking
that product, it being held in high esteem as their
chief article of sustenance. The Peruvians procured these fires by the use of a concave mirror of
polished metal, the sacred flame being afterward
intrusted to the Virgins of the Sun.

It was a natural feeling with the Indians to worship on "high places;" for this reason temples were
built over their dead, where they might come to
give expression to the reverence with which they
regarded the departed ones. Images for worship
were sometimes placed on the pinnacle of these
temples, as the one mentioned by De Soto near
Espiritu Santo Bay, upon which was found a painted
wooden fowl with gilded eyes, containing choice
pearls.

Near the outlet of Lake Harney was located the
residence of King Philip, a Seminole cazique, on a
shell plateau in rear of which is a burial-mount,
twelve feet high, surrounded by a trench. The following graphic description, taken from Professor
Wyman, will enable us to form an idea of its extent:

"This shell-mound is about four hundred and
fifty feet in length, with an average of one hundred
and twenty in breadth. It stretches nearly at right
angles to the river, borders a lagoon on the south,
and on the north merges into cultivated fields, over
which its materials have become somewhat scattered—its greatest height being about eight feet.
Fragments of pottery may be found anywhere on
the surface, and with these the bones of various

edible animals. Excavations were made at many points, from a few inches to several feet in depth, to ascertain if similar objects were within its interior. The most unequivocal evidence that this mound, while in process of erection, had been occupied by the aborigines was obtained from a pit four or five feet in diameter, and from five to six feet deep, which was dug near the center. Not only were fragments of pots and bones found at all depths, but at the distance of three feet the remains of an old fire-place were uncovered, consisting of a horizontal layer of charcoal, beneath which were perfectly calcined shells, and near these others more or less blackened with heat. Still farther off were fragments of the bones of deer, birds, turtle, and fish —all just as they would naturally have been left around a fire where cooking had been done for some time. In addition it may be mentioned, as a matter of negative evidence, that not a single article was discovered which could have been attributed to the white man."

Near the outlet of Lake Jessup are the remains of a mound nine hundred feet in length, with an average width of one hundred to one hundred and fifty feet. This structure has been much wasted by the river, but originally it must have been among the largest in the State. That the Indians confined their encampments, or at all events their cooking, almost entirely to these mounds, is proved by the fact that fragments of pots were found in large quantities along the shore wherever the shells are seen in the bank, and not elsewhere, though careful search was made for them. Fragments of deer-bones, turtle, and alligator, were also seen. The shells forming these mounds were chiefly *paludinas*, or fresh-water snails, although *unios* and *apellarias* are met with also.

Mounds on the sea-shore are composed entirely of marine shells, also containing clay-ware, ashes, and charcoal. On the St. John's, at different times, and by various naturalists, over fifty mounds have been explored, in some of which were seen human bones having the appearance of violence. As so few remains were found during these excavations that had the appearance of being subjects of regular interment, the question is suggested, What disposition was made of their dead, unless all the numerous vessels seen, which could not have subserved for cooking, contained the ashes of their friends which had been cremated?

Mounds have been opened in various portions of the State abounding in fluviatic muscles and clams, the inference being that they contained pearls, and for that reason had been opened. These mounds can be accounted for in two ways — the first and most important: they consumed the contents of these shells, of which they were very fond; the last was the necessity for elevated plateaus to protect them from the sudden inundation of streams when they were traveling through the country camping, consequently they utilized the *débris* as a prevention against accidents. In their journeyings they depended entirely upon the products of the forest and streams for sustenance, and for this reason followed the water-courses, stopping, like the migratory birds, wherever night overtook them.

Many copper weapons of warfare have been discovered in these earth-works, the metal of which was brought from the mines of Lake Superior, when the Indians followed the great river to the sea, three thousand years ago. These faint traces of mechanical and architectural skill favor the idea of a more enlightened race than that which possessed the soil when first discovered by the Spaniards—a society which, no doubt, sank amid storms, overthrown and shattered by unavoidable catastrophes. In Florida no discoveries have been made which evidence marks of a great nation, while in Mexico and on the Pacific coast, south, they increase.

The Creeks, Cherokees, and Seminoles all agree in attributing the mounds of Florida to a race anterior to their own, as their traditions are handed down "that they were here when their ancestors took possession of the country." It is also asserted that the Florida Indians formerly worshiped the sun, which fact has been ascertained by their heraldic devices; also the location of their temples in such a manner that the first morning ray from this rising luminary would flash upon their sacred edifice —the Medicine Man, or High-priest, being in attendance to present his invocations with symbolic gestures, whose mysteries were a sealed book to all those around him, but supposed to be well understood by the Great Spirit, whose favor they wished to obtain. The Everglade Indians now venerate the moon, which can be seen from the silver crescent ornamental emblems with which they deck their persons. Like the ancient Greeks, they deposited the remains of their dead in burial urns, the difference being that the Greeks always prepared the bodies by cineration, when the ashes only were entombed, while the entire bodies of Indian children have been discovered in clay vases in the Florida *tumuli*. In sepulchral mounds about Tampa were discovered large quantities of the heaven-born product called pearls, which created much interest and more cupidity among the Spanish settlers than we could well imagine. It is Pliny who tells us that dew-drops distilled from the heavens, or falling into the mouths of oysters, in certain localities, were converted into pearls. The Florida coast was looked upon by the adventurers who first landed here as the long-sought-for country which contained these treasures. After the arrival of De Soto on the coast of Espiritu Santo they were welcomed by the Empress, who presented them with pearls as the most costly offering from her domains, for which kindness these cruel creatures dragged her about as a hostage for their own security. However, when an opportune moment presented itself, she succeeded in making her escape, at the same time recovering large quantities of imperforate pearls which the Indians through fear had permitted them to rob from their dead. However much evanescent satisfaction these newly-found treasures supplied them with, history makes no mention of Spanish officials being enriched by the discovery. The enormous size which the fertile imagination of those explorers mention them does not come within the present limits of these precious gems of commerce.

The Indians understood the method of making beads from the conch-shells, their novelty and delicate color attracting the Spaniards—the size being equal to an acorn, and larger. The natives persisted in boring the pearls with a heated copper spindle, that they might be worn as ornaments for the neck, arms, and ankles, which rendered them valueless for other purposes.

Pearls are frequently found now on the south coast of Florida the size of an English pea, and less. Some of these are taken from clam-shells of immense size, weighing two or three pounds; also found in the oyster. These are all opaque, some of them slightly pink, a dull white, or the usual pearl color. Those examined by connoisseurs have never been considered of any positive value in the manufacture of jewelry. Both from study and observation we are led to the conclusion that, whatever might have been the impression received by the overwrought imaginations of the Castilian explorers, no pearls of great price, fed by heavenly dews, have ever existed or been discovered on the Florida coast.

Let us now pause and inquire, Who were the architects of these earth-works? What was their fate? and whither did they flee when overpowered? We have only proof that a nation has perished, leaving no record or history but these monuments. They must have had some knowledge of engineering, or they never could have reared such enduring, well-proportioned structures. While the subject furnishes food for reflection, the dark curtain drawn over their obscure presence has never been raised; however great the effort made by those who have desired to penetrate their unyielding secrets, the key to open these hidden mysteries has never been found. Whether called *tumuli*, plateaus, or mounds, they are objects of interest, in whatever locality they may be seen, of sufficient importance to engage the attention of the scientist when generations yet unborn shall walk the earth, and vainly try to pierce the portals of the silent past.

CHAPTER VIII.

THE upper St. John's commences after we pass Welaka, opposite the mouth of the Ocklawaha. Steamers leave the wharf at Jacksonville daily for this attractive portion of the country. An early traveler thus speaks of the wild animals he saw in this portion of the State, also the birds:

"The buffalo, the deer, the puma, and the wild cat; the bear, the wolf, the fox, the wandering otter, the beaver, the raccoon, the opossum, and many smaller animals; large flocks of water-fowl, the white and great blue herons, and their allied species, in large numbers standing along the shores; the wary turkey with his brilliant plumage; the roseate spoon-bill, sometimes seen, and the flamingo, once a rare visitor, but now no longer found; the wood ibis, the whooping crane, whose resonant notes are heard far and wide; the stupid and unwary courlan, disturbing sleep with its nightlong cry; the loathsome buzzard, circling, at times, gracefully among nobler birds, or, oftener and truer to its nature, quarreling with its kind as it gluts itself over disgusting food; also the snake-bird, of peculiar make and habit; the fish-hawk, whose massive nests of sticks and moss crown many a dead and shattered cypress; the bald eagle, soaring in the upper atmosphere, or robbing, in mid-air, the fish-hawk of its prize; the migratory birds, collecting in thousands for their journey northward; the alligator, drifting lazily with the current, or lying in his muddy wallow, basking in the sun."

THE SAURIAN.

All of these were seen during the visit of Bartram the elder, which must have made the St. John's one of the most beautiful and remarkable rivers in America.

It is now February, and a soft, blue mist frequently fringes the distant landscape, diffusing itself through the atmosphere, subduing the dazzling sunlight, when the sky and water appear to blend in one grand archway, like a half-veiled beauty whose charms are then most lovely.

A very happy family is on board to-day, and the lady has just remarked, "O we have a house on the steamer, taking it up to Mellonville for us all to live in!" She was a genuine Florida settler, who could look at the sand and say, If it can grow such immense trees and big weeds, it can produce food for us all to eat.

On our way we pass Lake George, eighteen miles long and ten miles wide, which the Indians called "Little Ocean," on account of the high, swift waves that are frequently seen here, attributable to the open country by which it is surrounded.

Many other interesting places, where new settlers

are constantly making improvements, are seen before we arrive at Enterprise, the terminus of navigation proper on the river, two hundred and thirty miles from St. John's Bar. A good hotel is kept here, while sportsmen find the vicinity attractive on account of the game and good fishing. Mellonville, on the right bank of Lake Monroe, was named for the brave Captain Mellon, who was killed here while at his post of duty during the Seminole war. He was buried with the only tribute he could then receive: "A soldier's tears and a soldier's grave."

Sulphur springs are numerous on the upper St. John's; one in the vicinity of Lake Monroe, several hundred yards in length, while at its source the water bubbles up like a fountain—a strong sulphurous odor being perceptible for some distance. The frightened alligators that retire here from their pursuers make terrible dives to hide, while in the transparent waters fish are seen distinctly as though going through the air. All of these upper lakes contain clear water, but none of it very deep.

The next waters are Lake Harney and Salt Lake. These are not the head-waters of the St. John's, but its source is farther on, down deep in some unexplored marsh or subterranean fountain. It requires a little patience to reach Indian River, either by rowing or overland, but hundreds of people are going there every year. During the Florida war the vicinity of Cypress Swamp and this river were some of the lurking-places in which the savages intrenched themselves, and from this point kept making incursions on the white settlements, which filled them with constant terror for their safety. In 1839 the citizens living in Florida prayed for peace, looked and hoped for it. They wanted rest, that favorite position of the Grecian sculptor's statuary, and when they thought it nearest then it receded again, flitting on the margin of their expectations like the *ignis-fatuus* which glimmered through the marsh. The Everglades furnished a natural fortress for the Indians, who were said to have been left there by General Jessup, as though one general was more to blame than another for their presence and murderous conduct. No confidence could be placed in the Indian promises; no security that the settlers could sow and harvest; all pledges given by them had been violated, and where should the line of their banishment be drawn, which would not be crossed by the murderous Seminoles, thirsting for human gore? Every person was indignant at the farce enacted by General Macomb, swallowing it as a sickening dose, or an amnesty with a cage of tigers. All projects for terminating the Indian war had failed, and the wail of woe went through the land, while the blood of murdered fathers, mothers, brothers, and sisters, cried for vengeance. As a supposed last resort, the bloodhounds, which had terminated the Jamaica war, were now sent for to Cuba by order of General Call. The Indians waged a warfare accompanied with so many irregularities that no tactician could designate or describe its method of attacks or retreats. To be always in danger of falling, but not on the field, and then being devoured by vultures, was not sought for by those who had dreamed of gory battle-fields, as there was glory in that. 'Affairs with the settlers had assumed so formidable an appearance that they did not think it necessary to be very scrupulous about the mode by which the warfare should be carried on against the Seminoles. Great horror was expressed in different portions of the States on account of the bloodhounds, which were going to "eat the papooses and squaws—then taking the 'breechless knaves,' whose tougher fibers would only be a last resort."

In August, 1839, a battle was fought on the Caloosahatchee River, between Colonel Harney and the Indians. All of the troops were killed but the colonel and fourteen men. Seventeen days afterward a detachment was sent out by General Taylor to bury the dead, when two of the missing troops were found alive. After the fight they remained concealed during the day in a mangrove thicket, and at night crawled to the margin of the river and ate sea-fiddlers. They died soon after being discovered. An Irish greyhound was also found, barely alive, which belonged to Colonel Harney. He had stayed to watch over the remains of Major Dallam, whose body was untouched, although the rest were much mutilated.

The following statement in regard to the Big Cypress Swamp and its occupants in 1841 will, no doubt, be an item of unsurpassed interest to those wishing to penetrate the Everglades, whether in imagination or reality:

The commencement of this swamp is thirty or forty miles south of the Caloosahatchee, extending within twenty miles of Lake Okachobee to the Gulf. On approaching the lake it terminates in thick mangrove bushes, uninhabitable for Indians. Between the Caloosahatchee the country is wet pine barren, with occasionally dry islands. On the south it is bounded by the Everglades, through which the Indians pass in canoes to the great cooutie-grounds on the Atlantic, south of the Miami River. This is a belt from five to eight miles in width and twenty miles long. To travel directly through the swamp to the Everglades from Fort Keas, which is upon the north margin, the distance is about thirty miles. Directly south of the fort, in the heart of the swamp, is the council-ground. South-east and south-west from this are the towns of the principal chiefs, Sam Jones living twenty-five miles and the Prophet within two miles of him. Trails communicate with their towns, but none with Fort Keas, the Indians knowing that would be the first point to which the whites would come. The entrance from the pine barrens to the swamp is twenty miles farther south-east. Within the swamps are many high pine islands, upon which the villages are located, being susceptible of cultivation. Between them is a cypress swamp, with water two or three feet deep. Many have cultivated outside toward Lake Thompson, as the fertility of soil and sun-exposure insured better crops.

The first reliance of the Indians is on their crop—peas, pumpkins, corn, and beans; next, roots, cooutie, and berries. They are now, in a measure, deprived of game, the powder being retained in the hands of their chiefs for defensive movements.

When troops are in the vicinity, they reveal their hiding-place by firing guns, which, in a country so marshy, can be heard a great distance. Their babies never cry when the whites are near, but, as if by instinct, crawl away and hide in the long grass like partridges. Fish, when the streams on the coast can be reached, afford them subsistence, but the movements of the troops deprive them of this luxury. Among them are a large number of horses, ponies, some hogs, and a few cattle.

The dry goods obtained from the massacre of Colonel Harney's men, and bartered by others who obtained a large quantity, clothe them richly as they desire. The specie has been sold, and manufactured into head-bands, breast-plates, or gorgets and bracelets. Among those Indians I have seen more rich ornaments than among any other Indians in Florida. Even in this murderous and lamentable massacre, when they all stood by each other, shoulder to shoulder, the same avarice and selfishness governed their actions. No feeling of friendship binds them to each other but the feudatory of Sam Jones and the necromancy of the Prophet.

There is, no doubt, much cause of dissatisfaction among them, from which they cannot escape. Their imperious laws, if violated, is followed by instant death, without the benefit of judge or jury. If one of their number evinces kindness toward the whites, the Prophet visits him or her, and, by various tricks with roots, a blow-pipe, and water, proclaims the designs of the individual. In some cases instant death has followed.

The Prophet is a runaway Creek, not fifty years of age. He escaped from the Creek country six years ago, and relates a long story of bad treatment from the whites. He has great influence over those around him, caused by his making known the approach of troops, healing the sick, finding game, and controlling the seasons. It is doubtful whether he has ever been in battle. In a garrison so well regulated as the one over which he presides, he must be of vast service, not only on account of his pretended ability to commune with the Great Spirit who controls their destinies, but for his happy talent as staff-officer, frequently feeding his followers on *faith in his necromancy*, when other troops, under similar circumstances, might demand "a more substantial article of diet." He has sufficient tact, as a Medicine Man, to convince his followers that he is, of necessity, a non-combatant.

Sam Jones is a distinguished Medicine Man, belonging to the Mikasukie tribe. He has numbered four-score years, and, for his age, is strong and active. He has great influence over his adherents, who respect his acts and obey his mandates with a religious sense of duty. His venerable appearance and bitter hostility to the whites have a tendency to elevate him in the estimation of his tribe. He plans attacks, fires the first gun, and retires to attend the wounded, leaving the head-warrior to fight the battle. He instigated the attack on Fort Mellon, performed his duty as head-man, and retired to execute the kind offices of his profession. The command devolved upon Wild Cat, who continued to fight until obliged to retire for want of ammunition.

Sam Jones says he is advanced in years; that his hair is white; that Florida belongs to his kindred; beneath its sands lie the bones of his people. The earth to him is consecrated; he has hallowed it with the best blood of his braves, and while his heart beats he will maintain his present position. His people were once numerous as the trees of the forest; they received and welcomed the white man, who, in return for kindness, have, it is true, extended the apparent hand of friendship, but within its grasp the glittering blade is clutched; dark stains are upon it, dyed by the blood of his children, who are now roaming abroad in the land of the Great Spirit, calling upon him to avenge them. "I am now old; in a few more moons I shall set out on the long journey; but I will not desert the land of my fathers. Here I was born, and here I will die!"

The hanging of Chekika and other Indians by Colonel Harney aroused the anger of the chiefs, who have declared hostility and savage brutality to any white man that came within their reach. Chekika was captured after being pursued through the grass-water until exhausted. He was six feet high, and weighed over two hundred pounds; considered the strongest man of his tribe. "We," said Sam Jones, "give them a decent death. We shoot them, or quietly beat out their brains with a pine-knot; never hanging them like dogs." The Indians which Colonel Harney's men left suspended were taken down by Sam Jones's men and buried.

The Cypress band is composed of the reckless, unbending spirits of the Seminoles, Mikasukie, and Creek tribes. The Mikasukie are the most numerous. They now mingle more harmoniously than at any previous period of their history, and willingly accept all others who will subscribe to their laws, and believe in Sam Jones as a wise man, doctor, and prophet—one who holds communion with invisible things, and controls their destinies. He is a skillful navigator of the Everglades; goes from the Cypress to the Atlantic in four days; knows all the great passages, and cultivates in their vicinity. He bestows blessings similar to the patriarchs. He has about one hundred and fifty warriors.

Persons prowling through the Big Cypress Swamp in search of pleasure will have some conception of the perils through which soldiers in search of Indians had to pass.

"*Dec.* 23, 1841.—The command under Major Belknap has just returned from a scout of seven days' duration in the swamps of the Big Cypress. The column was attacked by the foe on the 20th, who ambuscaded the trail on which it was advancing, in a cypress swamp two feet deep with water, when two men of the advance-guard were instantly killed. The Indians, as usual, fled immediately beyond our reach. The camps of the hostiles were near, and still smoking with their fires. They would, no doubt, have been surprised and captured, but for the stupidity of a flanker, who, being lost a few hours before, discharged his musket repeatedly—thus alarming the enemy, only two or three miles distant. The result of this scout has been, however, most important, in pointing out the hitherto mysterious position of the Prophet and his party, which enables us to entertain hopes that our forces may yet scour that country, so as to render their submission certain, even if they should fail in any attempt to surprise them. They have been trailed to their most favorite and secret fastnesses, and should now be soon harassed into submission. It is the belief of all, including some who have seen the most arduous service in Florida, that no march in this Territory has been attended with equal, or, at least, greater, severity than this. All pack-mules being left behind, officers as well as men carried their rations on their backs. The movements of the troops were amphibious rather than otherwise—marching in mud and water more than knee-deep from morning till night. The character given to this marvelous region of country has not been exaggerated, so far as the condition of its swamps is concerned. It is difficult to conceive of a region more admirably calculated for concealment than such a mass of dense hummocks and seemingly impenetrable swamps. Some of these waters have a perceptible current, thus being the heads of streams rather than swamps. The ax of the pioneer would never be attracted to this wet and mud-encircled region, and it may be fairly presumed that, so far as a knowledge of its topography is concerned, war has done more to expose it to our gaze than civilization would have accomplished in a century."

Indian River.—The following letter, dated Indian River, July 3, 1843, will give an idea of the impressions received by tourists from this river over thirty years since—coming to this place then being an enterprise of too much magnitude for any one to undertake but well-armed soldiers:

"This noble sheet of water is now constantly whitened by the sail of the emigrant in pursuit of land, and the stillness of its solitude broken by the splash of the oar, echoed by the merry songs of boatmen. At night the camp-fires of the adventurers are kindled on its banks, after which preparation is made for the evening repast, when, amid conversation and laughing, the toils of the day are lost in sleep. Refreshment ensues, and the morning finds them on their way, vigorous in frame and sanguine in spirit. Game abounds on its banks— the deer break through the thick growth on the margin of the river, and gaze with wonder at the visitors; the curlews give their short whistle and wing their way from the near approach of the intruders; the wild ducks, quietly feasting on the grass, take note of your approach, perhaps, to a place of greater security. Splash, splash goes the water. That's a mullet jumping at the prospect of being caught by us, or perhaps exerting its utmost activity to escape a hungry bass. If you are furnished with a harpoon or barbed piece of iron, you can have a fine supply of fresh fish every day during your voyage. Oysters are the staple of the stream, the banks being as numerous as though an improvident Legislature had created them, although they never suspend payment or protest a draft for want of funds. The lands north and south of Fort Pierce are rapidly filling up, and thus far, with the exposure of boating, felling timber, planting, and the thousand troubles of an emigrant's life, the best of health is enjoyed by all. Doctors are at a discount, and among the least useful things on the river."

Among other local peculiarities found near the Indian River is a kind of shell-sand, which hardens by exposure. The following is an interesting statement, made by a member of the engineer corps, who visited there in 1858: "While we were surveying a point between the St. John's, near Lake Harney, and Indian River, when watching the excavation of one of these pits, I carefully rolled a ball together from what appeared to be sand taken from the pit, and then threw it on the grass. Upon examination a few hours afterward, it was found to be extremely hard, and the surface covered with those minute shells, which is the principal component of the coquina-rock. Between Musquito Lagoon and Indian River there is a small artificial canal cut through the coquina, the portion exposed being very hard, while the submerged part is crumbling into sand."

It is an established fact that certain localities on the coast of Florida contain sand which concretes when exposed to the atmosphere. What the component parts of this cement contain no one has satisfactorily determined. It is certain all localities do not possess the same kinds of sand.

The lands in the vicinity of Indian River will produce bananas, pine-apples, oranges, sugar-cane, lemons, limes, strawberries, blackberries, grass, corn, indigo, sweet potatoes, garden vegetables, and tomato-vines that bear for three years, and bird pepper-plants which will grow into little trees, bearing all the time.

Hunters live well here on the wild game, while those in the first stages of consumption almost invariably fatten and recover on the diet and atmosphere combined. The following is a favorite dish: Take a fresh fish, without dressing; wrap in a damp paper; then place in the hot ashes; when cooked, pull off the skin while warm; season and eat. It is better than cod-liver oil, and can be swallowed without any winding up of the courage whatever, previous to making the attack.

Is it not pleasant for those who can, whether invalids or not, to spend a part of their winters, at least, in this portion of the State, where we are surrounded by trees clothed in perpetual verdure, loaded with native fruits, to refresh us when wearied with sight-seeing, and sated with tales of the marvelous, with which this country abounds? It is from association with scenes like these that a new impulse is given to our thoughts, which confinement within brick walls, with the smoke and changing temperature of coal-fires, cannot furnish. There is nothing like the soothing influences connected with letting our thoughts wander away with our eyes among the light, vapory clouds, that flit across the sky like floating islands, while we are inhaling an atmosphere soft as the dream of childhood's innocence, that can warm and stimulate vegetation into maturity at all seasons.

Tourists who go up the St. John's River, on returning always bring back something in accordance with their varied tastes. Imagine yourself a passenger on the Hattie Barker, a steamer of somewhat smaller dimensions than the Great Eastern, which can do more traveling in the way of making a fuss than any boat on the river, her progress being never less than four miles an hour. All kinds of travelers are returning from the upper St. John's—those who have trodden the wine-press of bitterness with suffering, and some who have sailed over the summer sea of life without a ripple. Prompted by the impulses which induce all tourists to bring something back when they return home, a quantity of curiosities sufficient to start a small museum has been obtained. No small steamer could ever have contained a larger number of tourists, with a greater diversity of tastes. Here is the sick man, with his nervous system, sensitive as the mimosa, who shrinks at the slightest harsh sound, and continues scolding about "such a crowd on the boat," as though some of them should have remained that he might have more room to fret and scold at his patient wife. Then there come the father and mother, with four little boys and two girls, besides the tiny baby and two nurses. How they rush about their limited boundaries! What a restless family of children, with the ruddy glow of health, keeping the parents and nurses in a constant state of trepidation for fear they will fall into the water! This family has no curiosities. With a long journey to their home in Canada before them, their hearts are full without other incumbrances. Two ladies sitting near us have a chameleon in a pickle-jar; one of them is catching flies for its dinner. What a pleasure it appears to give them when, darting out its coral-colored tongue, and winking its bright eyes, it gobbles them up so quickly! There is a lad, with two young alligators, who persists in taking water from the ice-cooler, to pour on them for fear they might die. The stewardess is on the alert to thwart his movements, by telling him, "Dat cooler-water is for de folks, and not dem ole black 'gaitors." The lad retorts by saying the water isn't clean. The stewardess says, "Yes, 'tis only a few settlements in de bottom." A sound comes from one of the staterooms, which is unmistakably made by young turkeys going North, in March. How the keen winds up there will pierce their downy coats! They had better save their voices for the cries they will have to utter then. The ornithologist is also represented, with his stuffed birds, having a flamingo, a plume-crane, an owl, eagle, and living red-bird. Another has paroquets, which he imagines, by some mysterious manipulations, can be made to talk like a South American parrot. One man, from Indian River, has an immense pelican, with an enormous flat bill, below which is a pouch attached, containing its rations. Some of the anxious mothers have heard it eats children. What terrible looks they give this poor fellow with the big bird, who appears so happy in the possession of his newly-found treasure, because to him it is so remarkably curious! Another has a blue crane, belonging to the order *Grus cinerea*, standing erect on its stilts, showing fight. How it snaps every thing which approaches it, like some crabbed people in the world! A young man has a slender, not grown, animal, which he informs us is a *Cervus Virginius*, or fawn, that he proposes taking to a friend. Among the number is an archæologist, who has been exploring the mounds of Florida, and procured a trophy from the recesses of a long-since departed Indian's grave. It is a stone hatchet, which was designed to hew trees and make boats, that the deceased might move not only with unrestrained freedom through the lands of the Great Spirit, but also across his pure streams. The most entertaining and original tourist of all is an unmistakable Dutchman, from Indiana, born on the River Rhine. He is a "bugologist," or beetle-gatherer. Hard-backed bugs and fresh-water shells are his hobby. He has collected and sent a barrel of specimens home in advance of him, and now he is carrying a big box, strapped tightly with the same care as a returned miner would his nuggets of gold. For our amusement he opened his treasure-box. The toilet articles of no lady were ever arranged with more care. Shells odorous with the remains of their former tenants, wrapped in cotton and tissue-paper, bugs and beetles with alcohol on them, or fastened to a card with long, tiny pins made for that purpose, and, last of all, a quinine-bottle in his pocket, in readiness to capture any stray bug that might happen to be out on an excursion. Numerous cages, containing young mocking-birds and red-birds, are sitting around, while the tables are piled with palmetto, air-plants, and American pitcher-plants. Every available space is occupied—baskets stuffed with oranges, lemons, and grape-fruit, while gray moss fills the interstices.

Many of the best people in our country are found traveling over Florida during the winter—some looking for homes, and others only pleasure-seeking, a few for health.

The number of old people with whom we meet while traveling here is quite remarkable. Some have sweet, sunny faces; others look as though life had been a continued struggle with them until now, when their solicitude was on the *qui vive* for fear they should get in behind time, or some impending danger might befall them, they do not exactly know what.

The indefatigable sportsman in Florida is ubiquitous. With gun in hand, he is constantly watching for game. If many a bird at which he aims flies away unharmed, the excitement of shooting with unrestrained freedom appears to give satisfaction, if nothing is killed.

CHAPTER IX.

IN coming down the river, we land on the east bank at Tocoi, for St. Augustine. There are no hotels here, as the cars always make close connection with the daily line of boats for the ancient city. Much ink and paper has been wasted about this unpretentious town on account of its unattractive appearance; but it is only a starting-point for St. Augustine, this point being more on an air-line than any other place on the river.

The distance to St. Augustine is fifteen miles, the scenery along the route varied, being interspersed with long-leafed pines, hummock-lands, with its heavy undergrowth, live-oaks, and wild orange-trees; the cypress, trimmed with its crisping, curling, waving gray whiskers, swinging and dancing in the sunlight of noonday, or resting in the somber shades of night, thus giving that grace and beauty to the landscape which is only seen in our Sunny South.

A short ride on the railroad enables us to see the country; and what mistakes some settlers make in planting orange-trees on hummock-lands without proper drainage, where the poor strangers, being neither amphibious nor aquatic, droop and die from wet feet!

Travelers, who imagine themselves greatly inconvenienced, and have so much to complain about for more profitable employment, after riding in the pleasant steam-cars from Tocoi to St. Augustine, will peruse the following, from which they can form some idea of the contrast within forty years in Florida:

"December, 1840—Notice to Travelers—St. Augustine and Picolata Stage.—The subscriber has commenced running a comfortable carriage between St. Augustine and Picolata twice a week. A military escort will always accompany the stage going and returning. Fare each way five dollars. The subscriber assures those who may patronize this undertaking that his horses are strong and sound, his carriages commodious and comfortable; that none but careful and sober drivers will be employed; also every attention paid to their comfort and convenience. Passengers will be called for when the escort is about leaving the city."

We have selected from among the many, one of the atrocious acts of violence committed by the savages previous to this arrangement, upon a worthy and respected citizen, Dr. Philip Weedman, whose three most estimable daughters are still living in St. Augustine:

"November 25, 1839.—Shortly after the mail-wagon left the city, Dr. Philip Weedman, sr., accompanied by his little son, a lad about twelve years of age, both in an open wagon, with Mr. H. Groves on horseback, left also for the purpose of visiting his former residence, now occupied as a garrison by a part of Captain

Mickler's company. On arriving at the commencement of Long Swamp, without any previous warning, he was fired upon and killed, having received two balls in his breast; his little son was wounded in the head, baring his brain; also cut with a knife. The mutilated youth, with the remains of the dead father, were brought in town to-day. The express, returning for medical aid, caused the Indians to run, as the wagon containing the mail was fired into, wounding Captain Searle, and killing a Polander who was riding horseback."

"Tuesday, November 26, 1839.—The funeral of Dr. Philip Weedman took place to-day, attended by all of our citizens, who sympathize deeply with his numerous family."

The Polander, Mr. Possenantzky, was buried the same day according to the Hebrew form. The Indians continued firing on the covered wagon-trains, calling them "cloth houses," their object being to obtain supplies, when a proposition was made to have fortified wagons. Hostile Indians were something which could not be worked by any rules; they were the exceptions.

On Saturday, February 15, 1840, we find a record of two mail-carriers having been murdered, one seven and the other nine miles distant—G. W. Walton, from South Carolina, while on his way to Jacksonville, and Mr. J. Garcias, near Live Oak Camp. The letters were undisturbed, although carried some distance. Both of the murdered young men were buried in St. Augustine. Afterward the mail was accompanied by an escort of five men.

We have tried to hold up some cause with the semblance of a shade to delude us into the belief that the Indians have less activity and enterprise than the white men, but facts stand forward in bold relief denying us even the poor consolation which such delusions might afford us. The lifeless bodies of our brethren speak trumpet-tongued in favor of their removal, and the wail of hearts blighted by their successes is stronger and more piercing than the fictitious surroundings of excited fancies.

Here is another thrust at the bloodhounds:

"These distinguished auxiliaries have received more attention than their services deserve, while great apprehension fills the minds of many for fear they should perchance bite a Seminole. We would state as a quietus that a competent tooth-drawer will accompany them, entering upon his dental duties very soon."

Another shocking murder occurred between Picolata and St. Augustine, before the St. John's Railroad was surveyed between Tocoi and St. Augustine.

"May 29, 1840.—On Friday last a carriage and wagon had been obtained to proceed to Picolata, for the purpose of bringing in some baggage and gentlemen connected with the theatrical company of W. C. Forbes, from Savannah. Leaving Picolata on Saturday morning, May 23, in addition to their own party they were joined by Messrs. D. G. Vose, of New York, and Miller, of Brunswick, who all reached the eleven-mile military post in safety. When within seven miles of St. Augustine they were fired upon by Indians, severely wounding Vose, Miller, and Wigger, a young German musician. While this work of death was going on, a wagon which had left the barracks that morning was seen approaching. It contained three persons besides the driver—Mr. Francis Medicis, of St. Augustine, Mr. A. Ball, and Mr. Beaufort. The Indians fired upon them near the six-mile post, when Mr. Beaufort and the driver escaped. The mules ran away with the wagon. The firing being heard at the little garrison of seven men, they turned out, when they saw distinctly twenty Indians. News having been received in town by a lad coming in on one of the horses, a party of gentlemen repaired thither. On reaching the ground, there lay Mr. Ball dead, while farther on was the body of Mr. Medicis, lying on his side, his hands clenched, as if in the attitude of supplication, his right shirt-sleeve burned with powder, and his face covered with blood. Mr. Francis Medicis was murdered the 23d of May, 1840, between the hours of eleven and twelve o'clock. The bodies of Messrs. Medicis, Ball, Vose, and Miller, were brought in at dusk, that of Mr. Miller about nine o'clock. The bodies of the strangers were placed in the Council Chamber. Mr. Forbes and his company passed over the Picolata road on the 22d of May, except Messrs. Wigger, German, and Thomas A. Line. Mr. Wigger was murdered. Thomas A. Line hid himself in a swamp, sinking up to his neck, and covering his face with a barnet-leaf, which he raised, to the great surprise of his companions, when they were searching for the survivors and gathering up the wounded."

The old citizens in St. Augustine now say that
when Mr. German, vocalist, one of the theatricals,
arrived in the city after his escape, his hair was
standing perfectly erect on his head, and in twenty-
four hours turned entirely white. As the Indians
rifled the baggage-wagon, they carried off a considerable portion of the stage-dresses and other para-
phernalia.

Now, we can peruse these tragic events as the
vision of some wild romancer, or relate them to
children as nursery tales, partaking enough of the
terrible to excite a desire for the wonderful. Wearied with waiting, and heart-sick of bloody murders,
we find the following piece of composition written
on this solemn occasion:

"How long shall the earth drink the blood of our
women and children, and the soil be dyed with the
ebbing life of manhood? Could they have looked
with us upon the mangled corpses of Indian wrath,
as they were laid upon the public highway, or gone
to the council-room and surveyed on its table, where
side by side the marble forms of four men lay, who
a few hours before were looking to the future as
filled with bright enjoyment, they would then have
whistled their philanthropy to the winds, and cried
aloud for vengeance. That was a sight never to be
forgotten. We have seen men killed in battle, and
perish by disease on the ocean, but amid the many
affecting and unpleasant incidents that have met our
gaze we have never seen a spectacle like that. Here
in the rigidity of death lay the youthful German, on
whom manhood had just dawned; also the compact

forms of muscular health, with the less vigorous frames of more advanced years. A casual glance might mistake it for a mimic scene, where Art had exhausted her powers in its production. But there was the pallid hue of faces; there was the gash the knife had made in its course to the heart; the cleft forehead parted by the tomahawk in its descent to the brain; and there the silent drop, dropping of crimson fluid to the floor—while our Secretary, with his usual imbecility, issues orders to 'muzzle the bloodhounds.' The funerals of these unfortunate victims took place on Sunday, attended by a large concourse of people, who expressed the keenest indignation at the repetition of such a scene so near our city. Wild Cat was the leader of this band, as he stopped afterward at the plantation of E. S. Jenckes, Esq., and told the servants he had committed the murder."

The troupe filled their engagement at St. Augustine, as only a musician had been killed from their number. History says, "The sterling comedy of 'The Honeymoon' was performed to a crowded house." Afterward the following notice appeared: "During the winter months we have no doubt that a troupe, embodying the same amount of talent which the present company possess, would find it profitable to spend a month with us each season."

Coacoochee, or Wild Cat, was captured with Osceola in 1836, and afterward made his escape, or he never would have been permitted to commit such a series of appalling atrocities as those which we have recorded. Wild Cat frequently visited the residence of General Hernandez, who lived on Charlotte Street. He also very much admired one of his beautiful daughters, and, like lovers at the present day, wanted an excuse for returning; consequently, on going away he would leave one of his silver crescents, which he wore on his breast as a defense and for ornament, to be polished, and when he returned, take the one he left before, and leave another. He delighted to stand in front of a large mirror which General Hernandez had in his parlor, and admire his person. He said if Miss Kitty Hernandez would be his wife, she should never work any more, but always ride on a pony, wherever she went; that Sukey, his present wife, should wait on her, but Miss Kitty would be queen. He frequently made assertions of his friendship for the family. When on one occasion some of them remarked that he would kill them as quick as anybody if he should find them in the Indian nation, he replied: "Yes, I would; for you had better to die by the hand of a friend than an enemy."

The following is an account of Coacoochee's escape and recapture: In all ages of the world there have lived those who laugh at iron bars, and defy prison doors—among whom we find the Seminole, Wild Cat, who appeared to be proof against bullets, with a body no dungeon could hold. He was very indignant on account of his imprisonment, denouncing his persecutors in no measured terms. He said the white man had given one hand in friendship, while in the other he carried a snake, with which he lied, and stung the red man. While in Fort

Marion he planned his escape in a most remarkable manner. He complained of illness, at the same time manifesting signs of indisposition, and made a request that he might be permitted to go in search of a curative agency. Accompanied with a guard, he was again permitted to breathe the pure air of his native home, but not in freedom. This movement furnished him with an opportunity for reconnoitering, and measuring with his eye the distance, outside the fort, from the loop-hole of his cell. After his return he resorted to the use of his herbs, and abstained from food, which had the effect of materially reducing his size. He selected a stormy night for the undertaking, when his keepers would be the least inclined to vigilance, and commenced making preparations by tearing his blankets into ropes, which he made fast inside his cell, and, by working a knife into the masonry, formed a step. This, with the aid of his companion's shoulders, enabled him to reach the embrasure—a distance of eighteen feet—through which he escaped by taking a swinging leap of fifty feet into the ditch, skinning his back and chest effectually. His companion, Talums Hadjo, was less fortunate than himself. After a desperate effort to get through, he lost his hold, and fell the whole way to the ground. Wild Cat thought him dead; but his ankle was only sprained, and, after enlisting the services of a mule grazing in the vicinity, he was soon far away from bolts and bars, which could restrain his wild, free-born movements.

Wild Cat had a twin sister, to whom he was much

attached. He said she visited him after her death, in a white cloud, and thus relates her appearance: "Her long black hair, that I had often braided, hung down her back. With one hand she gave me a string of white pearls; in the other she held a cup sparkling with pure water, which she said came from the fountain of the Great Spirit, and if I would drink of it I should return and live forever. As I drank she sung the peace-song of the Seminoles, while white wings danced around me. She then took me by the hand, and said, 'All is peace here.' After this she stepped into the cloud again, waved her hand, and was gone. The pearls she gave me were stolen after I was imprisoned in St. Augustine. During certain times in the moon, when I had them, I could commune with the spirit of my sister. I may be buried in the earth, or sunk in the water, but I shall go to her, and there live. Where my sister lives game is abundant, and the white man is never seen."

This chieftain was afterward induced to come in for a parley, to a depot established on the head-waters of Pease Creek. The following is a description of his appearance on that occasion:

About midday on March 5, 1841, Wild Cat was announced as approaching the encampment, preceded by friendly Indians, and followed by seven trusty warriors. He came within the chain of sentinels, boldly and fearlessly, decorated, as were his companions, in the most fantastic manner. Parts of the wardrobe plundered from the theatrical troupe the year previous were wrapped about their persons

in the most ludicrous and grotesque style. The
nodding plumes of the haughty Dane, as personated in the sock and buskin, boasting of his ancestry and revenge, now decorated the brow of the
unyielding savage, whose ferocity had desolated
the country by blood, and whose ancestors had be-
queathed the soil now consecrated with their ashes,
which he had defended with unswerving fidelity.
He claimed no rights or inheritance but those he
was prepared to defend. Modestly by his side
walked a friend wound up in the simple garb of
Horatio, while in the rear was Richard III., judging from his royal purple and ermine, combined
with the hideousness of a dark, distorted, revengeful visage. Others were ornamented with the crimson vest and spangles, according to fancy. He entered the tent of Colonel Worth, who was prepared
to receive him, and shook hands with the officers
all around, undisturbed in manner or language.
His speech was modest and fluent. His child, aged
twelve years, which the troops had captured at Fort
Mellon during the fight, now rushed into his arms.
Tears seldom give utterance to the impulse of an
Indian's heart; but when he found the innate enemies of his race the protectors of his child, he
wept. With accuracy and feeling he detailed the
occurrences of the past four years. He said the
whites had dealt unjustly by him. "I came to
them; they deceived me. The land I was upon I
loved; my body is made of its sands. The Great
Spirit gave me legs to walk it, hands to help my-
self, eyes to see its ponds, rivers, forests, and game;

then a head with which to think. The sun, which is warm and bright, as my feelings are now, shines to warm us and bring forth our crops, and the moon brings back the spirit of our warriors, our fathers, wives, and children." Wild Cat admitted the necessity of his leaving the country, hard as it was. After remaining four days, he returned, with his child, to his tribe.

General Worth commanded the army in Florida at this time. He established the head-quarters of his command in the saddle—only asking his troops to follow where he should lead.

Wild Cat had a subtle, cunning disposition, which gave the whites much trouble. They had deceived him, and his confidence in the pale faces was much shaken; but, being induced by General Worth, he was prevailed upon to meet in council. The General made a direct appeal to his vanity, by telling him he had the power to end the war if he chose, as they were all tired of fighting. Wild Cat was finally captured during the month of June. His camp was thirty-five miles from Fort Pierce, on the Okachobee Swamp. He had abandoned the idea of emigration, and his name was a terror to all the white settlers. He agreed to leave with the Seminole and Mikasukie tribes, who elected him their leader. His parting address, as he stood upon the deck, was as follows: "I am looking at the last pine-tree of my native land; I am leaving Florida forever. To part from it is like the separation of kindred; but I have thrown away my rifle. I have shaken hands with the white man, and to him I look for protection." Wild Cat, after being sent to New Orleans, was brought back to Tampa, that he might have a talk with his band, who numbered one hundred and sixty, including negroes. He was too proud to come from the vessel with his shackles, but when they were removed he talked freely with his people, and wanted all to be sent West without delay. He died on the way to Arkansas, and was buried on the bank of the Mississippi River. War to him was only a source of recreation.

The following spicy letter was written thirty-eight years since, contrasting the seasons in New York City with those in St. Augustine; also, a comparison can be drawn between the entertainments of the two places. In Florida Indian massacres were realities, and in New York they dramatized them for the amusement of pleasure-seekers and idlers:

"December, 1841.—A winter here in New York, and one with you, are very different matters; and were you disposed to question the orthodox character of my position, you need only make an attempt to promenade in Broadway now with thin breeches, to have this general relation of fact converted into a self-evident axiom. The wind searches you, sharp as the gaze of a jealous politician—every defect in your wardrobe—and, with a freedom which the other must sigh to attain, blows upon your person its icy breath, until the warm current of life feels almost frozen in its citadel, and your legs are scarcely able to perform the duties of their creation. Such is the difference of temperature with you and in this metropolis."

The same correspondent describes the manner of dramatizing the Florida Indian murders. *Scene*—Capture and killing of the mail-rider and wife in Florida:

"Having at one time witnessed some of the handicraft of our red brethren, I thought I would step in, and lo! the room was filled with some three hundred persons, anxious to behold this scene of blood. The Indians were veritable, stout, murderous-looking rascals; the mail-rider, a six-foot youth — oiled locks, beautifully parted, elegantly-combed mustache, white pantaloons, straps, and boots. This was the grandest specimen of a mail-rider ever seen in Florida. He might have personated some of those fictitious pretenders of gentility which sometimes visit you — but for a letter-carrier — Heaven save the mark! The wife was a pretty, plump, well-fed girl of sixteen, dressed in all the simplicity of girlhood, before fashion had desecrated its pure feeling with *tournures*, converting the human form divine into a monstrosity. Well, the chase was interesting; our six-footer stretched his legs and black coat-tails with effect. When fairly caught by his pursuers, he was bound, and his wife was likewise brought in captive. Then rose the loud and fierce yells of these demi-devils. The mimic scene was one of intense interest, and the quick dispatch of life argued something in favor of the captors, until the process of scalping commenced, when the blood rushed in gushes on the bosom of the girl, as her tresses were held up amidst the fiendish hurrahs of the Indians. Here there was a pause; the imagination had been wound up to the highest pitch, when something of a less gloomy character was furnished the audience."

It was then the Florida settlers prayed for the peace we now enjoy — when their streams should have the dreary solitude broken by the splash of the oar, and their moss-covered banks send back the song of the contented boatmen — when their tranquil surface should be rippled by the freighted bark, with white canvas bending before the breeze, sailing out to the ocean — when the watch-fires of their foes should be extinct, and the yell of murder give place to the melody of grateful hearts, as their songs of praise should rise from the hummocks and plains; that the land might be indeed the home of the Christian, the abiding-place of happiness and contentment.

CHAPTER X.

> Far in ether stars above thee
>   Ever beam with purest light,
> Birds of richest music love thee,
>   Flowers than Eden's hues more bright,
> And love—young love, so fresh and fair—
> Fills with his breath thy gentle air.

MANY writers who come to Florida copy an abstract of the most interesting portions contained in the guide-books, besides what they can hear, afterward filling up the interstices from their imaginations. We look to the old Spaniards for information, but, alas! they are like the swamp cypress which the gray moss has gathered over until its vitality has been absorbed—age has taken away their vigor.

This point appears to be a favored place for the stimulus of thought, where inspiration can be gathered from atmospheric influences, and not the heat of youth or the vapor of strong drink. Daily we are more impressed with the fact how treacherous are the links which connect the chain of tradition in a country where its earliest history is mingled with a record wonderful as the champions of knight-errantry who figured in the pages of romance.

The early settlers were lured here by legends of a fairy realm, where youth and beauty held perpetual sway, and mountains of gold reared their shining peaks. (See Frontispiece.)

From the 28th of August, 1565, when Pedro Melendez planted the broad banner of Spain with its castellated towers in the lonely settlement of Seloe, beside the waters which our Huguenots had previously dignified with the title, "River of Dolphins," to the present time, imagination has been on the alert to penetrate the past history of this country. On the site of the present plaza was celebrated the first mass in America by Mendoza, the priest, assisted by his acolytes.

The minds of the Seloes were much exercised with the appearance of their new visitors, the impression being received that they were immortal, with their steel-covered bodies and bonnets, which flashed like meteors in the sunlight, while music, more enchanting than any which had ever filled their most fanciful imaginations, floated on the silent air.

During the early history of St. Augustine it appeared to be disputed ground for all explorers—French, Spanish, and English. Sir Francis Drake in 1586 drove the Spaniards from here during the war with Spain, the Spanish retiring so hastily they left fourteen brass cannon, besides a mahogany chest containing two thousand pounds in the castle. During 1665, Davis, the buccaneer, captured the town again. In 1762 a writer describes it as being at the foot of a hill, shaded with trees, the town laid out in the form of an oblong square, the streets cutting each other at right angles.

In 1764 the Spanish left the town, and the English took possession, when we find this graphic account, from which observant visitors can note the changes:

"All the houses are built of masonry, their entrances being shaded by piazzas, supported by Tuscan pillars, or pilasters, against the south sun. The houses have to the east windows projecting sixteen or eighteen inches into the street, very wide and proportionally high. On the west side their windows are commonly very small, and no opening of any kind to the north, on which side they have double walls six or eight feet asunder, forming a kind of gallery, which answers for cellars and pantries. Before most of the entrances were arbors of vines, producing plenty and very good grapes. No house has any chimney for a fireplace; the Spaniards made use of stone urns, filled them with coals, left them in the kitchens in the afternoon, and set them at sunset in their bedrooms, to defend themselves against those winter seasons which required such care. The governor's residence has both sides piazzas, a double one to the south, and a single one to the north; also a Belvidere and a grand portico decorated with Doric pillars and entablatures.

"The roofs are commonly flat. The number of houses in the town are about nine hundred. The streets are narrow on account of shade. In a few places they are wide enough to permit two carriages to pass abreast. They were not originally intended for carriages, many of them being floored with artificial stone, composed of shells and mortar, which in this climate takes and keeps the hardness of rock, no other vehicle than a hand-barrow being allowed to pass over them. In some places you see remnants of this ancient pavement, but for the most part it has been ground into dust under the wheels of the carts and carriages introduced by the new inhabitants. The old houses are built of a kind of stone which is seemingly a pure concretion of small shells, which overhang the streets with their wooden balconies; and the gardens between the houses are fenced on the side of the street with high walls of stone. Peeping over these walls you see branches of the pomegranate and of the orange-tree now fragrant with flowers, and rising yet higher the leaning boughs of the fig with its broad, luxuriant leaves. Occasionally you pass the ruins of houses—walls of stone, with arches and stair-cases of the same material, which once belonged to stately dwellings. You meet in the streets with men of swarthy complexions and foreign physiognomy, and you hear them speaking to each other in a strange language. These are the remains of the Spanish dominion inhabitants, speaking the language of their country."

In 1757 no vessel could approach the coast of St. Augustine without running the risk of being taken by the French privateers. It has not always been the home of Spanish Dons and guitar-playing, as in 1777. Captain Rory McIntosh, the Don Quixote of the country, lived here, and paraded the streets in true Scottish style, dressed in the Highland costume. His home was with Mr. Archibald Lundy, then a merchant of St. Augustine. He was present at the taking of Fort Moosa, under command of General Oglethorpe, and mentions his share in the fight with characteristic bravado: "I am a scoundrel, sir! At Fort Moosa a captain of Spanish Grenadiers was charging at the head of his company, and, like a varmint, sir, I lay in the bushes and shot the gallant fellow."

On June 17, 1821, the American flag first floated from Castle San Marco. A meeting was afterward held in the governor's palace, where the exercising of a right was declared which had banished the Huguenots from the soil centuries before: "Freedom to worship God according to the dictates of one's own conscience."

The archives of St. Augustine were said to have been delivered to the United States Collector. They were sealed in eleven strong boxes, for the purpose of being sent to Cuba, but detained by Captain Hanhan, and afterward forwarded to Washington.

Dr. McWhir, an Irish Presbyterian preacher, visited Florida in 1823 and 1824, preaching at St. Augustine and Mandarin. He organized the first Presbyterian Church in the State, located at Mandarin. It was also mainly through his influence that the Church in St. Augustine was founded.

In 1834 St. Augustine answered to the following description: "Situated like a rustic village, with its white houses peeping from among the clustered boughs and golden fruit of the favorite tree, beneath

whose shade the invalid cooled his fevered brow and
imbibed health from the fragrant air." It was, indeed, a forest of sturdy orange-trees, whose rich
foliage of deep green, variegated with golden fruit,
in which the buildings of the city were embowered,
and whose fragrance filled the body of the surrounding atmosphere so as to attract the attention of those
passing by in ships at sea, and whose delicious fruit
was the great staple of export. The plaza then contained many orange-trees, one of which was over a
century old, producing, in a single season, twelve
thousand oranges—more than eight thousand being
nothing unusual for many of the trees in a year.

However, in 1835 there came a change over the
dreams of these independent, happy people, when
their source of income was gone in a single night—a
calamity caused by a cold, heartless invader from the
North, King Frost, which made them a brief visit,
and froze the trees to the ground. From an income
of more than seventy thousand dollars per annum,
the amount was decreased to nothing. Their trees,
being well matured, had produced an average of five
hundred oranges annually.

We feel as though, in trying to describe this place,
we were hovering on the brink of uncertainty, and
drifting along its shores, not knowing where to
land, that we might find the stand-point to commence our task. It is here we realize a kind of
traditional flickering between the forgotten and
neglected past, shrouded in awful obscurity, with
an intervening veil of myth and mystery—a pil-
grim shrine for those wanting relics to visit, where

many times large drafts are drawn upon the bank of their credulity, which look genuine if not honored with credence, or added to the store-house of useful information. Here we see more objects tottering upon the verge of existence and nonentity than at any other point in the State. The most venerable houses are built of tabby and coquina. Tabby, or concrete, is composed of two parts lime and coquina six parts, thoroughly mixed, and then placed in position between two planks, held together by iron bolts until dry. Walls of this kind were used as a means for defense in the days of Hannibal and Scipio, they being sufficiently strong to withstand the ancient battering weapons used in warfare.

Before the forest-trees which covered the grounds upon which New York City now stands were felled, St. Augustine was the seat of power. The streams of wealth and vast fortunes to be made as if by magic, had induced the adventurer to leave his home, and the pampered sons of power to pass the dangers of the deep. It is here, as in no other place, that two forms of civilization find a foothold—the Spanish dwellings of over a century, with the modern Mansard-roofs of recent date, all subserving the purpose of substantial residences. Many of the early settlers came like wandering sea-birds, wearied with their flight, and looking for rest.

This city is like ancient Rome, with which many found fault while there, but, from some kind of fascination, they always returned again. The inhabitants residing in other portions of the State formerly resorted to St. Augustine during the months of July, August, and September, that they might avoid malaria from the marshes. The fresh sea-breeze which comes out every morning they called "The Doctor," whose presence was hailed on account of its healthful influences. Its fine climate and orange-groves have always rendered it celebrated, although it has no fertile back country.

The powerful chemical ingredients, which exist in the atmosphere on the sea-coast, act as a neutralizer to disease. The chloride of sodium, compounded in the laboratory of the great saline aquarium and respired without effort, is freighted with the germs of health, which are productive of beneficial effect in many forms of pulmonic complaints.

During the Spanish rule, it was a place of importance as a military post, being the Government head-quarters, then containing a population of five thousand inhabitants.

As we look upon these old Spaniards our thoughts go back to the days of their sires, whose minds were ever on the alert in search of some new sources from which would flow fresh streams of amusement. Their manners, habits, and customs were once varied as their origin—having descended from the Spanish, Italians, Corsicans, Arabs, and French, possessing the peculiar traits of these nationalities. The carnivals, posy balls, and many other amusements in which they formerly indulged, have now in a great measure been absorbed by the Yankee element. The holiday processions no longer march around the plaza, bearing their bright banners and escutcheons blazoned with the ensigns of their kings, or with the names of their favorite patron saints.

The night before Easter in St. Augustine the observance of a peculiar custom is still retained, which the early settlers brought from Spain with them: it is that of the young men going around to the houses of their friends singing a song called Fromajardis. What a strange sensation steals over us to be awakened just before the old cathedral bells have chimed twelve by the sound of musical instruments, accompanied with singing, in a foreign tongue, a song which has echoed through the same town for more than three centuries! It indicates that the Lenten season is now over, and the young men are anxious to participate in feasting. Although it is customary, they are not always invited to partake of a bountiful collation after their song is finished, but are prepared to do so when the opportunity presents itself. The extreme poverty of the old citizens now renders it impossible for them to conform to the customs of palmier days, when large amounts of money were received from Cuba by the soldiery, and the labor of slaves furnished many with a genteel support. From these people we can see with what tenacity they cling to their home associations; although misfortune has crushed their spirits, and poverty lessened their desire for enjoyment, yet in their hearts still lingers the memory of a festive past, which now cheers them on through adverse fortune, and lightens life of half its burdens.

Most of the old inhabitants are persons of very

moderate means, moderate ability, and moderate their wishes by surrounding circumstances — who apparently live and grow old, ripen and die, with as little effort toward great designs or grand projects as the sweet potato in the hill. Many of them live seventy or eighty years, are born and die in the same house without forming any foreign attachments or associations—the machinery of their human frames not being moved with as much rapidity here as North.

On account of their early training being impregnated with superstition, the imaginary ghost that moves gloomily around at midnight is always their terror. The tongue or pen of critics is never prostrated when in search of material for feasts of faultfinding—a multitude of remarks being made with reference to the apparent indolence of the natives, not thinking that the atmosphere by which they are surrounded is in no way conducive to great physical exertion. The inhabitants follow hunting and fishing, besides cultivating their gardens, while some of them have cow-pens for their cattle, and land outside the city, which they till. They are a quiet, frugal people, retiring in their manners, and simple in their ways— the very opposite in every respect of the grasping, bustling, overreaching Yankee —devoted Catholics, warm in their friendship, but timid toward strangers. The young girls in the community have a type of feminine beauty which can be seen at no other place, except on the shores of the Mediterranean, or in the Madonnas of the Italian masters—in short, St. Augustine is an Italian town on the shores of America, and in that respect differs from any on the Western Continent.

The language spoken by their progenitors is supposed to have been identical with that used in the Court of Spain before the days of Ferdinand and Isabella. It has the terseness of the French, without the grandiloquence of the Spanish, being derived directly from the Latin.

There is nothing now remaining of courtly splendors. A few only of the ancient tenements are left, some of them tumbling down by degrees; those having occupants are a class of persons struggling for an existence, with adverse circumstances surrounding them which cannot be overcome, but must be borne in silent submission. Our imagination before visiting declining architecture is always to conceive that they have an air of the picturesque— a softness reflected on them by moonlight, or a panorama with dulcet strains floating somewhere in our fanciful dreams. All visitors come with an object, well or ill defined—the student to look, the historian to gather dates and make records, while the restless spirit that roves everywhere is here in search of something new or wonderful for his eyes to rest on a brief period of time. At this place there is an unchanging serenity of sky, a clear and harmonious blending of two colors—white and blue—with a soft shading, and the line of distinction lightly drawn. Long level stretches of sandy country lie before us on the beach, covered by the canopy of heaven, and lighted by the luminary of day. The Matanzas River is ever in view, and, like other waters, has its moods, with its surface sometimes smooth as the downy cheek of infancy, then wrinkled as the brow of age, or stirred like the impulses of an enraged partisan in a political contest. Every morning the same sun rises over Anastasia Light-house, and beams across the waters like burnished steel; the curtain of nature rises on the same scene, the early dawn brings the same worshipers; the priests read the sacred service, and we find it an easy task to banish bad thoughts, and become purer and better, if only for the time being.

A procession of nuns from St. Joseph's Academy, conducted by the Mother Superior, passes along daily, silently as the flight of a feather through the air. They have charge of two schools in St. Augustine for both white and colored pupils, which are well patronized, where much instruction, like the Jews of old, is given in the ceremonials of the ritualistic law. Their new coquina convent is pleasant, and the display of fine laces, made by their busy fingers, incomparable. The little chapel within the convent is very neat, containing a statue of their patron, St. Joseph, watching over it. They exhibited to us a shred of the Virgin Mary's dress, also a piece of the cross on which the Saviour was hung; but it required a greater stretch of our imagination than we were able to command to perceive the resemblance, particularly as we had never seen the original, or had any description of it.

The religion here is that which sprang into existence during the Middle Ages, when the minds of the people were unable to comprehend a disembodied spirit, an intangible, ideal substance somewhere; for this reason images were introduced to address their supplications. It is now the pomp of pontifical splendor, and not the strength of persuasive eloquence, that overawes the assembled multitudes— a scenic display metamorphosed into a religious drama, where " monks and priests are only players."

St. Augustine, unlike the European cities, bears no record of great prosperity or vanished splendors in the display of colossal buildings, or fine scientific skill, as the present period boasts of more fine houses than at any time anterior to this. What a host of past memories rise before us on every side as we walk its narrow streets, overshadowed by mid-air balconies! Here are the old palace-grounds, where the Dons from Spain paraded their troops, and exhibited them, with burnished armor and crimson sashes, before a queenly array of beauty seated on the verandas of the old Spanish governor's headquarters. It is here the fierce and warlike Seminoles made furious assaults, and were held in check until the women and children could take refuge in the castle.

The Seminole Indians lurked in the vicinity of St. Augustine during all the seven-years' struggle, but never, except as prisoners or to make purchases, did they enter it, which was quite different from other settlements which they depopulated and then destroyed. It is for this reason we see so many older buildings here than in other Florida towns, among the most ancient of which is the Escribanio, now called St. Mary's Convent, west of the cathedral. It was built for and occupied as El Escribanio, or business department of the governor. It was built of coquina and concrete, with a tile floor, much of the material used being brought from Cuba, and of the most durable quality. All business connected with the Government was transacted here. It was the annex building of the palace, but afterward occupied as a private residence until 1852, when it became church-property, being then purchased by Father Aubril. In 1858 Bishop Verot took charge of it, and then it was used only temporarily as a convent by the Sisters of Mercy, an order of French nuns.

The tale that is told of hard floors being for penance, where nuns had kneeled until the brick was worn away, is only a fabrication. The floor, like all those laid in Cuba, was the best burnt tiles. Also, that the groans of unhappy nuns who had died here from too much abstinence had been heard echoing through the arches at unseasonable hours, when spiritual visitants are supposed to be moving around, is another intangible story with which visitors are entertained who hanker after the mysterious. No nuns died in that convent, as the time they occupied it was too brief for any marked mortality.

This silent old town appears to sleep all summer, with an occasional lucid moment, when an excursion comes in for a day's recreation, until winter, when every thing is brought into requisition, with which a dime or a dollar can be turned from a visitor's pocket. It is then the dear old folks from a colder clime come to sit and sun themselves on the sea-wall, or balconies, while the young people walk, ride horseback, take moonlight strolls, and sail on the quiet bay or restless sea, talking, laughing, and singing as they go.

The hotel-keepers look cheerful again, the Spanish señoras smile sweetly as they exhibit their palmetto hats and grasses, while an orange stick and an alligator are the aspiration of the lads—the latter being a marvel to Northern visitors. When a genuine, live alligator cannot be obtained, a photograph has to suffice, taken after the animal has been captured and tied, to be made to sit for his picture.

It is true, many complain of the manner in which they are annoyed by all kinds of professions, from the boot-black—who screams in your ears, "Shine, sah!" until you feel like elevating him somewhere among the shining orbs, from which point he would not soon return—to the hotel bills. "Four dollars a day, sir; if no baggage, in advance." Then the carriages—"Ride, sir? take a nice ride?" The pleasure-yachts come in for their share of attention —"Take an excursion over on the beach? I takes over pleasure-parties."

These all swoop down on the defenseless travelers, like birds of prey over a fallen carcass, to the amusement of some, and the annoyance of many more. There is no lack of attention from interested parties, if you have the money to spend.

During the winter the old wharf, which shakes as though it had the palsy whenever a dog trots over it, has men and boys throwing out lines with a simple hook, and others with elaborate reels and silver hooks, amusing themselves; while the old Spaniards bask in the sunshine, on the sea-wall, resting from their night of toil in fishing on the rolling waves, as a means of support, like the apostles of old.

A good cart was formerly the highest ambition of the natives, while now elegant carriages, with liveried drivers, roll around the streets, decked with the trappings of wealth and show of fashion.

It is very amusing, many times, to hear the uncultured youths, reared in St. Augustine, make remarks in regard to the appearance and dress of visitors, frequently mocking them when they are speaking, particularly if the language is a little more refined than that to which they have been accustomed; but the most astonishing thing of all is the mysterious manner with which the natives come in possession of your name, the facts connected with your movements, where you stay, and, more than all, if you have any money. If you are not flush and free with funds, you can rest from any annoyances, except boarding-house keepers, who have adopted the motto, "Pay as you go, or go away."

The celebrated Florida curiosities are a great source of traffic, from the June-bugs to the head of a Jew-fish, including stuffed baby alligators that neither breathe nor eat, tusks from the grown ones, mounted with gold; birds of beautiful and varied plumage, relieved by the taxidermist of every thing but their coat of feathers and the epidermis, looking at you from out glass windows, through glass eyes; screech-owl tails and wings; pink and white curlew-feathers; saws from sword-fish of fabulous length; sharks' heads; sea-beans, supposed to have grown on Anastasia Island, but drifted from the West Indies; and the palm, wrought in so many varied and fanciful forms of imaginary and practical utility as scarcely to be identified as a native of the Florida wilds, whose rough and jagged stalks seem to defy an assault from the hand of the most expert explorer, being upheld by its roots of inexplicable size and length.

Most visitors think their tour incomplete without a palmetto hat; but who of the many that purchase asks, or cares, where these home-made articles were produced—what thoughts were woven by the light-hearted workers—what fancies flitted through the brain of the dark-eyed maiden, in whose veins flows the blood of a foreign clime.

The Florida pampas-grass, gathered from the surrounding swamps, is much used in ornamenting China vases and ladies' hats, together with the excrescent growths from the tall cypress-trees. Each countryman's cart has a marsh-hen, blue crane, or a box of live alligators, seeking to make money and divert the attention of curiosity-seeking persons.

All visitors will, no doubt, be solicited, freely and frequently, by the different crafts, to make an investment; but it is all nothing. Everybody has to make a support in some way—as the little boy replied to the Northerner who asked him how the people all lived down here in this sandy country. The lad replied, "Off from sweet taters and sick Yankees."

It has hitherto been a prolific source of entertainment for those who have been here to listen to the narrations of old settlers. The tide of memory never fails them. They can relate things that occurred long anterior to the current of their existence, with the same unbroken connection of circumstances as though they were among the events of yesterday. Most of the old settlers are dead now; but the legends live with the younger ones—the legendary transfer having been made without any apparent diminution of the marvelous.

Our days here pass in peaceful quietude, the time moving on with imperceptible speed; but the daily records would not fill a page in history, or supply material for a romance. An incident occasionally takes place, which stirs the under-current of life a little—as the capsizing of a yacht, catching a big fish, shark, or alligator.

Adventurers who come here seeking employment do not receive a hearty welcome. The natives look upon that class of persons as a kind of interlopers, who want to suck the sweets from their oranges, and lick the sirup from their bread, without paying them for it.

Persons here from Northern climes are expected to spend the winter in breathing the balmy air, canopied with skies clothed in the softest radiance of a summer sun, and praising every thing they see. If they have any doubt in regard to what they hear, let them lock it in secret, and keep silent until they leave; for the inhabitants think that this was once the paradise of the Peri, which will some day be restored to its pristine loveliness.

Visitors who are always ventilating their prejudices and preferences too freely, in any place, make enemies. Let none presume to tread upon the dangerous ground of expressing an adverse opinion with reference to what they see, in any of the small settlements with which Florida is filled, or in the larger towns either, if they wish to be fanned by the breath of popular favor. Always take the spirit of volatile indifference with you, to waft you through all the little inconveniences which you may have to encounter, resolving to accept and submit to every thing just as you find it, or fold up your blanket and steal quietly away where you can regulate things to your liking.

CHAPTER XI.

THE old St. Augustine inhabitants are very regular in their attendance at the cathedral exercises, which, during the Holy Days, appear to be their sole employment. The first sound that greets us in the morning is bells for mass. How those harsh tones, jingling like fire-bells run mad, break in upon our soft repose! The alarming speed with which they are rung attracts no attention, this being all the excitement we have in the way of a noise. The earliest sunbeams shine upon groups of worshipers going to offer oblations, while the shades of twilight deepen before vespers are over, and the throng of satisfied penitents move to the quietude of their homes. The most devoted are said "to live in the church." Surely their lives must pass peacefully, "Mid counted beads and countless prayers."

The cathedral is an object of interest on account of its ancient architecture more than age, having been commenced in 1793. The church in use previous to its erection was located on the west side of St. George Street. The engineers and officers belonging to the Government—Don Mariana and Don P. Berrio—directed the work, it being completed at a cost of over sixteen thousand dollars. During the many improvements made in the city, the main part of the cathedral has remained the same for nearly the past century, while time has touched it lightly—thus forming a link with the present in a useful state of preservation. The walls are built of coquina of no modern thickness, but as if designed to resist a siege. Its Moorish belfry with four bells, and the town-clock, form a complete cross. One of these bells was taken from Tolemato Chapel, it having been originally brought from Rome, as the lettering indicates. It bears the following date and inscription: "*Sancte Joseph, Ora pro nobis,* 1682." The cathedral also contains a crucifix, which is brought into requisition once every year on Good Friday, it being a relic from "*Nuestro Cano de la Leche,*" which is all that remains. The front doors of the cathedral are now kept locked, as it has been a resort for so many inconsiderate persons, who went there smoking and talking in loud, irreverent tones, as though it was a theater, where some kind of daylight drama was being enacted, instead of a house devoted to worship, and entered with purity of feeling, if not according to prescribed rules, which the faith of everybody induces them to adopt.

To the minds of these Church-devotees all other pageant fades into insignificance before the festivities and solemnities of the Holy Days connected with their Church-services, and the veneration due to their patron saints. Whatever vicissitudes or changes may take place with them in other respects, their religion remains the same; it is, indeed, a part of their being, without which their lives would be considered incomplete, their existence blank as the brutes, which die that others may live. Some of the worshipers rush to the cathedral with the rapidity of an opera-goer, who is afraid the seats will all be taken before he arrives, but enter with the same degree of veneration as the pilgrims who visit and kiss the statue of St. Peter—still clinging to their catechism and creeds firmly, as a part of their life, while their well-learned prayers are repeated as a talisman against temptation and violent death. These old cathedral walls have witnessed stately ceremonials, heard the prayers and confessions of many penitents, whose troubled consciences and sin-burdened hearts could find no relief except at the confessional.

The bishop is regarded by the Catholics as the Vicegerent of Heaven. He lives in the greatest seclusion and simplicity—never appearing in public except amid the glitter and grandeur of a ceremonial, but always accessible to those wishing the administration of Church-rites.

Many outsiders regard the adoration rendered to the priesthood as homage to man. This conclusion is incorrect—"all this effort at splendor and magnificence being wholly and purely a tribute of man to honor the religion which God in his love and mercy has given, and no part of it designed for man's honor." As evidence of this, none of the priesthood ever approach the tabernacle, or other holy symbols, except with marked demonstrations of the most profound reverence and uncovered head—thus rendering the same veneration to Christ which he requires from the people.

With an utter disregard for the fitness of things, on exhibition in this cathedral are two frescoes— one representing the "Death of the Wicked," the other the "Death of the Good." The good man appears perfectly composed, as though he were about to survey one of his Father's mansions, well prepared for the coming change, only waiting for the gates of glory to be opened for his entrance, when the words of welcome would resound through the peaceful abodes of the just made perfect, "Enter into the joy of thy Lord." "The Death of the Wicked!" Where the idea of so much that is horrible could have been conceived is difficult to be accurately determined. It has been conceded by all that there is nothing like it in Rome or the Vatican. Dante, with his vision of demoniac spirits, is not a rival. How these devils grin! How they stare at the distorted features of the poor, dying man, who anticipates soon taking a leap into the dark abode of these exultant beings, who are delighted at the prospect of having one more victim to slake their sleepless thirst, or on which to experiment with some newly-suggested torture!

Travelers, in coming here, must not imagine they can regulate the standard of religion in all climates by their own.

The old, time-honored custom, in Catholic countries, of spending a portion of Christmas Eve in prayer and praise to God for the unspeakable gift of his Son Jesus Christ, is still observed here with all the accompanying ceremonies of ancient times pertaining to the Holy Order of St. Augustine, transmitted, through the priesthood, to the present generation.

The high windows, which are nearer the roof than any other part of the building, will never draw wandering thoughts from their devotions, as their altitude would preclude any but angel eyes from looking through them. The modernized, cushioned, upholstered seats, upon which registered Church-members, with gilt-edged hymn-books in their hands, expect to slide from into the portals of glory, are not found here, but the genuine, old-time wooden benches, with a thick plank to sit on, and another to support the shoulders. No velvet foot-stool to kneel upon, but the bare floor for penitents to bend in their devotions, and the sin-stricken to derive comfort and seek forgiveness for their misdeeds. Outside the chancel, on the right of the altar, in a niche, is a statue of the Madonna, life size, with the God-child standing beside her, both looking very benignly. Beneath the niche is a representation of the lamb, of which our Saviour is the antitype. On an altar below this was a miniature stable, with an inside exposure, containing figures of the infant Jesus in a manger with Mary and Joseph, the whole surrounded by oxen, beasts of burden, and other things connected with the humble furnishings of a stable, while bending in front of all were the wise men worshiping.

In rear and above the grand "high altar" stands the figure of St. Augustine, dressed in all the insig-

nia of rank belonging to his holy order, decked in
azure, with gilt trimmings, above which is inscribed,
"Sancte Augustine. Ora Pro Nobis!" On each side
of this are two other saints with the same petition
over them. The altars were all dressed in an appropriate manner, with evergreens and flowers that
never fade. The choir made a fine exhibit of their
musical skill, singing *"Miserere Nobis," "Gloria in
Excelsis,"* very finely, with the organ accompaniment. On this Christmas the cathedral was filled
with a remarkably quiet, well-deported audience,
composed of citizens and strangers. The services
were conducted by Bishop Verot, who has ministered to them in holy things for nearly twenty years.
At this time he was dressed with more than usual
display, it being the crowning day of all holy days
—Christmas. His sacerdotal robes were of costly
materials, over which was worn the chasuble, elaborately embroidered with designs of the finest needlework, wrought in gold, and interspersed with numerous precious stones, while upon his head rested a
miter of corresponding elegance; in his hand he
held a crozier of costly and curious pattern. He
was assisted in the service connected with the ceremonies by two other priests, also twelve acolytes.
Bishop Verot made some very appropriate remarks
upon charity and the Redeemer's birth. He said
that no earthly king had ever made his appearance
in so humble a manner, and he was greater than all
kings or princes in the world.

Softly fell the rays of light from six tall wax candles,
supported by metal of ancient date, surrounded by

many lesser ones that lent their luster to reflect the solemnity of the scene. Heavenly thoughts should visit us when associated with so many holy emblems. Amid the stillness of midnight, surrounded by the symbols of this most fascinating religion, before the grand altar kneeled twelve nuns, draped and veiled with the sable-hued garments, indicating their abandonment of all worldly display. Before the tabernacle stood Bishop Verot, with a massive golden chalice in his hand, while slowly and distinctly from his lips were echoed the solemn words of the Lord Jesus, "*Hoc est enim corpus meum*," as each communicant received the blessed wafer.

A visit to Tolemato Cemetery, situated at the north end of Tolemato Street, is in reality going to a "garden of graves," on account of the large number of interments which have been made there. It was the Sabbath when we went, and, contrary to the usual custom in most towns and cities, there were no loafers prowling about the grounds, or sitting on the tablets reading novels, thus committing an act which in itself partakes so much of daring desecration. The custodian of the gate was a lizard, that lives in the lock, and crawls with astonishing rapidity to his hiding-place on application of the key. When the gates are open we enter "God's acre," where rest the remains of those who have lived and died for the past three centuries—priests and people, all sleeping side by side, awaiting that summons of which Gabriel will be the herald. Since the settlement of St. Augustine this cemetery has been the scene of a tragic event, which occurred in 1567, when Father Corpa, influenced by a desire to rescue the souls of the savages from the lurid flames which he imagined would hover around the delinquents in purgatory, rebuked them for their hostile and polygamic customs. His pearls were cast before swine, as the untamed red men had no prescribed rules from the Great Spirit in regard to their conduct. They could not adopt this new *régime*, and the propagator must be silenced. A council was called—the Sanhedrim of the savage—when a yell of triumph which penetrated the portals of prayer rang out upon the stillness of midnight. It was then the edict went forth, irrevocable and sanguinary as the laws of Draco, Father Corpa must die; and who should strike the fatal blow? Whose unflinching arm can rid us of this our peace-destroyer? The athlete of his tribe replied, "It is I!" Stealthily and silently they stole into Tolemato Chapel, where, kneeling before the altar, with a lone taper, whose feeble rays served as a guide, was Father Corpa. A single flash from the warrior's steel gleamed through the darkness; a single stroke sufficed.

Tolemato Cemetery now marks the spot where this act was perpetrated, baptized with the blood of its first missionary. The remains of this chapel have long since disappeared, except the bell, which hangs in St. Augustine cathedral.

Another chapel stands within the cemetery now, erected to the memory of Father Varela by his beloved pupils in Cuba. The architecture is Corinthian, while above the doorway is the following inscription: "*Beati mortui qui in Domino morientur.*"

This vault, when opened, is in reality a dark, chilly, awe-inspiring place, where service is held on "All Souls' Day," when Catholic devotees are assembled to repeat prayers for the repose of the souls whose bodies lie buried here. The following Spanish register is made upon the marble tablet which covers his remains: "ESTA CAPILLA, FUE, EREGIDA, POR, LOS, CUBANOS, EL ANO 1853, PARA, CONSERVAR, LAS CENIZAS DEL PADRE VARELA." Hanging over the emblematical representations standing upon the mahogany altar is a copy from Raphael's sublime painting, "The Ascension." The ravages of time have destroyed all the inscriptions upon the tombs which were placed here previous to 1821. One of the tablets being moved back from the top of the vault, a portion of the coffin was exposed. We concluded it might be the perpetuation of a time-honored superstition, which favored the idea that the soul visited the body, and watched over it after death. "*Vida Robles*"—a life of troubles—was inscribed on another tablet. From this epitaph a stranger would naturally suppose life had very few charms for the body deposited beneath it, and death a welcome messenger, that gave the care-worn frame a blessed rest.

A few years since, some workmen being employed to dig among the ruins where Tolemato Chapel once stood, discovered a medal, or medallion, in *basso-rilievo*, bearing the inscription, "*Roma.*" This sacred relic is supposed to have been attached to the rosary worn by the priest at the time when he was victimized before the altar. On one side of this medal is a kneeling figure, with an infant in his arms, around which is engraved, "SANCTUS JOANNES DE DEO"—St. John of God. C—who was born in 1495, a founder of the Order of Charity, and father of the eminent saints that flourished in Spain during the sixteenth century. His motto was, "Lord, thy thorns are my roses, and thy sufferings my paradise." On the opposite side is engraved "S. CHRISTOFORUS"—St. Christopher—represented bearing the Christ-child. This ancient relic comes to us blessed by the Pope, and in a remarkable state of preservation.

CHAPTER XII.

Can volume, pillar, pile, preserve thee great?
Or must these trust tradition's simple tongue?

THE ancient fortress of Castle San Marco, the name of which has been improperly changed to Fort Marion, is considered one of the most attractive and interesting objects in St. Augustine. It was constructed in the style of the strong castles in Europe during the Middle Ages, after the design of military engineering employed by Vauban. In 1762 it was called St. John's Fort, or San Juan de Piños, afterward San Marco, which name it retained until the change of flags in 1821, when it received the title of Fort Marion, in honor of General Marion, of Revolutionary fame. Its form is that of a quadrilateral, or trapezium, with bastions at each corner, the wall being twenty-one feet in height. Its extreme age, together with the durability of material employed, would be a subject of more interest to ancient architects, could they return, than to any of the present generation.

The battery is the boulevard of the city, where we can come and listen to the sea beating its great heart against the rocks, and see the snowy sails that glide so swiftly out to the solemn seas, while the white clouds float gracefully in their blue vault over our heads, like doves through the air, as the clear waters from the inlet flash in the bright sunlight, like burnished armor for a gala-day parade, and a pensiveness steals over our senses, which makes all earthly scenes vanish, like shadows in the distance at breaking of day.

We also find this a favored place for receiving serious impressions—this structure, formed by long-forgotten hands, which was a fortress of strength for the defenseless, a prison for treacherous captives, where they could pine and die far from the sound of human sympathy, with the gates of mercy forever sealed to them.

The mind embalms pleasant memories from this peculiar spot, when the skies are bright, bursting upon our vision like that day of which we read, whose "morning will dawn without clouds."

This structure was commenced in 1565, by the Spaniards, as a defense against the Indians. In 1732 Don Manuel Montiano, being appointed Governor of Florida, made application to the Captain General of Cuba for means to strengthen the fort, also more artillerymen, which were granted, the work being done under the direction of Don Antonio de Arredonda, a competent engineering official. In response to his request, two hundred convicts from Mexico being furnished him, six casemates were finished, of which there are eighteen in all, the remainder having been completed in 1756.

The impress of two eighteen-pound shot, low down on the eastern curtain, are now to be seen,

LAND APPROACH TO FORT MARION.

made from a battery placed on Anastasia Island by General Oglethorpe, who attempted by a regular siege to take the city. The bombardment was continued twenty days; but, on account of the lightness of the guns, and the distance, little damage was done. The siege lasted thirty-eight days, when the Americans withdrew their troops, and returned to Georgia.

General Oglethorpe returned two years after this, taking Fort Moosa, four miles distant, upon a broad river flowing under the fort; then advanced to the gates of St. Augustine, where he gave the garrison an invitation to march out and fight, which they declined.

In 1740 the castle is described as "being built of soft stone, with four bastions, the curtains sixty yards in length, the parapet nine feet thick, the rampart twenty feet high, casemated underneath for lodgings, arched over and newly made bomb-proof; and they have for some time past been working on a new covert way, which is nearly finished. The ordnance consisted of fifty pieces of cannon, sixteen of which were brass twenty-four-pounders. Thirteen hundred regular troops composed the garrison, also militia and Spanish Indians. In addition to this, the town was intrenched with ten salient angles, on each of which were cannon."

In 1769 it is again described as being completed "according to the modern taste of military architecture, and might be justly deemed the prettiest fort in the king's domain. It is regularly fortified with bastions, half-bastions, and a ditch; has also several rows of Spanish bayonet along the ditch, forming so close a *chevaux-de-frise* with their pointed leaves as to be impregnable. The southern bastions were built of stone."

The fort now, as then, is situated in the northeastern extremity of the old town, directly fronting the entrance to the harbor. On the west side is a broad and deep trench, or moat, connected with the moat around the castle extending across the town to the St. Sebastian River. This trench was used to flood the moat around the fortress, from the St. Sebastian River, and also to be filled with water when required, in order to obstruct the approach of assailants from the southern direction. On the south side of this trench very strong earth-works were erected, continuous with portions of massive walls on each side the city gate, which is now the best relic that exists in Europe or America—thus acknowledged by tourists who have visited St. Augustine. The form of the work is a polygon, consisting of four equal curtains, on the salient angles, on three of which are bastions, or turrets, the one at the northeast corner having disappeared. The moat around the castle is inclosed by the internal barrier, a massive wall of coquina, which also extends around the barbacan, following its entrant and reëntrant angles. An outer barrier extends around the inner, following in parallel lines the various flexures. Although a mound of earth is now raised against this outer barrier, inclosing the fort, there is little doubt, from observation of the remains, that the approaches to the castle were guarded, as in the Middle Ages, by an abatis, scarp and counter-scarp, frise, and all the defenses then employed, the traces of which are still extant. The barbacan in front of the entrance— called in modern phraseology the sally-port—is the only remaining specimen of a defensive work of the kind in this country, and to the present time has been an enigma to all visitors, which some tourists have committed the blunder of calling a demi-lune. This particular will be recalled by a reference to Scott's "Betrothed," which describes the castle of the "Garde Douloreuse." Traces of the "outer barrier gate" remain, also the draw-bridges, and machinery by which they were worked. Every thing is preserved but the "Warder's Tower" over the gate; the steps remain to prove the former existence of the tower. The draw-bridge, and even the pulleys by which it was raised, are there; also the ponderous portcullis, as an illustrated monument of Sir Walter Scott's description in regard to ancient castles.

The following Spanish inscription is to be seen over the sally-port in *alto-rilievo:*

REYNANDO EN ESPANA EL SEN^R
DON FERNANDO SEXTO Y SIENDO
GOV^{OR} Y CAP^N DE ES^A C^D S^{AN} AUG^N DE
LA FLORIDA Y SUS PROV^A EL MARISCAL
DE CAMPO D^N ALONZO FERN^{DO} HEREDA
ASI CONCLUIO ESTE CASTILLO EL AN
OD 1756 DIRI^G_AENDO LAS OBRAS EL
CAP. INGN^{RO} DN PEDRO DE BROZAS
Y GARAY.

Translation.—Don Ferdinand VI. being King of Spain, and the Field Marshal Don Alonzo Fernando Hereda being Governor and Captain General of this place, St. Augustine, of Florida, and its Province. This fort was finished in the year 1756. The works were directed by the Captain Engineer, Don Pedro de Brazos y Garay.

Every year hundreds of visitors rush into Fort Marion, and then the dungeon, with an awe-stricken feeling, as though the imaginary groans which are said to have been uttered here centuries since were ready to burst through the rocks and echo again, like the words of Plato, which his friends said froze in the winter, but on the return of spring thawed out again.

Several years after the cession of Florida to the United States the north-east bastion of this fortress caved in, immediately under the highest tower, disclosing a dungeon fourteen feet square. On the same day was made the discovery of a square rock, cemented in an opening similar to those in the casemates, only much less, which was undoubtedly the entrance.

> A tempest there you scarce could hear,
> So massive were the walls.

Some human bones and hair were then discovered and seen by volunteers from the ship Dolphin—a published account of which was forwarded to Washington, and deposited in the Congressional Library. The Smithsonian Institute has no knowledge of these cages, bones, or any thing pertaining to them ever having been placed there—which forever silences all inquiries in that direction. They told us, while in Washington, that when visitors came to the Institute asking information about them, the Professors were at a loss to know what they implied by their interrogations.

It has long been a demonstrated fact that some of the St. Augustine natives have a way of answering questions asked about them in accordance with their impressions, regardless of dates or historic records. The following description of the old fort mysteries is a change from the iron cages—the writer having visited the dungeon before the cage tale had been invented: "We were taken into the ancient prisons of the fort-dungeons, one of which was dimly lighted by a grated window, the other entirely without light, and by the flame of a torch we were shown the half-obliterated inscriptions scratched on the walls long ago by prisoners. But in another corner of the fort we were taken to look at the secret cells which were discovered a few years since in consequence of the sinking of the earth over a narrow apartment between them. These cells are deep under ground, vaulted over head, and without windows. In one of them a wooden machine was found, which some supposed might have been a rack, and in the other a quantity of human bones. The doors of these cells had been walled up, and concealed with stucco, before the fort passed into the hands of the Americans."

Many things, when related about it far away, sound tame, but have an awe-inspiring effect if surrounded by its grim walls, listening to the grating of rusty bolts, or the clanking of iron chains, and looking through the uncertain glare of the old sergeant's candles as he finishes his well-learned tale of horrors, in subdued tones, with the final paragraph, *"It may be so, or it may not; I cannot tell."*

That human bones have been discovered in the ruins of old churches and structures of various other kinds, placed there for sepulture, is a well-authenticated fact. While constructing the wall around the light-house at St. Mark's, Florida, in tearing down the old Spanish fort, a tomb was found beneath a tablet, containing a single body of much greater size than any living in the country at the present day. In the walls of the State-house, at Nashville, Tennessee, a niche was planned by the architect to contain his body, where his bones are now sealed in.

The iron cages about which so much has been said and written have come before the public with the enormous cruelties of the Inquisition and the mysteries of an almost-forgotten past. Many statements have been made and published in regard to them, without the shadow of truth for a basis. There are old citizens now living in St. Augustine, between eighty and ninety years of age, who saw those cages when discovered, and heard their parents state where they first saw them.

The following is, no doubt, the true version of the man-cages, direct from a most authentic source: About sixty years since, while some workmen were engaged outside the city gates in making post-holes for a butcher-pen, when in the act of digging, they struck a hard substance resembling iron, which excited their curiosity. They continued working until they uncovered two cages, made of wrought iron, welded together in a manner somewhat resembling the human form, and containing a few decomposed human bones. None of the New Smyrna refugees were then living, but there are those alive now who remember having heard their parents say that "two cages containing the remains of some pirates were hanging outside the city gates when they came to St. Augustine from Smyrna, after the English left it, and buried them just in the manner they were found by the butchers."

Although many inhuman acts have been committed by the Spaniards, they are not chargeable with all the atrocities perpetrated in the world. Señor B. Oliveros thus relates what he saw on the day they were dug out: "One evening, a little before sunset, I noticed a number of persons collected around the city gates, and proceeded there to ascertain the cause of so many people, when I spied the two cages standing against the city gate-posts." He, being a gunsmith, succeeded in obtaining one, which he said was most excellent wrought iron, of which he made good use. The other cage was taken in charge by the Spanish officers, and locked in the fort for safe keeping until it could be sent to Spain as a relic, where old persons now living here saw it with feelings of terror—they then being children. Thus, instead of being exhibited as a relic of the Spanish Inquisition at Washington, as has been represented so frequently, it is retained in Madrid as a specimen of English barbarity. The cages were no worse punishment than that of the old English law for aggravated offenses: "That the perpetrator be drawn and quartered alive." And who can number those that have perished in the English pillories?

No nation of people in the world can wash their hands entirely from cruel conduct, or show a clear record for the humane deportment of all its ancestry, remembering infallibility has left its impress nowhere except on the works and ways of God.

Some of those people usually designated as Indians, whose isolated existence is concealed in mystery, are here in Fort Marion, fettered with the forms of civilization, to which their adaptability of character conforms them with as good a grace as the circumstances will permit. That these tawny-skinned creatures have constitutions of iron there is no doubt, as their general appearance indicates a life of fatigue to which ease is a stranger. They are subjected to much exposure in pursuing the wild herds that rush with the precipitancy and speed of the mountain torrent, together with the days and weeks they spend with only the canopy of heaven for a covering, which increases their powers of endurance. Many times they retire supperless, and, when game is abundant, gorge themselves to gluttony, after which, like the stupid anaconda, they roll up for digestion, to supplant the place of more moderation. It is the testimony of all those who have lived among the Indians, that there exists a natural feeling of opposition to civilization, when not weakened by wars, or overpowered with superior numbers.

Did it ever occur to us highly enlightened people, while looking at the native dress of these savages, wrapped in their blankets, that clothing for the lower limbs was of but recent origin? Trousers were never worn by the Hebrews, Greeks, or Romans. The idea is said to have originated with the Gauls, the source from which our fashions are now received. The garment worn by the ancients was woven in one piece, about twelve feet in length and half the width, fastened on the right shoulder. It was secured with a girdle in folds at the waist when they started on long journeys, which was termed "girding the loins." This seamless coat was never out of fashion, and worn, if no accident happened to it, for generations. Think of a young man now wearing his father's coat, to say nothing of his great-grandfather's! It would be regarded as a synonym of extreme poverty, however rich the fabric from which it was formed might be woven.

The locality from which these Indians were brought was formerly designated The American Desert, located beyond the Arkansas River; but, as no remarkable barren country has been found there, the name was changed to Plains. The aborigines first found on the discovery of America, and those roaming through the Western wilds, are of quite different material. Those on the Atlantic coast were planters—cultivators of the soil. The Western Indians range through an area of two thou-

sand miles in extent, with no abiding-place but the
camp-fires, around which they gather at night to
rest, after shooting during the day the buffalo that
supplies all their necessities—clothing, tent-covers,
shoes, and strings for their bows; also an article of
commerce for trafficking with the whites. An attempt at a treaty with these children of nature
would have never been productive of any good.
The most feasible plan for the present has been
adopted—to capture a portion of them, which will
have a tendency to awe the remainder. Force is
the only weapon to be used. They are the Ish-
maelites of the West. The names of the tribes represented here are the Cheyennes, Comanches, Kiowas, and Arapahoes. The Comanches are the most
numerous of any tribe now existing, and have for
many years been a terror to Texas and frontier settlers. Entire districts have been depopulated by
them. While they exert a sleepless vigilance over
their own possessions, they are constantly making
predatory incursions upon their neighbors. The
Texas Rangers acquired the great skill, of which
we saw such frequent exhibits during the war, in
spending a portion of each day skirmishing with
these Indians. They are bold and warlike, with a
home on the grassy plains, whose kingdom is conquest, their throne a horse, upon which, when once
seated, with their arrows and lasso, they acknowl-
edge no umpire but death. More than three hundred years since, when first discovered, they had
dogs for beasts of burden—horses never having
been used among them. Plunder is what they live

for, and trophies what they fight for—it is considered disgraceful for them to return to camps empty-handed: no glory then awaits them, or words of kindness.

The Cheyennes have a rude system of representing their ideas by picture-writing, which may be traced up to the highest type of communicating thought by letter-writing. In this manner they have preserved legends, written history, and recorded songs.

The pantomimic movements of these Indians are all the language of signs. Each yelp has its import, by which means they can converse with one another, although their dialect may differ. Riding with the tails of their ponies braided is a key-note to hostilities. It is a remarkable peculiarity, in regard to their language, that they have retained it, however much associated with other tribes, which is illustrated by the Arapahoes and Cheyennes living in close proximity, indulging in freaks of fighting and friendship, as their inclination dictates, communicating with each other only by gestures or interpreters. They inhabit the valley of the Platte River, always ready to receive presents, talk in good faith of peace, but hardly have the words ceased to echo from their lips before they are holding a council of war, and making preparations for a descent upon any thing of value they may have discovered during their parley. They eat the flesh of canines with a relish that places all Government rations at a discount. Their visitors are expected to partake with them as a mark of friendship.

The Kiowa and Arapahoe tribes appear to have oratorical powers not possessed by the others, and their native eloquence has never been improved by education. Sa-tan-ta, a former chief of the Kiowas, when taken by the Government for numberless depredations, pleaded his own cause with such powerful effect he was dubbed "The Orator of the Plains." There is no doubt that the patriarchs among them prefer peace, but the young warriors are fond of fighting. With them it is an inborn instinct, like a bird for the air.

No life can be imagined fraught with greater dangers and privations than that of soldiers in search of Indians, to be found lurking with their missiles of destruction behind trees, grass-blades, or in any covert from which they can discharge these death-dealing weapons, in real or fancied security. The wild animals, driven by necessity, are always in readiness to pluck the bones of the first object they see, whether man or beast. Then the terrible thirst the poor soldiers endure, to be slaked with bitter waters, which destroy instead of refreshing them; the starving mules and horses of uncertain ages, whose flesh they have devoured like hungry dogs; the frosted limbs upon which they have limped until life seemed a burden. The fate of those who have preceded them is constantly in view; their companions are found lying near the last Indian trail with their bones bleaching, or their bodies filled with arrows, according to the number present when they were killed — no warrior is satisfied until he has pierced his bleeding, quivering flesh with a barbed point. Many of the arrows used have been poisoned by dipping them in the decayed hearts and livers of the buffaloes they have killed and then dried—a wound from one of them being equally as fatal in its effects as the virus from a dissecting-knife.

During the stay of these red men efforts have been made to teach them the use of boots and breeches, but the practical utility of either is of little import to them. Their first movement on returning West will no doubt be to drop their Government clothes, and resume the blanket and leggins.

CHAPTER XIII.

DURING the year 1690, after the appointment of Don Quiroga Loada as Governor of Florida, the water was discovered to be making encroachments from the bay into the town. A proposition was then made to the residents that a wall should be constructed from the castle to the plaza. At this time the sum of eight thousand dollars was raised, and a wall of coquina built, a portion of which can yet be seen. The present sea-wall, which is nearly a mile in length, extending below the barracks, was commenced in 1837, completed in 1843, at an expense of one hundred thousand dollars, the entire foundation being of coquina, mounted with a coping of granite, four feet wide. It is here young lovers delight to promenade in mid-winter, breathing words of tenderness and love, while the bright moonbeams silver the waves beneath their feet.

On the north side of the town, near the fort, stands what is left of the city gates, the most interesting relic that remains from a walled city. The gates are gone, the architecture of the two towers, or pillars, remaining being purely arabesque, surmounted by a carved pomegranate. Like the relics at Mount Vernon, if a protection is not built around these pillars, the hand of vandalism will soon have

REMAINS OF THE ST. AUGUSTINE CITY GATEWAY.

them destroyed, as so many careless visitors are constantly chipping off fragments. The sentry-boxes are much defaced, their foundation being a cement, the art of making it now being lost.

North of the fort, about one-quarter of a mile, on a slightly elevated plat of ground, there stood over three hundred years ago an Indian village, called Tapoquoi. Upon this spot now remains the foundation of a church, known as "*Nuestra Señora de la Leche.*" Two hundred and seventy-five years since a most inhuman act was committed here by the Indians. Father Blas de Rodriguez, a Franciscan friar, having administered reproof to a young chieftain for indulging in practices which did not belong to his profession, was warned in a menacing manner to prepare for death. He remonstrated with the Indians, trying to dissuade them from their wicked designs. However, all his tears and entreaties were unavailing. Finally, as a last request, he asked the privilege of celebrating mass before being forced to try the realities of another world. His fiendish, blood-thirsty persecutors crouched during the service like beasts of prey, waiting for an opportune moment to seize their innocent victim. Hardly had the words of supplication ceased for his enemies, before his murderers, as if impatient for the sacrifice, rushed upon him with their war-clubs, crushing him in a most shocking manner, bespattering the altar with his blood, while streams of his life's-gore covered his snowy vestments. They threw his mutilated remains into the field, but nothing disturbed them until a Christian Indian

gave them sepulture. An emotion of sadness is
produced in the mind of the sensitive visitor while
surveying the ruins of this chapel—"fragments of
stone, reared by hands of clay"—isolated from human
habitation, where no sounds now break the
silence but sighing winds and surging waves from
a restless sea.

The fact has long since been demonstrated beyond
a doubt that St. Augustine is the home of the rose
as well as the orange, which can be seen from the
following description of one called "La Sylphide,"
which grew in the yard of Señor Oliveros, on St.
George's Street: "This remarkable rose-tree before
its death attained to the height of about twenty feet,
the main stalk being fifteen inches in circumference
and five inches in diameter, the whole covering an
area of seventeen feet, yielding annually between
four and five thousand beautiful buds. But its
glory has now departed. While crowds gathered
to admire it, a worm was eating at the heart, thus
withering its creamy petals, blighting the tender
buds, which never opened their velvet coverings to
greet the sunlight, or kiss the morning breeze, as it
came from its home in the sea."

Many who have never spent a winter in Florida
think there is no religion, or churches either, which
is quite the reverse, as the finest pulpit-talent in the
North visit St. Augustine during the winter to rest
and prepare for the arduous and responsible duties
which await them on their return. The change
of scenery and surroundings give these clergymen
inspiration, when visitors often listen to some heav-

enly sermons. Imagine a Sabbath here in January, pleasant as a June holiday, North, among the roses, with a soft air floating through the house, which much resembles a new-born spring.

The Presbyterian church is a good, old-fashioned, well-preserved specimen of coquina walls. Many pleasant faces, whose homes are far away in icy regions, worship here every Sabbath. The table in front of the pulpit has a tall vase filled with the most beautiful flowers that ever bloomed in any clime—rose-buds, tinted like the sunset sky, orange-blooms, pomegranates, and snowy jasmines, all fresh from their bath in the morning dew, exhaling their sweet odors, mingled with the pæans of God's people — thus giving a holy peace to this blessed hour. The flowers are from the gardens of Messrs. Atwood and Alexander, who both have a cultivated taste for the beautiful. Two young men have just walked in, who are obliged to talk, whether they say any thing of importance or not. One of them remarked, "I think flowers in a church look too gushing!" This house, which is capable of containing over four hundred people, is filled nearly every Sabbath.

Dr. Daniel F. March, the author of "Night Scenes in the Bible," preached to-day. He always tells us something sweet to think of during the week, to lighten life of half its burden, that we can take along and travel its rough, rugged paths, singing instead of sighing. While associated with so much that is pleasant, the earth appears like a purified pedestal to a higher life, rather than a vale of wick-

edness. Dr. March has given a dissertation to-day
upon small matters, which make up the great sum
of life. He says: "Thousands of homes in our
land might be made heaven by kind words. One
little pleasant sentence spoken in the morning will
ring all day in a sensitive heart like the song of a
seraphim."

The Episcopal church, situated on the plaza, is a
neat Gothic structure, with stained glass windows
of exquisite design, which resemble the inner furnishing of an elegant city church more than a little
chapel down by the sea. It was commenced in 1827,
and consecrated in 1833, by Bishop Bowen, of South
Carolina. This church owns beautiful grounds,
filled with a tropical growth, adjoining it, on the
south-west side of the plaza. The land formerly
belonged to the Spanish Government, whose claim
ceased when the province was ceded to the United
States. This property, then, by a special act of
Congress, was given to the Church, to be under the
control and management of the wardens and vestry,
the act being confirmed February 8, 1827, when, in
1857, it was leased to a private party for the term
of twenty-five years. It is a piece of property that
involves a curious question—the Spanish or English
measurement of a few feet of ground, which takes
in or leaves out the veranda from the front of the
most desirable residence in the city, formerly owned
by Dr. Bronson. The question has never been decided who owns the veranda, but the Church, having no use for it, has never issued a possessory
warrant. Dr. Root, a venerable and most exem-

plary clergyman, is their pastor now, who ministers to them in holy things.

At no place in the world can a greater variety of peculiar people be seen during the winter, with their idiosyncrasies and eccentricities cropping out, for the amusement of some, and the annoyance of others, than at St. Augustine. One of these peculiar folks, of the masculine gender, can be seen every Sabbath morning in one of the churches. His devotions during the service are profound—his spiritual nature appears absorbed in humble confessions. At his side, on the cushion, reclines his constant companion — a little, black, shaggy dog, fastened to the seat. His master, having an aversion to strangers sitting by him, places his dog there as a protection against intruders. At the close of the service, the dog and master both leave the church with a regularity that has been remarked by all those who attend this place of worship. It was one Sabbath morning in March of 1878, while the orange-blossoms were exhaling their fragrance, the birds singing their songs of joy, combined with the perfection of a day which increased the desire for a stroll to the woods, and far away, that this dog and his master were seen approaching. The dog turned into the church, when the master stopped, beckoned, and tried to call him out, but all in vain—no effort could dissuade the dog from his regular custom of church-going, and the master had to attend church also, but against his own inclination on this occasion. This man is one of those harmless eccentrics whose freaks no one would think of interfering with, or trying to deprive him of, more than the crutch of the aged, or the spar from a drowning man. The most remarkable part of this story is yet to be told. His acquaintances in the North, who, seven years since, knew that he was an inmate of a lunatic asylum in New York, and supposing him there now, could scarcely credit the statement that he had been spending seven delightful winters in St. Augustine, chaperoning the ladies, with whom he is a great favorite, although the current of his matrimonial felicity has been stirred to the foundation, and never yet settled.

From the above facts, it can be seen that St. Augustine was not only supposed to contain the fountain of youth, but has, in reality, by its equable atmospheric influences, deprived the lunatic of his madness.

Among other attractions, St. Augustine contains a Public Reading-room and Circulating Library, both being the enterprise of kind-hearted, benevolent citizens and visitors, among the most prominent of whom we find the name of J. L. Wilson, Esq. The Reading-room is furnished with daily and weekly papers, together with periodicals from all parts of the United States, where time can be passed very pleasantly in obtaining a knowledge of the events taking place in the outside world. The Library contains about two thousand judiciously-selected volumes—most of them being late and standard works, from the best authors, in both Europe and America. Library-books are lent to responsible persons, who will return them within a prescribed time without injury. All contributions, either in books or money, will be thankfully received and properly used.

The important question with most visitors wherever they go is, What do we have to eat? as though the sole object of their lives was gormandizing. The market in St. Augustine is well supplied with eatables. Vessels from New York arrive weekly with groceries consigned to one or more of the va-

A SEA-CRAB.

rious firms of Messrs. Hamlin & Co., Genovar & Brother, Lyon & Co., large wholesale and retail dealers, which are furnished to their customers on more reasonable terms than purchasers would think possible. During most of the winter months fresh strawberries, cabbage, and lettuce, sparkling with the morning dew, are sold on the streets, besides celery, turnips, sweet and Irish potatoes, wild turkeys and ducks, together with plenty of venison and beef. It is a treat to visit the fish-market at early dawn, and see the boats come in with their live fish of various kinds—drum, mullet, flounder, sheephead, red bass, crabs, etc.

Fine Matanzar oysters are kept for sale in or out of the shell, as the purchaser may choose. If any appearance of starvation has ever faced visitors here, no one has perished here from hunger. It is true, there have been times when the demand for certain articles has exceeded the supply a day or two only, but now good, palatable, life-sustaining food can be obtained; also fresh milk, as some of the citizens are making dairies a specialty. Very sweet oranges are sold from Dr. Anderson's grove by the cart-load, while some others have almost every variety produced, including the Lisbon, Chinese, Maltese, Tangerine, Seville, and Mandarin, or Clove orange.

Hotels here, with high-sounding names and inviting appearance, are well kept. The St. Augustine, Magnolia, and Florida Houses, have the most rooms, while the Sunnyside has taken a front seat for first-class accommodations with all its patrons. Nearly every house rents rooms or takes boarders, and many of them feed well—among whom we find the names of Mr. George Greeno, Mr. Medicis, and Miss Lucy Abbott, as extremely popular.

Some who visit Florida expect gratuitous offerings from the residents for the great favor shown them in coming, and when they find every thing is cash on delivery, a general fault-finding is commenced on extortion—this exercise being the only escape-valve for their bottled wrath. The far-famed hospitality of the Southern people is a record of the past, from the force of surrounding circumstances, now obsolete, as Webster says with regard to some of his Dictionary words: with most of them it is a question of bread, and whatever produce or fruit of any kind is raised—from a ground-pea to a ripe sweet orange—the question is asked, How can I turn it into something by which my family may be supported? The South has now neither wealth nor much leisure to spend without value received. The inhospitality in not giving fruits is only one of the many sources of complaint—the boarding-houses and hotels being the most prolific cause for disagreeable remarks. The most eligible houses of entertainment, with scarcely an exception, are kept by Northern people, who have charged two dollars for a dinner with the most unblushing effrontery, while the Floridian is satisfied with fifty cents for a square meal. There are also those reared here who ask whatever they think visitors will stand, regardless of principle, but they always bear brow-beating, when they come down to prices within range of any ordinary purse.

Many speak of this favorably as a summer-resort, but when the season advances into May, the winter-visitors all leave. Then a painful silence pervades every thing, unbroken only by an occasional yawn from the residents, who are tired doing nothing. These demonstrations sound sad, as if from the tomb, and where the echoes cease to reverberate we have never been able to determine. The climate, from its insular exposure, is said to be lovely even in August.

We are now enjoying moonlight nights, about which so many have so much rhapsodized. There is no doubt that the nocturnal appearance of the heavens in this latitude contrasts with a Northern one in the same manner that two paintings differ—the warmth, richness, and brilliancy of the one being in opposition to the poverty and indistinctness of the other. On account of the latitude, there is no twilight—the "fairy web of day is never hung out"—but from blazing sunshine into darkness we are at once precipitated—no witchery or poetry to be found between the magic hours intervening.

Every season finds a large number of nice people at this place, who require a change of climate, from the severity of cold, piercing winds, to the blandness of an Indian summer. The care-worn come to rest, writers to find inspiration; for here, fanned by the sea-breeze, does not "light-winged fancy" travel at a swifter pace in the daylight? and when night comes, lulled by the surf, we can listen to the "great sea calling from its secret depths."

The inquiry is often made by those who have never visited here, How do you kill time in that ancient city? To the historian, there is no spot so well adapted to meditation on the past, where associations are awakened with greater rapidity, when the Indians held undisputed sway, only dreaming of plenty and the happy hunting-grounds beyond; but, suddenly as the Montezuma monarch, their territory was wrested from them by the Spaniards, whom these unlettered savages at first regarded as children of the Great Spirit; but when the ensigns of authority were unfurled, their country overran by myrmidons, and the power of their cazique sneered at, then the illusion vanished—the truth dawning that they were only sojourners whose presence did not add to the happiness of the newly self-constituted sovereigns of their country.

Three distinct classes of visitors come here—the defiant, the enthusiastic, and the indifferent. The defiant spend their time in assailing, "with vehement irony," every thing with which they are placed in contact, ringing changes upon any thing disagreeable to them, until their companions are wearied beyond measure. The enthusiastic rise more or less on the wings of their fertile imagination, when exaggerated accounts, highly colored, are written about Florida as it appeared to them—the change from the North to a land clothed in the perpetual verdure of spring-time being so great, they were enraptured in a manner that others of less delicate susceptibilities have failed to realize. The indifferent tourist is an anomaly to everybody. Why he ever thought of leaving home to travel, when with his undemonstrative nature he appears so oblivious to all scenes and sights around him, is an unsolved problem. He maintains an unbroken reticence on every occasion, the mantle of silence being thrown about all his movements, while his general appearance evinces the same amount of refinement as a polar bear, his perceptive powers the acuteness of an oyster, his stupidity greater than Balaam's saddle-animal.

St. Augustine, 1876.—The minds of the citizens

and visitors in the city have been on the *qui vive* for
several days, in anticipation of witnessing the realities, in miniature, connected with a buffalo-chase on
the prairies, in which princes from Europe have participated, regarding it as the crowning feat of their
exploits in the New World. For days previous ladies were discussing the propriety of their presence,
as the animal might be so unmanageable as to imperil their safety; very brave lads, who have been
sufficiently courageous to fire a pistol at an alligator
while in Florida, thought they might be safe in the
fort if they were to climb upon the walls, and very
small boys concluded their fathers would keep the
buffalo from hurting them.

Long before 3 o'clock the fort was enlivened by
those bent on sight-seeing. Here were the richly-dressed ladies and their escorts, with New-York-style mustaches, where only a restricted smile ever
rested, gazing through their eye-glasses toward every
thing that came near enough for them to take sight
at, as though a fixed stare through optical instruments was more excusable and allowable than with
the naked eye. Children of all sizes and colors came
in crowds. There were more old people present,
whose silvery hair looked like a "crown of glory,"
than could be seen in any other town at once in the
United States. Like Ponce de Leon, they visit St.
Augustine in search of the famous waters which
would give back their youth, restore and strengthen
their feeble limbs with renewed vigor, that would
be perpetual as the verdure and beauty by which
they are surrounded. Nor are they disappointed in

all respects; for if they do not grow younger, they prolong their days to enjoy more of God's pure air and sunlight, mingled with the perfume of flowers and singing of sweet birds, than they would in their own homes.

As the time for the chase approached, painted Indians peered from every part of the fort, most of them dressed in full costume, their heads trimmed with feathers from birds of varied plumage, the most conspicuous of which was the American turkey-tail. They were wrapped in gaily-colored blankets, profusely trimmed with beads, all of which trailed in a very *negligee* manner, while they seemed as much excited with the surroundings as any of the spectators. The Indians regard death with much less terror than do the whites. They say that if in hunting a horse falls and kills them, they will go where game is abundant, always living there — thus, like the Christian, making death the golden gate to glory.

No bugle echoed through the woodlands wild as a signal for the chase to commence, nor well-trained dogs, with the lead-hound barking fiercely from the excitement of a fresh trail which indicated a near approach to game. Their captain, to whom real buffalo-hunts on the boundless prairies are no novelty, led the van, followed by four painted, gaily-dressed, full-rigged Indians. They all rode as though their homes were in the saddle, and swiftly as if bright visions of fleet-footed game were feeding in green fields, only waiting to be captured by being shot at with their well-aimed arrows. They made some fine exhibitions of horsemanship, peculiar to their methods of warfare and hunting. In riding, they described circles, as if surrounding a foe in ambush, at the same time discharging their arrows, at a distance of two hundred yards, with great accuracy, while their horses were running at full speed. Their arrows perforated a small building, which they used as a target, penetrating so far they could not be removed without being broken. Gathered in groups outside the fort, near the hunting-ground, were many boys and young men of the more daring class, who displayed their bravery by a foot-race which put Weston, or any other walker, in the shade, whenever the buffalo looked toward them. Every thing was a success, except the buffalo, which was a small steer, that would not scare on any account. He was entirely too gentle for the fever-heat of excitement to which the feelings and imagination of the crowd had been wrought up. He shook his head once or twice, and started as though he might create a sensation, but would not keep far enough ahead for the hunters to make any thing like a good charge on him. Finally an arrow, sped from the bow of White Horse, pierced his vitals to the depth of four or five inches, killing him instantly. His throat was then cut, after which he was dressed and hauled into the fort, where ample preparations were made for his reception, with immense fires and kettles of hot water. Some of the Indians ate the heart and liver raw, which process did not look very appetizing to a delicate stomach. They always cook their food before eating it when in their native wilds, except the heart and liver, which they sometimes consume as a medicine. At a given signal among themselves, those not engaged in cooking commenced dancing. In their movements the poetry of music, or motion, has no votaries; but a slight approach toward it is made, as they all take the Grecian bend, and keep it, while going through their gyrations. When weary they group together around the fires, turning their right foot on the side, and seating themselves with an ease no studied art could teach them, and then they rest more free from care than the heart that beats beneath ermine, or reclines on velvet cushions. When their meat was cooked they terminated the day's exercise with a feast, which they all seemed to enjoy very much, each Indian consuming about four pounds of flesh, with a greedy gusto before which an epicure would retire in disgust. The grand wardance of the season came off after dark, when prisoners were captured and treated with sham hostilities. The mind of the imaginative could portray what would be done in reality to a helpless captive in their power.

We regard these poor savages as only a connecting link between the herd that roams the "verdant waste"—who see the Great Spirit in clouds, and hear him in the crashing storms—and ourselves. May we not inquire if their condition cannot be improved, and their voices, which only shout for conquest over a vanquished enemy, or in the chase while victimizing the huge buffalo with bleeding, gaping wounds, be taught to sing the songs of redeeming grace for a ransomed world?

CHAPTER XIV.

AT no other town in the State is the entertainment for visitors more of a success than here, and one of those pleasant occasions brought a large number of happy hearts together, to witness a grand opening of the Lunch-basket on the North Beach.

Many have been the devices, in all ages of the world, by every nation peopling the habitable globe, for a relaxation from the sterner duties of life. Among the first to which persons of various tastes have resorted is archery, which was practiced by that wild outcast, Ishmael, "whose hand was against every man, and every man's hand against him." We also read in the Pentateuch of a great and mighty hunter named Nimrod; while conspicuously prominent among the biblical characters Job poetizes upon drawing large finny monsters from the deep waters, and at a later date in the same profession of the apostles.

Many monks of the Middle Ages in France are said to have delighted more in the chase at times than the "trumpet of the gospel." Bull-fights, as an amusement, are supposed to have originated with the Moors, and are still practiced by the Spaniards, many of them being of Moorish origin. Grounds in the vicinity of St. Augustine have been located, beyond a doubt, where this cruel and barbarous

custom was indulged in by early Spanish settlers.
Archery has been the most popular pastime here
this season. The Indians have made the bows and
arrows for compensation and employment—more arrows having been thrown by the "sons of the forest" than hurled from the shafts of Cupid.

We can produce, as patrons of the hook-and-line
art, prophets and apostles in ancient times, kings
of more recent date, and Izaak Walton, who lived
nearly two hundred years ago, down to the truant
boy that throws his bent pin, baited with an innocent worm, or fly, into the clear running brook, at
which an old fish looks, as if about to nibble, then
wags his tail and sails away in search of something
that he can take in without being taken himself.

A very worthy divine, Bishop Hall, has wisely
remarked: "Recreation to the mind is like whetting to the scythe. The mind that is always mowing
becomes dull for the sharpening which relaxation
affords it; so the blade that is always cutting is
blunted for the want of an edge that grinding can
give."

The above remarks on recreation were suggested
by an attendance upon the opening of the Lunch-basket on the North Beach, opposite Anastasia Island, at a place called by the classic name of Parathina, from Homer's "Iliad": *Eban kerukes para thina tou poluphloisboio thalassees* — "The heralds
went to the beach of the high-sounding sea." A
long-looked-for and much-needed means of conveyance—a nice little steamer, called the Mayflower—
has made us happy already by its presence and busi-

ness-dispatching movements. She is a light-running little craft, that glides gracefully as a swan. Sailing and rowing are now lost sight of by visitors wishing to take a little ride on the water, as the wind never dies out and leaves them, or the oar-hands grow weary, on a steamer. The two first trips she carried over seventy passengers, which made the day pay very well.

Mr. J. F. Whitney, who, like all the editorial fraternity, is ever busy in trying to suggest something for either mind or body, being the prime mover in this undertaking, has erected four pavilions, and a cook-room, with a range. One of the smaller pavilions is carpeted, supplied with periodicals, rocking-chairs, and a bed for the sick to rest. The largest pavilion is nearly two hundred feet in length, and over twenty feet wide; in front is an extended view of the beach, beyond which the restless sea is rolling up new-born waves at every influx of its waters. Here are also detached dining-tables for the accommodation of parties coming together. The floor is level and smooth as it can be made, where, it has already been whispered,

> ———— youth and pleasure meet,
> To chase the glowing hours with flying feet.

The bill of fare for the occasion was equal to any New York restaurant. Broiled oysters vanished with the ejaculation, "Splendid!" All eatables shared a similar fate, with a superlative adjective attached, as the only one which could express the gratification of the guests. Champagne-bottles were relieved of their sparkling contents in a brief period of time. Ice-cream and pound-cake were soon reckoned among past pleasures, while everybody was eloquent on the subject of the surroundings.

The North Beach has now more attractions and amusements than any other point in the State, and when the arrangements are completed with a stud of riding and driving horses, it may well be styled the Newport of the South. Like Scīpio the Great, after the repast many wandered by the "murmuring sea," and gathered shells to take home with them as mementoes of pleasant memories in a sunny clime.

When refined hearts and well-cultivated minds meet in a spot made grand by the great Maker of all things, and rendered comfortable to our wants by the hand of Art, where only God and his heavenly wonders have dwelt in solitude for so many years, may we not say Scripture is being fulfilled—that "the wilderness and the solitary place shall be glad?" Yes, glad with happy voices in congenial companionship, and joyous with the sweets of social intercourse. It is, indeed, "a well in the desert"—a place provided, where persons in the pursuit of pleasure can assemble and forget all adverse religious tenets, political differences, or personal animosities—where secret and selfish purposes in life are lost sight of—whether gold is up or down, what are the last figures on the bulletin-boards of the "bulls and bears," the fractional variations of upland or sea-island cotton, being among the subjects absorbed in the enjoyment of the hour.

10*

218 *Petals Plucked from Sunny Climes.*

Among others came the never-tiring fisherman, with reel and fancy bait, who appeared much delighted with an opportunity of having sea-room for the exhibition of his skill. He did not have to follow the old rule of "fishing inch by inch," with an

FLORIDA RAY-FISH, OR SKATE.

indefinite idea of when he would have a nibble. Here is an illustration of his first bite, which caused him to retire, dragging his prize to shore, thinking, perhaps, he might have captured some Pythagorean metamorphosis, as it resembled neither fish nor flesh. Upon summoning those present to his relief, the following decision was rendered: A ray-fish, or skate, having a cartilaginous body, of nearly a white color, with pectoral fins largely developed, the caudal extremity being elongated into a whip-like form, armed with spine, which makes it an ugly customer for collision. The female, being oviparous, is provided with parchment-like cases, forming an extension, called by seamen "sailor's purses."

The moon rose that night and looked down upon a joyous crowd seated on the Mayflower, with a fine band from the St. Augustine Hotel. Music on the water—who can describe its enchanting influences! It was high tide when we arrived on the North Beach, when planks were put out for the party to walk on, while the gentlemen and steamer-crew assisted them to the shore. One lady remarked, in crossing, "Sometimes I take a black hand, and then a white one." We were not particular about color then; it was strong hands we wanted to keep us from falling in the water, as the waves were washing over our feet. The band played sweetly, the dancing was graceful, the refreshments abundant. When returning, the last trip, the steamer grounded on a sand-bar, as it was ebb-tide, when the Captain of the Bache Survey steamer kindly sent his long-boat and brought us all to the wharf.

St. Augustine, March, 1877.—The work of enlivening the old town, for the delectation of visitors and excursionists from other points, was undertaken here to-day. Everybody was merry, and it was almost incredible to see the number of dignified

persons, on other occasions, so completely carried
along with the tide of simple sight. All, apparently, had their laugh set on trigger, ready to go off
with the slightest vibration in the air. The streets
and sea-wall of St. Augustine, together with the
balconies, windows, and doors, in the vicinity, were
the scene of preparation for a grand gala-day of
sight-seeing. The vessels in the harbor were
dressed in flags of every nationality, and waved
free as the winds that tossed them to and fro. The
post-band played stirring strains, containing more
sound than sweetness, to quicken the impulses of
the occasion. At a given signal, cannons were
fired, when a fleet of snowy sails shot out from the
wharf, resembling a flock of sea-gulls. The yacht-
racing opened the day's sport. They all sailed
swiftly when first under way, but one after another
kept falling off and dropping behind, until the Wanderer and Seminole were left alone to decide the contest. They moved like something possessed with life,
more than canvas spread to the breeze for power to
propel them. Finally the Wanderer won, amid the
wildest shouts of joy from every side, and many congratulations for the owner. The cannons fired with
as much demonstration as though a great battle had
just been decided. A horse-race was announced as
the next excitement. Eight jockey-dressed men
and boys of different hues, mounted on bare-
backed horses of undistinguishable pedigree, but
marsh tackey predominant, were ready for the cur-
riculum. They darted off with the speed of a Grecian hippodrome, when they imitated the gait of

almost every untrained quadruped. On the home-stretch two of the riders rolled off easily, as though it was a portion of the programme for which they were prepared. Then came the hurdle-race, with the hurdles woven from cedar and scantling. The running was sport, but the jumping was without comparison. One of the horses caught his feet and plunged over, rider and horse together, but, neither being hurt, everybody shouted with glee. Another of the Arabian steeds carried the hurdles off victorious with his hind feet, but did not fall. A foot-race by the Indians was then declared with as much gravity as though a Grecian contestant, after all the abstinence and training of an ancient athlete, proposed to try his strength and speed for a victor's crown. Three or four big Indians, dressed with fancy caps and moccasins, walked to the pedestrian race-grounds, after which one started to run, but fell. The crowd was too big for them, and the reward too small. Two of the natives took their places, and made very good time, but not quite equal to a professional walker. Then came the hand-barrow race, with that unhistoric vehicle about which poets never sing. Ten black boys, with ten bright bandages over their eyes, started to run a race across the east side of the plaza. They all commenced at the word three, the band played, the people shouted, while the boys ran; the wheelbarrows were running a race, and so was everybody else. One boy went into the river-basin before he could be stopped; another rushed against a carriage, and set the horses to kicking and the ladies to screaming; a man was knocked down and run over—he was a prim, particular bachelor, with fine estates, whose birthday is best known to himself—it required the combined efforts of two servants to brush the sand from his clothes and place him in presentable trim again. Everybody in the vicinity was liable to be under moving orders without a moment's warning. Finally the race ended, and the victor crowned with greenbacks, which he could appreciate more highly than the laureate wreath of a conqueror, fresh from the goal with his coronet of fading glories.

The last performance was the greasy pole, with a fat ham on the top of it, placed in the center of the plaza. What a climbing, scrambling, and tumbling down, amid exclamations from the boys: "Bob, what made you let go?" "Tom, go up, and I will hold you!" "Put on more sand, and then we can climb!" The plaza was crowded with spectators—scores of grandparents, all clapping their hands and laughing—large families, with all their children, were there. The scene before them required no explanation. Finally, after a struggle of two hours, the ham and money were won, when all retired from the varied and innocent sports of the day.

St. Augustine demonstrates the fact, beyond a doubt, that the cat is a musical animal. They sit under your windows, climb on the neighboring roofs, scream in any strain, from the lowest bass to the loudest soprano, and never tire until the stars pale in the sky; do not become dismayed because a few pieces of coquina are thrown at them, glass bottles, or old boots—that only causes a change of position, when the voice rises an octave higher, on account of the escape from a little adventure. Here they congregate in crowds; they rehearse their exploits in excited strains, with untiring assiduity, for the entertainment of visitors, to prevent their receiving the impression that *St. Augustine is a dull old place.* Then the digestive organs of the departed are manufactured, and made to imitate the same dulcet tones in the halls of mirth, where so many derive pleasure, by turning themselves into more shapes than a captured sea-eel. At the St. Augustine Hotel they swallow all kinds of condiments to the sounds coming from these membranous strings, stretched beyond all marks of their former identity. With a satisfied smile, and no fears from indigestion, the invalid or consumptive consumes every variety of food, whether from land or sea, compounded into the latest styles of the *cuisine*, to the music of "*Il Bachio*," or "A place in thy memory, dearest!" while ice-cream vanishes like dew to the melody, "Thou art so near, and yet so far!" or "Some one to love me!"

CHAPTER XV.

THE longevity for which the inhabitants of St. Augustine have been remarkable is a proof of its healthfulness; indeed, the tenacity with which they cling to life, as well as the uncomplaining manner in which they endure every thing, is really wonderful. Several years since, an aged lady, who had been helpless for years before her death, remarked that Death seemed to have forgotten her—she remained here so long.

Some who have heretofore imagined that St. Augustine had no attractions but its antiquity must remember that new industries are constantly being developed, among the most recent of which is the manufacture of marmalade and wine from the native wild orange fruit. We had the pleasure of visiting both these enterprising establishments—first the marmalade factory, in charge of Señor S. B. Valls, a Cuban exile. His father, Señor Jose Valls, under the well-known brand of "El Pavo Real, Fabricada de Dulces," or Sweetmeat and Guava Jelly-maker, in Havana, has won a world-wide reputation, having received the Paris Exposition medal, 1867. His method is original, and his sweetmeats better adapted to the American taste than those of Scotch make. The enterprise has met with great success, the de-

mand always exceeding the supply, and the moderate
charges being also an attractive feature. He pre-
serves lemons, limes, and figs in such a manner that
they will keep for years. He makes an orange-
bloom cordial, which must be, without doubt, the
original nectar of the gods; for certainly there is
nothing like it, the flavor perfectly resembling the
odor of the orange-blossom; the sensation produced
in swallowing it is like sailing on a summer sea.

The orange-wine manufactured by Genovar &
Brother well deserves to supplant the miserable,
adulterated, yeasty preparations which are sold and
drunk daily by those whose minds are afterward in
a constant state of doubt as to the amount of harm
incurred by the potion imbibed.

It is April, and the season has arrived when visitors commence leaving; all amusements in which
they delighted have become stale—even the yacht-
races, which contributed so largely to the entertainment of those fond of boating; while outsiders are
constantly under the impression that the boats are
trying to tack for another course, making an effort
to anchor, or turning in for a nap.

The Southern Indians imprisoned here for the
past three years have been a subject of comment
and amusement for most of the visitors, while their
presence in the city was any thing but desirable to
certain aggrieved persons, who succeeded in obtaining an escape-valve for their feelings by the following expressions, printed in the *Savannah Morning
News*, entitled, "A Page from the Unwritten History
of the Ancient City":

"*St. Augustine, Fla.*, March 4, 1878.—While the prominent points in St. Augustine, which present themselves to visitors, are written threadbare, there is an undercurrent, although felt by the suffering, that has never been stirred by the anxious inquirers after information. It is God's poor—those reduced by circumstances over which they have no control. Many exclaim, Lo! the poor Indian; but none consider the avenues to employment which the presence of these scalping, murdering, human heart-eaters, are causing in this water-locked city by the sea. When teaching the Indian to appreciate the value of a Government which proposes to protect them, at the same time enabling them to participate in all the privileges of an enlightened organization, why cannot they be made self-sustaining, and hired out, as other convicts? What heroic deeds of greatness have they ever achieved, that they should be treated like prisoners of State, instead of inhuman fiends, at whose record of crime Satan would grin with delight? Many of them are permitted to roam with freedom, not only in every portion of the city, but in the country around, thus terrifying timid citizens with their presence, causing them to change their habitations to the town for protection. While they are fed and clothed by the Government, free, they hire themselves out at lower wages than poor laborers can work for, and be sustained. This has become a great source of grievance to the community, which they desire to have redressed by their removal. Much of the money they make is only to buy food for a pampered taste, which has been acquired since

they came here, and not to sustain their existence.
If labor has to compete with crime, the hand of industry with the bloody hand, where is the hope on
which honesty is to hinge and work its way through
the world? The whole can be told in a few words:
While these sixty savages are here being employed
in every department of manual labor, thus taking
the bread from the mouths of dependent women and
children, it is productive of suffering in our midst,
whilst those advanced in life look in vain for a support to their sons, whose hands are tied by these
savage oppressors."

Two weeks after the news of the pope's death had
been received in other cities, and the drapery of
mourning become dusty, the cathedral bells here
commenced tolling at sunrise, and continued the
entire day until dusk. The chimes in Rome were
never struck with more regularity, and when the
sun sank to his home in the west a sigh of relief
was felt, that every thing has an end. If the day
was spent by the Catholics in mourning for the pope,
the night was spent by the visitors in giving expression to the most jubilant demonstrations of joy—
the festivities being gotten up by the Yacht Club,
which appears to be the only central live-figure head-
light in the city now. On this occasion the Yacht
House was illuminated with Chinese lanterns, which
encircled it over the water's edge; calcium lights
blazed with overpowering brilliancy, and the most
dazzling rockets shot through the air like meteors,
while the brass band discoursed very loud, stirring
strains, and the little boats glided about on the bay,

like *ignes-fatui*, with lights suspended on their masts or on their bows, glittering through the darkness, resembling a distant constellation. With the freedom of uncaged birds, fresh from bondage, every one appeared buoyant, giving themselves up to the pleasure of the hour with a kind of *abandon* as if, after all, it might be a panoramic view produced by some Eastern Magi. After the illumination on the water was ended, the string-band commenced playing, when busy feet kept time to the harp and viol, without a thought of the confessional which would have to be met before the next sacrament.

For a few days past the weather has been rather capricious, the sunshine hidden behind damp clouds, and the wind more boisterous than sight-seekers enjoy. We imagine some of the tourists' note-books are full enough of complaints. The weather is delicious now, the air all balm, the sky all blue, the bananas waving in the gentlest of breezes, the sea heaving softly under the sunlight. We shall miss this changeful sea at St. Agustine, the reviving air, the lovely palms, the mocking-bird upon whose happiness the day closed too soon, as from his perch in a neighboring orange-tree he trills his song of joy until the night is far spent.

St. Augustine, April, 1878. — The Indians have gone! Yes, the pets of some and the pests of others have left St. Augustine amidst the sympathetic demonstrations of a crowd, followed by the best wishes of all, that they may arrive safely at their points of destination. The marks of improvement are evident on the outside of them; but none need nurse the delusion that it has struck in. On being asked what they were going to do with their clothes when they went West, they replied, with a symbolic jerk, "Tear them off, and throw them away!" Think of Mrs. Black Horse and Mochi, with their heads dressed in fashionable Mother Goose hats, with plumes and white tissue veils, that had been given them by lady-visitors, their bodies rolled up in a buffalo-skin, before a campfire, after a long march in the rain, or fresh from a war-dance, with the dripping scalps of white men hung from their waists as trophies of bloody triumphs! They were delighted at the prospect of freedom; beating against rock walls and prison-bars was too much pressure for them—to which they yielded in sullen despair. They left their literature —religious picture-books and buffalo-hunts not being in harmony—"Moody and Sankey" song-books suddenly losing all charm for them, "Hold the Fort" being changed to "Leave the Fort." They said, "Me man, no school." Some of them could speak Spanish, and while here learned a little English. They corresponded with their kindred on the plains by picture-writing. A lady-visitor wished Minimic, or Eagle's Head, to give her a letter written him by his wife, when he replied, "What white squaw do with my squaw's letter?" The poetry of the idea was evidently lost on him.

The "noble red man" of the novel-writer and these coarse savages, whose rough nature repels all polish, are quite different. Three of these Indians, who have taken to the customs of the whites more kindly than the others, are to be sent North and educated, the expense incurred being the enterprise of private individuals.

A year previous to their departure, while the work of civilization was supposed to be progressing very rapidly, in the midst of untiring efforts on the part of Church-missionaries to convert them, one of the tribes was discovered plotting mutiny. They could not endure the strain of civilization—it was too much for them. White Horse, chief of the Kiowas, reckoning the number of moons long past since he had the promise of freedom, excited an insurrectionary movement among the Kiowas, twenty-four in number. When their intentions were manifested by insubordination, a squad of armed soldiers were ordered from the barracks to seize them after they had entered their mess-room in the casemate. The Indians were marched out in pairs, and searched, to which they submitted without resistance. A number of barbed, steel-pointed arrows, and pistols, were found on their persons. They did not intend a general massacre; only those who opposed them in their efforts to escape were to be murdered. The fort was closed for a day or two only, when White Horse and his principal accomplices — Lone Wolf, Woman's Heart, and To-Zance — were put in irons. These Indians pined for their homes; their lofty, aristocratic natures revolted against the discipline to which they were subjected, as unmanly and unsuited to the dignity of a warrior, who had roamed with unrestrained movements over the plains, free as the herd which he killed. Most of the Indians, while here, employed their time in making bows and arrows, and polishing sea-beans, while the women worked over old bead moccasins, and freshened them up with new soles and buckskin linings, all of which were bartered to visitors — thus making their bondage more endurable, besides furnishing themselves with pocket-money.

As in time past, the old fort, that has lifted its turrets unmoved for centuries to the fierce gales which visit the coast, will again become the home of the lizard, a resort for bats, the abode of the owl, whose shrill screechings and weird movements make the darkness of night more suggestive of a ghoul-haunted castle, where unhappy spirits are supposed to assemble, when "coarser spirits wrapped in clay" are snoring to the ascending and descending scale of unwritten sounds.

Opposite St. Augustine is situated St. Anastasia Island, which was named for a celebrated saint in the Roman calendar of favorites. On this island is found the coquina, or shell-rock, from which the fort and many of the houses were built; here also roam the fleet-footed deer, catamount, and wild hog. At low tide the ponies and marsh-cows resort here to feed upon the long grass which grows so luxuriantly at all seasons. The cattle, while in pursuit of it, frequently become bogged, and die; but the horses, when reared here, are not so unfortunate, being lighter and more nimble-footed; when they get beyond their depth, and are sinking, they throw themselves on their sides, and commence floundering and rolling until they find a surface sufficiently solid to sustain their weight, when they rise and quietly resume eating, as though nothing had occurred. Like all other places in this vicinity, it has historic records. It was here, in 1740, General Oglethorpe erected a battery of five pieces, four of which were eighteen-pounders. When he had made the preparations necessary for an attack on St. Augustine, he gave the Spanish Governor an invitation to surrender. General Oglethorpe received the reply that he would "be glad to shake hands with him in the castle."

The new light-house stands on this island—being constructed because the old one was found to be undermining by the action of the waves. The old coquina light-house was designed to subserve the double purpose of a fortress and a beacon, having strong walls and loop-holes, with a cannon on its summit, to be fired as a signal on the approach of a vessel. At night a light-wood fire was kept burning, which could be seen by vessels at sea for several miles.

On the coast below St. Augustine, surrounded by the briny waves, some distance from shore, bursts up a fresh-water spring, from which ships can obtain their supplies before going to sea. This remarkable fountain of fresh water is produced from one of those subterranean currents so frequent throughout the State, north of the Everglades, coming to the surface only when they reach a point considerably below the level of their sources, sometimes forming lakes, and at others channeling their way to the sea.

The coral reefs, so abundant in Florida, are the

Petals Plucked from Sunny Climes. 233

work of a tiny insect which operates only under water, after which the water deposits the lime that constitutes the limestone of Florida—many portions of the State having been subject to upheaval since the deposit of lime between the coral reefs. This

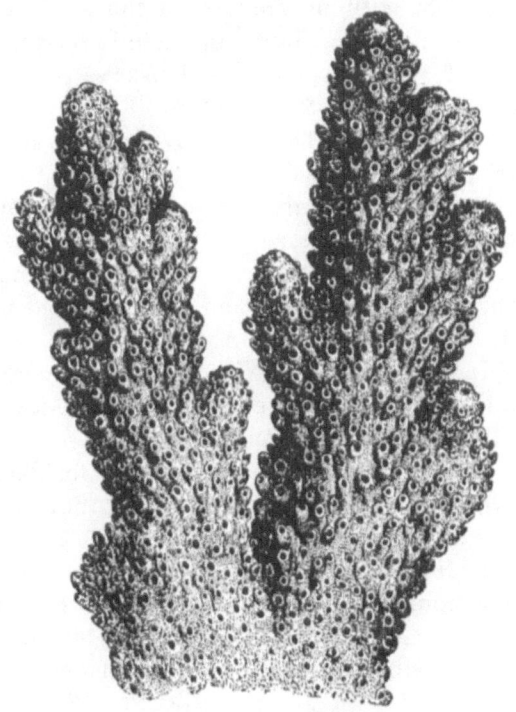

FLORIDA REEF CORAL.

lime formation being undoubtedly very recent, and having little solidity, is entered by the surface-water, which forms channels through it; thus, by the force of accumulated waters, it reaches the sea, these channels being constantly enlarged by the lime combining with the water, together with the abrading action of the currents; and when the rock is so weakened as to be unable to support the weight above, it falls, and the lime-sink is formed, or fresh-water springs, with no feeders on the surface, but supplied from below, burst up in mid-ocean, with sufficient force to displace the denser salt-water, or change the position of a vessel.

About sixty miles below St. Augustine, at Fort Moultrie, a council was held by the whites, in 1823, for the purpose of limiting the movements of the Seminoles to the southern portion of the State, thus interposing a white element between them and the Georgia Indians, to prevent an alliance in the event of war.

The Indians were the Nimrods of our country; they did not require large bodies of land for culture. The murder of McIntosh, in Georgia, caused many of the Indians to leave that State for Florida. Here they were called Seminoles, or runaways, being only refugees and fugitives, without a country or language. They adopted a dialect resembling the four Southern Indian tongues of which they formed a part—it being still retained by the remnant of the tribe inhabiting the Everglades.

CHAPTER XVI.

FROM the following account we can imagine under what difficulties young men went on hunting-excursions a century since in Florida:

"The Spanish Governor's son, living in St. Augustine, together with two other young men, arranged a trip on the coast for the purpose of hunting and fishing. Being provided with a convenient bark, ammunition, fishing-tackle, etc., they set sail, directing their course south, toward the point of Florida, putting in to shore and sailing up rivers, as a conveniency or the prospect of game invited them. The pleasing rural and diversified scenes of the Florida coast imperceptibly allured them far to the south beyond the fortified post. Unfortunate youths! regardless of the advice of their parents and friends, they entered a harbor at evening, with a view of chasing the roebuck, and hunting up the sturdy bear, or solacing themselves with delicious fruits, and reposing under aromatic shades, when, alas! cruel and unexpected event—in the beatific moments of their slumbers they are surrounded, arrested, and carried off by a band of predatory Creek Indians, who are proud to capture so rich a prize. They are hurried into bondage, being conducted, by devious paths through dreary swamps and boundless savannahs, to the Nation."

It was at this time the Indians were at furious war with the Spaniards—scarcely any bounds set to their cruelties on either side; in short, the youths were condemned to be burnt. An attempt was made to rescue them, by some English traders, from their unrelenting persecutors, who petitioned the Indians in their behalf, offering a great ransom for their release, acquainting them, at the same time, that they were young men of high rank, and one of them the governor's son. Upon this the head-men or chiefs of the whole Nation were convened, and, after solemn and mature deliberation, they returned the traders their final answer and determination, which was as follows:

"Brothers and Friends:—We have been considering upon this business concerning the captives, and that under the eye and fear of the Great Spirit. You know that these people are our cruel enemies; they save no lives of us red men who fall in their power. You say that the youth is the son of the Spanish Governor. We believe it—we are sorry he has fallen into our hands, but he is our enemy. The two young men are equally our enemies—we are sorry to see them here, but we know no difference in their flesh and blood; they are equally our enemies. If we save one, we must save all three; but we cannot do it. The red men require their blood to appease the spirits of their slain relatives; they have intrusted us with the guardianship of our laws and rights—we cannot betray them. However, we have a sacred prescription relative to this affair, which allows us to extend mercy to a certain degree: a third is saved by lot. The Great Spirit allows us to put it to that decision; he is no respecter of persons."

The lots are cast. The governor's son was taken and burnt.

Hunters now go on excursions down the Florida coast as a pleasant pastime, with no fear from human foes, and no inconvenience, save a few musquitoes and sand-flies, which furnish a feast of merriment for their friends when they relate their adventures after returning. There is a decided difference between coming here in 1774 and 1874.

Matanzas is situated eighteen miles below St. Augustine, at the mouth of the Bloody Matanzas River. In the vicinity a boarding-house has recently been erected, for the accommodation of visitors. The echoes from busy life are so faint and far away, and so long in reaching us here, that we feel as though we were in another state of existence—the outside world only affecting us like a spent wave, as it dies away on the shore. The fishing-boats steal slowly by with nets and lines; the fishermen are silent, although their lives are not sad; but they snare the voiceless dwellers of the deep, which have peculiar habits to be studied, and baited for with cautious movements, before they can be captured. There is no crowding, no jostling, no dust—all is peace, and the pure air is life. An occasional schooner approaches from New York; it comes like a good angel on a mission of mercy, laden with stores for the sustenance of citizens and strangers.

Fort Matanzas, although cracked and seamed

from turret to foundation, is ever redolent of past memories. It is about twenty feet in height, and formerly had brass cannon mounted on the ramparts, designed to command Matanzas Bar. During the Spanish rule of 1800, to the time of its cession to the United States, it was occupied by a company of soldiers, who guarded the entrance to St. Augustine; also for the punishment of officers or soldiers who had been drunk, or wandering from the path of duty in any way. Its last commander was Captain Christobal Bravo, whose son, bearing the same name, is now a worthy citizen of St. Augustine, and can relate incidents which occurred during the time his father was stationed there. This fortress, inferring from facts furnished by the old French records, is, no doubt, the one commenced by the two hundred who escaped the night previous to the fatal massacre by Melendez. It never had a portcullis, or sally-port, but was entered by an escalade from the outside, after which the ladder was drawn up and dropped down inside, where were casemates for the soldiers' quarters and rations, also an ordnance department, and lock-up for delinquents to cool off from their potions and meditate upon the uncertainties of all earthly pleasures — particularly that of taking a glass too much! It is partly concealed by vines and foliage — reminding us that Nature, when not interrupted, comes to close the yawning gaps of busy-fingered Time, planting a twining ivy, a hardy cactus, or a climbing rose, covered with blooms and verdure — thus teaching us the lesson of resignation,

which clothes our misfortunes in the garments of
grace, producing the flowers of fragrance, although
the jagged edges of rough, rugged paths surround
us. Here we have a fine view of the sea, where the
sun rises fresh every morning as the day after its
creation; and we can imagine Aurora scattering
flowers before his chariot as the fleecy clouds,
decked with the purity of the day-dawn, burst
upon our delighted vision.

NEW SMYRNA.—Dr. Turnbull obtained a grant
from the English Government for settling a Greek
colony in Florida, which had been ceded to them by
Spain in 1763. He sailed to Peloponnesus, and obtained permission from the Governor of Modon, for
a consideration, to convey to Florida a large number of Greek families. In 1767 he sailed with one
small vessel from Modon; putting in at the islands
of Corsica and Minorca, he recruited his numbers to
fifteen hundred. He agreed to give them a free passage, furnish them in good provisions and clothing;
at the end of three years' service to give each family
fifty acres of land, and in six months after their arrival, if they were discontented, to send them back.
Many of the old people died during the voyage of four
months. Sixty thousand acres were granted them by
the Governor of Florida. As it was then winter, they
built huts of palmetto to shelter them, and the following spring commenced planting their gardens. This
settlement was about sixty miles south of St. Augustine—they named it New Smyrna, for a Grecian
city from which they came, in Poloponnesus, where
they all contended Homer was born, but, unlike its

namesake—being ten times destroyed, always rose from her ruins—it has never been rebuilt since the indigo speculation proved a failure. The first year they engaged in the culture of indigo, when the crop amounted to nearly forty thousand dollars, but the price declining so rapidly, it was soon abandoned. Turnbull did not treat them kindly; he appointed drivers from the Italians, reducing them to the lowest slavery, when they were assigned tasks and drew weekly rations. When the clothes they had brought with them were worn out, they were furnished with a suit of osnaburgs, giving the men shoes, but the women none, although many of them were accustomed to affluence in their own country. This servitude continued for nine years. The cruelties exercised over them were equal to those of the Spaniards of St. Domingo. For the most trifling offense they were cruelly beaten, negroes being chosen mediums for this torture. If they ran away, they were brought back, the one who returned them receiving a reward. At the termination of nine years, only six hundred remained of the fifteen hundred brought over. Finally three of them escaped, and, after swimming the Matanzas River, arrived in St. Augustine, when they made known their business to Colonel Yonge, the Attorney-general of the Province, who gave them protection. A change of governors had taken place, Grant being superseded by Tonyn. Grant was supposed to have been connected with Turnbull in the speculation. Tonyn interfered in their behalf, setting them at liberty. Mr. Pallicier was chosen their leader when they marched out of bondage, like the children of Israel, from what to them had been an Egypt. The governor treated them kindly on their arrival in St. Augustine, giving them lands in the north part of the city, where they built houses and cultivated gardens, which are occupied by their children to this day.

Not far from this we find the Halifax River country, near which is Daytonia and other settlements, said to be remarkable for the selectness of its settlers, no rough adventurers having drifted in there. Below New Smyrna is the famous Colonel Douglass Dummit plantation, from which, a half century since, he raised and manufactured two hundred barrels of sugar in one season, which he sent to the city of Boston, Mass., and sold for eleven cents per pound. It was only rich planters, then, who could afford to buy seed and pay three or four thousand dollars for an engine to make sugar. An acre of cane here has been made to produce three thousand pounds of sugar in one year.

INDIAN KEY MASSACRE.—Adjectives expressive of the horrible were exhausted in Florida during the Indian war. Some of the contemporaries of the Indian Key murder are still surviving in St. Augustine, and to hear them relate its terrors produces a chilliness which to us is quite overpowering.

August 15, 1840.—The steamer Santee arrived on Wednesday—Captain Poinsett commanding—bringing the family of Dr. Perine. They were living on Indian Key, a small spot not over seven acres in extent, situated near Matacomba Key, about thirty miles from the mainland, on the Southern Atlantic coast.

When the attack was made by the savages, seven of its inhabitants were murdered, the island plundered, and its buildings burned. About three o'clock on the morning of the 7th instant a Mr. Glass, in the employ of Mr. Houseman, happening to be up, saw boats approaching, after which, on closer inspection, it was discovered they were Indians. They immediately commenced firing on the residences of Mr. Houseman and Dr. Perine, the former of whom, with his family, and that of Charles Howe and family, succeeded in escaping to boats and crossing over to Teable Key. The family of Dr. Perine passed through a trap-door into their bathing-room, from whence they got into the turtle-crawl, and by great effort removed the logs, and secreted themselves among the rocks. The bathing-house above them was set on fire by these fiends, when with the greatest efforts only they were kept from being roasted alive by putting mud on their heads and cheeks. Mr. Motte and wife, and Mrs. Johnson, a lady seventy years of age, fled into an out-house, from whence Mrs. Motte was dragged by an Indian, and while in the act of calling on her husband, "John, save me!" was killed. Mr. Motte shared the same fate, and was scalped. The old lady, as she was dragged forth, suddenly broke his hold, and escaped under the house. Her granddaughter, a child of Mrs. Motte, aged eleven years, was then killed with a club—the infant strangled and thrown into the water. This was seen by Mrs. Johnson from her hiding-place; but the Indians fired this building, when she was again obliged to flee, escaping to Maloney's wharf, where she secreted herself until she was finally rescued. Joseph Sturdy, a boy twelve years of age, concealed himself in the cistern under the residence of Mr. Houseman, and was scalded to death by the burning building heating the water. The remains of an adult skeleton were found among the ruins of Dr. Perine's house, supposed to be the doctor—also a child, thought to have been a slave of Mr. Houseman. The perpetrators of this deed were Spanish Indians, headed by Chekika, the same who made the attack on the Caloosahatchee. They obtained a great amount of plunder from the houses and stores, and whilst engaged in obtaining these articles Mrs. Perine, with her two daughters and little son, reached a boat partially loaded, and put off to the schooner Medium, lying at some distance. On Mr. Houseman reaching Teable Key, Midshipman Murray, U. S. N., started with his only available force of five men and two swivels, hoping to cut off the boats, and thus prevent the escape of the Indians. On the second fire of his guns they recoiled overboard, when the Indians commenced firing on his boat from a six-pounder belonging to Mr. Houseman, charged with musket-balls, driving back the officer. Dispatches were sent to Key Biscayne, but the Indians had retreated, after holding possession of the island twelve hours, carrying off large quantities of powder and other things, besides laying a little settlement in ashes.

This act was regarded as among the boldest feats of the war—that a force of seventeen canoes, with five Indians in each, should make a voyage thirty miles from the mainland, plunder, murder, and retire in perfect safety! Dr. Perine was a man of learning, a botanist, whose observations and notes on Florida will be a great loss. We see daily in our streets armed men in the employ of the Government, we hear of company after company being formed, and why are not operations commenced against the enemy?

CHAPTER XVII.

THE Indians inhabiting the Everglades before the Seminole war had been driven there from the adjacent islands by conquest. They did not belong to this tribe. They spoke Spanish, and many of them had been baptized in Havana. Their pursuits were quite different—they fished and followed the sea as a means of support, having never been ten miles from the shore. No account has ever been written by modern explorers in that region which gives the reader as correct an idea of the topography of the country as the one given by the engineer who accompanied Colonel Harney, Jan. 1, 1841. Those who visit there now and return, appear to have a commingling of scenery—the flowers, the grass, and water, all being blended, the quantity of each not designated. This grass-water country is said to be like no other place in the world—a sea of water filled with grass and green trees, that can only be approached by canoes, which must be pulled through the mud and saw-grass, and then paddled when the water is of sufficient depth, with a black soil of measureless extent.

The following interesting extracts will enable us to form an idea of the energy and enterprise required during the Seminole war to penetrate the fastness of a country where the foes intrenched themselves, and from which they made sallies upon the unwary more to be dreaded than any disease which visited them. The expedition was conducted by Colonel W. S. Harney. His forces were distributed in four or five large canoes, carrying from six to ten men each; the greater number went in boats made for the purpose, containing five men each. Orders were given that every man should be provided with twenty days' rations, sixty rounds of ball and cartridge, with the necessary blankets, etc. The most perfect silence was to be observed by all; orders communicated by signal-whistles, with which the officers were supplied; the boats moving in single file, twenty paces apart, every man ready to drop his paddle and seize his gun at a moment's notice. The dragoons were armed with Colt's repeating rifles, and, being under command of Colonel Harney, formed a well-tried band of experienced Indian-fighters. Half an hour after sunset, and during a shower of rain, the command left Fort Dallas, which is situated on the bay at the mouth of Indian River, eight miles above Key Biscayne—Colonel Harney in advance, with Mico as guide, and negro John as interpreter, the army next, and the navy in the rear. After passing up the bay seven miles, they entered the mouth of Little River, a tortuous and extremely rapid outlet from the Everglades, where they struggled against the current until after midnight, when they reached their first resting-place—the site of an old plantation—where they landed.

January 2.—The guide says that by not starting from here until toward night, we will reach Chitto—Tustenuggee's Island—an hour or two before daybreak to-morrow; we therefore retained our position as much as possible in the grass and thickets until 4 P.M., when we started, but in reversed order—the colonel in advance, the navy next, and the army in the rear. After passing up a few miles of swift rapids, we entered the Everglades at sunset, and, skirting along a projecting elbow of the pine barren for two miles, lay concealed behind the point of it until quite dark. We then moved forward swiftly and noiselessly, at one time following the course of serpentine channels opening out occasionally into beautiful lagoons, at another forcing our way through barriers of saw-grass. After several hours of hard paddling, we came in sight of Chitto's Island, when the signal was passed "to close up." Moving cautiously, we took our positions around the island, and lay in anxious expectation of the signal to move up and effect a landing. An advance-guard, having been sent in to reconnoiter, after some time reported that the enemy had left the island, and, in a tone of bitter disappointment, the colonel gave the word, "Move up and land; the Indians have escaped."

January 3.—Chitto—Tustenuggee's, or Snake Warrior's Island—is a most beautiful spot, containing from eighteen to twenty acres; the soil is extremely rich, and about two feet deep, with a basis of rotten limestone. The center is cleared, but the circumference is well protected by immense live-oak and wild fig-trees, with an almost impenetrable thicket of wild mangroves. There are two towns, two dancing-grounds, and one council-lodge, on this island. With the exception of the dancing-ground and a small patch of fine Cuba tobacco, the whole clearing is overrun with pumpkin, squash, and melon vines, with occasionally Lima beans in great luxuriance, and of a most excellent quality. The Indians have been gone at least two weeks, having left behind them all useless articles, such as war-dance masks, supernumerary baskets, kettles, fishing-spears, etc. At 11 o'clock the colonel dispatched a small force to reconnoiter Tuconee's Island, which lies about three miles west of us. They returned at 4 P.M., reporting recent signs of a woman and child. The only trophies they obtained were some ears of green corn and a few stalks of sugar-cane.

January 4.—Started this morning for Sam Jones's Island. He is said to hold a strong position, having seventy warriors with him; the only fear entertained by officers or men is that he may have left the island and gone to Big Cypress. After paddling until 3 P.M., we reached a small cluster of trees, from the tops of which the guide said that Sam Jones's camp was visible; he was accordingly sent aloft to make an observation, and soon pronounced the place deserted. This information changed the colonel's programme, and, instead of waiting until night should conceal his movements, he advanced immediately toward the island; however, not omitting to send out flanking parties, and an advance-guard to reconnoiter. Before sunset we had all landed, and were enjoying our biscuit and bacon, in the midst of an Indian village.

January 5.—Sam Jones's possessions consist of a group of several islands, differing in size and separated by narrow sluices. Upon the largest of these, which is about one hundred and fifty yards in width and half a mile in length, are three villages and dancing-grounds, the general features being the same as Chitto's Island, but the soil sandy. There are no villages on the other islands, but they have been cleared in the center and planted with pumpkins, melons, and corn, which were all destroyed. Our greatest annoyance at this place was the immense number of fleas, cockroaches, and musquitoes. Every thing you touched—even the ground—was alive with the former, which, with the musquitoes, attacked our persons, while the roaches luxuriated on our provisions. The whole group of islands, called Army and Navy Group, is nearly a mile and a half in length, and presented no recent signs of Indians.

January 6.—At 8 A.M. passed over three miles to the Pine Keys, and scoured the whole extent; returned at night, hungry and fatigued, to Sam Jones's camp. Started early the next morning for the Prophet's Island, which, according to Mico, is two suns from there. At 11 A.M. stopped and destroyed a flourishing crop of young corn. At 3 P.M. came to another small island uncleared: upon sending John up a tree to look out, he reported two Indians in canoes, two miles distant, approaching us.

Orders were given to lie close, as they were evidently coming to the island. In a few minutes John reported they had seen us, and were going back. The colonel gave chase, but, finding there was not water enough for his large canoe, transferred the guide to Captain McLaughlin's boat, and directed him to move on in pursuit—the light-boats of the artillery to accompany the captain and his command. The colonel, with the large canoes, returned to the island, and sent up a lookout, who reported the Indians not visible, but our boats still going at speed, and rapidly nearing a small island about three miles distant. Colonel H., becoming impatient, and feeling confident that he could find a passage across without any guide, left for the other island, and reached it just as some of the advance boats flushed a party consisting of four warriors, five squaws, and two children; each warrior had a separate canoe, containing his family and worldly possessions. They left the boats to the care of the women, and took to the grass-water, loading and firing as they ran. Three of the warriors were soon shot, three squaws and one child taken, and the other drowned by its mother to prevent its cries leading to her detection. Night approaching, one warrior and two squaws, favored by the darkness, escaped. Only one soldier was slightly wounded in this enterprise. Early this morning Colonel H. sent out a small force to follow the trail of the other warrior, and endeavor, if possible, to take him alive, as he had ascertained from the squaws it was Chia, one of the best guides in the whole Territory. After following the trail five miles, they came up with a squaw (Chia's wife), and took her; a few yards farther beyond, on hearing a rustling in the grass, several of the men leaped into the water, when one of the marines, in the act of springing from the boat, was shot in the side by the Indian, who ran a few paces, reloading his rifle, and, as Sergeant Searles, of the Third Artillery, rushed toward him, he turned and fired at only five paces, wounding the sergeant mortally, who, however, did not retreat. Chia then struck at him with his rifle; but, blinded and fainting as he was, from loss of blood, he quickly rallied for a last effort, and threw himself upon the Indian's neck, crying, "I have him!" Chia then drew his knife, and was about to stab his captor, when a soldier arrested his murderous hand. After securing the captive, the sergeant was lifted into a canoe and brought back to the island, where his wounds were examined and dressed by the medical officer. The ball was found to have passed through the right arm, entered the right side, breaking a rib, opening the right lung, and passing into the liver.

January 9.—Last night we were obliged to sleep in our boats, and, in addition to this discomfort, it rained hard, with a cold south wind all night. Chia says that Sam Jones, on hearing of Colonel Harney's first expedition, had sent over to the Seminoles for powder and lead, saying that he would go into the Big Cypress, where, if pursued, he would fight until death. Chia and his party were going to join him, and he (with a gallows in prospective, should he prove false) promises faithfully to guide us thither. In consequence of this information we returned to Sam Jones's Island, which we reached at noon.

January 10. — The description given of Sam Jones's present position is such as would intimidate almost anybody from attempting to dislodge them but Colonel Harney. At 8 A.M. we started for the head-waters of New River, which we reached at sunset, and passed down the stream to Fort Lauderdale, where we arrived at midnight.

January 11.—Having disposed of the wounded men and female prisoners, we left Lauderdale at sunset, and ascended the New River, entering the Everglades by the right-hand branch, an hour before sunrise.

January 12.—After allowing the men two hours' rest, we moved to a group of keys, lying between the expanse of the Everglades and the edge of the Big Cypress. It was here that Chia expected to find the main body of the enemy; but, upon examination of the signs, he pronounced that they had gone on to Okee-cho-bee. With a heart full of disappointment, Colonel Harney found his schemes thwarted by the cowardice of the Indians, who had fled panic-stricken upon hearing of Chai-kai-kee's fate, and deserted their inaccessible retreats. At noon the navy left us, taking with them Mico and negro John as guides across the Everglades, in the direction of the first expedition. After dinner we bore away for Lauderdale, and, aided by the swift current of New River, reached our destination at 8 P.M.

January 13.—Colonel Harney this morning started with twenty men to search for a reported passage from the New River into the Hillsboro Inlet; the low stage of the water proving an insurmountable obstacle, he returned at sundown, giving orders to prepare for moving homeward to-morrow.

January 15.—At early dawn the canoes were hauled over from the beach into the bay, when, in passing down it, we reached Fort Dallas at noon. The Pay-hai-o-kee (grass-water, or Everglades) comprises a large portion of Southern Florida, lying south of the twenty-seventh degree of latitude, and separated from the Atlantic, or Gulf of Mexico, by a pine barren, varying in width from five to twenty or more miles. There are a number of outlets on the eastern, or Atlantic coast, while on the western, or Gulf coast, there is only one, now named after its first navigator, Harney River. The appearance presented upon entering the Everglades is that of an immense prairie, stretching farther than the eye can reach, covered by thick saw-grass, rising six feet above the surface of the water, which it conceals—the monotony varied by numerous snake-like channels and verdant islands, scattered few and far between—the average depth of water over the whole extent being from two to four feet. The channels vary in width from ten to twenty feet above the usual water-level, though, no doubt, in very wet seasons occasionally overflowed—the water all being clear and wholesome—and even where no current was perceptible there was no appearance of stagnation.

The results of this expedition, although apparently not very brilliant, have only been surpassed in usefulness by those of the first Everglade expedition, undertaken and prosecuted with such untiring energy and eminent success by Colonel Harney. The knowledge acquired of the nature of the country, the localities of the lands, and strength of the positions, occupied by two of the most formidable chiefs, is of itself ample reward for the privations and sufferings necessarily encountered during a movement in open boats, with no tents, a limited supply of blankets and provisions, exposed to the sun by day and the dew at night, to the drenching rain and chilly blast, but rarely allowed the luxury of fires, and eating food which it required a strong appetite to relish.

The Everglades extend from the head of the St. John's, on the north, to within ten or fifteen miles of Cape Florida, on the south. This land is believed to be twenty or thirty feet above the level of tidewater, and is susceptible of being rendered perfectly dry by deepening and widening the various outlets or rivers that flow through it, from the lakes to the sea. The lakes near the center of the Everglades are deep and navigable, connecting with one another throughout the entire distance.

The tropical region of the peninsula reaches from Cape Florida about two hundred miles north. The soil of the country has been pronounced by all explorers very rich, it being only covered with water in the rainy season. When the resources of this tropical region are utilized, the importance of Florida can hardly be appreciated too highly. Besides the growth of cultured fruits, the Manilla hemp is one of the indigenous products of the soil; the Indians used it in making ropes and mats, and formerly supplied the Spaniards with halters, lines, and bedcords, at cheap rates—it was called grass-rope. The cotton-plant found here is the same as that raised on plantations, differing only in the smallness of the leaf and pod, length and fineness of the fibers— it produces two or three years without being replanted.

January, 1841.—Colonel Harney has been on two expeditions in the Everglades; captured thirty-nine Indians; pressed into service a slave, formerly the property of Doctor Cruise, as a guide, he having been in the hands of the enemy. He conducted the colonel to a camp where the Indians were assembled, who fought, but were soon overpowered, when Colonel Harney hung ten of the warriors, Chekika among the number, who led the attack on Indian Key.

St. Augustine, January, 1841.— An ovation was given to General Harney, after his return from the Everglade expedition, when the St. Augustine Market-house was brilliantly illumined. A large transparency bore the inscriptions, "Lieutenant-colonel W. S. Harney, Everglades!" "No more Treaties!" "Remember Caloosahatchee!" "War to the Rope!" with the device of an Indian suspended from a tree. A band of music played in the plaza, cannon were fired, together with many other loud demonstrations of joy at the prospect of peace.

The few may have smiled, but the many wept in tears of blood, and wailed in sackcloth and ashes, over the long train of evils that followed the Treaty of Payne's Landing—a compact of which many had never heard until they began to suffer under the ineffectual attempts to carry it into execution. What a tale of sorrow could the poor, suffering soldiers unfold, who had to march through the saw-grass and saw-palmetto, with their serrated edges, which seized their clothes and flesh as they passed, marking their pathway with tatters and blood!

In South Florida, bounded on the north by Lake Ogeechubee—the largest body of water in the State, it being fifty miles in length, and twenty in width—is a tract of country known as the Everglades, comprising an area of six hundred miles. Here dwells the remnant of a race of men which required more time to subdue, and cost the Government more money, than the Colonial war with Great Britain. They are ruled by chiefs, according to their ancient patriarchal custom, the royal line being transmitted from parent to child, as in monarchical governments.

Old and young Tiger Tail are both living now, the senior chief being almost a century of age. It was his father that built an Indian village where Tallahassee now stands, and in which place he first saw the light.

Old Tiger Tail murdered his sister, who favored emigration, to which he was opposed. After going to the West he became much dissatisfied, when he made his way to the wilds of Mexico, where he intrenched himself in the natural fastness among the mountains. From this fortress he made frequent sallies upon the inhabitants, killing when he met resistance, and carrying away whatever plunder of value he could seize upon. He was joined by others, who were living as outlaws in their own country, thus combining the cunning of the Indian with the brigand spirit of the Mexican, forming an alliance more to be dreaded than the wily movements of the Chieftain Osceola. He is a battle-scarred warrior, and can relate with much accuracy every different engagement where he was wounded. He is friendly with some visitors; has a summer and winter home, where he camps each season.

The Indians visit Fort Pierce, on the Indian River, as a trading-point, when they bring buckskins, potatoes, pumpkins, and honey, to sell. The wild honey brought to market from all parts of the State is a sufficient proof of its adaptability to the production of that commodity for settlers to engage in the enterprise of bee-culture. In addition to the blossoms of annuals and orange-trees, a honey-dew exudes from some of the trees at certain seasons—the magnolia, poplar, wahoo, and sweet-gum — from which the bees can gather largely.

Father Dufau recently visited the Everglades as a missionary, but, meeting with poor encouragement, returned. He does not bring favorable reports in regard to their mental or spiritual improvement. The Indians regard the "pale faces" with suspicion and distrust. They have been duped so often by the whites that their chief forbids the females speaking to them. They have no forms of religion, but worship the Great Spirit and planets, wearing devices of the moon. Father Dufau had a pair of silver ear-rings, made by them, the pendant portion resembling a crescent. These were formerly owned and worn by Tiger Tail, who sold them for whisky.

Slaves are still regarded as property with them, the difference in caste between master and servant not being distinguishable. Polygamy is becoming unpopular with them now. Tiger Tail has two wives; but the oldest squaw claims priority, causing the stream of harmony to flow in divided currents. She says, "Two squaws no good." The soil teems with verdure all the year, and they live without solicitude, either temporally or spiritually. In hunting, they require neither guns nor dogs, but imitate whatever beast or bird they propose to capture, and when their prey approaches near enough, shoot it with arrows. The water found in the Everglades is very clear, thus enabling them to fish without hooks or nets, by shooting the fish, which they do with great skill.

The men dress in deerskin breeches, wearing calico coats, with long skirts, and various patterns sewed on them. The squaws are all clothed like our cracker country females—the younger ones displaying their fondness for beads by wearing four pounds around their necks. The funniest of all is how they received that irrational style of having their hair *banged* like white girls, and surprises visitors very much. Some of the younger warriors expressed a desire to be taught to read, measure, and weigh. They speak little English, but communicate mostly by signs.

Father Dufau had to walk wherever he went, after leaving Key Biscayne Bay, his speed at times being accelerated more than was agreeable by water-moccasins and alligators.

The Everglades still retain their primeval state, guarded with ample care by towering live-oaks, the majestic grandiflora, and the aromatic bay, from which the yellow jasmine swings her airy bowers, and where the polyglot bird trills his joyful notes, the velvet-plumaged paroquet chatters to his mate, and the red-bird whistles shrill sounds of joy, while high above all, swinging in mid-air, the golden oriole is listening from her pendent bower for the first sounds of vitality which will echo from her nestlings. The foot of man, in his march of progress, has never penetrated these wilds of natural beauty —a solitude tempered by sea-breezes, unvisited by wintry winds, where moonbeams sleep on glassy waters, unmoved by the tempest's roar or the trident of Neptune.

CHAPTER XVIII.

IN leaving Jacksonville for Cedar Keys, we first take the Florida Central Road, which is thought by some to ride very rough, but the controlling element which had it in charge treated it rougher than any jolt which passengers receive in riding over it. Soon as the road can recover from the raids upon its earnings, preparations will be made to accommodate the traveling public so well that they will always prefer riding on the Florida Central from choice. Baldwin is the first noticeable station on the road, twenty miles from Jacksonville. We arrive here in time for breakfast, which the vigorous ringing of bells indicate — the Berger Family is nowhere in comparison to the noise they make. As we had no free feeds, we are not obligated to puff the eating-houses; but the moderate charges and fine fare constitute an attractive feature to the hungry traveler. The depot and telegraph-office windows are said to furnish amusement for the agent and operator, where they can spend their leisure in fishing.

The attractive alligators and moccasins are hibernating now, as it is February; occasionally a stray one comes out, like Noah's dove, to see if winter has gone. The junction of roads is what makes the town—the A. G. & W. I. T. Co. Road is taken here, in order that the Mexican Gulf, one hundred and seven miles distant, may be reached. Northern passengers complain of the snail-pace by which the trains are propelled, but no accident ever occurs to endanger life or limb. The piney-woods scenery predominates, which gives the country a very unpicturesque appearance; and the land, that in some places appears poor enough to make squirrels sad, changes as we advance toward the Gulf.

Trail Ridge is noticeable for its high location, being over two hundred feet above sea-level, always celebrated for its healthfulness and pure water. Lawtey, four miles from Trail Ridge, has recently received a large accession of immigrants from Chicago. The lands are considered among the best in the interior of the State. One great advantage in living on the Transit Road is free transportation for self and family, together with the superior facilities for sending produce to market. Starke, seventy-three miles from Fernandina, is a place of some importance, containing a lumber-mill, turpentine distillery, and several stores, besides boarding-houses. What a multitude of disagreeable sounds break upon our morning slumbers in these plank habitations! The cats, which have been vigorous in their serenading during the night, now prepare to quit the field by a final contest, which Dinah interrupts with the broom. The pigs, that lay piled in the yard so quietly during the night, are calling for their rations, while the chickens have been cackling a chorus in advance of the supplies which they will furnish for hungry visitors. Never, apparently, did dinner-pots require such a vast amount of scraping. Then the old coffee-mill sounds like a ten-horse-power flouring-mill. These little innovations upon our morning nap are soon forgotten after we have eaten our breakfast, and witnessed what a beautiful day is before us.

Waldo now appears to be settling more rapidly than Starke. A large hotel, called the Waldo House, has been built here, which is well kept. Croquet-grounds are laid out, shade-trees planted, in a tasteful manner, presenting an inviting appearance to travelers as they approach the town. This station is destined to be a place of prominence. A canal is in process of construction to Lake Santa Fe, four miles distant, thus connecting it with the main artery of communication in the State. This region of country is attracting no small amount of attention at present, the high ground it occupies being one of its most desirable features — which fact is demonstrated by the waters, instead of settling, flowing east and west, then emptying into the Atlantic and Gulf of Mexico. This lake contains nearly thirty square miles of water, being about nine miles in length, its greatest width four miles. The depth of the water is from twenty to sixty feet, being pure freestone, palatable all the year with a little ice. Superior inducements are offered to those who wish to come as actual settlers, fine lake-sites being very reasonable, and the present inhabitants the best of people.

We next come to Alachua county, the richest and now the most important on the route, containing hummock-lands, covered with phosphates, indicating a fertility of soil, where the long staple will flourish, and silken cotton-bolls open their tributes of wealth to reward the industrious planter. Tiny floating islands are visible on each side of the track, while the lily rises from the dusky waters of the morass, as though upheld by some invisible hand. Long-legged Florida cattle are grazing upon the fresh grass, while the yearlings run races with the cars, to the annoyance of all concerned. Visible signs of impatience are manifested by the lady-passengers, when the following colloquy takes place between a Bostonian and a very black train-hand:

Lady—"Say, sir! are there no refreshments coming in soon?"

Negro—"What is dem, Miss?"

Lady—"Why, something to eat."

Negro—"I reckin dar 'll be some groun'-peas gwine 'roun' 'fore bery long, or some cane-stalks."

Lady (very indignant)—"I wish you to comprehend I came from *Boston;* we do n't eat such things up there in our part of the country!"

During the year 1750 a Creek chief retired from his nation, named Secoffe, and settled in Alachua, he being attracted by the game and natural fertility of soil. He was a sworn enemy of the Spaniards, but a friend to the English up to 1784. He visited St. Augustine on hearing that Florida had been sold to the English, at which time, not thinking himself treated with due deference to his rank in life, he returned, swearing vengeance to all the whites. He died soon afterward, which frustrated his projects of revenge. Before dying he called his two sons, Payne and Bowlegs, to whom he intrusted the mission of killing fourteen Spaniards, which, added to eighty-six—the number already killed by himself—would make one hundred—the requisite amount which the Great Spirit had revealed to him would insure happiness to his soul. His sons, not being of a revengeful spirit, lived in peace with the Spaniards, and died much respected. Another band came in 1808, under Micco Hadjo, settling near Tallahassee—from this date the Florida Indians were called Seminoles, or Runaways.

This county contains a great sink, called by some a lake, in which congregate during the dry weather large quantities of alligators, together with fish of all sizes, that cannot escape into the subterranean rocky passage. This sink is situated in a savanna about fifteen miles in length. The Indians formerly had a town near this locality, which they moved on account of the stench from decayed fish in summer, that had been driven there by the alligators. These Indian settlers were busy during the war, like their companions. The following are some of the fruits of their conduct: "The Rev. McRae, a Methodist preacher, and two other persons, while riding from Waccahootee to Micanopy, when at the Juggs, within three miles of the fort, were fired upon by a party of fifteen or twenty Indians. Mr. McRae's horse was wounded and fell, when he was overtaken and scalped by the Indians, but his scalp was left on the ground. The others escaped with four balls in their clothes. In five more days a citizen and soldier were murdered within four miles of Fort Micanopy, their hearts taken out, and their bodies horribly mangled." June 5, 1839, on the Newnansville road, Mr. Ostein, Mr. Dell, and Miss Ostein, were killed. After this tragic event, the following notice speaks in trumpet tones:

"The injuries of the citizens of Alachua and Columbia counties have been of a nature that can never be forgotten or forgiven. The white man and the Indian can no longer occupy the same territory in peace; one or the other must be removed or annihilated, and the General Government will justly decide the question. FRANCIS R. SANCHEZ."

During this year all flags of truce and peace movements were lost sight of, as Indian murders were every day occurring. At this time two volunteers were killed near Micanopy, their bodies much mutilated, and their tongues cut out. General Jackson at this time estimated a force "of four hundred Indians, which could be whipped out by a battalion of women armed with broomsticks."

The approach from the depot to Gainesville is very unattractive, particularly in the winter season, having the appearance of being inaccessible either by land or water. Black, marshy-looking places, containing a muddy fluid, fail to give travelers a pleasant impression, and for this reason draining should be commenced by building causeways to the city and the frequented places in the vicinity. They have not put the best side out here. Gainesville was named for General Edmund P. Gaines, a Florida Indian-war veteran. Mrs. Myra Clark Gaines, who for many years has been litigating for a portion of the ground on which New Orleans stands, was his wife, who by a special act of Congress receives a pension, whether married again or remaining his widow.

Many invalids have a preference for Gainesville, on account of its even temperature, over localities on the bays, rivers, or lakes. It has fine accommodations, containing two good hotels, besides comfortable boarding-houses of various dimensions. The Arlington House is first-class in every respect, being new, while Oak Hall, for good eating, cannot be outdone. The dining-room serving-man has waited here for twenty years, which is very remarkable in consideration of the various vicissitudes through which that race has passed. The quiet of country life is found in this locality; the sound of wheels is hushed in the streets, the sand being so deep it has no echo when wheels pass over it. Protestant Churches are well represented in numbers and houses of worship. The Presbyterian pastor, the Rev. Mr. McCormick, has ministered to his people for a quarter of a century. Through what numerous changes has he passed! What sad memories linger around his ministrations, but sometimes mingled with joy when a sinner for whom he had long been solicitous has been born into the kingdom!

More of the *Tillandasia*, or hanging moss, which sometimes grows ten or fifteen feet in length, is found here than in most other portions of the State. Two moss-factories, preparing it for commerce, are doing a thriving business. It closely resembles horse-hair when properly cleaned and curled — is quite elastic and inodorous. It is used extensively in upholstering, and is quite profitable to those engaged in the enterprise.

Dry-goods stores, groceries, and drug-stores all do a lucrative business with the people living in the back country. Lands lying in the vicinity of Gainesville are very fine, one acre of ground being capable of producing fifteen hundred pounds of sugar and three hundred gallons of sirup.

By taking the stage at Gainesville, Orange Lake, "the natural home of the orange," is easily reached. This lake is a vast lime-sink, draining a large extent of country, having no visible outlet. The inducements and facilities for orange-culture are probably unsurpassed in any other locality. One man owns over a hundred thousand budded trees, and a million more yet remain in a state of nature. The native orange-growth has been a source of wonder to all modern explorers. Nothing can be imagined more beautiful than one of these natural groves in March —the golden orbs in a setting of green, while creamy blossoms, like clouds of incense, rise in overpowering sweetness to welcome us with their choicest oblation. The whole forest has a tropical luxuriance, the abundant vegetation being well sustained by a rich soil of sandy loam, with a layer of marl and decomposed shells. Besides the orange, we see the live-oak, magnolia, hickory, bay-tree, and many other native woods, interspersed with grape-vines measuring three feet in circumference, climbing to the tops of the tallest trees, forming a dense shade,

where sunbeams can rarely or ever penetrate. As
we walk between its stately colonnades, our minds
revert to the silence of "God's first temple." It is
in this vicinity lime-sinks abound, which are formed
from subterranean streams of water constantly flowing, thus washing away the sand, which causes the
coral formation supported by it to fall, frequently
exposing large lakes of immense depth, many of
them containing fish.

Malaria is said to prevail here sometimes, "although it is perfectly healthy." Let settlers plant
the *Eucalyptus*-tree, which is no experiment, but a
success, in other places, being a powerful absorbent
of miasm, converting sickly, malarious localities
into healthful, happy homes. A seedling orange-
tree is considered the most hardy, and will produce
in five years, while a budded tree bears in two or
three years. It is well to have both kinds, in order
to fully realize the golden dreams of a successful investment. The manufacture of citric acid from the
wild orange has been attempted here several times,
without any great results as yet, but marmalade is a
decided success. All information on the subject of
groves in this locality can be obtained by address-
ing John F. Dunn, Ocala, Marion county, Florida.
There are many homesteads in all parts of the State.
For particulars address United States Land Agent,
Gainesville, Florida.

After leaving Gainesville, before reaching the
Gulf, several places are passed, bearing important
names, their locality and present appearance of
thrift now giving promise of future prosperity.

Cities in the prospective: Orange City, Arredondo, Battons, Archer, and Albion—all stopping-points and new settlements. Albion has been settled mostly by young Englishmen, who have come here to engage in grape-culture—these being the first invoice of a large colony from Europe. Bronson appears to have a larger population than any of the other towns, except Gainesville. It is the county-seat of Levy, where can be found among the actual settlers energetic Christian people. A diversity of crops can be obtained from this soil, much of the land inclining to an undulating surface.

Otter Creek, one hundred and thirty-four miles from Fernandina, is the dinner-station, kept by a most worthy gentleman—Captain Mason, formerly of the United States Army Indian war service. We are now entering the great Gulf Hummock, the vegetation changing from a semi-tropical to an entirely tropical character. Here the cabbage-palmetto and hard-wood trees rear their tops high in the air—a characteristic of the rich hummock soil. We see no trailing vines killed every winter by frost, but giant climbers twining around tree-trunks so closely they appear like a portion of them. This heavy growth converts the route here into an interminable forest, where only occasional spots or fragments of sunshine peep through slight openings, that appear to be at no greater distance than the tree-tops over our heads. These fertile lands are awaiting the muscular development which has been productive of such marked results in almost every portion of the State.

CHAPTER XIX.

CEDAR KEYS is the terminus of the West India Transfer Railroad—that comfortless, unlovely, much-abused sand and water place—where people always heretofore have paid a big price for a small equivalent. There is life in the old town yet. She supports a newspaper now, and has a good hotel, kept by Dr. McIlvaine, who knows how to serve the traveling public, without robbing them, when they are in his power. The memory of the fresh fried fish, they can serve up so fresh and hot, will make visitors who go once have a desire to return. Then, to think of oysters twenty-one times in a week! Consider on it, those who never ate enough fine, first-class bivalves in their lives. Visitors who come here will find sailing and fishing very fine amusement. Cedar Keys is going to have a big hotel—then everybody will want to come, if they can only regulate the prices according to the amount of accommodation. There is, no doubt, a bright future before her yet.

For the benefit of those who imagine Cedar Keys never had a citizen in it with an idea much above an oyster, I have copied the following, which is a specimen of the toasts drunk by the patriotic to the military, July 4, 1843. They contain something so genuine, in the way of word-selecting and arranging, that it really reads refreshing in these days, when such a surfeit of fulsome flattery is considered the only current coin of the day:

"Mr. Speaker. Freedom's Anniversary: The wilds of Florida, where echoed the Indian's war-whoop and the revengeful battle-strife, to-day bring forth their festive offering. We celebrate a new jubilee.

"By Mr. Thompson. The champions of Florida's restoration from the desolations of war—Generals Jessup and Worth.

"By Mr. Brown. Colonel Belknap: The red man's friend in peace—the terror of the savage in war.

"By William Cooley. Colonel Wm. S. Harney: The brave and gallant avenger of savage atrocity and barbarity.

"By Augustus Steele, Esq. General Worth: The peaceful fields we till, the quiet roads we travel in happy security, the waving corn and lowing herds that gladden our senses, bespeak our remembrance and admiration of the skill and intrepidity, also the indomitable perseverance which, under difficulties little less than insurmountable, have secured us these blessings."

The "moving impulse" from Cedar Keys for a long time was in a weak condition, the H. Cool being the only craft to convey passengers from here to Manatee and Tampa. However, now two regular steamers, with good accommodations, are to be had, without the prospect of a dive beneath the briny waves.

Many imagine that a trip to South Florida is an enterprise which would require the fortitude of a Stanley to undertake. It is true, the inaccessible position of some localities in this portion of the State would be rather impracticable for feeble invalids; but what more could craving humanity demand than a climate where the thermometer never rises over ninety, and rarely descends lower than sixty? By taking a creditable steamer at Cedar Keys, we can reach Manatee, the point of our destination. Sometimes the gulf is a little rough, but very often smooth as a mill-pond, when we glide along gently as a sail across a summer sea.

Clear Water Harbor, the last point before Manatee, was first explored by Narvaez, whom the Indians received without demonstrations of fear or hostility. After the Spaniards landed, they were attracted by the gold worn upon the persons of the Indians, which they said came from the far North. These Spaniards, being both sailors and soldiers, wearied with maritime pursuits and fighting, now resolved to try their fortunes on land. They started with three hundred men, in a north-west course, to search for the mountains of gold. In their travels they discovered nothing but fatigue, privation, disappointment, and death, wherever they went. But four of the number survived, who became medicine men among the Indians—finally making their way to Mexico, after an absence of six or seven years.

Nothing of particular interest occurs to break the monotony during our voyage to Manatee, one hundred miles distant from Cedar Keys. It is situated on a river of the same name, fifteen miles from the gulf. It was named from the sea-cow, which was found there, and used as an article of food. Visitors or immigrants may have the fondest dream of their imagination realized in finding here all the natural accompaniments for a pleasant home.

The view of Manatee, as we approach the town, is not particularly imposing—the houses being scattered in every direction, like the forces of a retreating army, while each settler appears to have taken possession of what land he could cultivate as he came. The dwellings are embowered in orange-trees, which in March freight the air with a perfume that permeates our very existence, producing a kind of luxurious rest, when time and all objects around us move as though in dreamland.

Perennial spring-time keeps vegetation growing all winter. The *Palma Christi*, in this locality, becomes a large tree, yielding its beans perfectly every year; while tomato-vines grow to an immense size, twining into shady bowers, fruiting, without cessation, until three years old, when the tomato has a strong flavor, resembling the vine. The guava, from which the jelly of commerce is manufactured, grows spontaneously, and it is said the mamma of all in South Florida still flourishes at this place. The lands in the vicinity are pine, hummock, and prairie. The pine-land requires fertilizing—the hummock, clearing and ditching—when two hogsheads of sugar and seventy-five gallons of sirup are the average product of an acre, which, to those who never in their lives had as much sugar as they could eat, is a sweet item.

The prairie-lands furnish sustenance for the lowing herds, which are wild as deer. They are captured by a song the "cow-boys" sing, resembling nothing else in the world. Where it originated, none can tell; but the cattle gather from afar whenever it is sung, and are then driven at will by those long rawhide lashes that pop like pistols, many times cutting out pieces of quivering flesh, at which the sight of humanity would shrink.

The lusciousness of oranges produced here is incomparable, particularly when contrasted with those sour, stringy products of commerce. We have tasted this fruit from every clime, but never have the Manatee oranges been excelled. How ripe and delicious they grow on those tall trees, where they hang constantly exposed to the rays of a tropical sun until March! Messrs. Gates, Whittaker & Lee have old bearing groves, while hundreds of others are coming on.

When we reflect upon the superabundance of natural products that flourish in this locality, with which to supply the necessities of life, can we wonder why one of the wrecks of once powerful tribes so long resisted the encroachments of white settlers, contesting for territory until nearly extinct, many of them suffering with the calmness of Christian martyrs, or the bravery of Roman heroes—thus regarding death with a lofty disdain? The Indians, like the wild beasts in whose skins they were clad, have been driven, by the march of civilization, farther and farther into the grass-water country, where, like a lion deprived of his claws, resentment has died for want of strength to assert its prowess, while, by contact with an enlightened race, their original independence has been brought into a state of subjugation.

In this portion of Florida the cactus-pear grows to an immense size. History mentions a peculiar tribe of Indians who once lived here with as little solicitude for their support as the birds of passage, especially in the pear-season, which was hailed by them as a period of feasting—their only labor being to obtain the pears, which they afterward peeled and roasted for present use, or dried and packed like figs, to eat on their journeys, while the remaining portion of their time was passed in the observance of their various festivals and dancing—their houses being made of palm-matting, which they carried on their backs—thus moving their habitations, every three or four days, without the slightest inconvenience.

The inducements for immigration here are equal to any in the State. Adventurers do not flourish on this soil, the residents, taken as a mass, being the best that can be found. Many of them from the Southern States, uprooted from their old homes by the reverses of war, but not disheartened, have come down here to take root and thrive again. Church privileges are enjoyed, in a church where quiet Christian people assemble for worship. Also three well-taught schools in the town and vicinity. Two good resident physicians, but dependent on visitors for a support—one of them from a malarious country, who came here to escape death. Here, as in other localities, settlers have to sow before they can reap, but the natural growth in the hummocks evidences great fertility of soil.

The Manatee boarding-houses are sanitariums, where more trouble is taken to please visitors, at less expense, than at almost any other place in the State. The tables are supplied with food visitors can eat, that will nourish them—not what the host chooses to furnish. I well remember with what a troubled look Mrs. Gates took me into the larder one day after having dined on lemonade. There was a quantity of provisions to gladden the hungry: almost an entire roasted wild turkey, stuffed quarter of venison, fresh-baked fish, home-made light-bread and biscuits, pound-cake, rich lemon pies—any of which would tempt an epicurean taste. "You are eating nothing hardly," said she; "now, whenever you wish, come and help yourself."

The remoteness of this point from the principal resorts is the only objection. Every one who comes says the climate is perfect. The streams and gulf swarm with fish. Visitors sit on the wharf and recreate in catching twenty-pound snappers, while at low-tide the rheumatic old men wade about in the warm salt-water, happy as boys just entering their teens. Let all those who dream of sand-hills, and only starvation staring them in the face while in Florida, come to Manatee. A pure sea-breeze pervades the whole surrounding country, the evenness of temperature producing a very genial and happy influence in pulmonic diseases, more than all the drugs compounded by any pharmaceutist in the world. The moon here shines with a clear, luminous light of two common moons—an indescribable brilliancy that transforms the darkness of night almost into a continued day, which has a tendency to bewilder, and make us think we are in a land of fabled beauty, more than a troubled world, to be tossed again by the tempests incident to life. This appears to be the native home of the grape-vine, where all varieties flourish finely. Think of the money that is expended every year in sending to foreign countries for the one article of wine, and what a miserable, adulterated mixture is brought over, only dashed a little with pure grape-juice, while the drugs introduced would cause any one with delicate sensibilities to shrink from the thought of swallowing! If a reliable firm were to come here and undertake the culture of vineyards, manufacturing pure wines, it would be found more remunerative than orange-growing, the risk being not half so great, as the wine is improving with age, while fresh fruits decay very rapidly, when being transferred. Invalids, in coming to Florida, bring their wines; whereas, if they could be furnished with a better article at much less rates, they would soon find it more advantageous to patronize a home-product, the compounding of which they knew to be genuine as the far-famed vintage of the Rhine. Wine has always been in use from the days of Noah to the present time, although brigades of men and women-crusaders have screamed themselves hoarse in proclaiming its evils and wicked influences. If the manufacture of wines from pure grape-juice was encouraged, this beastly drunkenness from strychnine whisky would very soon be abandoned.

Sometimes here, as in other places, the laborer is not rewarded in his efforts to raise a good crop, which, in this far-famed country for fertility and productiveness, is pronounced a fraud practiced by somebody in holding out inducements for them to come to Florida and starve. No person has ever been known to suffer for food in this portion of the State—as an illustration of which, one man has lived in the vicinity nearly thirty years, reared a large family, and none can testify to his having done a whole day's work during that time. The safe way is to cultivate a variety of vegetables and fruits—something will thrive. Sweet potatoes are indigenous, and never fail, making fine food for man and beast. Sugar-cane is a sure crop, ratooning without replanting for six years, if properly cultivated, and, as it is never injured by frost, blooms and perfects seed.

Bees can be successfully kept, on account of the mild climate, as they can work all the year. Much wild honey has been taken from trees, which is a proof of their adaptation to this place. Patent hives have not been introduced, or perhaps these old-fashioned bees would not fancy so many apartments in their palaces; but it would, no doubt, be worth the experiment to try them. Bee-gums made from a hollow log, set flat on the ground, are principally in use. A good swarm is said to yield seventy-five pounds of honey in a season. No apiarian societies have been yet established, and very little attention is given to the bee industry in any way. Some planters have twenty-five or fifty colonies. Bee-culture will be introduced as the industry of the country is developed, and the sweet tastes of the people demand it. When you are asked by the Floridians if you will take "long sweetenin'" or "short sweetenin'" in your coffee, remember the "long sweetenin'" is honey, and the "short" sugar.

Let all those who wish to avoid the long, dreary, drizzly days during March and April, in more Northern latitudes, when the warm current of life is almost chilled into frigidity, come to South Florida, and roam by the river-side, or glide across the quiet lakes in light canoes; ply the oar at night, when the bright moonbeams kiss the parting waves, or while the iridescent rays of dancing sunbeams shimmer under the brightness of a tropical sky.

It is now the last of February, and the sunny side of nature is beaming upon the oleanders that are bursting their pink petals, while the orange-trees are sending forth fresh leaves that envelop the germs of the far-famed Hesperidean fruit. The wild orange is in bloom, which freights the air with delicious odors, although the fruit is only used for making beverages and marmalade. The banana, which is cultivated as corn is farther North, has commenced putting up fresh shoots, whose leaves are to take the place of those rent in shreds by the rude winds that have spent their fury on this coast during the Northern winters.

The air is now soft as a sleeping zephyr on a summer sea, while the earth is covered with a fresh carpet of green, mingled with white and blue violets, the tiny forget-me-not, the wild verbena, the purple and yellow crocus, and other flowers of less humble growth, and more varied hues than can be described, deck the landscape with beauty, gemming the wild woods with loveliness, and filling our hearts with delight. Sounds of melody echo from sunlit bowers, where birds of song flit on airy wings, and the gentle cries of fledglings arouse the maternal instincts to greater exertion.

Every settler is busy gathering oranges, which will be ruined if left on the trees when they commence blooming, as the juice is required to perfect the future blooms. Young trees are being transplanted, palmettoes dug out, cows penned for milking, calves caught and marked—as no one can recover the value of a stolen animal not branded. Poets have called the rose "a child of summer." Those rhyme-writers never visited Manatee, where new-born roses open every day, and summer lingers all the year. This vicinity, like most other places, has its historic record of various *data*. It is here the pirates Ambroister and Arbuthnot were captured, and afterward hanged by order of General Jackson. These lands were once the hunting-grounds of Billy Bowlegs, who defeated General Taylor at Ocheechobe Lake, during the Seminole war. When Bowlegs was being taken through the Capitol-building in Washington, he gave only a stupid stare or grunt at all other objects except an oil-painting, where, among other figures, was General Z. Taylor, at which he grinned with a look of satisfaction, exclaiming, "Me whip!" The old chieftain was a great hunter. When expostulated with for hunting game on Sunday, he very promptly replied, "White man have good book to read, and he work on Sunday."

From this place Hon. Judah P. Benjamin, Secretary of the Confederate States, now Solicitor-general for the Queen of England, made his escape. Here he remained six months under an assumed name, with the pretext of desiring to purchase hummock-lands. During his stay newspapers were shown him by his friends, in which were large rewards offered for his capture; but his protectors scorned treachery for gold. He left Manatee, disguised as a cook, on board a sloop. Before they reached Key West their little craft was overhauled by a United States revenue-cutter. The powerless foe for whom they were searching, not being recognized in his galley disguise, ran the gauntlet in safety. While on his way to Nassau the schooner in which he was sailing, not being able to resist the heavy seas that it had to encounter, sunk, when he was shipwrecked, losing all his personal effects, and was rescued from drowning only by escaping to a small boat, from which he was afterward picked up by an English vessel. He was recently solicited to write an account of his adventures before escaping to Europe, but replied, "It is too soon."

In this portion of Florida have been discovered bones of immense size, belonging to an order of animals now extinct—these being fragments of the mammiferous mastodon and megatherium, which furnish material for study that takes us back to the

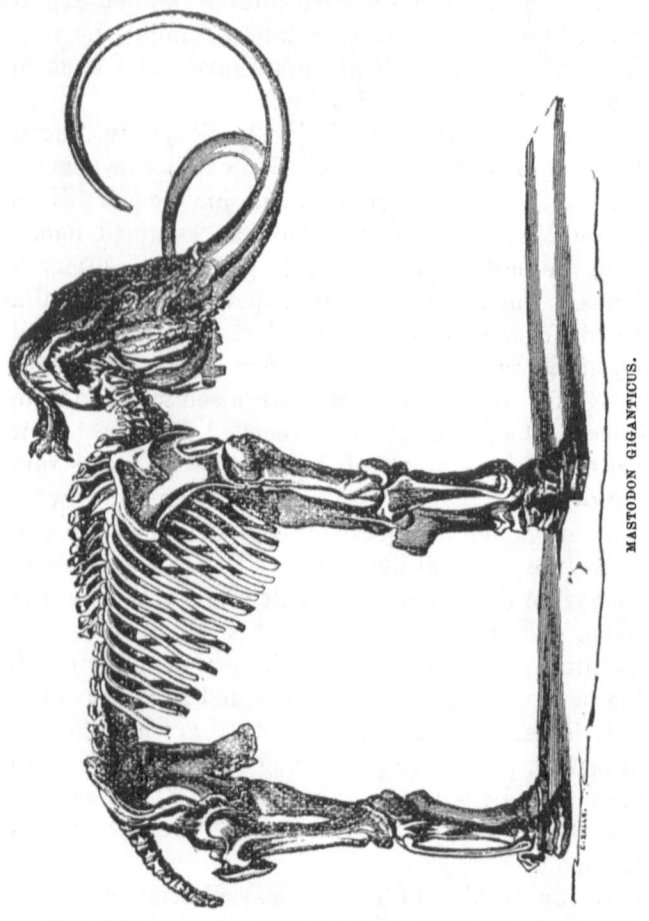

MASTODON GIGANTICUS.

earliest history of the world, before giants lived, or Adam was made out of the red clay, to enter Eden

and participate in its primeval glories. When those
creatures, that now only excite our wonder, walked
the earth, covered with their piles of flesh, moving
with majestic tread the uninhabited globe, the sloth
was then the size of an ox, the bear as large as a
horse. Portions of vertebræ belonging to the mastodon *giganticus*—a race of elephants that lived during the tertiary period—have been discovered here,
measuring eleven feet in height, with a body seventeen feet in length, and a huge tail over six feet
long. The bones of this animal, when exhumed,
were found in marl-pits, or salt-licks containing
saline matter, to which may be attributed their remarkable preservation. Their grinding-teeth were
adapted to a much coarser article of diet than that
consumed by elephants of the present period. They
have also been called "the hairy elephant." Was
it not the mammoth megatherium that furnished
the aborigines with material for pointing their spears
and manufacturing their bone implements, the remains of which are now frequently found beneath
the *tumuli* of Florida? The megatherium was a
contemporary of the mastodon—a few bones having
been exhumed in South Florida; but Skiddaway, on
the coast of Georgia, has furnished remains of the
most perfect and interesting specimens of this animal ever found in North America, discovered in
1855. This herbivorous creature belonged to an
extinct species of sloth, which had ribs measuring
more than three inches in width, and teeth nine
inches long, its thigh-bones being three times the
thickness of those of the largest elephant, with fore-

feet one yard in length, a body eighteen feet long, and its massive tail two feet in diameter, which enabled the animal to balance its body while feeding, and also use it as a weapon of defense. The weight of its hind-legs and tail prevented it from somersaulting while cutting down trees with its teeth.

CHAPTER XX.

FORTY miles from Manatee is to be seen the remains of Tampa. Your morning slumbers will not be interrupted here by the hammers of rude workmen, who are usually so inconsiderate for the comfort of others in their noisy movements. During the Florida war this town boasted more prosperity than at any subsequent period. It was then a military station for the soldiers, and depot for army supplies; also a kind of central point for this portion of the State. Here the Indians were ordered to report before being sent West. Its early settlement was commenced under difficulties by Navaraez, who, in 1828, landed at Tampa Bay, and, after penetrating some portions of the interior, returned and sailed for Cuba, leaving one of his companions—Juan Ortiz—whom the Indians had captured without his knowledge. The extreme youth of Ortiz excited sympathy among the Indian women, who rescued him from being burned, but the men made him feel the bitterness of bondage, until his life became a burden. They required him during their festal-days to run the gauntlet for their amusement, his celerity on these occasions saving him from death. As a variety in his servitude, he was employed to watch through long, wearisome nights in the graveyard. The In-

dians then buried their dead above ground in boxes,
placing only a rock on the lid—the bodies being frequently dragged out by animals. Poor Ortiz had
been so miserable while among the living that he
now looked to the dead for an amelioration of his
condition. Armed with his bow and arrow, he
stood as sentry over the silent slumberers, when,
unfortunately, one night he sunk into a somnambulistic state himself. The body of an infant was
missing, the falling lid awakening him. Ortiz followed in the direction of the retreating footsteps,
when he discovered a panther, which he instantly
shot, and secured the corpse. For this act of bravery he was taken into favor by the Indians, and soon
afterward rescued from their caprices and cruelties
by De Soto, who landed in 1539, he having sailed
from Cuba. He came with more display of pageantry than America had ever seen before, entering
the waters of Tampa Bay on Whitsunday—hence he
named it Espiritu Santo. The geography of the
country fought against those who tried to penetrate
its recesses—passing through morasses below sea-level was accompanied with greater difficulties than
they had imagined before trying the experiment.
After their arrival, most of their time was spent in
feasting and rioting, more becoming a returning triumph than an entrance into a new country. The
Indians made a descent on them one night after a
bacchanalian revel, wounding three of their number,
notwithstanding the heavy armor in which their
bodies were incased. De Soto soon left this country in search of other conquests and greater treas-

ures than awaited him here. On account of the remoteness of Tampa from the other early settlements in the State, it was occupied almost entirely by Indians until during the Florida war. Billy Bowlegs was chief of the tribe here, but lived near Manatee. His last visit to the commander was performed under great difficulties, the army head-quarters being in Tampa. He was permitted to remain in the territory, on account of his peaceable inclinations, after his tribe had been ordered to the West. Such was the desire and anxiety of this aged chieftain to see the military commandant face to face, and give him renewed assurances of fidelity to his engagements, in hope of silencing the clamors of white alarmists, a report of which had reached him, that the weight of infirmities under which he was laboring was insufficient to stop him, the journey being performed under circumstances that gave conclusive evidence of his peaceful intentions. So great, indeed, was his decrepitude, that during his last days—being wholly unable to travel, even on horseback—he was borne on a litter on the shoulders of his men.

In consideration of the fine timber which surrounds Tampa, two mills are employed — one in sawing cedar, the other pine. The cedar here is of much finer quality than the upland, containing more oil. At the mill it is sawed into pencil-lengths, after which it is packed in boxes, and shipped to New York, and other points, for making pencils. The cabbage-palm grows in the vicinity, and is much used in building wharves—it not being effected by the sea-water, and resisting the attacks of the *Teredo Navalis*, which destroys the hulls of vessels when made of any other timber but this, which it never molests.

The schools here are not considered by many as important institutions, consequently are in rather an embryo condition. We visited one taught in the court-house. This structure, not unlike many others in the vicinity, is among the things that lack symmetry and sound timbers. The present incumbent in charge of this school is a genuine specimen of the Illinois backwoods race. His visage looked blank as the door before which he sat chewing the Virginia weed, and firing jets of juice, evidently making a bigger effort with his jaws than his brains. His pupils were undergoing a heavy cramming process. Meaningless, incomprehensible words were being wedged into their heads so tightly they never could be got out, either for use or ornament. How those bright-eyed little boys were martyring auxiliary perfect passive participles and verbs! One fact was evident: if they had a better auxiliary to instruct them, they would have a more luxuriant growth of intellect than they were obtaining under the present regimen.

We do not take leave of this place as of a dear friend. Its deep sandy sidewalks are any thing but inviting for promenaders. The decaying structures and dilapidated fences remind us of old age, "when the keepers of the house shall tremble." The place looks discouraged from sheer weariness in trying to be a town. The hotel-keepers are wishing for a few guests which they could relieve of three dollars *per diem*. The merchants appear anxious, as though they wanted somebody to come and make purchases. They are of that class which look at everybody with an eye to business, wondering how much money they can grind out of each customer in a given space of time.

Old Tampa, many years ago, was considered a famous resort for consumptives. Persons advanced in life, from all parts, now speak in glowing terms of the uniform temperature of its atmosphere. But indifferent houses of entertainment, charging exorbitant rates, will soon ruin the popularity of any place. Fort Brooke, of Indian fame, is found here. It was originally designed as a means of defense during the Florida wars. It is now a desolate, tumble-down old place. The fine site it occupies, together with some ancient-looking water-oaks, standing like sentinels, is all that is to be seen in the least degree attractive. The Federal Government has been paying eighteen hundred dollars per annum to keep the place from being destroyed, while no one would be willing to make an investment of that amount for the entire contents, land and all.

When Coacoochee was captured the last time, he was brought to Tampa. General Worth, on receiving the information that Wild Cat was a prisoner, visited him, with a number of his officers, for the purpose of an interview. The general, with his staff, appeared in full uniform, that the scene might not be lacking in pageant. They met upon the deck of the vessel, and, taking the chief by the hand, General Worth spoke as follows:

"Coacoochee, I take you by the hand as a warrior and a brave man. You love your home as we do; it is sacred to you; the ashes of your countrymen are dear to you and the Seminole. These feelings have caused much bloodshed, distress, and horrid murders: it is time now the Indian felt the power of the white man. Like the oak, you may bear up for many years against the strong winds, but the time comes when it must fall—it has now arrived. You have withstood the blasts of five winters, and the storms of thunder, and lightning, and wind, for five summers; the branches have fallen, and the tree burnt at the roots is prostrate. Coacoochee, I am your friend; so is your Great Father at Washington. What I say to you is true. My tongue is not forked like a snake's. My word is for the happiness of the red man. You are a great warrior; the Indians throughout the country look to you as a leader; by your counsels they have been governed. Much innocent blood has been shed. You have made the ground and your hands red with the blood of innocent women and children. This war must end now, and you are the man to do it. I sent for you, that through the exertions of yourself and your men you might induce your entire band to emigrate. I wish you to state how many days it will take to effect an interview with the Indians in the woods. You can select three or five of these men to carry your talk: name the time, it shall be granted. But I tell you, as I wish your friends told, that unless they fulfill your demands, yourself and these warriors now seated before us shall be hung to the yards of this vessel when the sun sets on the appointed day, with the irons upon your hands and feet. I tell you this, that we may well understand each other. I do not wish to frighten you; you are too brave a man for that; but I say what I mean, and I will do it. It is for the benefit of the white and red man. *The war must end, and you must end it!*"

A profound silence pervaded the company after the general ceased speaking, when Coacoochee arose and replied in a feeling tone:

"I was once a boy; then I saw the pale face afar off. I hunted in these woods first with a bow and arrow, then with a rifle. I saw the white man, and was told he was my enemy. I could not shoot him as a wolf or bear; yet, like these, he came upon me: horses, cattle, and fields, he took from me. He said he was my friend; he abused our women and children, and then told us to leave the land. Still he gave me his hand in friendship; we took it; while taking it he had a snake in the other; his tongue was forked; he lied and stung us. I asked but for a small piece of these lands — enough to plant and live upon, far south — a spot where I could place the ashes of my kindred, a spot only sufficient where I could lay my wife and child. This was not granted me. I was put in prison; I escaped. I have been again taken; you have brought me back; I am here; I feel the irons in my heart. I have listened to your talk. You and your officers have taken us by the hand in friendship. I thank you for bringing me back. I can now see my warriors, my women and children; the Great Spirit thanks you—the heart of the poor Indian thanks you. We know but little; we have no books which tell us all things, but we have the Great Spirit, moon and stars—these told me last night you would be our friend. I give you my word; it is the word of a warrior, a chief, a brave; it is the word of Coacoochee. It is true I have fought like a man—so have my warriors—but the whites are too strong for us. I wish now to have my band around me, and go to Arkansas. You say I must end the war! Look at these irons! Can I go to my warriors? Coacoochee chained! No; do not ask me to see them. I never wish to tread upon my land unless I am free. If I can go to them *unchained*, they will follow me in; but I fear they will not obey me when I talk to them in irons. They will say my heart is weak—I am afraid. Could I go free, they will surrender and emigrate."

General Worth then informed him that he could not be set at liberty, nor would his irons be removed, until his entire band had surrendered; but that he might select three or five prisoners, who should be liberated and permitted to carry his talk, with a respite of thirty or fifty days, if necessary. "Lastly, I say if the band does not submit to your last wish, the sun, as it goes down on the last day appointed for their appearance, will shine upon your bodies hanging in the wind."

Coacoochee selected five of his warriors to carry

this message to his band, making the following appeal to them:

"My feet are chained, but the head and heart of Coacoochee reaches you. The great white chief will be kind to us. He says when my band comes in I shall again walk my land free with them around me. He has given you forty days to do this business in; if you want more, say so—I will ask for more; if not, be true to the time. Take these sticks; here are thirty-nine—one for each day; this, much larger than the rest, with blood upon it, is the fortieth. When the others are thrown away, and this only remains, say to my people that with the setting sun Coacoochee hangs like a dog, with none but white men to hear his last words. Come, then, come by the stars, as I have led you to battle. Come, for the voice of Coacoochee speaks to you."

The five Indians selected were started on their mission, accompanied by old Micco. Before the month expired, seventy-eight warriors, sixty-four women, and forty-seven children were brought in. Coacoochee was relieved when told his band had arrived. "Take off my irons," said he, "that I may once more meet my warriors like a man." Upon the removal of his irons, he gave one wild whoop, and rushed on shore. "The rifle is hid," said he, "and the white and red man are friends. I have given my word for you; then let my word be true. I am done."

The appeal of General Worth to the vanity of Coacoochee was more efficient in closing the war

than all other moves from its commencement.
Wild Cat was more cunning than brave—strategic than bold and daring; but a vulnerable chord
had been struck, and he responded with apparent
alacrity.

Many Seminole Indians were shipped from here
to the West at the close of the war. The following
anecdote is related of Wild Cat after he left Fort
Brooke, to be banished forever from his home in
Florida: The steamer James Adams encountered
rough weather as soon as she was outside the bay.
The waves of the sea rose to a great height, the
steamer labored much, and four feet of water was
reported in her hold. Every thing that was on
deck was cut loose and cast into the sea. The
faces of the crew became paler than usual. Wild
Cat was on deck, an attentive observer of the increasing consternation of the white men, when
suddenly he accosted the officer in these words:
"Be not afraid. The Great Spirit will not suffer
me to die with the pale faces in the manner you
now apprehend. Tell me from what quarter you
wish the wind to blow, in order that the big water
may become quiet and the fire-canoe paddle on."
The officer, although attaching little importance
to what the chief said, complied with his request
to keep him quiet. He was taken to the binnacle
and shown the compass, by which means he was
made to understand from what quarter the wind
must blow in order to produce a calmer sea.
Thereupon, Wild Cat commenced making signs in
the air, and other demonstrations. Fifteen or

twenty minutes elapsed, when, to the astonishment of all the whites, the storm abated, the winds hushed and almost lulled. The exertions of the crew stopped the leaks, and enabled the boat to proceed in safety. We do not ask you to believe in the power of Wild Cat to control the elements; but this anecdote shows at least self-possession, and the desire of distinction, and reverence for the Great Spirit, to be prominent traits in the savage character, where others would only think of the peril before their eyes.

CHAPTER XXI.

Meantime the steady wind serenely blew,
And fast and falcon-like the vessel flew.

DOES any one know what a sailing-voyage, in a coasting-vessel, from Tampa to Key West—a distance of two hundred and fifty miles—implies? Some may suppose it to be a kind of flying motion through the air, or skimming swiftly over the waters, like a sea-gull in rough weather; but those who have tried the experiment find it quite the reverse. It means a little good sailing, an occasional fine breeze thrown in, with many disagreeable things to be encountered and forgotten as soon as possible. For instance, the first night after leaving, under favorable appearances, the wind dies out, the mainsail hangs flabby as a beggar's rags in a thunder-shower; the sailors lower the canvas, put out the anchor, and all retire. Numerous drum-fish select the hull of the vessel as their camping-ground, where they serenade us all night with a peculiar drumming noise, while the loon from the shore catches the refrain, and utters its unearthly screams, which disturb our repose, mingling with dreams of hideous mien. The mattress is hard as Pharaoh's heart. Bilge-water keeps the cabin supplied with an odor resembling sulphur-spring surroundings. Fleas enter the list of perplexities, to draw rations from our perishable nature, run races, and practice acrobatic movements on our bodies, with astonishing facility. Roaches as long as your little finger look at us as if meditating a fierce attack, which, if executed, must result in our annihilation. Three small children lying close by are screaming alternately, from interrupted slumbers, caused by advances from the insect tribe. Their father, who is a Methodist preacher, applies hand-plasters, which silence the batteries temporarily. This will be found a charming place for the exercise of patience, without the fortitude of Job to endure trials. Day dawns, and with it comes breakfast. Strong coffee, seasoned with highly-colored sugar, the mixture stirred with a table-knife, and drunk from a tin cup, together with well-salted meat, fried eggs, and hard-tack, furnish the repast. Unpalatable as this food appears to an epicurean taste, the sailors devour it with a relish, as it gives them strength to endure many hardships. The morning wind is fair, although light, and we are sailing again toward Terrasilla Bay, which is a portion of Tampa, bearing another name. The sugar-crop is waiting for shipment to Key West, and our invoice not being full, we stop for freight. Numerous bars line this bay, where oysters of a delicious flavor, and clams of immense size — some of them weighing three pounds, with the shell — are obtained at low tide without dredging.

For the benefit of those lady-passengers who, perchance, may travel this way, and have never been

borne in arms since they were children, we can tell
you there are no wharves here, no throwing out of
planks, no stopping-places for ladies, between water
and land. The vessel sails as near the shore as possible without grounding, and then the passengers
on board are carried to *terra firma*. This is done
by two sailors, who make a kind of seat by clasping
their hands together, after which they receive the
living freight. You put out each arm, and clasp
your improvised sedan around their necks, to keep
from falling. Sometimes one of the sailors is as
black as tar; but it makes no difference—"civil
rights" is not the question at issue now. You cannot wade, or wet your feet, and they will carry you
safely, this being a portion of their duties, for which
they are paid.

Terrasilla Island is one of those charming spots
which all admire, but none can describe. The principal inhabitant is Madam Joe, a German lady, celebrated for her hospitality. Here she came, with
her husband, after the Florida war, to occupy lands
given them by the Government. An adventure of
some kind was then of daily occurrence. Nature
poured forth her beauties in solitude, and from the
dark recesses of the primitive forest-wilderness were
echoed and reëchoed the war-whoop of the Indian,
the howl of the jaguar, the scream of the catamount,
and the threatening growl of old bruin. The rough
hands, stalwart frame, and nut-brown face of this
lady, indicate a life to which ease and idleness are
unknown. Her home is now transformed from a
wilderness to a place which recalls our youthful im-

ages of fairy-land. Here you constantly feel as though you were having a beautiful dream, which may be dissipated by some external irruption, and the spell broken. How delightful to any one who has a constant warfare with life to keep himself master of the situation is a visit to this beautiful island, where only the winds and waves strive for victory, and the excesses practiced in refined society are unknown! where orange-trees grow as tall as Lombardy poplars, and are laden with fruit hanging in luxuriant loveliness, designed to delight all those who partake. It is now February; new Irish potatoes, tomatoes, with green peas, and egg-plants, are abundant. Fresh flowers are in their bloom and beauty; the earth is enameled with the white petals of the forget-me-not, in lieu of the snow-banks which cover the ground farther North. Roses of immense size are open, together with verbenas of varied hues, geraniums, salvias, periwinkles, and corkwood-trees, all exhaling their fragrance in the open air. Here in this beauteous bower Madam Joe, after her day's duties are done, walks, with the bright moonbeams shining on her pathway, singing those German patriotic melodies so dear to the heart of every wanderer from the historic shores and vine-clad hills of the River Rhine—thus forming a symphony with the ebbing tide of briny waters by which her home is surrounded.

A young couple from Alabama are staying here, who have come with the intention of settling. Romance has never written any thing more rural, nor the imagination of a poet conceived thoughts which savor more of poesy, than the real life which they lead. He lost an arm while battling for his country, but his courage has never failed him. With a little assistance he has built a palmetto and pole house, which subserves the purpose of sitting-room and bed-room. The white sand blows in sometimes, during the day, from the beach, falling on the bed, converting the pillows into friction-brushes, and the young wife's temper into an irritated condition. She cooks their food under rustling palms, while he reads to her from some interesting book. She accompanies him in his hunting expeditions, to carry home the game, which is their principal subsistence. Adam and Eve, when first placed in the garden of Eden, were not less solicitous for a support than this couple appear in their rustic home. The land bordering on Sarasota Bay contains some portions of country as uncivilized as when the savage glided across its green waters, or his voice rang through its uncultured forests. The climate is delightful beyond description—the air "soft as the memory of buried love." Here, in appearance, must be located the Enchanted Isles, where cold, heat, or hunger were unknown, where roamed the white deer, which the red man worshiped as a god, that lived and fed from the delicate mosses, silken as a mermaid's hair, slender and feathery as a pencil of light when it first reaches the earth at the early blush of morn. Some old fogies, who have lived here for many years, express opposition to new settlements being made, and say "it will spile their cattle-range." Stock-raising has been the only money-making employment of the population since they lived here. They are not informed with regard to other branches of industry, or their successful prosecution. Broad acres, with pastures green, on which range the wild herds, have been the standard of their wealth heretofore. Persons wishing to settle in a country always inquire about its healthfulness. There exists no malaria, or disease of any kind. The settlers live mostly on the bay, where, from constant evaporation, the waters are more briny than the Atlantic. The land is interspersed with rich hummock, underlying which is a stratum of marl. A great variety of wild fruits are found in the woods, the principal kinds being the fox-grape, octagonal cactus that produces a delicious fruit, tamarinds, sugar-apples, poporea, and sea-grape—all indigenous. The Lima bean bears during the entire year. The pine-apple culture has proved a success. The *Palma Christi* and bird-pepper grow into perennial plants, living and producing many years. The change of seasons in South Florida is imperceptible, while in more Northern climes autumn, with stately tread and Tyrian-dyed train, assumes her sway, bearing fruits of scarlet and gold, that are gathered in haste, for fear the rude blasts will freeze out their luscious, juicy qualities; but here there is no suspense of vegetation. Many times during the winter months a soft haze, accompanied by a more tender and less glaring light, overspreads the land and sea, when the sun shines as it shines in the Northern Indian summer. It is during these halcyon days, when nature appears transfigured for a time into an abode fit for angels, that we love to sit and muse upon this lovely scene, with feelings too sacred for confidants, too pure for earth. Many tourists, in traveling, expect all their schemes to roll on electric wheels, without rocks or ruts in the roads, or any hilly eminences to impede them; but we must all remember that patience is a plant which flourishes in a pure atmosphere, with its petals fanned by the breath of heaven, while its roots are nourished by the great moral principles that radiate from a pure heart. As the motive-power that takes vistors through and about this country bears no resemblance to a "lightning express," many exclamations are made by those who have to endure these irregularities incident to a new country that would read badly in print.

Off the shore of Sarasota Bay fishing-smacks are engaged at all seasons in obtaining supplies for the Havana market. These little vessels contain a well where the water can be changed, and the fish kept alive until sold. The most delicious fish of all found in these waters is the pompano, which resembles the California salmon, both in color and flavor. It is only taken at night by striking with a harpoon. In some portions of the bay the finest oysters grow that are found on any coast.

Mangrove-thickets also abound, which in some places form an almost impassable barrier to navigation. This tree resembles the banyan of India, in throwing out stolons, besides the leaf-bearing limbs, that incline downward, thus taking root, and producing other plants, which grow into trees. They are only natives of a tropical shore, where they root in the mud and form a dense thicket to the verge of the ocean. Oyster-shells and sea-urchins attach themselves, hanging in clusters, which form an unapproachable defense.

New settlers are frequently found here, living in palmetto-houses. Think of a family composed of ten persons staying in a house made of leaves, with a finely surf-beaten shell-floor, the whole structure nearly fifty feet long, twelve feet high, divided into rooms by pieces of sail-cloth, the roof impervious to water, and no rude winds to blow on them. We have wandered far to find the home of contentment, and here it dwells. How heartily they all eat fish, clams, and oysters! How soundly they sleep on their mossy beds! How happy they appear, building boats or cultivating their lands! How merry they whistle when starting out to fish, or strike in their little canoes! They look exceedingly picturesque gliding about with their torches in the bow of the boat, resembling *ignes-fatui* more than tangible substance. When they approach the shore the hogs, dogs, and cats all run to meet them, knowing their supplies are coming. Hogs are fattened on fish, and penned a month before killing, when they are given other food to prevent the meat having a fishy flavor. Here conchologists, and persons fond of shell-hunting, can be gratified. After you pass the keys which abound in this bay, you come to a wide beach of snowy whiteness, formed from the *débris* of shells and coral, worn by the waves which open to the Gulf of Mexico. There is no place in Florida which has such a variety of rare and beautiful shells. Here are also numerous layers of rock, extending into the water, very nearly resembling the St. Augustine coquina, which is used in building chimneys, also house-foundations.

All visitors that come to Florida, who are not confirmed invalids, have their hobby, or favorite amusement, with which they propose to be entertained during their stay. Some love to fish, and require choice morsels to tempt their prey. No rivulet, however remote, if a minnow moves in its sluggish waters, is proof against their explorations. The crabs are pulled out with a celerity that astonishes their crustaceous lordships. The sea-fiddlers cannot come from their holes for a quiet dance on the beach without being jerked up to a tune they never heard before. These are all used for bait, which delights the silly fish very much, until he finds himself a captive in an element which relieves him of vitality. Others are fond of capturing alligators, and many an unfortunate animal is found lying on his back, with his teeth drawn out, his head cut off, and skin missing. The deer-hunter is in for his share of amusement: he loves to camp at night, and, when he can "shine the eyes" of the unsuspecting animal, send a bullet with unfailing certainty through his head.

The most indefatigable, persistent, unrelenting, and unyielding, to any obstacle, is the naturalist. No mire or mud, filled with shapes however monstrous or ugly, is proof against his encroachments. The eagle in her eyrie, with a nest built on the tallest pines, is reached with ropes, the young eaglets captured, to be cut in pieces, their wings measured from tip to tip, feathers counted, and bodies embalmed. Mr. and Mrs. Snake have no privileges, except in their dens, but that of being gobbled up in a very unceremonious manner, their striped hides taken off and stuffed, then carried to the Smithsonian, or some other museum of less celebrity. The ugliest and most repulsive-looking worms have no chance to measure their length outside their dark places of repose with the prospect of ever returning. No butterfly, if discovered, is permitted to pass through its transitions in freedom, for oftentimes, before its wings are spread to the breeze, it becomes a helpless, hopeless prisoner, where in its captivity it can metamorphose much as it pleases, and then yield its life a sacrifice to science. The bugs, with their various shapes and sizes, cannot try the strength of their wings, or compare their green, velvety jackets, with their more plainly-dressed neighbors, without being seized like culprits, and pinned to pasteboard.

Sailing and stopping, how care is lightened of its burden in the life we are now pursuing! There is nothing expected of us, but we are anticipating a great deal of pleasure from the trip. We are now landing at Egmont Key, which is an insular domain —a kingdom bounded by deep waters—a residence among turtles and birds of varied notes. This island is five miles in circumference, and seven from the mainland, commanding the entrance to Tampa Bay. Latitude — north, $27° 36'$; longitude — west from Greenwich, $82° 45'$. A light-house was erected upon this island in 1848. It is built of brick, and is eighty-six feet above sea-level—lens of the fourth order—the light being a fixture, visible twelve miles. The high tower looks as though it was trying to reach the sky, which overhangs its solitary turret. In this retired spot the ocean-birds resort to build their nests, or rest their pinions for longer flights; and the turtle comes to deposit her eggs, to be fostered by sunbeams, and afterward caressed in emerald waves, when their maternal shells are broken. Here the most frequent sounds are from sighing waves and heavy seas; but, when the weather is calm, feathered songsters of varied notes come from their coverts of safety to sing songs of joy.

Naturalists from every State visit this point—among the number the late lamented Professor Agassiz ranked as the most distinguished. Among the many marines with whose habits we have become conversant, the hermit-crab, also called the soldier-crab, appears the most peculiar. At low tide we saw a large mollusk-shell traveling toward the shore, and wondered why such unaccustomed speed in its movements. We soon discovered crab-claws projecting from its shell, and recognized it as a hermit-crab, an original freebooter. How strangely he looked, with his confiscated house on his back, moving about like a sailor in his boat, using his claws for oars! When the shell he is occupying gets too small for him, like a land-liver he goes house-hunting. If he finds one tenanted which will answer his purpose, he pulls out the occupant with as little ceremony as a fellow-man kicks his drunken brother into the street. He then darts into the shell with great speed, leaving his companion, bruised and homeless, to die at his leisure, or secure another, if he is able.

In this favored spot the eagle teaches her eaglets to face the sun and soar from sight, while the sea-gulls flap their wings in silence, the cormorant gorges himself to gluttony, and the pelican takes on her cargo of fish, which she carries to a platform

A FISH-HAWK FORAGING FROM A PELICAN.

raised in front of her nest, that the fledglings may draw their rations without leaving their downy beds, where they remain until they are grown.

Rare sea-shells are found on this beach, and rarer birds; but the rarest of all that is seen on this island is the light-house-keeper, Captain Coons, who is a Spiritualist, a curiosity, a mixture of singularities combined, an enigma of the human species. His presence reminds one of a moving panorama, or kaleidoscope, with a great variety of coloring and adaptations, always changing, and designed to please the crowd before which it is placed. He has much versatility of talent — can scrape almost any old-fashioned tune out of catgut, blow plaintive notes from a flute, and draw "Yankee Doodle" from that unclassic instrument upon which we never read of David the son of Jesse having performed—an accordion. Spirits of persons that have been drowned in the vast deep are said to visit this island more than others: perhaps the proximity favors their coming; and sailors, never remarkable for their piety, while wandering in darkness, and weary of the gnashing teeth in their unhappy abodes, if they do come, it is only seeking rest.

This point is the best for spiritual circles that could be imagined—no affinities that are inharmonious to come in, and prevent those mystic rappers which have been promising to benefit the world so wonderfully for more than twenty years, but never, as yet, developed any important truths.

The united family live here. The spirits have revealed to the husband that in another world "they will be married, as in this." He says "he never wants another wife but the one he has got." His well-chosen consort has lost nearly all her teeth, and the spirits which she has interviewed on the subject of dentistry have promised her a "new set" when she commences her spiritual life. If all the toothless people in the world were to wait for a new supply of grinders until they arrived in another world, the dentists would soon starve out in this.

No part of the world furnishes a greater variety of the finny tribe than this coast, and fisheries are being established in the vicinity. Sharks, sixteen or eighteen feet in length, make their appearance in company with devil-fish of enormous size. Jew-fish, weighing three or four hundred pounds, together with tarpons of one hundred and fifty or two hundred pounds, are quite common. Schools of mullet swarm in these waters, constituting an article of commerce. Green and loggerhead turtle are taken, and form a lucrative traffic.

An old Spanish sailor on duty tells us he can remember when the buccaneers landed on this island with their stolen goods and secreted them. This class of people were descended from the French, and subsisted upon a kind of smoked meat called boucan, from which they derived their name.

These buccaneers assumed martial names, known only among themselves. Their clothing was of a most repulsive character, consisting of a filthy shirt, colored with the blood of animals they had killed, belted with a leather-thong over trousers to match, while hung to their belts were Dutch knives and a saber; a brimless hat and hog-skin shoes completed their toilet. They never attacked vessels on their way to America, but on their return, grappling the largest and firing into their port-holes with such accuracy the gunners were unable to return the fire. They cherished a great antipathy to the Spaniards, because they had captured the portion of country from them that they claimed. They were a terror to all commercial enterprises in the Spanish

Colonies, also crippling the agricultural prospects. Jean Lafitte, their leader, died at Appalachicola, where his body lay in state several days, when it was visited by many people from long distances.

The breeze is now freshening a little: raise the foresail, mainsail, and jib, when we are moving at the rapid rate of a mile in two hours. Even in midwinter, at noonday, the merry sunshine comes beaming down in this latitude with intense fervor. Finally a dead calm ensues, and we are prisoners on the high seas. The zephyrs are nooning in their sylvan bowers, while the heat has to be endured peaceably as possible—like all other things, it terminates. The great orb of day has performed his duty well—resembling a successful conqueror, he descends triumphantly, in his chariot of fire, beneath the briny waves—a golden train of glory is left behind him, while the charming blue sky and sunset are mirrored upon the sea, each alternate wave being a reflection from the sunbeams. Poets may sing, "Beautiful isles of the sea," but before they had spent much time in this desolate spot, it would be, "Lonely isles of the sea, when shall I be where the face of human beings will gladden my heart, and the smiles of friendship beam upon my pathway again?"

We are hopeful yet, as Boca Grande is reached—the entrance to Charlotte Harbor—then Point Blanco, afterward Point Kautivo, where a poor preacher was captured and murdered for money. Now we are sailing through seas once the hiding-place of pirates, where much gold is said to be buried which was captured from a frigate on her passage to France.

One of these numerous islands is now the residence of a professional privateer in by-gone days, but who has since returned to private life, pursuing a civilized vocation. On another island in the vicinity lived Felippe, a Spaniard, with his three Indian wives. After the close of the last Seminole war, when orders were issued by the Federal Government for the savages to leave Florida, his wives, belonging to the tribe, were included in the edict. The Federal officers induced Felippe to leave home, that they might rob him of his concubines and fourteen children. After his departure all were more easily persuaded than Polly, his last love, whom he had seduced from an Indian guide. However, after much persuasion, she was reconciled by a purse being made up for her benefit. When Felippe returned he was perfectly inconsolable for the loss of his wives and children, and, on being informed Polly was prevailed upon to go by giving her money, he replied, "O Polly go to hell for money!"

Punta Rassa, our landing-place now, is situated over one hundred miles from Key West, and twenty-two miles from Fort Myres, opposite Synabel Island. The waters of the gulf here, being confined in a small compass, rush with fearful rapidity during a gale. The Federal Post was destroyed in 1844. From this point also were collected and shipped, during the Florida war, many of the wives and children of the Seminoles.

Here the land part of the International Telegraph Line terminates—the wire leaping from mid-air into the Gulf of Mexico, to remain in old Neptune's bed, undisturbed by winds or waves, and only agitated by the most important events taking place in the world. There is but one house here of any size, built by the Government during the late war for commissary stores, and now occupied by the telegraph company. The musquitoes are so thick the clerks have an operating-room, partitioned off in the center of the building with thin domestic, containing their apparatus. These insects being of such gigantic proportions, and making such vigorous moves, netting would offer no obstruction to their blood-thirsty operations. They can jump through an ordinary net as easily as a frog breaks a spider-web. Here is a signal-station, the agent stopping in a tent. All that induces any of the operators to remain is the high wages they receive, which compensates them in a manner for the deprivations they suffer in the loss of society.

From this point large quantities of cattle are annually shipped to Cuba, the facilities for loading being superior to any on the coast.

CHAPTER XXII.

> The sun now rose upon the right—
>   Out of the sea came he,
> Still hid in mist, and on the left
>   Went down into the sea.

WE have been sailing near land since we left Tampa Bay, but now we are in water sixty fathoms deep, and past wading or swimming out, let what will happen to us. We leave Ten Thousand Islands and Cape Roman without landing, as they are uninhabited, and so lonely it seems God alone visits them. A night on the water alone with God and the stars, who can describe it? The sun has left his sentinel, Venus, soon to descend, with her evening charms, after delighting her admirers only a short while. The atmosphere at sea being so pure, this planet looks as though it had silver steps leading to its portals, upon which fancy might climb without wings, or the Muses catch inspiration without effort. What a grand sight to watch those far-off worlds, as they silently rise before our unobstructed vision, gemming the canopy of heaven with their grand glories for a few hours, and then retiring, while others take their places to dispel the darkness with their continuous rays!

We read of golden waves, and silver waves, but

phosphorescent waves exceed all. When the salt-waters of the Gulf are much agitated, and the vessel plows the "breaking foam," it appears surrounded with a sea of most brilliantly-lighted waves, extending far as the agitation reaches. The lead and line, when dropped in the water, is followed by a flash resembling electricity from the clouds. The luminous particles which compose this light are found floating in the water when it is dipped up in buckets, and adheres to the sides of any vessel in which the water is placed. It is produced from a species of animalcule called *arethusa plegica*, and when collected in large masses resembles flashes from an electric body, or balls of fire. Sailors regard the passing of these lights under the hull as ominous of adverse winds, and danger of being swamped from heavy seas. We are nearing Sand Key Light, seven miles from Key West, and sixty from Cape Sable. From Punta Rassa to this place nothing breaks the monotony of our movements but the sea-monsters darting under and around our vessel—sometimes a whale, spouting water; a dolphin, playing hide and seek with his companions—all enjoying the freedom of their native element near the surface, as though the great luminary and smooth waters had charms for these voiceless denizens of the deep as well as ourselves.

Here we see the Southern Cross just above the horizon, although many suppose it visible only south of the equator. The principal stars composing it are very bright and unmistakable as the constellation of Ursa Major. The coral formations in these waters are what make sailing dangerous and shipwrecks frequent. Many a vessel in sight of port, with golden prospects before them when they should anchor in the harbor, and reap a rich reward for their toil, has sunk or stranded here, and then been robbed by men unsympathizing as Hottentots. The early records of Key West say that it was inhabited by a different tribe of Indians from those on the mainland, in evidence of which human bones of a larger size than those belonging to the present race of red men have been discovered here in ancient fortifications and mounds. The Indians living on these islands and along the coast visited the mainland for the purpose of hunting, when a dispute arose between them, which resulted in war. The Indians on the mainland, being the most numerous, pursued those from the islands, until they were obliged to take refuge on Key West. Here they were compelled to make a stand, where they had a battle which nearly exterminated them—a few only escaping to Cuba in boats, and it is said were seen there during the early settlement of the island. As the conquerors did not remain to bury their enemies, the ground was strewn with bones; hence the Spanish name *Cayo Hueso*, rendered by the Americans Key West. It is called the "Gem of the Sea," and distant from Cuba ninety-seven miles—latitude, 24° 32' north.

The lands are of coral formation, consequently very sterile, although presenting a verdant appearance, caused by artificial fertilizers. Tropical fruits grow the entire year without interruption. Here we find the sugar-apple, alligator-pear, sapodilla-guava, limes, lemons, tamarinds, bananas, and plantain—the cocoa-nut tree, with her tessellated leaves, fanned by the breath of eternal spring-time, and ripening its refreshing fruits to nourish the thirsty residents, who would languish were they not supplied with the juices from fruits. The cocoa sheds its fruit when ripe, endangering the heads of those passing. Parents having children who play under the trees are constantly uneasy, as a full-grown cocoa-nut, falling forty feet, would nearly annihilate a child. They are gathered by means of long poles, attached to the end of which is an iron hook—sometimes with ladders and ropes.

To a person who has never visited this island it is almost impossible to imagine that only sixty-five miles from the mainland of Florida is a city so nearly in appearance resembling the Spanish dominions of the Old World—where hardly a sentence of English is heard, business transactions conducted in a foreign language, produce bought and sold, together with fruits from the adjacent islands cried in Spanish by the auctioneers. The wharf is a busy place. Here are vessels from various ports, with the ensigns of different nationalities—schooners, ships, and steamers, carrying from ten tons to many thousand, loaded principally with provisions and lumber.

The chief of the Seminoles is among the traders, from his Everglade home, inhabited by the deer, which leaves its "delicate foot-prints" on the margin of the streams, or the "slow-paced bear," which drinks and then leaps across the lagoons in search of prey, or to be captured by his savage enemies. Tiger Tail has come to market with sweet potatoes, pumpkins, cabbages, venison, honey, and buckskins. The honey is in one of nature's own receptacles—a deer-skin, taken from the animal whole, one of the fore-legs being used as a mouth for this natural bottle, containing the captured sweets. He does not cultivate the soil in person. His wives, together with his two negro women, who have never heard of the "Emancipation Act," raise the vegetables, while he and his warriors engage in combat with the untamed beasts that roam in their native wilds, or wage destruction upon the finny inhabitants of the dark, sluggish waters.

The population of Key West numbers seven or eight thousand. The streets indicate a populous place — the number of inhabitants having been greatly increased since the insurrectionary movements in Cuba. Cleanliness is a prevailing characteristic of the streets, there being no deposits of *débris* permitted. As there are few vehicles, and no sidewalks, pedestrians use the center of the street for promenading. The ladies do not wear covering for their heads, except a few, who use thin black lace veils: all wear their dresses trailing a long distance behind them, presenting a most *dolce far niente* appearance walking about in the golden sunlight, fearless of its burning rays as the eagle which gazes upon its dazzling splendors. Many new houses are in process of erection upon the island, and the march of improvement is making rapid strides among the vacant lots. The architectural style of these buildings is adapted only to the necessities of a tropical clime—a shelter from the heat and rain. They have no chimneys, consequently no bright, cheerful firesides, with their fanciful shapes described in the curling smoke, leaping flames, or expiring coals, about which poets love to write and dream Conchs were the original English settlers of this place, who came here from New Providence and the adjacent islands of the Bahama group. "Conch" is not, as many suppose, a term of contempt, but a local distinction. When the first regiment of colonial militia was organized at Nassau, they adopted the figure of a conch-shell in gold, with a blue field, for their regimental colors, thereby declaring the protection of their natural position; from this the term is applied more particularly to those from that city. They are a temperate, frugal, industrious class of persons, accustomed for generations to procuring a living from the sea; but many of them on this island have turned their talents in other directions, controlling a large part of the commercial business of the place. The greater portion of them are engaged in wrecking, sponging, or fishing for the Havana market, many owning fine vessels, and being men of respectability, although belonging to those classes whose names, to one not acquainted with them, appear an equivalent to buccaneers or pirates.

Wrecking was conducted for many years at Key West in a most ungenerous manner, with the old adage, "Freight is the mother of wages." Whole-

Petals Plucked from Sunny Climes. 319

some laws have since been enacted for the protection of the unfortunate owners who are stranded; also for compensation of wreckers who come to the rescue. Many of these accidents occurred from preconcerted action between the sailing-master and the wreckers, or carelessness in crossing the reefs, together with the changing currents. Now, a forfeiture of license for frauds in accounting for goods, embezzling, or bad sailing, has produced a stringency which precludes dishonesty.

The United States District Court for the Southern District of Florida holds its sessions here, and is constantly open for the adjudication of cases in Admiralty. Scarcely a week passes but its services are called for in deciding the claims of some salvor against property which has been rescued from peril. Over seven hundred cases in Admiralty have been heard and decided within the last year. Judge Locke, who wears the ermine gracefully, is the presiding official in these courts, dealing out justice according to the judicial requirements of the applicants.

The International Telegraph has its principal head-quarters at this point. Among the many facilities for the union of interests, and the transmission of news, this route is considered the most important. The survey was commenced from Jacksonville to Miami, from Miami to Key West, inside of the reef; afterward from Gainesville to Cape Roman found the route to Punta Rassa the best, following far as known the Washington meridian. The cable from Havana to Punta Rassa *via* Key West was laid in August and September, 1867. In 1869 a second was laid. During May, 1871, one of the working cables failed between Key West and Havana. In attempting to pick up the end in five hundred fathoms of water, they caught the working cable and broke it, after which the International Company had a dispatch-steamer running regularly, carrying messages to and from Havana. Several efforts have been made to pick up and repair the broken cable, spending over $150,000 without success. A new cable now, however, obviates all difficulties. This connects the United States with Cuba, running to all the West India Islands. There are also other cables laid along the south coast, by which means the United States Government communicates with its vessels of war and consular agents in the West Indies, also Spain and the colonies. The "Conchs" heretofore have not been interested in general education; but recently a desire for the knowledge of something besides reefs, keys, sponges, and turtles, has rapidly increased, while general intelligence and "book-learning" are now considered as among the essential requisites. The public-school system has been introduced with excellent results, and two flourishing schools are continued for ten months each year, where the common and higher English branches are taught, and Latin. There are other schools of lower grades, besides several private schools, and the Sisters of Mary and Joseph.

Cigar-making is extensively carried on in Key West, thus giving employment to hundreds of exiled Cubans. The establishment of Seidenberg & Co. is the largest in the city, employing six hundred operatives. Upon the first floor are seated eighty females, engaged in stripping tobacco from the stems. Here mother and daughter work side by side, the daughter earning five dollars per week on account of her more nimble fingers, and the mother three. The daughter puffs a delicate cigarette, while the mother smokes a huge cigar, it being considered a disgrace for the young ladies to use—only cigarettes. Two hundred and fifty men are occupied in one room upon the second floor, all forming those cylindrical tubes through which is to be drawn so much enjoyment in the present, while a perfect *abandon* of all anxiety for the future is felt. These operatives employ a reader, who reads aloud from newspapers printed in Spanish, while they are working, for which luxury each one bears his proportion of the expense. When any news favoring the cause of the insurgents is read, the house echoes with shouting and stamping of feet. The remaining laborers are employed in assorting and packing the cigars for market. Only the choicest tobacco is used in this factory—each first-class cigar made here being warranted equal to any Havana brand. Thirty-five thousand cigars are manufactured daily, consuming thirty thousand pounds of tobacco monthly. The most amusing sight of all is to see these workmen drink water: it is contained in a kind of earthenware vessel which they call a "monkey-jug," made from a porous earth obtained in Cuba, and shaped something like our American gallon-jug, only the orifice is on the side. These jugs are suspended by a cord in some cool place, where the air circulates most freely, a slight percolation constantly taking place from the water inside. When they drink, the vessel is raised to an angle of twelve degrees above their mouths, and, after setting their heads back on their shoulders, with their mouths wide open, they turn the water down their throats, without any perceptible act of deglutition. After they have finished drinking, they close their mouths with a peculiar "umph," at the same instant exclaiming *"Ave Maria!"* to indicate the act is finished, and returning thanks to the Virgin for the privilege.

The cochineal insect is indigenous here, and is found upon the *Cactus opuntia*. In appearance it resembles a tiny ball of cotton attached to the plant; but, on being pressed, a scarlet fluid exudes, which is the life-blood of the insect, produced by the colored cactus-fruit upon which it feeds. This furnishes the beautiful dye of commerce, for which it yields its life.

Sponging is another important branch of industry centering here—the entire coast being composed of reefs and keys. The numerous sounds and inlets abound with sponges of an excellent quality, one class of which has won an established reputation in commerce, being known as the "Florida Sheep's-wool." The cheaper qualities are the "Yellow-boat," "Glove," and "Grass"—the last two being the kinds used particularly by the American Sponge Company, very extensively, in the manufacture of upholstery. Many tons of these sponges are shipped annually for that purpose. This product of the sea is found growing in water from ten to twenty-five feet deep. It is detached from the bottom, and brought to the surface by means of iron hooks fastened to long poles. When first found they are solid, and resemble a jelly-fish. They are then thrown on the deck of the vessel until they die, when they are beaten, washed and wrung out, leaving, as it were, but the skeleton of the original article—this constitutes the sponge of commerce. The amount realized from the sale of sponges gathered and sold at this place, yearly, exceeds one hundred thousand dollars, which costs nothing but the labor of gathering, cleaning, drying, and packing. The rough life these people lead does not make them appear as though they had been fed on mountain-dew, or nurtured on the wings of love; however, they are kind-hearted creatures to their friends.

Key West being the entrance to the Gulf of Mexico, it is well fortified by Fort Taylor, thus using every precautionary measure for its protection. Here stands this fort, with its frowning battlements, upon which are mounted the most formidable artillery used in modern warfare. The construction of this fortress was commenced in 1845, and it now protects an important harbor and naval depot. It is built entirely of brick, with two tiers of casemates, and one in barbette. The most exposed and weaker parts of the walls have been strengthened by making them twelve feet thick—solid masonry—which has prepared it to resist any thing but a continued bombardment. There are now mounted for action one hundred and thirty guns; three three-hundred-pound Parrot, thirty ten-inch Rodman, and two fifteen-inch Rodman guns have been placed in position on the barbette tier, in the form of a trapezoid, with bastions at the four angles. The remaining guns are of smaller caliber. The defenses have recently been increased by two land-batteries, exterior to the fort, commanding the western and northern approaches. One of these batteries mounts twelve, and the other seventeen, fifteen-inch Rodman guns, with magazine traverses. There are also two towers, with casemated batteries, in which are twelve ten-inch guns, to prevent boats landing. All these works are under the supervision of a most accomplished engineer—Colonel Blount, of the United States Navy.

Key West is also fortified with a Curiosity Shop, in the event of an attack from curious people in search of something to gratify their tastes in that direction. The name was adopted from Dickens—the difference being that one existed in the imagination of the writer, and the other is a reality. Here we find the *fac-simile* of the veritable clock which ticked the hours away, mentioned by Dickens. In appearance, it has size enough to be a "bed by night and clock by day." May it not have the misfortune of its namesake to time the sheriff's entrance, and keep tally to the auctioneer's hammer! Also a pair of andirons, said to have been used by George Washington. Imagine him and Martha in front of these grotesquely-patterned fire-supporters, the gen-

eral just returned from Yorktown, Virginia, and
relating the news of the capitulation of Lord Cornwallis. The sword of General La Fayette graces
the rubbish of this curious medley, instead of a
brave general's side; pistols a century old; cannon
of four-pound caliber, which were used anciently to
announce the Fourth of July; flint-lock muskets,
of Revolutionary fame; flags that have floated over
victories, and surrendered with defeat; silver coin
made in 1799; gold coins of 1803, together with
coins of all nations and dates, from Julius Cæsar
down; Russian signal-lanterns; a model of the
steamer Sumter; a bird-cage, Gothic style, containing nearly five thousand pieces; turbot-skins;
horned frogs; chicken-spurs, the property of a warrior never beaten; skeletons of sea-horses and sea-cows; sharks' teeth; books two hundred years old;
a parrot speaking Spanish; the devil in a bottle, besides a thousand other things too numerous to mention. When you survey all you can see, and don't
discover what you want, call for the owner, John
Dixon, who is more of a curiosity than any thing
his shop contains. He is a genuine Greek, born on
an island of Greece. Is it an impossibility that the
same crimson current which courses through his
veins may not have descended from Solon or Socrates? Perhaps his ancestors might have been among
the brave number who opposed Xerxes in his efforts
to subjugate Greece—may be a relative of the cynic
philosopher, Diogenes, whom he more nearly resembles in his peculiarity of independence and contempt
for common things in general, or any thing which is

not extremely old or curious. He has for a sign a full-sized ship's figure-head of the Virgin Mary, on which the gilding is much defaced, it having been washed ashore many years since from the wreck of a Spanish ship.

CHAPTER XXIII.

Soft the shadows slowly creeping
  Through thy dim and spectral pines;
Pure thy lakelets, calmly sleeping,
  Save a few light rippling lines,
When the water-lilies move,
And fairies chant their early love.

AFTER leaving the St. John's River and traveling westward, we approach what is called Middle Florida, fanned by the gulf breezes, and protected from the northern blasts with heavily-timbered lands. The first town of importance through which we pass is Lake City, fifty-four miles from Jacksonville, this being the county-site of Columbia. This city was named from the beautiful sheets of water by which it is surrounded, where naiads and fairies could come to dwell, and lovers do resort to whisper. These lakes are distinguished by the names of De Soto, Isabella, Hamburg, and Indian. The waters abound in fish, while alligators are daily seen, plunging about in them, as happy persons are rowing in light canoes upon their smooth surfaces. The population numbers about two thousand. It has eight churches of various denominations, a creditable court-house, and three hotels—the Thrasher House being the most agreeable and roomy in every respect. A weekly paper is published here. It is also the terminus of the submarine telegraph, and contains an "old probability" office. The citizens are refined, intelligent, and friendly toward strangers.

The architectural style of dwellings in Lake City are more truly Southern summer-residences than any other city in the State. They are built up from the ground, with a wide passage separating the two apartments—the floors being made of pine plank, which the combined efforts of woolly artisans with shucks and sand manage to keep invitingly clean. This style of structure, to an artistic taste accustomed to the modern cottages, dormer-windows, and pigeon-like apartments, covered with slate-roofing, thus converting the upper story into a fiery furnace after a hot day, suggests a kind of rudeness, characteristic of the locality, which is quite the reverse: like the whispering gallery, they are made to catch the slightest agitation in the atmosphere, it being duplicated, within this long receptacle, into a most grateful breeze. However, here, as in other tropical climes, it is observable at noon, each day, that the softest winds are lulled to rest, when a general stagnation steals over every thing, from the house-dog to the tallest pine, with its green plumes kissing the midday sunbeams; but after the day commences to decline, a breeze springs up, which enables us to appreciate its presence and survive better during its absence. The soil in the vicinity is fertile—thus enabling the inhabitants to engage largely in the culture of early vegetables and strawberries, which are shipped North. Oranges weighing a pound are not uncommon. Many invalids find the atmosphere of Middle Florida exceedingly conducive to their comfort, as the temperature is less variable than many other points in the State, and for this reason fine for asthmatics, who say they can sleep all night here, while in most other places day dawns with no perceptible transition into a somnambulic state. The strong scent of resin from the pineries, after we leave Lake City, is quite perceptible, it being a fine lotion for weak lungs. Malaria visits some portions of Middle Florida, where, anterior to the recent immigration, it was almost unknown. This has been the history of all newly-settled countries—the decomposition of much vegetable matter producing chills and fever.

West of the Suwanee is usually designated as Middle Florida, it formerly being more densely populated than now, evidence of which is furnished us from the ruins of buildings. For many years a jealousy existed between the settlers of East and Middle Florida, in regard to their landed estates. The commissioners in East Florida were more interested in selling than settling the country—the lands in Middle Florida being considered superior for agricultural purposes, and the titles good, which is more than can be said of all the East Florida lands even now.

Some have looked upon this portion of the State as a kind of lottery, the value of which would be realized after the drawing had occurred, while there are those who come to stay, and when they find the visionary ideal dream in which they have indulged is not realized to its fullest extent, then they are ready to say, "We have been inveigled here." These should remember, "There is no spot which combines every desirable characteristic, with the absence of all that is undesirable. It not unfrequently occurs in life, when unhappy spirits, chained in diseased bodies, which cause them to settle into a sullen melancholy, whose presence would discolor the face of all nature, and tinge with a sickly hue the flowers of paradise, or the glories of the eternal throne."

After leaving Lake City, the next town of note before Tallahassee is Monticello, one hundred and thirty-eight miles from Jacksonville, situated at the terminus of the Monticello Branch Road, four miles distant from the main line. It is the county-site of Jefferson, surrounded by fertile farming-lands, this being the head-center of traffic for a large extent of country. A population of not quite two thousand inhabitants reside here, with every appearance of content. Good churches of various creeds are well attended when open for service. The former wealth of this county cannot fail to impress visitors who happen here on Saturday, when great numbers of freedmen, formerly owned in this locality, from habit leave their work and come to town for a holiday. They go marching about the streets orderly as a procession, or file into the stores until there is scarcely standing-room, getting on very quietly until late in the day, when some of them, while under the influence of badly-adulterated whisky, become noisy and obstreperous — thus ending their day's frolic in the lock-up. A good hotel is kept here, where bountiful tables, well patronized by appreciative guests, daily attest its merits.

After sunset the frogs will be found the most demonstrative inhabitants, at times, on the route to Tallahassee, which, strange as it may seem, almost drown the car-whistle with their croakings—thus reminding us that happiness, with some creatures, is not yet extinct in the world. Probably no place

MIDDLE FLORIDA MUSICIANS!

can furnish a greater variety of frogs belonging to the same genera, among which we find the bell-frog, speckled frog, green frog, some of them being nine inches in length, measuring from the tip of the nose to the terminus of the hind-foot toe, which amphibious quadruped, when full grown, will weigh over a pound. The bell-frog is supposed to have been named from the voice, which is fancied to be exactly like a loud cow-bell. The following statement from a naturalist on frogs will give us an idea of his impressions: "The bell-frogs being very numerous, and uttering their voices in companies, or by large districts, when one begins another answers—thus the sound is caught and repeated from one to another a great distance, causing a surprising noise for a few minutes, rising and sinking with the winds, then nearly dying away, or is softly kept up by distant districts—thus the noise is repeated continually, and as one becomes familiarized to it, the sound is not unmusical, though at first, to strangers, it seems clamorous and disgusting." Englishmen sent them home, more than a century since, as Florida curiosities. The following is taken from the record of one's arrival: "The pretty frog came safe and well, being now very brisk. Some more of these innocent creatures would not be amiss. But pray send no more mud-turtles—one is enough. The water-turtle is a pretty species—came very well." Here is what Bartram wrote about our dirt-daubers, which build their nests in the crevices and corners of every neglected tenement: "I have sent you a variety of the clay cells which the singing wasps built last summer, that I consider very curious." All tourists have made Florida a point of scientific research, in various ways, for many years.

> Far in ether, stars above thee
>   Ever beam with purest light;
> Birds of richest music love thee,
>   Flowers than Eden's hues more bright;
> And love, young love, so fresh and fair,
> Fills with his breath thy gentle air.

Tallahassee cannot be pointed out as the place where great literary works first saw the light—such as the Commentaries of Cæsar, or where Cicero rounded his periods, or Horace gave the last polish to his Odes, or Milton conceived the grand idea of his Paradise Lost; but from its choice shrubbery the golden oriole trills its melody, and the mocking-bird warbles in the sky and on the house-tops, or fills the air with song from neighboring trees at night.

De Soto, after discovering Espiritu Santo Bay in 1539, came through the country to an Indian village called Auhayca, now the site of Tallahassee—the name signifying "old field"—where, with his army, he spent the winter. While here he secured the services of an Indian guide, who proved to be "a most elaborate liar on various occasions," in regard to gold-mines which only existed in his imagination. The Spanish soldiers accompanying De Soto were encased with armor, which creates a wonder in the minds of all who have seen it, how they were able to march through a country offering so many obstacles, with such an immense weight on their bodies. One winter's sojourn in this locality was sufficient to satisfy De Soto that no treasures could be discovered hidden away in the hills around Tallahassee; consequently, the following spring he left.

Tallahassee is situated in the center of the State. The first house erected after the cession of Florida to the United States was in 1824, the Legislature convening there the following winter. In 1825 it became an incorporated town. In January, 1826, the corner-stone of the State-house was laid, and one wing of the building erected during the year. The growth of this town, after its incorporation, equaled any in America. It was situated on an eminence which commanded a fine view of the surrounding country, with picturesque scenery, and on a stream of water fed by bold springs. The State Governor speaks of its early American settlement as a place "where the emigrants crowded, the rising walls of the capitol being the attraction"—"the woods yielding their shade to the saw, and their silence to the hammer."—the vicinity rapidly changing from native forest-land to well-cultured fields.

On account of being situated twenty miles from the Gulf, the prospect of its ever becoming an important commercial point for business was not anticipated. The surface of the country around Tallahassee changes from the flat lands of Florida to an elevated and undulating country, and from sand to red clay. A gentleman-passenger who had retired to sleep during the night where the land was level, on awaking in the morning, and noticing the change in the surface of the country, called out to the conductor, "Look here, boss! haven't you got this machine turned around, and taking us back into Georgia?"

Persons perusing the following will be enabled to see the material of which Governors' messages were made, in the Executive Department, during the Indian war in Florida:

"*Tallahassee*, February, 1840.— Since you have been in session a number of our people — among them a woman and children — have literally been

butchered by the Indians, many of whom occupy
the swamps and other fastnesses of Florida, from
the Appalachicola to the Suwanee, while in East
Florida the murder of the mail-carriers within a few
miles of St. Augustine, proves how unavailing has
been every effort to restrain the enemy in that quarter. Indeed, it would seem that the cruelties of
these wild beasts — for so they deserve to be regarded, and their thirst for blood places them beyond the pale of humanity — are becoming more
and more audacious, their deeds of horror rather
accumulating than diminishing. They venture to
assail houses, and appear in our public roads in the
open day; they press beyond military posts to per-
petrate their murderous purposes, starting up like
evil spirits when least expected to appear, destroying the brave, virtuous, and innocent. Their numbers can only be conjectured: it is not doubted that
some sent to the West have returned; but be the
number great or small, every thicket and deep forest
is liable to be occupied by them; they elude pursuit; driving them from one place to another is
impracticable, as within the past year they have
planted near military posts. Our situation is desperate; men sleep with arms under their pillows; a
sense of insecurity accompanies the traveler in his
journey on the highway; every neighborhood has
its tale of blood, and those in authority look around
them in pain and distress, because they are powerless to afford an adequate remedy for the evils
thronging around them in every direction. This is
no **exaggerated** picture of our present condition.

Romance lags far behind the realities we daily witness, and it becomes our duty to consider what shall be done for the relief of the country. No occasion has yet occurred for testing the usefulness of the dogs brought from Cuba. It is still believed, however, that they may be used with effect; and why should they not be used? If robbers and assassins assail us, may we not defend our property and our lives, even with bloodhounds? Shall we look upon our ruined dwellings—upon the murdered and mangled remains of men, women, and children—then meekly say, 'The poor Indians have done this; we must be merciful and humane to them; we will not set our dogs upon them. O no! that would be more horrible than these butcheries.' Those who are safe from Indian alarms, in distant cities and peaceful lands, may indulge in gentle strains of humanity and brotherly love—were they dwellers in the log-cabins of Florida, they would attune their notes to harsher measures. Let these men, in whose hearts there is such a gush of the milk of human kindness, consider attentively a scene recently exhibited upon the Appalachicola. Mr. Harlan's dwelling was burned, and his family murdered, in the afternoon of the 20th of last January. Mr. H. was absent, and the following is from an eye-witness: 'On arriving at the spot, we found every house reduced to ashes—at the kitchen-door the bones of a human being, nearly consumed. Upon examination, we saw the track of the moccasin. On the trail, not far off, we saw articles of clothing, potatoes, and papers, dropped. Soon afterward about twenty-one armed persons arrived from Iola, among them Mr. Harlan, who in a wretched state of feeling proceeded to examine the burnt bones, believing them to be the remains of his wife and son, whose knife he found amongst them. One of the men, in searching behind a tree about one hundred yards distant, called out, "Come here, Harlan! here is your wife." Joy sprang to my bosom as I ran to see the dead come to life; but there was Mrs. H., with her throat cut, a ball shot through her arm, one in her back, and a fatal shot through her head. Her youngest son, eight years of age, lay near her side, with his skull fractured by a pine-knot. He exhibited signs of life, and I had him carried to a shelter, water given him, and his feet, which were cold, bathed in warm water; slight hopes are entertained of his recovery. Had you witnessed the heart-rending sight—the father embracing and calling his son, "Buddie! Buddie!" with the solemn sound of parental affection, sunk to the lowest ebb of dejection, and then running to his wife, with his arms around her, shrieking, "My wife! my wife!"—I know your feelings would have given way, as mine did. I had heretofore felt a sympathy for these savages, but my mind then assumed a stern fortitude foreign to its nature, and I felt not like leaving an Indian foot to make a track in the desolation they had caused.' Who can witness such atrocities without admitting it to be lawful to use blood-hounds against such hell-hounds? It is my solemn conviction that the only mode of conquering the Indians is to hunt and pursue them, in every direction, with a competent force of brave and hardy men devoted to the service, and generously rewarded by their country for the perils and privations they endure. R. R. REED, *Governor.*"

"GENUINE BLOOD-HOUNDS.—*Tallahassee*, January, 1840. The blood-hounds, with their twenty leashmen, have arrived from Cuba, and are landed in Tallahassee. They have been tried, and follow a trail with accuracy twenty-four hours old."

"*November*, 1840.—On last Monday one more of these animals arrived from Cuba. He is mouse-colored, strong-limbed, and with a nose that could scent the trail of a butterfly. He was whelped and raised in the mountains on one of the sugar-estates, and is known to be of the best pedigree. His propensities for blood are of the highest order, having slain and eaten two negroes entire, besides one-third of his own tail—a mistake which has somewhat marred the beauty of the graceful appendage. Two Indians were caught in the neighborhood of Tallahassee with the blood-hounds. They, no doubt, have not had a fair trial."

The poor blood-hounds were ridiculed on every side—read the following: "Seven peace-hounds left Black Creek for the Ocklawaha on Thursday."

The whole country at this time was in a state of trepidation; the feelings of the people could not be described; but an order was republished which had been issued during a similar exigence, in the year 1764, by William Penn:

"BOUNTIES ON HEADS.—Whereas the Six Nations of Indians have been at amity with Great Britain, but now, having broken their most solemn treaties," etc., "for the scalps of every male Indian, above the age of ten years, produced as evidence of their having been killed, one hundred and thirty-four pieces of eight, or Spanish dollars. God save the king!"

Some amusing incidents are related in connection with the Florida war, as well as those not so very ludicrous. In Tallahassee they were subjected to frequent scares from the Indians. The approach of the foe was to be announced by the ringing of the Planter's Hotel bell, the only one then in the town. This bell was the tocsin for an instant assembling in the market-house of the Home Guards, let the hour be midnight or noonday. These Guards held a convocation every night at 8 o'clock, to receive orders and be detailed for duty — each sentry to stand guard four hours, being at his post by 9 o'clock, and a corporal appointed to go on a tour of inspection, to see if the men on duty were not asleep. Each object that moved or breathed was magnified into a wily Indian. A gentle William-goat could not graze in peace after nightfall without being in danger of receiving a bullet for his temerity. The following incident is the most stupendous scare of the war: Mr. T. Barnard, being on duty one night, saw a dark object approaching, which, from its cautious tread, he was certain could be nothing but the long-looked-for and much-dreaded savage. According to a previous arrangement, the enemy's approach was to be announced by the firing of a gun. He fired, then followed a terrible tramping, which he considered unmistakable evidence of a retreating foe. When day dawned the citizens were in a state of great fear, which was much increased after a moccasin track had been seen marked with blood. Armed men patroled the streets, while women, children, and servants, were rushing, in the wildest confusion, to the State-house, as the only place of safety. When the truth became known, and the facts explained, everybody had a good laugh over their fright. The sentinel, having lost his shoe the night before in his encounter with a goat, returned to search for it, when he saw the track made by himself in the soft sand while in his sock-feet, the impress resembling an Indian moccasin, the ground having been stained by a lame mule in cropping the herbage.

Besides the constant state of alarm in which the citizens lived, there were tragic occurrences happening in their midst too true for jesting, and too shocking for sensitive nerves to hear related, without shuddering for their own safety. We find this one, among others, bearing date January 22, 1842:

"On Sabbath a band of Indians, supposed to number thirty-five or forty, attacked two wagons loaded with salt, whisky, etc. They stripped the negroes of their clothes, except their shirts, taking every thing from the wagons. Whilst engaged in their work of plunder, Mr. Solomon Mather rode up, when the Indians pursued him, firing five or six times, wounding him slightly in the shoulder. In the meanwhile the negroes put whip to their mules and escaped. This affair took place at the Flat Branch, on the Magnolia Road, about fourteen miles from Tallahassee, near the residence of Mr. J. H. Byrd."

The lands lying around Tallahassee evince marks of taste, having been inclosed by the Cherokee rose, which forms a fine hedge, whose evergreen foliage lives all the year, while its snow-white blooms crown it with beauty in their season. The magnolia grandiflora, queen of the forest, with its smooth, glossy, green leaves and immense flowers, grows without culture; while the sickly, dwarfed oleander and cape jasmine, of Northern culture, is used here to shade the avenues of pleasure-grounds. The fine brick residences, of extensive proportions, add testimony in confirmation of its past prosperity. Churches of different denominations, substantially built, speak for the morals of the community, while the kind-hearted people can speak for themselves. The installation of the first Presbyterian minister in Florida took place on the 28th of March, 1841, in Tallahassee. Although many persons have lived here who were, no doubt, celebrated, in their own estimation, yet none of royal blood has ever been traced with certainty but Colonel Napoleon Achilles Murat, whose last residence was about one and a quarter miles from town—the place now being owned by ex-Governor Bloxham. He was a son of Joachin Murat, King of Naples, who was shot in Castle Pizzo for insurrection. When required to meet his doom, a chair was offered him, and a bandage for his eyes, to which he replied, "I have braved death long enough now to face it with my eyes open and standing." Achilles Murat, with his mother, came to America in 1821, settling near Monticello, Florida, naming his plantation Liponia, but afterward retired to Bellevue, near Tallahassee, where he lived several years, with his wife, who was a relative of General Washington. Having witnessed the vanity of pomp and display in his youth, he assumed very little style during the last days of his life. A short time previous to his death, the bishop from Mobile made a visit to Tallahassee, he being apprised of the fact that upon a certain day Colonel Murat would make him a visit, dressed in his robes of State, to receive princely blood, as officers of both Church and State are entitled to a certain amount of consideration from each other, in keeping with the dignity of their position. The morning advanced until nearly midday, with no appearance of Colonel Murat, when finally a thin, bony old horse, with a thinner, more shadowy old man on his back, was seen approaching the avenue to Dr. Barnard's residence, accompanied by his body-guard, a very black negro named William, who was walking. The colonel was attired in country home-spun, known as brown jean, in Southern vernacular. His hat and shoes both indicated marks of wear, while age had robbed him of all desire for pageant, as the day had dawned when priests and princes were alike, in his estimation. After a long interview with the bishop, Colonel Murat retired to his rural home. Mrs. Murat was much annoyed with the irregularities and eccentricities of his conduct during the last years of his life, which, in common people, would

have been termed craziness, but in royalty, or
genius, it is relieved with a border, and termed peculiarities, or idiosyncrasies. Many amusing anecdotes are related in regard to the common people
who lived near Colonel Murat. Having been informed that a king's son lived not far from them, they
often went purposely to see him, relating the object
of their mission as soon as they arrived. When
they found the colonel dressed in country clothes
and cowhide boots, his rustic visitors were unable
to discover any apparent marks of royalty, and invariably, after entering his domains, asked to see
Prince Murat. On being told that he was the man,
they would respond, "Why, you don't look like a
king." Colonel Murat died suddenly, April 15,
1847, on his plantation, and was buried near Tallahassee, in the cemetery, without ceremony. His
wife survived him several years, living in town.

In Leon county, sixteen miles from Tallahassee,
Mrs. Mary E. Bryan, one of our best Southern
writers, was born. She was the daughter of Major
John D. Edwards, one of Florida's first and most
honored members of the Legislature. Her father,
being a man of wealth, wished every thing in keeping with his position; for this reason he reared a
mansion, known as "Castle Folly," on account of
its immense size and costly material, the wood-
work inside being of solid mahogany, its location
almost isolated from all other residences even of
humbler pretensions. Her early life was not spent
in a wicked city, where the morning papers teemed
with sad tales from the depths of depravity, fished

up from the slums of vice, which keep high carnival under cover of darkness, hiding their foul forms in the glare of sunlight, and holding their fetid breaths when the dewy freshness of morn wafts its odors on the new-born day; but where the gay pomegranate glistened, with its pendant flaming bells, and the snowy tribute of cape jasmine, loaded with its perfume of overpowering sweetness; while, like a shower of heavenly blessings upon every zephyr, was borne the fragrant treasures from the orange-blooms, gentle as a pure spirit in a holy trance, which leaves our minds in a blissful, dreamy state, as though we were floating in mid-air. Her home was one around which childhood loves to linger, environed by primeval forests, where the placid waters of the land-locked lakes reflected the fitful shadows of the towering pine, or wide-spreading live-oak, where the graceful vine hung in festoons, or the gray, swaying moss hung from its drooping limbs, and danced to the music of the soft-sighing winds, as they swept through the evergreen foliage and died away in the dense thickets. It was when, from one of those crystal lakes, she saw the evening star, as it stole through the gleam of the dying day, reflecting its pale, trembling light alone, that she felt the throbbings of unrest stirring the depths of her soul. In these placid waters the virgin lilies bathed their beautiful heads, while the golden gates of day were closed, and the voices of night whispered themselves to rest on the balmy breezes. Many of her happy girlhood-days were spent in "Salubrity," the home of her aunt, Mrs. Julia McBride, whose many Christian virtues and philanthropic acts still live in the memory of those who knew her. However, the longings of her thirsty soul were never satisfied until she had held communion with the spirits of those whose grand thoughts she found recorded in the volumes of her uncle's library. It was while reading from the pages of classic lore, or the more enchanting strains of poetic rhythm, during the absence of Colonel R. B. Houghton, her mother's brother, that a happiness unknown to coarser clay was realized, and her spirit found repose. Mrs. Bryan is one of those flexible, trusting spirits, equal to any emergency in the struggles of life, which sorrows, however deep, may bend for a time, but, like the flower too much freighted with rain-drops, only bows its head until the sunshine comes with its welcome beams to kiss away the moisture, when its bright petals open, and again it looks heavenward. A presence diffuses itself in all her writings sweet as the perfume by which she was surrounded in her own lovely home, pure as the heavenly-lustered orbs that overshadowed her pathway. At twilight, when

> Venus, robed in clouds of rosy hue,
> Flings from her golden urn the vesper dew,

she rises on the wings of fancy, and the rich, mellow streams of thought flow freely, buoyed up by visions which shadow no tumultuous cares, or sounds of woe, the fires of genius burning brightly on the altar of thought, as the blazing meteor which, at

God's command, guided the wandering Israelites
to their promised rest. The versatility of talent
she exemplifies so remarkably is really wonderful,
while she may be classed among that gifted number who, in spite of prejudice or criticism, fastens
the minds of her readers, taking them captive at
will. She is now the *star* of the *Sunny South*, published in Atlanta, Georgia, from whose columns her
pure thoughts are sparkling every week, to illumine
the home circles of many Southern families. All
her writings are characterized by that chaste freshness of originality, that earnestness of feeling, emanating from a truly pure heart, which have been
poetically and truthfully described in the following
lines:

> Bryan! hers the words that glisten,
> Opal gems of sunlit rain!
> So much the woman, you may listen,
> Heart-beats pulsing in her brain!

About sixteen miles from Tallahassee has been
discovered another of those remarkable springs
found in Florida. In order to reach it, we take the
St. Mark's train, sending a carriage in advance to
meet us at Oil Station, six miles from Wakulla
Spring. Few objects of interest are seen on the
way; but here, where the woodman's ax and the
turpentine still are not silencing the sounds that
have echoed through the airy forms of these forest-trees, which have stood as sentinels for centuries, we can listen to the music among the pines—
a strange, unearthly moaning, vibrating movement
of lanceolate leaves, the sound produced being at-

tributable to the loose manner in which they are
attached to the bark of their stems.

> You may as well forbid the mountain-pines
> To wag their high tops, and to make no noise
> When they are fretted with the gusts of heaven.

The spring is reached at last, where we can feast
our eyes with its pearly hues and changing, shim-
mering waters, dancing in the sunlight. It is about
seventy-five yards wide and sixty in length, its greatest depth being one hundred and twenty-five feet.
The water is blue limestone, but looks green from
reflection, and very cold, said to produce a numbing
effect upon those who try bathing in its transparent
depths. It is the head-waters of Wakulla River,
forming a bold stream at a single bound from its
subterranean home. The following description of
this spring, by a writer who visited it over a hundred years since, will give the reader a more correct
idea than any recently-published articles, although
many who visit it now think they have the keys of
all knowledge in delineation, and a vast amount of
wisdom will cease to illumine the world when their
existence is extinguished:

"This charming nympheum is the product of
primitive nature, not to be imitated, much less
equaled, by the united effort of human power and
ingenuity. As we approach it by water the mind
of the inquiring traveler is previously entertained,
and gradually led on to a greater discovery—first,
by a view of the sublime dark grove, lifted up on
shore by a range or curved chain of hills at a short

distance from the lively green verge of the river on the east banks, as we gently descend floating fields of the nymphea in lumbo, with vistas of the liveoak, which cover a bay or cove of the river opposite the circular woodland hills. It is amazing and almost incredible what troops and bands of fish and other watery inhabitants are now in sight, all peaceable, and in what a variety of gay colors and forms, constantly ascending and descending, roving and figuring among one another, yet every tribe associating separately. We now ascended the crystal stream, the current swift; we entered the grand fountain, the expansive circular basin, the source of which rises from under the base of the high woodland hills, near half encircling it, the ebullition being astonishing and continual, though its greatest force or fury intermits regularly for the space of thirty seconds of time—the ebullition is perpendicular, upward, from a vast rugged orifice, through a bed of rocks a great depth below the common surface of the basin, throwing up small particles or pieces of white shells, which subside with the waters at the moment of intermission, gently settling down about the orifice, forming a vast funnel. After those moments when the waters rush upward the surface of the basin is greatly swollen, and then it is impossible to keep the boat, or any other floating vessel, over the fountain; but the ebullition quickly subsides — yet, before the surface becomes quite even, the waters rise again, and so on perpetually. The basin is mostly circular, sending out a constant stream into the river fifteen yards wide, and ten or twelve in depth. The basin and stream are both peopled with prodigious numbers and variety of fish and other animals, as the alligator, manatee, or sea-cow, in the winter season: part of the skeleton of one, which the Indians had killed last winter, lay upon the banks of the spring; the grinding teeth were about an inch in diameter, the ribs eighteen inches in length, and two inches and a half in thickness, bending with a gentle curve—these bones being esteemed equal to ivory. The flesh of this creature is considered wholesome and pleasant food. The hills and groves environing this admirable fountain afford amusing subjects of inquiry."

At this time it was called by the Indians Manatee Spring.

Twenty miles west from Tallahassee on the railroad we arrive at the town of Quincy, situated on a hill commanding a fine view of the surrounding country. The population numbers about twelve hundred; the houses are built of wood, painted very white, which gives them a refreshingly-neat appearance. The citizens have a welcome for visitors which is home-like. On account of the undulating surface of the lands a diversity of scenery is found here not seen in other portions of the State — numerous streams, which flow with a musical cadence from their homes under the hillsides, running far away to swell the streams that are soon lost in the great gulf below them. During the early settlement of this portion of the State cotton-planters were not attracted to it, as the broken lands were not as

favorable for its culture as the more level—for this
reason : we find an independent class of settlers who
raised what they consumed, never buying meat or
bread from abroad. Those who have tried growing
cotton were successful, the long staple producing
very well. Before the war Cuban tobacco was cultivated with a rich reward, as they supplied dealers
from New York, also a foreign commerce. The
scuppernong grape is commencing to receive attention, for which enterprise the adaptability of the soil
is favorable—wine having been produced here equal
to the famous California product.

Twenty miles west from Quincy, situated on a
river of the same name, is the town of Chattahoochee, this being the terminus of the Mobile & Pensacola Railroad. The State Penitentiary is located
here, but the convicts are farmed out. The rough
condition of the railroad has been a barrier to travelers going there much since the war; but a prospective change, when effected, will make it more
agreeable for all parties concerned. The region of
country below contains some fine orange groves.
Those shipping oranges say they prefer Columbus
or Atlanta to New York, on account of more rapid
transit and less expense.

The route through Eufaula and Montgomery,
North, taking a steamer at Chattahoochee, is becoming more popular every year, as tourists are fond of
variety. A line of stages connecting Quincy with
Bainbridge, a short day's ride, enables those desirous of locating to see the country to better advantage. The overland passage appears robbed of its

monotony by the long hedges of Cherokee rose-
bushes, crowned with their pink and white petals,
which lend a brilliancy to the country through
which we pass, not soon forgotten. Yards, gardens,
and avenues, dressed in floral robes, are frequent;
but miles of roses who can describe! The lands on
our route are diversified, also the timber, but the
yellow pine predominates.

Bainbridge is at last reached, when a wonder fills our
minds. What made this town so big? It was once
the center of trade for a large, fertile country around
the Appalachicola River, this place being the medium of communication where fine steamers could be
seen loading the wealth of a prosperous people. The
war came and robbed them of their labor—the railroads then turned the tide of communication in another direction, leaving them above high-water
mark. However, the trade is now reviving, as proof
of which it is a favorite resort for commercial tourists of all kinds.

Thomasville, about twenty-five miles west of Bainbridge, is a pleasantly-located town, where visitors
can be accommodated with most of the modern improvements in hotel-keeping; also palatable, tooth-
some dishes, which finely-pampered appetites require.
The Mitchell House makes Florida tourists a specialty, this being a point where they can come to in-
hale the healing, balsamic odors from the surrounding pines, and refresh their perishing natures with
the good things raised from the best of lands by a
most excellent people. The Gulf House has an old
and honored reputation for fine fare, also a kind-

hearted host, who anticipates the wishes of his guests. The town is substantially built—laid out tastefully and elegantly—the dwellings being models of neatness and culture, embowered in emerald retreats of perennial foliage, which, seen from the cleanly sidewalks, cause many strangers to sigh for a welcome which they could not expect while far from home. The yards teem with flowers in midwinter, blooming from rockeries, mounds, and twining vines, where occasionally an artificial fountain, with its sparkling silver veil, echoes its cooling voice as it falls into the reservoir below. Trade is brisk here—large stores, well filled with costly goods, find ready purchasers from a well-to-do people living in the town and country. The town can boast two newspapers and one periodical—indeed, we have heard it whispered that some of these writers think they have the keys of knowledge on certain facts pertaining to agriculture, etc. A female college has been established in this vicinity for many years, which has sent from its halls of learning many creditable scholars, who are now filling important stations in the spheres allotted them. Several tall-spired churches of various denominations have been erected in this community, where gifted heralds of the cross proclaim the glad tidings of salvation to large, attentive audiences, which is a good key-note to their spiritual condition. Thomas county made an exhibit of its former wealth immediately after the war, in a representation entirely of colored members—the white population being so greatly in the minority they could not elect one of their own color.

But the ambition of colored politicians in this section is visibly on the decline, most of them having such thick lips, and, like Moses, "slow of speech," they now prefer speaking by proxy in the legislative halls. Thomasville has no facilities for water communication with the outside world, but, being located on the Atlantic and Gulf Road, should therewith be content, as a few hours' ride will furnish them an opportunity of taking a steamship for England or any part of the world.

As we leave Thomasville going east, we pass through the wire-grass country of South Georgia, containing towns, if not of great importance in external appearance, contain the best of citizens with the kindest of hearts. Quitman comes first, with its plank walks, shaded by live-oaks, its home-like hotels, and hospitable, law-abiding people. A paper is published here which would do credit to a place of more note. A cotton factory is in operation; indeed, every thing in the town moves around with the vivacity of college-students out taking their first holiday. Valadosta is the last town of any size before Savannah. The soil looks so sandy, the grass so wiry, the pine-trees so tall, with such mournful music sighing through their airy forms, awakened by the slightest zephyr that passes, which produces a kind of melancholy in our minds as to whether we should have any thing to eat or not if we stopped. All fear of starving can be dispelled, as the country in the vicinity produces well, which can be proven by the immense sweet potatoes on which we are fed, and the well-grown sugar-cane for sale, from which sirup and sugar are made. A very newsy weekly is published in Valadosta, the editor being the author of the Okafinokee Swamp Expedition, which trip has furnished him with material to fill out many an interesting column in his inimitable paper. On public days such a crowd comes to town, the mystery is, Where do they all stay? In pleasant homes scattered through the country, where happy hearts beat with much less struggling than those in higher life, boasting greater attainments.

A trip on this road at night is not unpleasant, as so many light-wood fires are burning bright near the track, kept up by the lumbermen and signals for the switch-tenders. Collisions from sudden curves never occur on this road, it being built so much on the air-line that the head-light can be seen in many places over twenty miles distant. Frequent repetition with familiar surroundings blunts the accuracy of the perceptive powers; but the first time I traveled this route it appeared like a kind of unreal scene, as the moon shone with an apparently unwonted brilliancy that changed all external objects into an epitome of the "Arabian Nights' Entertainment."

CHAPTER XXIV.

MANY other places may possess their varied amusements, but Pensacola can be reckoned among the cities having attractions sufficient to render a sojourn very agreeable. It is here the sun gently declines, leaving a train of glory behind. The clouds then loom up lazily in serried ranks, and the breakers from Fort Pickens roar in the distance, like unhappy spirits of strife, when a swift breeze comes from the surrounding forest, and warns the sails to come to their moorings for safety. While we are impressed with the thought that this has been a spot around which many historic records have clustered —that the days of its departed grandeur are forever gone—still an invisible presence encircles it, which appears sacred, while a solemn echo comes from the remembrance of past pomp, that reminds us of the perishable nature of all earthly pageant.

Pensacola was first explored, and a settlement commenced, by De Luna, in 1561, who landed on the bay as it now appears, naming it Santa Maria. This feeble colony, on account of hardships, became discouraged and returned home. The first permanent settlement was made by the French in 1691.

The present city of Pensacola stands on a bay of the same name, which contains a safe and capacious harbor, where vessels drawing twenty-one feet of water can enter at low-tide, and find shelter and fine facilities for anchorage. It was formerly named Ochusa, from a tribe of Indians who lived here. Where the city is now built it is fine siliceous sand, supported by an understratum of clay, which is of varied colors. This clay is manufactured into brick, from which some of the houses are built, also pottery, and the monkey-jug, or water-cooler, so much used among the Spaniards in Cuba and Key West. The present plan of the city was laid out by the English in 1763, after they took possession of it. The streets cross each other at right angles, making squares of two hundred and fifty by four hundred feet, with a bay front of nearly a thousand feet. Many fine buildings were erected at that time— among which might be mentioned Casa Blanca, the residence of the Governor. The gardens attached to the city lots, the strong fortifications, and the edifices of different designs which graced the streets and squares, were the pride of Florida. The Governor rode in his chariot, making pleasure-trips to his landed estates, six miles from town, escorted by his postilions, and surrounded by his companions in authority, thus deporting himself like a genuine scion of royalty. During these days of prosperity Pensacola was attacked and conquered by the Spaniards under Count Galvez, in 1781. The place was defended by General Campbell; but the magazine at Fort St. Michael being blown up, resistance was useless, and the town surrendered. This event marked the commencement of its decline; the work of twenty years was blighted, and the prosperity of the city waned. When Florida was ceded by Spain to the United States, St. Augustine in East Florida, and Pensacola in West Florida, were the only towns of any importance in the State. The country about the city was poor, the good lands of the interior being occupied by the Indians; besides, the original settlers were not as enterprising a class of people as those in East Florida. The above considerations, together with disease, fierce contests with foes of other nations, its inaccessibility, and no large watercourse connecting it with the interior fertile cottonlands, are the combined reasons why Pensacola is not equal in size to any town on the Gulf.

Fort Don Carlos de Barrancas—the word Barrancas signifying *broken ground*—was so named on account of the rugged appearance of the site on which the fort stands. The first fortification is supposed to have been built by a commander named Auriola, in 1687, as a defense against the French. It was a square, with bastions, situated near the site of the present Fort Barrancas. What remains of the ancient fort was built by the Spaniards—it being a tetragon, with salient angles at each corner, and formerly had a tower one story higher than the curtains, which served as a point for reconnoisance. It has an outer scarp, or glacis, surrounded by a barbette twenty-two feet wide. It contains an embrasure, the firing being done from the loop-holes and parapets with flank defenses. The barbette is overgrown with weeds and cactus, all armed with projectiles more to be dreaded than any other weapons of warfare in position here now. A deep dry-well is visible near one corner of this barbette, supposed to contain the buried treasure of the Spanish Governor, and for which it is said he ordered three of his men to be killed to prevent their divulging the secret. No guns are mounted on the parapet but two Rodmans of one hundred pounds caliber. The entrance to the old fort is through a scarp gallery several hundred feet in length. At the terminus are three arched rooms, the arches constructed without nails, from native pine boards, the grooves being fitted to each other. Here was the Governor's chamber for council, the ordnance department, and barracks. The materials employed for the walls were only brick and mortar, both in the old part built by the Spaniards, and the new constructed by the Americans. From the form and thickness of one part of the fort, it is supposed to contain a dungeon, but no efforts have yet been made at excavation, to explore its hidden secrets. The entire fortress, both ancient and modern, is surrounded by a dry moat, the main entrance having a portcullis.

The present fortification of Fort Pickens was built in 1830. It is situated on a strip of land fifty miles in length, and only one-half mile in width, called Santa Rosa Island. This ground has been the scene of various conflicts during its early settlement, of which we have a record for nearly two centuries. The contests between the Spanish and French were always severe, the victor destroying the forts and devastating everything within reach—which accounts for the disappearance of the ancient landmarks.

Fort St. Michael and Fort St. Bernard were other works of defense built in the rear of Pensacola, but designed originally to protect the town and harbor, and also to serve as a safeguard against the Indians. The principal fort, St. Michael, was attacked in 1781 by Don Galvez, when a bomb-shell struck the eastern glacis of Fort St. Bernard, and, in rebounding, blew up the magazine, destroying the principal redoubt, which compelled the garrison to surrender by capitulation.

It is but little more than half a century since Colonel Nichols, a British officer, came to Pensacola, and issued his proclamation, offering a reward of ten dollars each for the scalps of colonists. However, the career of this bold usurper and ambitious adventurer was soon terminated by General Andrew Jackson and his brave men, who marched into the town, then defended by a fleet of seven armed vessels, three forts, block-houses, and batteries of cannon defending the streets. The center column of Jackson's army was composed of regulars, and presented as formidable a front in appearance and strength as the ancient Grecian phalanx. The battery was stormed by Captain Laval, who, although severely wounded in the engagement, afterward recovered from his injuries. The Spanish Governor, Marinquez, met the American forces, and begged that quarter might be shown the citizens. To this proposition General Jackson acceded, protecting individual property as far as possible. At this time Fort Barrancas was blown up, all the guns being spiked but two. This enabled Colonel Nichols to escape with his fleet. All the fortifications being now destroyed, General Jackson left, after holding the place two days. The Spaniards then commenced building Fort Barrancas, when Colonel Nichols proffered his aid; but the Governor refused, telling him his friend General Jackson would do better.

In 1818 Jackson received information that the Spanish would not permit supplies for his troops to ascend the Escambia Bay, while the Indians were supplied from Spanish stores. The Governor warned General Jackson against making an attack, saying he would be opposed by all their forces; but, with his usual go-ahead zeal, he marched in and took possession of the town without opposition. The Governor had taken refuge in Fort Barrancas, whither Jackson proceeded during the night, and commenced erecting breastworks. The Spaniards fired upon them, which was returned with good effect by a howitzer. In a few hours the fortress surrendered, and, by the terms of capitulation, the garrison was sent to Havana. Soon after Jackson came into possession of Pensacola, he was told that the Spanish Governor, Callavea, was in the act of sending papers relating to land-titles away to Cuba, in direct violation of the treaty. General Jackson demanded these documents, and, upon being refused, he ordered Callavea into the calaboose, but released him on the papers and boxes being returned. Afterward several of the Spanish officers, suffering from outraged feelings, sent a remonstrance to General Jackson on account of this unheard-of indignity toward the Spanish Governor. For this movement

twelve of them were banished, thus establishing the
authority of Old Hickory beyond a doubt. The old
camping-ground of General Jackson is still pointed
out as historic ground. It was situated on what was
known as the Blakely Road, which passes the old
sites of St. Bernard and St. Michael.

Pensacola once contained a plaza, which was an
ornament to the city and the admiration of all visitors.
The grounds were in a high state of cultivation,
where flourished the orange, lemon, olive,
banana, guava, and Japan plum-trees, ornamented
with pleasure-walks, where the gay cavaliers promenaded
and made love to the beautiful señoritas,
where the delicate nonpareil displayed her painted
plumage, the gay mocking-bird sang her songs of
joy, and the humming-bird sipped honey from nectarine
flowers, whose petals perfumed the air with
fragrance. But stern want, whose decrees are as
unyielding as the Medean and Persian edicts, was
staring the Spanish garrison in the face at this time,
and the commissary stores being exhausted, the
largest portion of these beautiful grounds were sold
to furnish the army with supplies. All that remain
vacant are the extremities of the old plaza, which
form two squares, known as Ferdinand and Seville,
that are as barren of ornament as the municipality
of means to appropriate for its embellishment.

It is singular that a country whose original settlers
were celebrated for their chivalric daring and romance
should preserve no vestige of their former
characteristics or peculiar nationalities. It is thus
with the present appearance of Pensacola. One

portion indicates the march of improvement, while the other, near the bay, has a faded appearance of weather-beaten plank, except out on the wharves, where may be seen many new buildings used for various purposes connected with shipping operations. There are no fine blocks of elegant stores among the number, but many one-story houses, some containing two, and a few three.

The old houses now standing are decidedly of Spanish architecture, with the long verandas in front, accessible only at the ends by steps, the jail-like double doors being made of wood, riveted with iron bolts, not designed to look beautiful, but to be very substantial, or resist a siege of small arms. The dormer-windows are frequent, while a few old roofs are covered with tiles. A wide, substantial walk is built through a portion of the town, stopping at no place in particular, but a favorite promenade for ungallant sailors, where they reel like drunken elephants, seven abreast, sometimes elbowing other pedestrians into the marsh. A few brick pavements have been made, but the bricks present their edges and ends uppermost as often as the flat sides, while sand-wading, in many places, is the only alternative, street-crossings being an unknown luxury. Pensacola is almost the only town in Florida where no fabled fount is supposed or represented to exist, whose waters heal all infirmities and rejuvenate declining years—where no tales are told of elysian elegance to fascinate visitors into their houses of entertainment, or invitations given to take strolls on the beach, and breathe the sea-air with its breezy

freshness, always warranted more beneficial to the
invalid than all other atmospheres that ever fanned
a hectic cheek, or had been inhaled by consumptives, that will enable them to recover sooner than
any other influence by which they could be surrounded. The principal employment of persons
here is maritime, from the fisherman, who spreads
his tiny sail and dances on the waves, fearless as a
sea-gull, in his bateau that looks only a speck on
the waters deep and wide, to the full-rigged ship
which plows the angry waves, and "thrills the wan-
derers of that trackless way." The prosperity of
this place is dependent upon the adventitious condition of the changing and fluctuating trade in other
places, together with a demand for their only commodity—lumber. No appearance of pomp in fine
turnouts is seen—no matched spans or grand phae-
tons. Those who ride go in one-horse vehicles,
which move noiseless as the midnight assassin,
through sandy streets of an uncertain depth. A
majority of the people are both plain and practical
in all their movements. Their misfortunes seem to
have soured them, embittered their lives and saddened their hearts, making them sullen, while others
converse as though they had settled into an apathetic
despair, mingled with clouds of darkness, and peopled by phantoms of pinching want. This season
business is terribly dull. Stevedores without employment are as abundant as plank without purchasers, and uneasy as a mullet out of water. The profession of gambling is well filled, which can be seen
by the glare of diamonds and watch-chains on sus-

picious-looking men, with no vocation but to come
here and prey on the hard earnings of poor, unsuspecting sailors. A ship coming in the bay creates
as much commotion as a big wreck in Key West.
Unoccupied boarding-houses for workingmen are
numerous. What is lacking in accommodations
can be supplied in charges. There are one or two
boarding-houses, called hotels, designed for the better class, charging three dollars *per diem*. Visitors,
or persons of leisure, do not often come here to remain long, consequently no grand hotels for their
entertainment. But there is one attractive feature
in Pensacola even now, and that is the bountiful
supply of rich pine. "What a beautiful fire!" we
hear every one exclaim, as the boarders take their
seats in the recently-illumined parlor after supper,
when all without is dark and drear. Then they
give us wood in our rooms, where any one can
make a fire in a minute, when sickness drives away
sleep. How it lights up the pale faces of our friends,
as though the glow of health had suddenly wafted
her magic touch over them, dispelling the pallor of
disease and marks of suffering! How it softens the
gloom of night and diverts our minds with its cheerful blaze, as it permeates every thing like the visit
of a bright messenger, when the winds howl as
if they were demons from the realms of Erebus!
What a cheerful greeting it gives us from the old
fire-place, with its burnished massive fender and
brass andirons! Then it flashes and faints on the
wall, or in the corners, hides in the curtains, to be
replaced with another flash, followed by a report

like the distant roar of artillery. The Indians loved to dance around its bright light in celebrating their fiendish orgies, or howl their rude songs of welcome for the return of harvest, as the well-filled ears of maize roasted before their camp-fires of resinous wood. With what lingering looks of sadness did they see the last spark waft its tiny ray into the heavens, as the morning dawned and the nightshades fled away, on which they were to bid farewell to the happy home of their birth they loved so well, and relinquished with such reluctance, when they thought of the grand old *lightwood* fires which had glistened away the gloom of dense forests, or rendered powerless the malaria of swamps, and kept the approach of wild beasts at bay!

All day constantly before our eyes is Ferdinand Park, which manifests visible signs of a decline. Four old Spanish pieces of artillery are planted in the center, and fastened with ropes, to balance the standard-bearer of a powerful nation, and place in position, high in mid-air, a pole, on which to unfurl the ensign of a great country. The park-inclosure is dropping down as quietly as a rose-leaf in May. Here stock ramble to graze with their bells on, presenting a rural landscape of rustic life, and tired, bony old horses stray for sustenance; hogs, with very thin sides and bristling backs, root about for herbage, or roam through the streets, gathering, with eager haste, any thing like a decayed apple or potato, of which some kind-hearted huckster has relieved his stall or cart; while the cows wander in front of dry-goods stores, trying to replenish the well-springs of vitality with stray wisps of straw, bits of paper, or pasteboard, which have been swept out. The lacteals of the poor brutes receive a small amount of sustenance from such an uncertain source of nutritive matter—for that cause nearly everybody in this region uses condensed milk. The William-goats promenade with unrestrained freedom, giving concerts with their loud treble voices, while the refrain is echoed by the young ones, resembling the cries of a baby. If these sights and sounds, with variations, do not always give pleasure to visitors, they break the monotony and furnish a variety.

This town boasts a very substantially-built market-house, the material used being brick. Only a few of the stalls are occupied, as the produce is hauled about the streets in huckster-carts and sold, or kept in stores by provision-dealers. During the lenten season, fishermen go out soon in the morning, and, when they are successful, return singing, by which means those wishing supplies can come and buy; but when they have taken nothing, they row silently to shore, looking as though they had toiled in vain. Sometimes the fish are too large to be conveyed whole, when they are cut up and sold by the pound. Frequently two fishermen are seen carrying a fish suspended between them, a portion of it trailing on the ground. What a triumphal entry they make! What a proud look they have, as they find themselves "the observed of all observers!" They could not be induced to change places with the governor. Smaller fish are carried in tubs, swung on a pole suspended

between the shoulders of two very brawny-looking
men. They announce their approach by blowing a
large ox-horn, which is heard in the streets on Sabbath as other days. The minister, invoking a blessing on his worshiping congregation, is liable to have
the interludes filled with the echo of trafficking trumpets. Common fish are cheap. The pompano and
red snapper, being the choicest, are held at high
prices. Beef and venison are plentiful, but the
beef is of rather a sinuous texture. Most vegetables would flourish here during the winter, but,
from a lack of enterprise, they are not much cultivated. The only dream of prosperity ever indulged
by these people is ships coming in from foreign parts
for lumber. One thousand feet from low-water mark
in Pensacola Bay is found fresh water, which is obtained by boring or driving iron tubing through the
salt water and several strata of earthy deposit. The
upper stratum is composed of sediment, the second of quicksand, the third of blue clay, the fourth
of coral, the fifth of gravel, in which is found pure
freestone water, unadulterated with foreign matter,
and clear as crystal. This water is obtained at a
distance of seventy feet below the surface of the
earth. These fresh-water fountains are of recent
date, having made their appearance among other
improvements which are constantly being discovered in this progressive age. These wells possess
many advantages over the old custom of hauling
water from the springs in barrels through the
streets by hand, which furnished a means of support for those employed to deliver water on the

wharves for sale to ships, it being their only vocation. The barrel was prepared by inserting a piece of wood outside the head, in which were placed iron pivots. Two iron rings were attached to the end of a rope that revolved upon these pivots. The water-hauler threw the rope over his head and shoulders, then marched along with the speed of an Andalusian pony—the barrel following like a cart. A few water-barrels are to be seen rolling about the streets now, but it constitutes only a precarious means of support to the "drawers of water," when compared with the past.

Porpoises — belonging to the class *Phocæna* — abound in the vicinity of Pensacola. They range with other monsters of the deep, sporting in the shoals, and playing around vessels anchored near the wharf, at times approaching the shore gentle as cats. They are said to take their prey by strategy, darting under an unsuspecting school of fish, and with one stroke of their tail stunning enough to furnish them a fine repast. The astonished fish is soon swallowed by the porpoise, without perceiving the change that has taken place in his existence, when, instead of searching for nourishment himself, he has commenced to sustain another. Porpoise-oil contains the same properties as sperm, but porpoises are not killed here, they being very harmless, and are said to act as a protection against sharks to persons who bathe or fall in the bay.

The culture of tropical fruits has never been a success in Pensacola, since so much of the timber has been destroyed. The few orange-trees here have a stinted appearance in comparison with those in other portions of the State. A constant strife is going on between the north-west and trade-winds, the former sweeping down from the Rocky Mountains, freighted with frost, which destroys the fruit and foliage of the orange-trees. However, a suitably-arranged grove, with only a southern exposure, would bear under ordinary treatment. Persons now owning bearing-trees say they have been killed down three or four times The winds are too rude for the banana—it grows here only in summer, with winter sheltering.

A little stream, called the "Washing Bayou," winds its way through the town, gurgling as it rushes among the bushes, and noiseless as the flight of an arrow when it glides over the snowy sands. Tiny fishes live here unmolested, sporting in its clear waters, until they leave the quiet home of their birth and go into the great sea, where many of them are eaten by the big fishes that are constantly on the alert. Besides the poetry in this musical stream, there is much practical utility connected with its presence, as it subserves the purpose of city laundry, where most of the soiled clothes are cleansed. More than a hundred barefooted women can be seen at one time here, with short dresses, standing in the water, their wide tables in front of them, battling with unclean linen. After the garments are washed in this water, which is said to possess peculiar cleansing properties, they are spread on the green grass and bleached. No ordinary agitation affects the stream, or makes the waters turbid, while it re-

mains clear and warm during the whole winter.
Here Spanish, French, Creole, and *L'Africane*, all
combine together, working in harmony. Patrons to
this branch of industry can have their apparel ma-
nipulated in such language as they prefer, or whatever shade of color belonging to the human species
they hold in the highest esteem. Hunters resort to
this portion of the country, where they spend weeks
in camping and killing game. Every one who comes
to Florida imagines the supply of fish and flesh inexhaustible, notwithstanding the heavy drafts that
are made every year. Complaint was made by the
Indians of game becoming scarce within certain localities during 1835, and the wonder is now that any
thing remains to be killed.

Ribaut, while describing his travels in this State,
mentions the waters of a great river as "boiling and
roaring through the multitudes of all kinds of fishes." Thoughtless persons having heretofore caused
such a wanton destruction of deer, laws have now
been passed for their protection. The method
adopted mostly among hunters of running game
with hounds until exhausted, has a tendency to
terrify the poor scared animals, thus making them
more shy, and retire farther into the fastnesses of a
country to a place of greater security. Old hunters
say they would just as soon eat a piece of dog-meat
as deer killed when overheated. The Indians resorted usually to still-hunting, taking the stag-heads
and hides to conceal themselves, and, with the use
of their imitative powers, induced many a thoughtless animal to approach them, when the well-aimed

arrow secured the victim as a prize to their skill. The murderous guns now in use will soon destroy all the wild game in Florida, as in other old-settled places, when stories of the nimble-footed fawn, that gamboled with the calves and cattle while feeding side by side, will be related as tales of the past history of this country. Several times since Pensacola has been in possession of the United States, that malignant form of disease known as yellow fever has made it some unwelcome visits. During 1822 it was terribly fatal, taking whole families and streets. It spread at this time like wild-fire, and was supposed to have originated from a cargo of spoiled cod-fish! In 1853, 1866, 1873, and 1874, it returned. Its last appearance—in 1874—took them all by surprise. It commenced in August, and continued until December. Different reasons have been assigned for its last calamitous visit in 1874. Some say it was brought from Cuba; others, that it was occasioned by the removal of a hospital from the navy-yard, where yellow-fever patients had been sick. It was no respecter of persons. The boatman in his bateau, the guard at his post of duty, the soldier on drill, the colonel commanding, or the commodore with his floating navy, all yielded to the fell destroyer. Three Sisters of Mercy died in one day, the highest number of deaths during the space of twenty-four hours in the city being ten. Persons who occupied houses that had been closed and vacant during the fever, sickened and died after the disease had subsided. The quarantine regulations now are inefficient, while filth from every street and alley lies undisturbed, thus inviting disease. The municipal authority is now thoroughly Africanized, consisting of mayor, aldermen, and police force, while a negro postmaster bears unblushingly the honors and emoluments connected with his position. Before the last war (1861) many orange and fig-trees were growing in private yards; but the Federal forces destroyed nearly all of them, together with many of the houses and fences. The squares—most of them — are now grown with opopanax, yapon, scrub, and live-oak, while the twining grape-vine, climbing above its evergreen foliage, produces a nearer resemblance to hummocks than the surroundings of civilization which characterize refined life.

Perdido, or Lost Bay (so called from the bar at its entrance being closed by quicksands), is thirty miles in length—the main tributary of this bay being a river of the same name, whose banks are covered with inexhaustible pine forests. This river furnishes excellent communication with Perdido Bay, upon which are built several fine lumber-mills. These mills are a recent enterprise, having been in operation only about four years, thus giving employment to many operatives, and furnishing an article of commerce to every part of the world. During the winter of 1873 one hundred and fifty square-rigged vessels could be counted loading with lumber, also spars over one hundred feet in length, to assist in floating ships from every part of the world. Wild game is abundant in the forests about Perdido River, such as panthers, deer, black bears, wild ducks, and turkeys.

Escambia Bay is another of the beautiful sheets of water by which Pensacola is surrounded. It is eleven miles in length, and four in width. It has a tributary of the same name, which courses through rich hummock-lands, until it reaches the clear waters of the bay. The lagoons and marshes that lie near this river abound in the remarkable amphibious animals called alligators. The roaring of these creatures in spring-time is deafening. They are of slow growth, but eventually attain an immense size—a full-grown one being fifteen or twenty feet in length, with an upper jaw, which moves, three feet long, the lower jaw remaining stationary. Their skin is impenetrable to a ball, the whole body being covered with a kind of horny plates, but the head and under the fore-legs is vulnerable, and not bullet-proof. They build nests in the form of a cone, three or four feet high, and five feet at the base. They commence these nests by making a floor upon which they deposit a layer of eggs, then a stratum of mortar, seven or eight inches in thickness, then another layer of eggs, until the whole superstructure is completed. They are said to deposit over one hundred eggs in a nest. These are hatched by the heat of the sun, together with the fermentation of vegetable matter produced in the hillock. The mother-alligator watches near during the period of incubation, and has been known to attack persons who interrupted her embryo. When her young are hatched she marches them out like a hen with her brood, leading and protecting them, while they whine and bark around her like young puppies. Their mother belongs to the cannibal species, eating up her young in their babyhood, which precludes but few of them attaining their full size. They move rapidly in water, although clumsy on land, wallowing in mud-holes like a hog.

There are five churches in Pensacola for public worship—Presbyterian, Methodist, Baptist, Roman Catholic, and Protestant Episcopal. No other town in the State can produce so large a number of old members as the Catholics in Pensacola. During the early history of this country the devotees of this faith made pilgrimages to the Convent of St. Helena, a religious order established by the Franciscan Friars. They spent weeks in performing the journey to St. Helena, in St. Augustine. It was to them what Jerusalem was to the Jews, or Mecca to the Mohammedans—their holy city, their revered shrine for worship, where the *"Ego te absolvo"* gave solace to the troubled conscience, and comfort to the sin-burdened heart.

The demand for schools in the Pensacola market has hitherto been limited; consequently the quality is not always of a superior kind. The free schools are avoided by all who can do better. They are now under the supervision of George W. Lindsley, county superintendent. He belongs to the African class of humanity, and acquired his education while acting in the capacity of body-servant to Judge Plantz, of the First Judicial Circuit of the State of Florida. Four schools are supported here by the public fund—two for each sex and color. The one for white boys is taught by an old man who has evidently lost his temper and outlived his days of usefulness as an instructor. His pupils looked spiritless and indifferent to any thing like mental effort. They recited badly, and appeared stupid. The female department is taught by a lady of youthful and humble appearance. The timid little girls came to recite with the admonition, "Now, if you don't know this lesson, I will switch you." Numerous rods were lying about the floor, as though warfare had been progressing, with weapons of very ancient date, recommended by Solomon. The rooms occupied for the schools are two apartments in an old private residence, the building in about as waning a condition as the popularity of the institutions. Fifty children, all told, comprise the number in this metamorphic condition. The citizens say they are taxed beyond endurance to support schools, but never know what becomes of the money. Perhaps they never try to ascertain in the right place, or at the proper time, what disposition is made of the funds. Two colored schools here are supported by the public funds. The building in which they are are taught was erected for the purpose—light, airy, and roomy—more provision being made for the education of the colored race, all over the State of Florida, than for the white. The great difficulty now is to have the negroes brought up to the standard of appreciation. Only a few can be prevailed upon to attend the schools provided for them, and they belong mostly to a class of numskulls whose heads are so thick that an idea could not get into their brains unless it was shot there with bullet-force. Both the male and female schools have colored teachers. The copy-books were handed me for inspection. Here is a specimen of the copies: "Virtue is the persute," etc.; "Do a good child tell stories?" The chirography was unmistakably original and inimitable, but the spelling was not from Webster, nor the grammar of Butler's approval. The pupils were in tolerable order—the secret of which, no doubt, lay on the table, in the form of a huge leather strap—that relic of barbarism revived—and a piece of plank for the more incorrigible cases.

The Catholics have two separate schools for the education of males and females, besides a mixed school for colored children. The female school, containing about sixty pupils, is under the direction of the Dominican sisterhood. The children all arose and bowed politely when I visited them; but no opportunity was offered for ascertaining their method of teaching, or the proficiency of the young ladies, although I politely asked to hear them recite. These wimpled teachers veil their movements also. The Catholic school for boys is under the tutorage of an old gentleman of the Irish style, whose looks resemble the description given by Goldsmith of the "village school-master." The children were talking aloud, caricaturing on slates, and exhibiting it to their companions, whistling, and shaking their fists behind the teacher's back, these employments being the principal exercises during my visit. The teacher was energetic in his efforts to preserve order and hear the recitation. He placed one offender on his knees for penance, and struck some more of them with an immense ferule which he carried in his hand. When the din and confusion drowned his voice, he resorted to jingling a bell and screaming "Silence!" He evidently had a bigger contract than he knew how to manage. The Pensacola boys are said to be very bad, whether from association or the original sin born in them, has not been decided —probably a combination of both.

Let no one imagine that in all this dross there is no pure gold. Mrs. Scott, wife of the present rector of Christ Church, teaches a parochial school, patronized by all, irrespective of creeds or forms of worship, being always open to inspection for the friends of education. The pupils exhibited a thoroughly progressive knowledge of all the branches which they were studying. This school is governed by a direct appeal to the elevating and moral qualities of the heart and soul, which lead the mind upward, thus restraining their natural impulses. The pupils evinced a surprising familiarity with blank verse, by transposing and parsing lines from Paradise Lost— the work of that colossal mind whose soul, illumined with inward light, soared beyond the star-lit domes of space, to commune with chaos and the great mysteries of its unrevealed depths.

CHAPTER XXV.

TO walk upon the beach and see the bright golden waves rolling beneath our feet on a sunny day, and hear the gentle surge moving like the soft cadence of dying echoes, creates in us a desire to be wafted into other climes, where we can see untold wonders, and be regaled with something new to feast our senses. It was from the promptings of a restless spirit that we embarked on a fine sailing vessel for Cuba as the morning tide was receding. An escort of sea-gulls, with their white pinions and unwearied wings, followed us far from land, as messengers of peace, wishing us a *bon voyage*.

We soon commenced to feel contented in our isolated moving habitation, with its strong canvas buoying us up in the breeze, like a huge bird of passage in its aërial flight, and we looked out on the "waste of waters" as only an untried experiment, about which very fearful things had been said, but not so bad after all. While we were watching for new wonders, the sun sunk into the sea, and the stars came out one by one from their canopied homes in the blue sky, the larger, brighter ones rising first, like the stronger spirits in life, which leave their beds with the dawn, to make preparation for the feebler little footsteps that now open their eyes tim-

PORTUGUESE MAN-OF-WAR.

idly on the great world into whose magnitude and
mysteries they are just entering. The monotony
of a sea-voyage is always broken by the daily revo-
lutions of the earth on its axis, if not more stirring
events. Our second morning at sea the winds and
waves were hushed quietly as the calm which pervades a sinner's sensibilities when the angel of peace
first speaks comfort to his sin-burdened soul. Our
sails hang loosely as a gambler's conscience, while
the surge swings us around freely without taking
us forward. The spars squeak, twist, and groan, as
though in distress at our condition. The sailors are
busy tying up ropes, mending sails, and climbing
about in the rigging like cats. A kind of sea-
polyp, *Physalia utriculus*, or Portuguese men-of-war,
which move passively on the surface of the water,
have been in sight all day, with their bubble sails
of rainbow hue, supported by emerald hulls, with
their anchors steadying them in their swift, uncertain voyage over the sea. How fragile and ethereal
they look! These little creatures only trim their
sails in fine weather, but when the wind blows they
descend into more quiet quarters. The sailors look
with suspicion upon their movements, as they say
their appearance indicates foul weather. They present a concave surface above the water of three or
four inches that is guided by purple rudder-bands,
which descend about two feet into the sea. These
filaments are very poisonous when handled — the
sailors, while in bathing, being sometimes stung by
them, which is accompanied with a very painful
burning sensation, like the nettle. They may be

classed among the many other curious and wonderful beings that inhabit the great deep, of which we know but little or nothing.

The old tars have been singing to-day,

> Mackerel skies and mares' tails
> Make lofty ships take in their sails.

Last night, as we were retiring, the sky was banking up black clouds, which indicates a nor'-wester. Now, when we look across the crested surface of the deep, dark sea, our thoughts are too sacred for bosom-confidants, and too serious to bear much sounding by ourselves, being shadowed by forebodings, not unmixed with melancholy, when we think on the fate of many who have sailed before us. Our rough old captain, who commences his day's duties before sunrise by giving the steward a cursing for what he has done or left undone, as a kind of recreation when he is drinking his coffee, has been giving his oracle, the barometer, some mysterious looks all day.

The sun has gone to her home in the west, and we now feel that a night of darkness—it may be destruction—has drawn her deepest shadows over us. The wind is blowing a gale, above which is heard at the wheel aft the same cross old captain screaming his orders through the storm-trumpet, which sound dismal as death: "Lower the foresail!" "Take down the topsails!" "Put out a watch!" "Let her drive before the wind!" Old Neptune has commenced his fearful frolics in earnest, rolling the white caps in every direction. The vessel has commenced plunging through a trackless pathway, while the sea boils like a pot.

> And whistling o'er the bending mast,
> Loud sings the fresh'ning blast.

It is when messengers from the realms of King Storm are abroad in the land—when the sea rises at his call, and the winds meet from their hidden coverts, to exercise their strength and contend for victory—that the poetry of sailing on deep water vanishes, and we look stern reality in the face, and feel the danger of being swallowed up, which overbalances all the adventurous spirit for sight-seeing.

The tempest which was now shrieking and howling in its fury bore no resemblance to any thing disagreeable enough by which a comparison could be made, except falling clods upon the coffin of an only friend and protector, or the click of a pistol that sends a soul into eternity. In imagination I could hear the gnashing teeth of fighting fiends, in reality the roaring thunders, threatening with their stunning proximity, while torrents of water were descending—thus bringing a yawning abyss before us under circumstances of appalling nearness, when the sea, in its fiercest moments of fury, has often plunged the ship and mariners into an open chasm, with cold, cruel waves for a winding-sheet, while the winds sung a requiem. It was an epoch in the history of my life, when I felt my grasp upon tangible substance weakening, and at any moment that I might be hurled into that shoreless, fathomless depth, from whose uncertain soundings and unexplored domains there would be no return. As the wind increased the sea commenced washing over decks, which movement would not be mistaken for purling streams meandering through green lawns and "flowery meads." The pantry contributed its share to the general din—the plates all falling down, the tumblers, cups, and bowls, never ceasing to roll over—at the same instant a big wave coming in washed the tinware from the galley, while the cook-stove, with its legs nailed fast to the floor, remained a mute spectator. The chairs gathered in groups and skated across the oil-cloth at each lurch of the vessel. Nothing revealed those terrible troughs in the sea before us but the vivid lightning, which also enabled the sailors to see the spars, and keep a portion of the sails reefed. The deep waters resembled liquid mountains piled in pyramidal forms, dissolving like dew with every wind that passed, at which we were not dismayed while the vessel could leap over them. Meanwhile there came a heavy sea that shipped down the gangway and commenced washing out the cabin—at the same instant a gust extinguished the binnacle lamp. As a precautionary movement, to keep the mast from being jerked out, the foresheet was secured. The beating billows, rattling chains, and inky darkness, combined, were suggestive of a passage contained in the Epistle of Jude, where the fallen spirits are spoken of as "reserved in everlasting chains under darkness unto the judgment of the great day." The hour of midnight, when the clock shall have struck twelve, is looked for with much solicitude during a gale. How the men worked! How the

pumps groaned! Our vessel was only a toy with
which the waves were playing as a pastime, whose
angry waves we were willing to appease by a promise that we would come no more, if only spared from
a dive beneath their surface.' Storms and adversity
are both great levelers in life. How all social barriers of distinction vanish as we feel our dependence
upon the roughest tar that climbs the mast at sea,
or rolls like a swine in the gutter on shore! With
what eagerness we notice every movement of the
officers in times of peril, and listen for their foot-
fall on deck, or the rustle of their rough-weather
tarpaulins, as they walk through the cabin, watching to see that fire does not break out from the
lamps, or spontaneous combustion take place in the
hold, which then severs the last gleam of hope, except that which awaits us beyond a grave in the
sea when we sink beneath the waves, where all is
peace! While we are certain a commander, in
times of danger, will do all in his power to save the
lives of those on board, is it not then we should lean
on that One all-powerful to aid, and feel for the Hand
"that holds the waters in its hollow?" A little after
midnight the captain, worn out with his duties, "had
turned in." The winds seemed to lull, and except
very heavy seas, a fair prospect of peace overshadowed us. However, we soon afterward found we
had been nursing a delusion, as a little before 2 A.M.
the breeze freshened; it came in gusts, increasing in severity, and the vessel becoming unmanageable, the captain was called on deck, while
the mate rushed forward to take in sail. He had

proceeded but a short distance when a heavy sea struck the ship, and the bow-hatches were five feet under water, with the mate swimming against the deck-railings, and the trumpet-toned commands issued to a powerless crew. It was a fearful moment, never to be forgotten in the history of a lifetime, when all hopes, joys, sorrows, and past recollections, are merged into an instant of time, to be swept away by a breath.

A little after daybreak we sighted an English vessel on her course for South America. She sailed swiftly, never stopping to tell us the danger she had passed, as a chopped sea was running, which denoted the expiring struggle through which it was passing in trying to calm its fury. The sun rose at last, and our rent sails were all that told the perils we had encountered; for the same Voice that could command "the winds and the sea" to obey was with us, and we were saved.

About midday we passed the Isle of Pines, whose proximity our quadrant indicated before we saw it. In making for the south side of Cuba, this land is all we see during the passage. It is said rain falls here when the weather is pleasant in every other place—to which is attributable its unusual appearance of verdure and its fine streams of fresh water, which first attracted the attention of the early Spanish settlers. The large amount of rain which falls here is accounted for by the trade-winds in these seas blowing from the north-east. Marble and jasper of various colors are found on this island. It was formerly frequented by pirates, the last of whom was Bernardo del Soto, who was a Spaniard, and commanded the band. They named their cruising-ship the "Pinta," which in Spanish implies a point. Their closing exploit was robbing and destroying the brig Mexican, near Cape San Antonio. All the crew were murdered except two, who were spared on condition they would join the pirates. These two unfortunate survivors afterward escaped to the United States, when they gave information in regard to their companions who had been so cruelly murdered, and also the rendezvous of these high-sea pirates, which led to their capture by the brig Summers. The buccaneers were taken to Boston, and tried for murder, of which they were all convicted and executed, except the commander, whose wife came from Cuba and interceded with President Van Buren, that the life of her husband might be spared. Her entreaties were not unavailing, and his existence was prolonged, only to reward her solicitude by murdering her in a fit of passion, for which crime he soon atoned with his life.

Mexican Gulf.—Soon after dinner we noticed an unusual appearance in the sky, like fog and mist. The sailors, with a terrified look, were standing in a group together on deck, while the captain took the helm. A storm on ship-board, strange as it may appear, develops more profanity than reverence among sailors; but water-spouts are something with which they never presume to trifle. Two of these were plainly visible. One passed aft the vessel, missing it about fifteen feet; the other presented a most peculiar phenomenon, which is said to be caused by the reciprocal attraction of the cloud above and the sea beneath. The water rises toward the cloud, which elongates itself in the form of a tube to meet and receive the fluid below—this ascending column resembling in form a speaking-trumpet, with its base uppermost. They were called *presters* by the ancients, which word in the Greek denotes an igneous fluid—the more singular on account of those who applied the term having no knowledge of electricity. These terrible missiles of destruction often annihilate every thing in their pathway, although only a few drops of water reached us from these. They are fearful objects, unlike most others which come clothed in darkness, they being only veiled in thin mist, rising like a mysterious presence from the depths of the sea to join the forces in the air, thus making the combined influences doubly formidable. The ship had been tacked to port side just as the water-spouts had been discovered, and we were sailing southward away from them. They may be properly termed "sea-cyclones, carrying up drops of water which they have separated from the surface of the waves." The beauty, terror, and grandeur accompanying these visitants can never be imagined by one who has not witnessed them, much less definitely described by a terrified spectator. The sun shone brightly during the time, as though the storm-fiend was not abroad in his chariot, riding swiftly on wings of wind, ready to hurl the missiles of death at any hapless mariner who crossed its pathway. Ever shall I remember how utterly undone those poor sin-hardened, rough sailors appeared while waiting for orders that would give expression to their feelings, no words coming from those uncultured lips which could furnish any conception of their mental agitation.

Cuba, February 28.—The most precious jewel of the Antilles is the Isle of Cuba, which we are now approaching. It is about seven hundred and ninety miles in length, its greatest width being one hundred and seven miles. The mountains add beauty and boldness to its scenery, the highest elevation on the island being about eight thousand feet. It was first discovered by the famous Columbus, in 1492, but not conquered from the Indians until 1511, at which time the Spaniards killed nearly five hundred thousand of the natives. From the following well-authenticated account we may be enabled to form some idea of the barbarity which characterized these movements: "One morning, as the Spaniards were tying an Indian cazique to the stake for the purpose of burning him alive, a Franciscan Friar approached, and informed him that if he would embrace their religion he should go to heaven, but if not he must burn in hell forever. The prince then asked him if there were any Spaniards in heaven. The friar responded in the affirmative—to which he replied, 'If that be so, I would rather be with the demons in hell than the Spaniards in heaven; for their cruelty is such that none can be more miserable than where they are.'" The cause of the Indians being so cruelly destroyed by the Spaniards was their covetous wish to possess the entire island, with its supposed wealth in silver and gold. Unfortunately, after they had murdered the Indians, their visionary dreams of vast fortunes were never realized, as very little precious metal was discovered, which many have supposed was a judgment on them for their cruelty.

The soil in Cuba is itself a mine of wealth, on which can be produced from five to seven crops yearly, spring-time and harvest continuing all the season. There are mines of copper ore here, from which the early settlers made their cannon.

About two hundred miles from Cape San Antonio Light, upon the south side of Cuba, is an entrance called Fernandina Del Jauga Bay, the coast being lined with rocks of a coral formation. Ten miles from the Mexican Gulf, at the head of this bay, surrounded by a country of unsurpassed fertility, is the city of Cienfuegos, named in honor of the general to whom its present prosperity is in a great measure attributable. The fort which guards the entrance to this town impresses us with its entire inefficiency to resist an attack from our modernized implements of warfare, or to even make a show of strength for any length of time during a siege. One lone sentinel rushes upon the parapet, and presents arms, when a vessel approaches, as though he had a hundred-pound ball, which could be sent with sufficient force to sink any ship that should make an attempt to enter the port. The harbor upon which the town is situated is commodious and safe. Two gun-boats are anchored here, which, judging from their shape and size, look as though they would require assistance to advance, but are said to make six miles an hour when under full headway. They are not regarded as formidable by military men. The report from the guns would, no doubt, be more demoralizing than the effect. The houses in the city are built mostly of brick and concrete. They have no yards in front, the walls of the residences being even with the streets, only a narrow sidewalk sometimes intervening. The buildings are painted blue or green, straw-color, and white—the doors being differently colored from the houses. The windows have no glass, as it would make the dwellings warmer, and the ladies could not look from the folds of their curtains into the streets so easily without being seen as they do now. The windows are protected by iron rods and bars, which give them a cage-like appearance—the houses have no chimneys or fire-places, and the apartments are furnished in a very simple manner. The floors are made of marble and tiles—the carpet is only a large rug in the center of the room, upon each side of which are placed two rows of chairs, most of them being willow-work rocking chairs; also a center-table and sofa, with a willow back and seat, sometimes a piano, embrace the list of parlor fixtures. At night the doors and windows are thrown open for ventilation, the rooms being lighted by gas chandeliers—every thing can be seen, even to the beds on which the family sleep. The bedsteads are made of iron, and are very light, upon which is placed a wooden frame with a piece of canvas tacked across it. There are no mattresses or feather-beds used. A sheet of Canton-flannel is the first appearance of bedding, over which are spread linen sheets of snowy whiteness, pillows filled with cotton or moss — the whole being overhung with pink and white-lace curtains, to keep out the musquitoes, that never leave on account of climatic changes. But few of the dwellings are more than one story high. If the ancient Spanish custom were to be observed here—that the rent of the first floor was for the king—there would be no income left to the owners. Many of these structures have ceilings twenty feet in height. They build them as airy as possible, and afterward dedicate them to the god of the winds, whose presence is many times oftener invoked than received. However, the land-breeze at night, and the sea-breeze during the day, render the climate more delightful than can be imagined by one who has never visited here. In this locality days and weeks steal imperceptibly away, leaving no visible impress except a feeling of repose, as though earth had no cares or pains which would ever torture our minds again with their unwelcome visitations. The great amount of leisure every one appears to command is really surprising. The rich enjoy their condition to the fullest extent of the term—no titled lords or ladies have more courtly grace and elegant manners. The poor ape the rich in their movements, as though it were undignified to be brisk, or manifest any haste, going about quietly as though at peace with all the world. Every thing in their houses is exceedingly neat, the lower part being stuccoed several feet from the base with designs, no doubt intended as the escutcheons of royalty. The floors are also laid in tiles, ornamented with flowers of sapphire color, being connected with each other by patterns which, when in position, are plainly seen. May not these be identified with the sapphire foundations of which the Prophet Isaiah speaks? Among the recent discoveries made in the Moorish ruins of Italy are also found similar floors.

It is a novelty to look in the houses and see the family circles gathered in their homes, all smoking and talking but the babies. The cares of life apparently rest very lightly on them, while their clothing is more airy than all—the little baby-girls with only a pair of ear-rings, the boys dressed in the shadow of the nurse, or night falling softly on them. What a multitude of unformed thoughts enter our minds as we look at the novel sights appearing before us, where only a foreign language is sounding in our ears! They all speak the Spanish, which is derived mostly from the Latin, and resembles it, except some words from the Arabic, which came into use with them after Spain was conquered by the Moors. The pantomimic efforts made by salesmen and servants, in trying to make us comprehend that they would like to be attentive and please us, is very amusing. The marketer explains the price of his fruits by showing us a corresponding piece of silver. If we shake our heads, he reduces the amount, and writes it down in figures. Although we can feast our eyes on the various scenes which come before us while in Cuba, we must remember the natives are looking at us, uttering a jargon of words, not much of which we can comprehend, except *Americano* and *sombrero*, which implies that we are Americans, and wear hats. The Spanish ladies wear veils, the men only wearing hats.

Cruelty to seamen while in Cuban ports is an evil which needs reforming. The vessels in whose service they are engaged are mostly from a frozen clime, that return loaded with cargoes of sugar and molasses. The change of climate to a person of leisure is very perceptible, but when required to perform the heaviest of labor under a tropical sun, it is too overpowering—it is cruelty! The sailor is frequently sent aloft to grease the mast at midday, when he is overpowered by heat, and drops on the decks, gasps once, and is gone! Poor fellow! Only a man! There is an Irishwoman living in Cienfuegos, called by the sailors "Mother Carey," and the duped sailors her chickens. She is married to a Spaniard, and keeps a Sailor's Home, or saloon. She employs runners to inveigle mariners into her shop, and then for fifty cents' worth of whisky will take a good pair of boots, or any kind of clothing, from the stupid wretches. After robbing them in this unfeeling manner she turns them out, to find their way back to the ship as best they can. The sailor has few inducements for doing right, but the avenues for his destruction are never closed night or day.

Cuba has been on the altar for sacrifice several years. The United States have been looking for some time toward the event of its severance from Spain, when it would gravitate toward her for protection. The present movement is being made because the people have no voice in their own government; they are overburdened with taxes to support declining royalty from Spain, for the purpose of making laws and administering them. Would an embassy of Americans, with authority from Washington, be more acceptable to the Cubans than their present rulers? Does our administration now evince that efficiency, justice, and prowess to protect the unprotected, and strengthen the weak, which would encourage a feeble foreign principality to seek an asylum beneath the "stars and stripes," where a shelter free from discord and contention could be furnished as a refuge in times of danger? Does not the successful warfare in which it has been engaged for a number of years indicate the first fundamental principles of self-government and defense? How terrible the fate of all insurgents when captured, at the sight of which humanity sickens! and yet they neither appear intimidated nor appalled. The victim for execution is led out at the dawn of day, with no escort but the priest and executioner. Upon his bended knees he repeats his prayers after the padre. The condemned man is then shot in the back, his head cut off, his body thrown in a cart, and carried to a pit, where it is tumbled in and left. No words of extenuation, no excuse or quarter, is tolerated for an instant.

Within twenty miles of Cienfuegos, among the mountains, there has numbered a force of rebels somewhere in the vicinity of twelve thousand. Their movements show both strategy and strength —their mode of warfare the guerilla. Over a month since four hundred troops were landed here

from Spain, and shortly afterward ordered into an
engagement, or to make an attack upon the insurgents. They were not regulars — some of them
beardless youths. When the fray was over, it is
said but one escaped, because he had a better horse
than his pursuers. The destruction of this force
was only a before-breakfast pastime for the rebels.
They are now constantly making incursions upon
the planters, firing fields of cane, sugar-mills, and,
before the work of destruction is half finished, they
are miles away, strewing desolation wherever they
pass. The Cuban rebellion is no longer of infantile
growth; the entire inefficiency of the volunteers,
who go racing about the country, is plainly to be
seen. Every thing pertaining to military movements is shrouded with an air of mystery. When
the wounded and dying are brought in on the cars,
guards are placed at the doors—no person but surgeons admitted, no questions answered, or satisfaction given to outsiders. It is shocking to see a
country of such luxuriance and beauty fall a prey
to the unrelenting hand of war, which gluts itself
with human gore, and is only satiated when the fiend
of destruction has no more blood to shed, or conquests to make.

"La Purisima Conception" is the name of the
only church in the city. It has two towers and ten
bells. The tallest tower was erected to contain a
clock, and afterward the church was built around it,
thus rendering the style of architecture any thing
but imposing. The materials used are stone and
brick, with marble floors. It is singular to see a

people among whose progenitors in Spain the Christian religion was first planted by the apostles themselves, cherish so little zeal in regard to the observance of its ordinances in any way. The congregation outside is larger than the number of worshipers inside, on Sabbath morning. The men stand about the entrance, and make remarks about those going into church, as though they were engaged in the path of duty. Their conduct is a reminder that the chivalric days of elegant address and lordly demeanor are passing away from the Spanish people who reside this side of the water. At 8 o'clock A.M. the best society residents come out to worship. In a population of ten thousand souls a goodly number might be expected to witness the imposing ceremonial of a high mass on Sabbath morning. The church has an elegant interior, the architecture being Doric, the arched roof supported by numerous pilasters. At the terminus of the nave is placed the grand altar, ornamented with images of dazzling brightness and golden candlesticks of gigantic proportions, containing immense wax candles, which, when lighted, shed a star-like luster. There are also eight other altars of less dimensions, where the more humble kneel to receive consolation. The priest looks as ancient as the religion he represents, and chants mass with an intonation that would be creditable to one less in years. With fine music, choice paintings from Spanish and Italian masters, representing saints preceded by a record of unsullied purity, upon which were beaming subdued rays of light through stained glass of rare design and workmanship, be-

sides all that could be attractive in a church and
service combined, there were only about fifty persons
present, including white and black. The edifice
was designed to seat only a few of the congregation.
A noticeable peculiarity in attending worship
here is that each lady-worshiper is accompanied by
a servant, who carries a low cane-seated chair for
her mistress to occupy during service, and an elegant
rug made of long, soft cashmere goat's hair,
beautifully dyed, which is placed in front of the
chair. On this mat the mistress kneels to repeat her
devotional exercises, with an ease which would have
been considered quite sacrilegious by St. Francis,
or any of those old hair-shirt-wearing friars. The
servant in attendance, if young, kneels by the side
of her mistress upon the marble tiles, where she is
expected to repeat all the prayers connected with
the ritual. If she is seen gazing about, as an admonition
to give attention to her religious duties,
she receives a tap on the head from her mistress's
hand, which causes her lips to move again, and her
eyes to cease their voyages of discovery. Old servants
kneel behind their mistress, and go through the
forms of worship as a religious duty and safeguard
against sin. At 11 o'clock A.M. the poor people attend
church in the same place; the heat is too fervent
for the rich to venture out then. Spiritual
consolation is a commodity not much sought after
in this market by rich or poor, if the numbers in
attendance are any criterion. What few are assembled
go through the service in a hurried, business-like
manner, which has no soul in it.

The plaza in Cienfuegos is the largest on the island. It is kept in order by the coolies—a race of people brought from the mountains of Asia, which forms the most numerous servile population in the country. At night it is the scene of a grand display, or military parade. The band comes from the barracks, surrounded by a military escort, near which no one is permitted to pass. The guards are all extremely tall, dark, well-formed men, being of Moorish origin. While on duty they stand as mute and motionless as statuary, with their guns pointing upward, but ready for instant action at the word of command. It is here the chill winds never come, and drape the foliage in somber hues—the flowers are always blooming, sweet as dreams borne on angels' wings. To this plaza, at night, the entire population of the city resort for recreation, and to breathe the fresh air. The grounds are divided into parterres, laid out at right angles, through which are wide avenues, paved with flat rocks. In the center is a fountain and grotto, near which are four marble statues representing the seasons. No fabled habitation of the genii, or enchanting description of the Isle of Calypso, could fill the imagination with more delightful emotions than the real scene before us. The bright moonbeams come stealing softly through the scarlet hibiscus, and feathery palms wave their graceful wands above our heads, while the most gentle zephyrs fan our brows with their blandest breeze, and every thing seems tipped with silver sheen, and too unreal for earth. The gay and beautiful señoritas soon commence promenading, many of them dressed in white, with long, starched trains to their robes, and skirts that swept over the paved boulevards with a rushing sound, like the waves plashing against a vessel, although the accompaniment of shuffling sandals and slip-shod slippers of the men make a grinding noise nothing suggestive of grace or elegance. The music soon struck up, with its most fascinating strains; everybody seemed to partake of its harmonious cadence, and commenced moving about with the grace of sylphs. The soldiers and police, with their *brusquiere* movements, were the only ones present not given up to the most perfect *abandon* for enjoyment. Among other choice and beautiful pieces, the band played *Il Trovatore*. The melody seemed intensified by the same pathos that seized the mind of the great composer when he wrote it; and as its sounds died away among the moonbeams and perennial foliage, while its echoes lingered in the air, the surroundings appeared too beautiful for any thing but the culmination of all on earth that might be termed grand.

CHAPTER XXVI.

SEEKING information with reference to distances while in Cuba will be found an adventurous enterprise. The answer you receive is, "Far as the voice of a countryman, or the crowing of a cock," which you find after traveling two or three leagues just beyond. The following are the correct distances across the island by railway: From Cienfuegos to Cruces, nineteen miles; from Cruces to Santo Domingo, twenty-four miles; from Santo Domingo to Matanzas, eighty miles; from Matanzas to Havana, sixty-six miles. Many suppose Cuba has no railroads, except some on which an attempt to ride would imperil their safety, which is a great mistake. The roads are in the hands of the Government, being well built, and the speed all that could be desired. Three kinds of passenger-cars are placed at the disposal of travelers —first, second, and third class. The first class are not cushioned, but have willow-wrought backs and seats to make them cool. Few, except foreigners, ride in them. The second class have cushioned seats, and more passengers. The soldiers also ride in these. The third class cars have seats without backs or cushions on them. The majority of Cubans have no pride in regard to their mode of traveling. These uncomfortable cars are literally packed.

Here we see the elegantly-dressed lady, with her crape shawl and embroidered veil—gentlemen-planters, coolies, the blackest slaves on the island—all listening to the blind musician playing on his guitar, while his wife and he are singing their Spanish melodies and gathering up the *dinero* which the kind-hearted people give them.

The smell of garlic and tobacco are two odorous substances with which travelers in Cuba must become accustomed. Passengers all smoke in every car—the interrogation never being used, Is smoking offensive? Everybody seems trying to pull the greatest possible amount of pleasure from the Havana weed. A vast number of cigars and cigarettes vanish in a short space of time.

As the train started from Cruces, a quiet shower distilled itself. It rains in Cuba without threatening skies or any visible preparation. There is no rolling up of squadrons into threatening ranks, the moisture appearing to come from nowhere. The shower was like beauty blushing through tears, the skies were so lovely, and the rain-drops very gentle. It is harvest-time now on the island. Every thing is hurry and rush, while both men and beasts are, many of them, driven to death. When we stopped at the first station it was early in the morning, and day was breaking. Carts, drawn by oxen and loaded with sugar-hogsheads which had come from miles away, were standing there. Poor brutes! What a look of subjugation they all have, with an immense ring through their noses, and no yoke around their necks but a small one fastened to their heads and horns, by which the loads are drawn! These oxen are of immense size, with tremendously long horns. They are not the Florida stock of cattle, but brought from Mexico. They drive them with goads, or sharpened pieces of iron, which are very severe. Nothing is treated so badly here as the patient ox, the mortality among them being greater than all the other animals combined. Acres of sugar-hogsheads now cover the grounds around the depots. The wealth of the country—that before which all other products sink into insignificance—is the rich sugar-cane, supplying more than half the world with its saccharine deposits. The cane raised here is three per cent. richer than that raised in the Southern States. It grows from four to eight feet in height, according to the fertility of the soil. It is now March, and the summit of the cane is crowned with its useful blooms, which are gathered and dried for upholstering purposes, while the leaves are cut and used for the sustenance of stock, which are herded, watched, and fed, night and day, when not working. In passing through the country we frequently see, remote from any dwelling, small tents stretched over a cot-bed. Here is where the coolie cattle-herder sleeps. The heavy dews, with the hot sunshine at midday, to which they are exposed, must finish out the existence of these poor wretches very soon.

The mornings being a little airy now, the agents come out, on the arrival of the train, dressed in the *capa parada*, or long brown cloth cloaks, with capes which hang over their shoulders. Below is seen a

pair of legs dressed in white, supported by a pair
of feet covered with their birthday stockings and
leather sandals. This constitutes the uniform of
both agents and loafers, worn by them when making their *début* from a hasty morning toilet. Travelers, in going through the country now, pass the
day in varied vicissitudes of thought and feelings.
It is no secret that a war is progressing in Cuba
which may end in a Santo Domingo massacre, or,
like the Kilkenny cats, continue fighting until they
destroy each other. More soldiers are traveling
on the trains than citizens — their uniforms being
made of light-blue striped linen, with scarlet cuffs,
and their hats of Panama, turned up on the left
side, on which is fastened a red and yellow cockade.
This style of dress seems to be intended as a mark
of loyalty to the Spanish Government, used more
for a badge of their principles than a uniform designed for those in actual service, as it is worn by
men too old for duty, and boys too young for enlistment. The men are all armed with guns, knives,
and pistols, until they look like moving arsenals.
Barracks are stationed on the railroad at every
town of any size, while cavalry soldiers, armed
with carbines, go dashing about in all directions.
The Cuban saddle-horses are evidently related to
the Arabian stock brought from Spain; they are
pretty, graceful, docile, easy-gaited creatures. The
cavalry braid their horses' tails, then tie them to the
saddles with red and yellow ribbons. When they
ride up to a store or hotel, they hitch them under
the front veranda. A Spaniard told me "that it

was because they were too lazy to walk, and they rode into the house."

The insurgents are more to be dreaded, in the adoption of their present tactics, than regularly organized troops. They are acquainted with every portion of the country—all its defiles and elevations—with their methods and places for secure retreat always selected. They dart about like sunbeams, dealing destruction to every thing in their reach with the celerity of hurricanes. The regular vocations of life are interrupted—all the energies of the nation being expended on arms, and not on arts, which has already sounded the death-knell to their national prosperity. Many Spaniards are now nursing the delusion of peace, but it is only a shadow, evanescent as the gorgeous hues which deck their evening skies. Foreigners, as they pass through the country, feel some anxiety for their safety when they approach the track of the insurgents so close as to see the smoking ruins of burning sugar-houses. Strangers who visit here now, with proper passports and correct deportment, will be protected. Persons who either cannot or will not give any account of themselves are regarded with suspicion, which is the same in all countries that are in a state of insurrection.

In traveling two hundred miles we change cars four times. On the trains we have none of those insinuating, untiring, vigilant, prize-candy boys, to thrust their wares in our faces, just as our nerves are settling from the last jolt, to worry us until we have to make an investment in their sweet flour-

paste and brass jewelry, to be rid of them. The
coolies seem to do the peddling at the stopping-
places. They have for sale sponge-cakes, peeled
oranges, bananas, goat's-milk cheese, and guava-
jelly. What a medley of all nations is seen when
we halt! There is something in the atmosphere
opposed to silence, yet everybody keeps in a good
humor. When the train stops there is no hurry or
bustle—all the ladies sit down, while the men walk
up to the bar for a drink. The favorite beverage is
made from the *penalis*, or "*long kiss*"—a hollow-
shaped banana, molded from sugar, mixed with wine
and water. There is no drinking behind screens—
it is all public, in a large room, with seats for passengers to sit on. The Cubans drink small quantities each time, yet no one gets drunk, the wines
being so light and pure. Each departure of the
train is announced by the ringing of a large dinner-
bell held in the hands of a negro. The coolies are
employed on the cars, both as firemen and brake-
men. Our coolie brakeman went to sleep between
each stopping-place, but never was behind time when
the engine whistled down brakes. The depots are
not large; but each one has a flower-yard, or garden, attached, arranged with taste, where the scarlet hibiscus blooms with its showy petals, that flame
like "mimic suns." They gave us flowers freely
when we motioned for them; but they gave us looks
too, as the inhabitants in the center of the island are
not much accustomed to seeing foreigners. Although it is only the first day of March, every thing
has on a midsummer dress—all the flowers, like the

national colors, are of the grandest hues. The favorite shade-tree is the orange, of which nearly every cabin, however humble, has a few. One arbor had tomato-vines trained over it, hanging full of scarlet fruit, forming a fine contrast with the green leaves. Miles of banana-trees are passed on every side, maturing rapidly. Immense fields of corn give promise of an abundant harvest. The plantations are inclosed by hedges of Campeachy and Brazil wood, besides sessile hemp, Spanish bayonet, and cactus, while some have rock walls. The hedges formed from vegetation are constantly clothed with verdure and flowers: any attempt to penetrate them would be a hazardous enterprise for man or beast, as well as a damaging encounter for all fleshly or furry coverings. The tropical atmosphére which pervades this island is favorable to the growth of plants of various species from all parts of the world. The royal palm, with its curling plumes, rearing its lofty head two hundred feet in the air, stands in rows on each side of the avenues that lead to the dwellings. Its leaves are used in thatching houses, its fruit in fattening hogs, and its stately trunk for troughs. By means of ropes these immense trees are climbed by the natives, with the celerity of monkeys. The acacia-tree also sheds its fragrance in the woods and cultured gardens. The virgin forests are teeming with such a superabundance of vegetation, it has no room for development. The trunks of the trees are covered with moss, ferns, and parasitic plants, which perfume the air, and delight us with the most exquisite odors, while above all climbs the convolvulus to dizzy heights, interweaving and forming arches to crown the rank growth with its perpetual-blooming, campanulated flowers. Here the cactus family, with its collaterals,

NATIVES GATHERING PALM-FRUIT.

assume immense proportions, armed with weapons, the appearance of which is sufficient to fill the mind of any explorer with terror. The old man's beard, with its swinging pendants hanging from the tall trees at the mercy of the winds, flourishes as though its resting-place was something more substantial than the caprice of every fickle breeze. There are no large streams of water flowing through the country; but springs abound, some of which are supposed to possess curative properties. The most airy tales emanating from the pen of the wildest romancer have never equaled the real beauties of this modern Eden. It seems to have been designed as a haunt for the Muses, or a resting-place for ethereal messengers, where they could meet and hold converse before proceeding on their missions of mercy, in administering comfort to the afflicted. The residents of such a land, instead of destroying each other, and manifesting the unfeeling, restless disposition which we see here, should be as contented as crickets, to feed upon dew-drops and bask in sunbeams.

That slave-labor is employed here, and slavery exists, we have sufficient proof in traveling through the country. Negroes being naturally a discontented race, they run away whenever an opportunity presents itself. One planter left us with a black slave at Colon. She had a rope tied around her waist, with which her master was leading her. She was well dressed, had some bundles in her arms, and looked very indifferent, generally. The laws forbid their being whipped; but the plantation-drivers all have huge lashes, which, when popped, sound like the distant report of fire-arms. The slaves are formed into ranks when they go to and return from their work; sometimes a hundred are

seen in a drove, composed of both sexes. They are
now employed in cutting cane, and load from thirty
to fifty wagons at once before they move them to the
mills for grinding and boiling. The mules grind
the cane with veiled faces and sour looks for such
sweet work. Cane only requires renewing here once
in five or ten years; consequently, but few are planting or plowing. We visited one plantation for the
purpose of seeing them work. Every thing was in
a rush. Some had on chains for bad conduct; but
their tasks had to be performed all the same. One
coolie was pointed out as having been run away two
years, hidden out at work with the colliers in the
mountains. He was kept in the stocks at night, and
made to work with his chains on during the day, of
which he complained to the overseer's wife. She
replied, "If they give you liberty you will go away
again." He responded, "I will." The slaves were
never treated with half the severity in the States
which they receive here. Their quarters are miserable thatched huts, with earth floors, furnished with
only an inclined plank for a bed, sick or well. Their
principal food is rice and cassava-root, ground and
baked in thin cakes. Slave-property has depreciated
very much in Cuba since the insurrectionary movements, and at present none appear anxious to make
investments in such precarious property. The im-
portation of more coolies has been forbidden. Negroes from Africa have been landed here this winter.
The coolies cannot learn to speak English well, but
catch the Spanish language directly. Small negroes
are plentiful; they all come around us, with their

rude, naked, black bodies and woolly heads, to steal a sly glance at the strangers, and then run away. Many traveling monkeys look brighter, and manifest more signs of intelligence, than these creatures. As soon as they can walk they receive about the same attention as puppies—upon which they thrive very well. There is no Sunday on sugar-plantations, and all the slaves look as though they did not have sense to comprehend it, if any one should tell them they had a soul. They are only taught to work, and if they refuse, the stocks and chains are ready for them, and other punishments too, although the laws make a pretense of redressing their wrongs and ameliorating their condition.

Chicken-fighting is practiced in Cuba as a means of subsistence. When a young man forsakes the paternal roof in the States, to engage in games of chance, he usually carries a pack of playing-cards in his pocket, which are not seen. The young Cuban leaves home attired in his best clothes, with a thorough-bred fighting-cock under his arm, from the body of which all the feathers have been plucked, his wings and tail-plumage only remaining. These chickens are carried with an evident feeling of pride, and for the purpose of display, as an American jockey would show a fine horse. The owners have an ear of corn in their pocket, with which they feed them. When the cars stop they always crow, as if trying to challenge a champion for fight. These fights are not considered disgraceful here, as in other countries, and hundreds of dollars are bet on a single chicken. The Cubans laugh when any thing is said about cruelty to chickens, and reply, "No law has yet been passed here for the prevention of cruelty to animals. When Bergh visits Cuba, no doubt, his first and warmest sympathies will be enlisted in behalf of the poor chickens, with their bare backs deprived of the natural covering to prevent others with which they fight from holding them by their feathers. The Spaniards, being a nation of strong passions, require something more than mental exhilaration to stimulate and satisfy them—hence the resort to chicken and bull-fights.

Matanzas is situated on the north-west coast of Cuba, latitude 23° north, and sixty-six miles from Havana. The sea-approach to Matanzas Bay is indicated by two singularly shaped hills, called The Pan of Matanzas, which appear to stand like sentinels guarding the entrance. The harbor is fine, affording protection from all winds but the north-east. The surrounding elevations of land give the city the appearance of an amphitheater, or half circle. The soil in the vicinity is the richest in Cuba. The range of mountains here evidences marks of convulsions in nature, and they have, no doubt, been the seat of volcanic action. The rocks forming the basis of these mountains are limestone—some of them containing caves, one of which is said to extend under the town. As we approach the depot, what a medley we see! A regular Pentecostal illustration of olden times, where every one hears his own tongue spoken! We noticed an official on duty whose services are much needed in many places. It was a man with a moderate-sized rod, which he used in clearing the car-shed of idle boys and lazy servants—making porters, carrying bundles, move with accelerated velocity. A subordinate race here has no show for the development of their slothful proclivities; the authorities arrest them when discovered, and, without any appeal, send them to work, miles away, on the sugar-plantations—vagrancy and vagabondism being dangerous experiments in Cuban cities.

I am unable to explain the cause, but all the Cuban men wear visages as though their bodies were the abode of numerous pains, which distorted their facial nerves, while their attenuated limbs look like the home of rheumatics, whose frequent twitchings had absorbed the flesh, leaving only a little parchment-covered bone and muscle, resembling a has-been foundation of an aristocratic family. No smile sleeps or wakes on their faces; if one should, perchance, light on them, it soon leaves, for want of encouragement. The ladies all look plump and well kept as any scions of royal blood. Care rests lightly on them as their clothing, which entire outfit resembles the lace and gauzy drapery for the more substantial ornamenting of an American lady's toilet.

Here we see the coolies engaged in all kinds of servitude—cooking, waiting on tables, attending in sleeping-apartments—always moving in that snail-pace which, apparently, nothing less than a tornado would cause them to vary. What a sad, solitary, sullen-looking race they are, with a cloud of discontent always hanging over their faces, rarely, if ever, engaging in pleasantries with their companions, but always creeping around with a shadowy frown, which resembles a graveyard-parting more than any thing with which we are familiar! A pleasant look on their features would be as foreign to them as a ray of sunshine to their hearts.

When we pass the gateway through which all passengers are required to enter and surrender their tickets, how reviving the prospect to strangers the notice, "English and French spoken," which enables them again to hold intelligent communication with the outside world, after spending a whole day in a crowd, with only their own thoughts and suppositions on subjects and novel sights, surrounded by a Babel of unmeaning sounds! The above direction, designating the languages spoken, is the only requisite sign for a hotel. As we enter, a reception is given us by the proprietor, who is a keen, sharp, smiling French Creole, with the clearest of ideas in regard to the amount of funds he can extract from every guest. A lovely and refreshing breeze passes through the house, coming from both mountains and sea. Here it meets us like a welcome friend, to fan the warm and refresh the weary traveler with its combined influences. Let all the contracts of those who come to Cuba be made in advance; it will save much unpleasantness, as the proprietors charge in proportion to their avarice, if no previous terms have been agreed upon by both parties. Four dollars per day, in gold, will give a guest the full benefit of all accommodations furnished, including wine for dinner. You can receive your attentions in Spanish, French, or English. Dinner commences at 4 P.M.,

of which we will now avail ourselves at a later hour.
The table is spread with a white linen cloth and
damask napkins. The little ants have been inspecting the premises, and many of them are still exploring the precincts. Some have selected the caster as the most prominent point for reconnoitering,
where they are still taking observations. These are
all soon brushed away by the waiter without ceremony, and then comes the repast. The cooking is
on the French restaurant order. The savory odor
of onions and garlic exhales from soup and meat
on every side—chickens cooked in all styles that
a connoisseur could invent—beef, mutton, Irish
potatoes, tomatoes, and squashes, besides other
vegetables of all kinds. After having our plate
changed ten times, the meats are all removed for
dessert, which consists of cheese, guava jelly, cocoanut grated and cooked in sirup—the meal concluding with a cup of *café noir*. The Cubans laugh at
the Americans for mixing flour and sugar into pies
and sweet-cakes.

After dinner we went to visit some friends on
the bark Adelaide, anchored in Matanzas Bay.
The process of being pulled on board from a small
boat would be a hazardous experiment for those
whose arms were not well fastened. It makes a consequential person feel very diminutive, as though
he were about the same size and importance as any
other fish, dangling at the end of a line, previous to
being taken in and served up for chowder.

Over eighty vessels are anchored in the bay—all
waiting for cargoes of sugar and molasses. The

captains are complaining on account of the low
bids made for freights. Every day fifty of them
can be seen in the consigning-office of Mr. Sanchez.
They all have an anxious, care-worn look, and some
of them so old, seasoned, and toughened, by hardships and exposure, that, if they were to fall overboard, the shark that would have the temerity or
skill to seize them, would never survive a similar
experiment, unless a Jonah miracle were wrought
in him. Each captain, as he arrives, gives the
morning salutation by asking his companions in
turn, "Is your vessel entered?" "Are you chartered?" "Where you going to sail for?" Most
of the vessels are from Maine and Massachusetts.
Strange as it may appear, many of these captains
have their entire families with them. The ladies,
while in port, extract some sweets, despite the
rough life they lead, in making calls, visits, and
even giving dinners and concerts — all the invitations being limited to their maritime acquaintances
from the four quarters of the globe. Then they
take little excursions, in their long-boats, up the
beautiful and historic valley of Yumori, or walk to
the city in crowds of fifteen or twenty, accompanied
by all the children who are not too small to go with
them. Batteries of black eyes are leveled at them,
as they pass, from every side. No hippodrome, in
making its grand entree, was ever scrutinized more
closely. Clerks leave their counters to gaze at
them; servants forget their business; pack-mules
endanger the wares of their owners; coolies drop
their cakes of ice in the river when unloading ves-

sels, as the foreigners cross the bridge, while idle boys and girls follow them, to take a good look! The gratification is mutual—each gazer is happy, and, apparently, satisfied in the enjoyment of sight-seeing. Some of these ladies have sailed with their husbands for years, under stormy skies, or crossing polar seas. A few of them have learned how to compute latitude and longitude by the quadrant. They speak of wrecks as we would heavy thunder-showers on land.

The time for leaving the bay soon arrived. Nature had veiled her face, like the Cuban beauties, with a tissue so transparent that, instead of concealing her charms, they were only increased. The darkness seemed like a mist, produced by the enchanting movements of some invisible spirit, more than the shades of night in other places. The lights beamed from the shore in the distance. All the ships had their signals, of varied hues, burning brightly, while the stars shone with the same unfading, brilliant luster as when their first song echoed through the ethereal vaults of heaven, and "all the sons of God shouted for joy." The process of being returned into the little boat, at night, appears like a leap in the dark, as I stepped backward down a rope-ladder until the pilot says, "Let go," when my hands unclasp; at the same instant a very uncertain hold is taken, with my feet on something that moves, but I am safe. Before us lies a scene in which our imagination has reached its culminating point, where enthusiasm gains the ascendency, when an approach is made toward extravagance in the use of language—the barge of Cleopatra, borne on the placid Cydnus—which, in musical cadence, echoed no more sweetly than the plash of our oars with the brilliant phosphorescent light by which each stroke was followed, and the train of silvery waves that marked our movements through the illumined waters of Matanzas Bay. Near the wharf we obtained a carriage, without difficulty, that conveyed us to the plaza, and, afterward, to the hotel. The plaza resembled a panoramic view, drafted from the imagination by some skilled artist—the beautiful señoritas, with no dull, meditative moods in their eyes, but merry flashes of the sunshine, in which they spend their lives, reflected back to beautify the world in which they live. Decked in their pink and creamy robes, floating through the avenues among gorgeous flowering plants, they resembled a festival in fairy-land more than the enjoyments incident to real life.

Our hotel is soon reached, where quiet rules the hour, all the inmates having gone to the plaza, or slumbering in the arms of tired repose, but the majoral and a few of his assistants. A tall, ebony-colored servant conducts us to our apartments, and turns on the gas, which, in the jail-like rooms, is much needed. I commenced speaking English to the *valet de chambre*, when he looked at me as if in distress, and said, "*Pourquoi ne vous me parlais en Francais!*" "*Vous parlez Francais!*" I relieved his anxiety by giving all our orders in French, to which he responded with much alacrity. The bolting of blinds and doors, combined with the high, substantial brick and mortar walls which surround us, savors very much of captivity—all the oxygen we have at night passing through a small square made in the apertures of the blinds. The canvas-framed stretchers, designed for reclining, and the accommodation of only one person, are canopied over with beautifully-wrought lace, looking both clean, cool, and inviting, to our weary frames. The atmosphere at this place is said to be conducive of sleep. Every thing sleeps, no difference when or where. The driver nods on his cabriolet, which might be attended with direful consequences, but the poor brutes are so jaded they are sleepy too. The salesman snores on his stall, sometimes stretched out full length. The cooly nods over his chopsticks and rice, after he has eaten his dinner, while the more elegant matron inclines her head gracefully, saying, *Siesta*. Morning dawns, leaving no marks of intervening space, but every thing is full of life and business. The butler's voice is heard above the din of dishes and kettles, giving orders, while his busy hands are preparing delicate loin-steaks, mutton-chops, and veal-cutlets, for broiling, and 9 o'clock train from Havana. The coffee is prepared on a separate range near the dining-tables, close to the call of every new applicant for the delightful beverage; it comes steaming out into the big China cups, the servant holding in one hand a kettle of boiling milk, and one of coffee in the other, furnishing us milk and coffee, or *vice versa*. "*Mi café*," at six or seven in the morning, accompanied with a small French roll, fortifies the inhabitants for any movements which they wish to make until breakfast-time. While drinking our coffee the porter, hat in hand, announces *El Volante*, which we had ordered the night before for the purpose of visiting the cave. All efforts to describe that curious conveyance must fail, when compared to the reality of riding in one—it being a vehicle of Cuban origin, not in general use on the island now, except in the country. It is drawn by two horses, one placed between the shafts, the other on the left in rear of the first, upon which a booted, liveried postilion, called a *calesero*, is seated in a diminutive saddle. The center of gravity is nowhere in a *volante*, while it swings and vibrates along softly as a boat on smooth water. When the wheels strike a rock it is accompanied with no unpleasant jolts, like our American carriages. Fancy could not conceive of spirits borne on the wings of an ethereal messenger being wafted more gently. As I was carried through clouds, illumined by the morning sun, which ascended sweetly as incense from the altar of devotion, I was seized with indescribable sensations, elevating emotions, comparable to nothing—partaking of no other event of which history has any record, except the transit of a perfect man, who passed beyond the realms of space, and never returned. It is materialized enjoyment, the realization of momentary happiness, at peace with all the world; our feelings are pure like the air that surrounds us, which comes direct from its heavenly home on cloud-like wings. If permitted to live longer, I feel prepared to tread paths of life with fortified strength, meeting its exigencies "with a more calm and virtuous majesty." If the angel of death were to come, he would find me ready in feelings—the mowing-blade of Time could cut me down and swing me off without a pang. Every sound appears harmonious, from the bird-orchestra, tuned by the voice of God, to the cricket that chirps from the rock-wall as we pass.

That remarkable cavern of *El Cueva de Bellamar* was discovered over twenty years since, under the following circumstances: A slave, having been engaged in the preparation of a lime-kiln, accidentally dropped one of his tools in a cavity near the place where he had been collecting rock. Hoping soon to recover it, for fear of punishment, he commenced reaching where he had last seen it. All his efforts proved useless. He then threw in rocks, which were a long time finding soundings. The next day excavations were made, which revealed a cave over two hundred feet perpendicular below the surface of the earth, and a mile in length. This remarkable subterranean passage has, no doubt, been the work of centuries, the water dripping on the lime-rock, which dissolved it—all these beautiful transformations taking place in midnight darkness, under the guidance of the great Architect whose omnipotent hand formed all things, whether above or under the earth. While descending the steps which lead into the cave, a singular phenomenon is observable. It is an intense, stifling heat, which increases as we advance, and oppresses us until we become accustomed to it. This descent may be compared to an approach into the lower regions—the torches in the hands of our guides flickering and snapping like fiery serpents. Any fears of having found the realm of his Satanic majesty are soon dispelled by the prismatic view presented to us. As we enter the cave two avenues describing a triangle are seen, it being the commencement of an apex with converging lines, which terminate not in regions *inferno*, but the "Devil's Gorge," near which stands *El Organ*, with its silent pipes reaching to the dome. We come in contact with rough edges on every side, while narrow passes almost obstruct our progress, when suddenly we are ushered into *El Cathedro*, forty feet in height, and nearly the same in length, with a variable width of twenty feet. Here is found the basin of holy water, blessed by no earthly priest, fed by a fountain whose innermost recesses have never been penetrated, or measureless depths fathomed. The palace halls of princely dwellings, decked with costly gems of priceless value, shine with no more dazzling luster than the icicle-shaped pendants of snowy whiteness hanging from the arch and sides of this remarkable underground temple. The stalactites in many places form solid columns of transparent crystals, which meet the stalagmites, and extend to the earth. Oyster-shells and sea-urchins of immense size are found imbedded in the rocks, which demonstrate that this has been the home of the restless sea, where old Neptune combed his "hoary locks," and beat his foaming billows. To enter this subterranean cavern seems like standing on the brink of a volcano, our only hope of escape being a fickle flame extinguished by a breath, looking into the domains of futurity, not knowing how soon we might be called upon to try its realities. No one can conceive the period of time which has been consumed in the production of this remarkable formation—a drop of water, containing the fractional part of a grain of lime, leaving an imperceptible deposit in its downward course, thus forming the stalactites and stalagmites of fantastic forms and delicate proportions, which the ingenuity of no human hand, however skillful, can imitate. A kind of awe-inspiring sensation seizes our minds while surrounded by the oppressive stillness in these depths, where mighty forces are fulfilling their great purposes in producing mountains by infinitesimal accessions.

As we approach the lake, the atmosphere becomes cooler, when a virgin sheet of water presents itself, on whose surface no heavenly zephyr has ever danced, or rude winds plunged into maddening strife. Here, stretched before us, is a body of water nearly two hundred feet long, thirty feet in width, and eighteen feet in depth; while firmly attached to its bed are blooms perennial as the plants of paradise, resembling double dahlias, not less than eight inches in circumference, with variegated petals of delicate pink, violet, and straw color—the coloring attributable, no doubt, to the mineral deposit contained in the waters which trickle from above. As we gaze into its pearly depths, we are impressed with the thought that here all is peace.

Many visitors who come here have the grasping relic-hunting propensity so strongly developed for wanting every thing attractive which they see, that they can only be restrained from breaking the finest stalactites by the guides threatening to extinguish the lights, which is sufficient to terrify into submission the stoutest sea captain that ever walked the quarter-deck of a vessel, or any of his *attachês*. As in other explored caverns, names have been given by the natives to the different formations found here, which so nearly resemble English that they can be readily translated. The resemblance of these curious figures to the objects indicated by the names they bear are sufficiently striking to produce an increased emotion of admiration:

"Cathedral de San Pablo."

"Manto de la Virgen."

"La Sagua bordado."

"El Organ."

"El bano de la Americana."

"Los Apostles."

"El Altar de la Virgen."

"El Confessionario."

"La Boca del Diablo."

The almost overpowering glare of sunshine, accompanied with other unpleasant sensations, resulting from a return to the outside world, was a disagreeable reminder that I had not been translated, or presented with a new body which never ached, or a heart that always beat in harmonic measures to the tasks imposed on it. Persons must never imagine that no rough places are to be gone over, or fatigue endured, when exploring the recesses of this wonderful cavern; but all slight obstacles overcome will amply repay those who make this cave a visit. It is about a league distant from Matanzas, accessible by land or water.

We will now have to descend upon our light wings of ecstatic admiration and delight to the plainer realities of earth. The bay, like a restless spirit, always in motion, rolls up its deposits of seaweed and shells almost under the *volante* wheels as we pass, while the golden waves of borrowed brightness, reflected from the shining orb of day, rise to recede again, and keep time to the evolutions of the great universe, of which they form a part.

CHAPTER XXVII.

WE departed from Matanzas shortly after our return from the cave. The scenery along the route to Havana leaves the impression that the country is declining. The buzzards fly close to the train, apparently gentle escorts, and sufficiently numerous to be the national emblem—a heavy fine being the penalty for injuring one of these scavengers. They are styled the red-crested vultures of Cuba, for grandeur.

The island is surrounded by a chain of keys, reefs, and shoals, which make it inaccessible except to the experienced pilot. Havana was permanently settled by Velasquez, and named in 1519. At the point of entrance to the bay is a rock on which stands El Moro, or Castellos de los Santos Reyes, the lighthouse, and signal-station, where an excellent revolving light can be seen from a distance of more than twenty miles. The following description is given of Moro Castle when it was first built: "It was of triangular shape, containing some heavy pieces of ordnance, which produced a perceptible quaking in the vicinity when fired." Forty pieces of cannon, of twenty-four pounds each, were mounted on the parapet. From the main castle there runs a line, or wall, mounted with twelve very long pieces of cannon, lying almost level with the water. These are all thirty-six-pounders, and most of them brass, being called "The Twelve Apostles" by way of eminence. At the point between this castle and the sea stands a tower having a round lantern at the top, where a sentinel is constantly on duty to see what ships are approaching the harbor, of which he signals by hoisting as many flags as they are in number. In 1691 the whole fort was surrounded by a moat filled with water, when it was captured and destroyed by an English fleet under Sir George Pocock, after a siege of twenty-nine days, at which time a thousand Spaniards were killed. The present Castle del Moro guards the bay on the east side, and is able to resist all attacks by sea, having two bastions toward the water, and two on the land side. Around this old structure lingers as many unpleasant memories as the Venetian Bridge of Sighs, which led from the palace to the prison—it being the prevailing opinion that whoever crossed it never returned. Those against whom any accusation can be brought of sufficient magnitude to thrust them in the Moro will find the chances greatly against their ever seeing the outside world again, or enjoying their freedom. Another castle, built opposite this, is called El Punta. This communicates with the city, and is usually well filled with soldiery. It has four regular bastions, and a platform mounted with sixty pieces of brass cannon.

The city of Havana, a hundred years since, was the most important port in America for the Spanish commerce, where a thousand ships could anchor in nearly forty feet of water, it then being a rendezvous for other fleets when coming from the Spanish possessions of the Western Continent. All the Spanish galleons and merchant-ships met at this point every year, in September, to obtain supplies and water, that they might return to Spain together. They held a kind of carnival during their stay, which lasted until a proclamation from the governor was issued, forbidding any who belonged to the ships remaining in the city on pain of death, and at a given signal they all retired on board. This fleet was regarded the richest in the world, carrying several million pounds sterling. They came from Spain laden with merchandise, and were frequently attacked by pirates and buccaneers. These galleons were only factors for the other countries among which this wealth was distributed when they made a successful voyage. In 1796 the Santo Domingo massacre drove twelve thousand families to Havana, which now has a population of two hundred thousand. The dwellings are built entirely of rock, or brick, which is furnished from the island. The substantial manner in which the most common tenements are constructed is really remarkable, looking as though they were designed to last forever. The style of architecture now in use was originally of Moorish origin. The windows descend from the ceiling to the floor, with iron rods extending the whole length, more nearly resembling cages for wild beasts, but are retreats from which beauty casts many sly glances. In private residences curtains are drawn during the day, but in stores and market-houses the windows and doors are closed only at night, thus exposing the inside movements of the occupants all day. The dwellings for private residences have only one entrance for man or beast. The mistress and *volante* come in together, when the horse is stabled on the first floor, and the lady walks up-stairs to her parlor. The narrow streets and narrower sidewalks keep the minds of visitors in a constant state of trepidation for fear of seeing some one crushed under the fast-moving vehicles. The mules, while waiting for a load, turn their heads from instinct, to let conveyances pass. Gradually the city proper has crossed the old wall boundaries, and now the outside is more attractive in appearance than inside. Soldiers are seen all about the city, but they are very peaceable. A censorship is kept over the newspapers, and letters from way-stations are delivered into the hands of the mail agent, instead of bags, while a dark veil conceals its politics and movements, in every way cherishing with jealous care the condition of all its internal troubles.

El San Carlos is situated nearest the bay, and most convenient for travelers. This hotel is four stories high, commanding a fine view of the city and Moro, where we are now promenading for the purpose of sight-seeing. The roofs of the houses are mostly flat, and a favorite resort after sunset. The surrounding scenes entertain us. Children and chickens are seen in close proximity on the neighboring house-tops, where they live and sport apparently happy and hearty in their contracted boundaries. This resort being protected by a high wall around the outside, which prevents any accident to the occupants, whole families resort here to smoke and talk, it being more private than any fresh-air resort on the premises. The rear of all the residences is a kind of labyrinthian retreat of avenues, accessible by an indescribable variety of movements, together with flights of steps of different altitudes. In these coverts swarms of human beings are born, live, and die, in this condensed condition, regardless of comforts. At night, when the curtains are raised, heads are seen in these tenements as thick as rows of pins in a paper. Neither stoves nor fire-places are used in Havana: the cooking is done on a furnace in the back-yard — charcoal, made by the colliers in the mountains, being the only fuel required.

The firing of heavy cannon from the English man-of-war anchored in the bay, and echoed by the Moro guns, agitate our thoughts and break the quiet of the dying day. The panorama before us is changing. An invisible hand behind the scene has dropped a shadow over the light of day draped in its brilliant and gorgeous glories. When the curtain rises again, the Queen of Night, more lovely than any queen of kingdoms, arrayed in her robes of royalty—for God has dressed her with the glories of heaven—appears, reflecting her full orb in the water, when an unbroken trail of silvery light apparently connects the two worlds. El Paseo, where the wealth and fashion of the city come at the close of the day for an airing, where are seen the beautiful señoritas, their eyes sparkling with the bright thoughts of their hearts, giving signals to their friends and lovers with their fans, which are readily comprehended and returned, although not a word has been spoken. The liveried postilions, with jack-boots, bare legs, brass buttons, and blue coats, accompany the Cuban *volantes* in which they ride. This vehicle has been superseded to a considerable extent by a lighter conveyance known as "El Coche," or the French coach. This coach is capable of containing two persons with ease; sometimes three are seen riding in it. A screen of canvas, buttoned to the back of the driver's high seat, and then fastened to the top of the conveyance, excludes the rude gaze of the vulgar, gaping throngs, through which we are driven. The residence of the Captain-general is situated on the edge of El Paseo Militaire. Here, amid the song of birds from the aviary, the falling waters of the cascade, cooling echoes from the numerous *jets d'eau* and fountains, the sweet odors that freight the air from the flowers, and the picturesque landscape over which the royal palms watch with their waving wands, we should expect to find the home of happy hearts. It is quite the reverse: the general has a care-worn visage, beneath which beats a troubled heart. He rides in a fine coach drawn by matched iron-grays, and guarded by armed postilions. He walks with an escort, for his kingdom is filled with insurrection. He is invested with almost unlimited power, being in command of the civil, military, and religious authorities, and from his decision there is no appeal.

Many tourists appear desirous of getting over the greatest amount of space in the least possible time. It was that class of persons composed our party in visiting this object of interest. How they rushed about as though a policeman **was on their** track, in hot pursuit, and they could not stop to look at any thing! "O supper will be ready!" they kept constantly exclaiming, as though eating was the sole object of their existence. El Salle de los Mercaderes is the street on which the banks are located, the ladies resorting there only in their *volantes* and coaches for the purpose of shopping. They never display their charms by alighting; it would be considered immodest: all goods which they wish to examine are brought to them while seated in their conveyances. The prevailing religion here is Catholic. Several years since this city contained more priests than people, more holidays than working ones—this kind of government basis requiring indulgence in order to insure allegiance. The scenes enacted on Sunday in the market-house are the same as on other days. The cobbler, seated on his bench at the door, made fun of us as we entered, thinking we could not comprehend him. "*Sombreros Americanos!*" said he. I looked at him, repeating the words, "*Vaya usted.*"—Begone! when, as if taken aback, he ceased his impudence and commenced sewing. What a profusion of fruits is seen here! bushels of oranges, immense bunches of bananas, cocoa-nuts by the wagon-load, plantains —until we wonder what will be done with them all— but when fried they form an important article of diet among the Cubans—besides many fruits for which we cannot find a name or use. Meats of any kind were not exposed in quantities, but much fish, among which the gar appeared most abundant. Much of this produce is brought here in panniers on the backs of mules or horses, while long lines of moving bundles come filing in, with the animals that bear them invisible, except their legs. These pack-mules are more used than wagons, on account of the narrow streets, the danger in passing being less than with loaded vehicles. The amount sold to each purchaser appears small: a piece of meat wrapped in a paper, and a little fruit tied up in a handkerchief, is all. When a purchase is made a present is expected, which they call *cuntra*. In proceeding to the cathedral we pass the stores and shops, all of which are open. The tailor sits, with his legs crossed, sewing as earnestly as though he was repeating his *Paternoster*. They are all Roman Catholics, who have already been to receive the supposed requisite supply of grace for the week, and have now returned to their business vocations.

A CUBAN ORANGE-MARKETER.

The drinking-saloons are open, with their patrons in full view, seated at the marble-topped tables, chatting with their friends, their favorite beverages in front of them, while the blind beggar, with his wife, stands outside singing Spanish ballads. The drays and wagons are not running, which is all the contrast between work-days and Sunday in Havana. The proximity between wealth and misery here is close, and the contrast so visibly marked that the impression received is more lasting than in America. Beggars expostulate and importune us until our hearts sicken with the sight of our surroundings. "*Lottera!*" is cried on every side by miserable-looking men and women selling tickets, which may be blanks or prizes, to be tested in the great Havana Lottery.

The cathedral occupies a fine position in the city, being located in the *Calle del Ignacio*. It has stood so long, and withstood so much, that it has become an historic record, uniting the past and present. Here happy hearts have plighted their vows, and many times the last tribute of tenderness rendered to loved ones. Here the faithful follower of this religion has counted her beads, while the penitent knelt, confessing his crimes, and tarried for absolution. It contains numerous altars devoted to different saints. In rear of the cathedral is a monastery for the Padres. The cathedral, with its mystical scenes, causes our thoughts to revert to the times of Aaron, when, with his priestly vestments trimmed with tinkling bells and pomegranates, he stood before the altar and burned incense as an oblation for the sins of the people. The plate and ornaments of the main altar are silver and gold. The candelabra are of the most curious workmanship—some of them weighing nearly a hundred pounds. The bishop, assisted by twenty-four fathers and acolytes, conducted the service. Mass was read in Latin, the acolytes composed the choir, the members responding audibly. Worship, like other things in Cuba, is conducted with a zest. The number of worshipers in attendance was small. Those who came assumed the most devotional of attitudes, kneeling, during the entire service, in a promiscuous manner, on the hard tiles, if they had not provided themselves with soft rugs for the occasion. I could not determine where the line of distinction in color was drawn—white and black all supplicating together. The most elaborately-dressed señoras and señoritas bend before the confessional. A poorly-dressed Cuban woman, among the number, kept prostrating herself lower and lower until she kissed the marble tiling, when she rose with a look of satisfaction, as though the act of humiliation had unburdened her soul. The organ sent forth its thundering tones from behind the colossal pillars, playing the "*Te Deum*" and "*Miserere*"—thus enabling us to comprehend, to a certain extent, the grandeur of the music at St. Peter's Church in Rome.

On the right of the main altar is a tablet, on which is engraved the following inscription: "*O restos è y imagen del grande Colon! Mil siglos duraran guardados en la urna y en la remembranza de nuestra nacion.*" "O ashes and image of the great Columbus! You will be guarded for a thousand centuries in the tomb and in the heart of our nation." The great injustice done him while living cannot be atoned for now when dead by dragging his remains about the world. He died in Valladolid, Spain, where he was buried. His body was exhumed and taken to Seville, then to Santo Domingo—afterward, with great ceremony, to Cuba, and deposited in the cathedral, where it will, no doubt, be kept until some other idea seizes the minds of his impulsive countrymen. The cathedral walls are hung with the choicest of peaceful, benign portraits, of their glorified saints, looking with calmness upon us. Among the number is a life-size, finely-executed painting of St. Christopher, or Santo Christobal, who flourished during the third century A.D., and is the guardian saint of Havana. Immense statues of St. Christopher are still to be seen in many cathedrals. He is always represented as girded, with staff in hand, for a journey, which gives expression to his allegoric wanderings through the sea of tribulation, by which the faithful intended to signify the many sufferings passed before he arrived at the Eternal Gate.

This saint was formerly implored against pestilential misfortunes or distempers. He adopted the name of St. Christopher as an inestimable treasure. His martyrdom is commemorated on the 9th of May. Many paradoxical things are related of him: "That he was a giant with a dog's head, and devoured men, but a transformation occurred when he believed on Christ. He is said to have been instructed from heaven in the way of right; that he was baptized by the moisture in a cloud which came from the sky, an invisible voice uttering the sacramental words." He is related as having had numerous contentions with Satan—his majesty's presence only being kept at bay by crossing himself. He was advised by a hermit, as an act of penance, to pray. "That I cannot do," he replied. "Then you must carry travelers over deep rivers." While performing his assigned tasks a child applied to him, to whom, when seated, he said, "You seem

heavy as the whole world." The child replied, "I
created the world, I redeemed the world, I bear the
sins of the world." Then Christopher saw that he
had borne Christ over the river, and for this reason
he is always represented with the infant Jesus on
his shoulders. It was common, during the Middle
Ages, to place effigies of him in statuary outside
the gates of a city, as he who looked on this figure
of St. Christopher was safe from sudden death that
day. The following inscription accompanies the
figure of St. Christopher:

> Christophori sancti faciem quicumque tuetur.
> Illa nempe die non morte male morietur.

Monday morning I ordered a coach for the purpose of visiting Cemetario de Espeda, named for an
ancient bishop in Havana. The entrance to this
cemetery is through a fine rock archway, designed
only for pedestrians, and not carriages. The office
has to be passed, and money handed in, before any
corpse has a Christian burial in these consecrated
grounds. Whatever might have been their virtues
while living, the dead one here is to have wealth to
take the body into a vault and the soul through purgatory. This cemetery contains not less than fifty
acres of ground, around which is built a rock wall
eight feet in height and about the same thickness.
These walls are made of well-dressed rock, in which
are vaults for interment. Inside the main inclosure are built other high walls for the same purpose.
Paved walks cross each other through the grounds,
covered with square-cut rock, which give a hollow
echo when stepped upon, and, no doubt, contain

other tombs. Vaults of sufficient size to admit a coffin are made in all these walls, which are afterward sealed, then a tablet of marble is fitted in, being secured with mortar, on which is placed the inscription, chiseled in Spanish. This tablet is arranged in accordance with the taste of the friends of those deceased who survive them. Some contain glass cases, with pictures of the Virgin; others, wreaths of black beads strung on wire, hung over the tomb. In one I saw a chameleon cozily ensconced, as though the wreath was made for him. Lizards were crawling in all directions; harmless little creatures, they liked the retirement of death's victims! The inscriptions were mostly very simple. Here are two of them: "A NUESTRO QUERIDO, HIJO TOM." "To our beloved son Thomas." "HIJA, MIA." "My beloved daughter." No mounds of earth mark the resting-place of any. Many birds of varied plumage were singing their songs among the roses, cape jasmines, pride of China, and mimosa trees.

As we alighted, two bodies had just preceded us into the cemetery for deposit—a rich and a poor man, distinguishable by distinctions in death as in life. The rich man was in a fine casket, with his name engraved on the lid, and six silver handles, borne by liveried attendants, dressed in black clothes, trimmed with wide white stripes. No women were present, but a large number of dignified-looking Spanish gentlemen. The casket was placed in a vault, after which workmen, with brick and mortar, commenced closing up the orifice, which was witnessed by those in attendance until it was finished, when they retired with the same manifestations of grief as though a dead leaf had dropped from a tree. The poor man was borne on the shoulders of four rough-looking fellows, who grunted as though the body might have weighed a ton. They trotted away into a corner with the bones, and no mourners, as if it were a log, instead of a human being, where once dwelt the breath and likeness of the Eternal God.

A hundred dollars is considered a remuneration for the use of a vault twenty years—at the expiration of which time, if there is no renewal of funds, the remains are taken out and thrown into a common pit, or potter's-field, where the poor are buried without coffins. The corpse of a pretty little girl, dressed in white, her head wreathed in flowers, was brought in a coffin with no cover, accompanied by a few poor, sad friends, when a rock tablet was raised by means of ropes drawn through iron rings, and the child's body thrown into a deep pit—the coffin being taken away, which could be used again in bringing many more poor children for burial. Protestants are not permitted sepulture here, on any consideration, if the fact is known to those in charge. We retired from this "garden of slumberers" to the entrance, where sat the Padres, one of whom smiled and called *el coche* with a peculiar p-s-t-s-c-h, which sound goes whizzing through the air like a rocket.

There are persons with whom we meet in life whose smile means mischief, whose friendly grasp is a covering for treachery, which fact is, alas! true in regard to the Cubans, for they rarely mean what they say to you. Ah! it was only a promise. Then there is so little manifestation of repentance with them, if you are disappointed. They pile up excuses for all untoward acts until you are led to believe it was not a reality—only a mistaken idea of your imagination.

It is thus in Havana. Orders are given to be called in time for the early train. Soon after retiring, peaceful slumbers possess your body and pleasant dreams your mind, until finally, on awakening, you come to realize the facts that too much time has passed, the train gone, and a day longer before you, where the thought of remaining had not crossed your mind. It appears to be a preconcerted plan, on the part of landlords, to retain paying patrons. Persons having a large amount of patience will find frequent exercise for it while traveling in Cuba.

A Ramble into the Early History of Florida.

IN trying to ascertain the distribution of tribes during the early explorations of the Florida settlers, we feel as though the veil of obscurity had never been lifted. However, three divisions have been traced, with some degree of certainty, after the extinction of the original Caribs, or Cannibals, whose works are seen so extensively on the St. John's and sea-coast of Florida. In the northern part lived the Temuncas, on the eastern coast the Ais, and the Cobooras on the south-western. It was these Indians who were found occupying the soil when the Spanish and French explorers first landed on the new continent. Their presence in this country was, and still continues to be, an unsolved mystery. Different tribes have their peculiar legends, which date back for centuries. Some of them say their ancestors walked out from a cave; others, that they came from the clouds, consequently were of heavenly origin.

Whatever may have formerly been the difference of opinion in regard to the first discoverer of Florida, the honor is now awarded to Sebastian Cabot, who was born in Bristol, England, A.D. 1477. He was the son of John Cabot, a Venetian pilot, who in the pursuit of his vocation spent a portion of his time in Italy, but his home was in England; hence the erroneous statement made by writers that he was a Venetian. The fact has been well authenticated that the continent of America was discovered by Cabot, 1497, although Columbus first landed on some of the islands. England poorly requited Cabot for the great discovery of the New World. Henry VII.—whose ruling passion was parsimony—then being king, could not comprehend the magnificent prize which lay within his grasp by right of discovery. It is stated Cabot died about 1557, aged eighty years. During his last illness, just before his spirit took its flight, his mind being illumined with the radiance of another existence, he remarked that "Divine revelation was an infallible method of ascertaining the longitude he could then disclose to no one." After this great discovery of Cabot the adventurers returned with tales of the wonderful, before which fiction paled into insignificance. They all thirsted for riches, and the wildest fantasies of the imagination could not keep pace with their golden dreams, to be realized in this far-away El Dorado. The sojourners at home seized upon the information with the same avidity as the explorers.

The discovery of Florida has usually been given to a companion of Columbus, Ponce de Leon, a daring cavalier, whom fortune had favored in all his undertakings. Having been promoted to the highest official position on the island of Porto Rico, his declining strength was a bitter potion, which remained in the cup of his closing life. Failing in the realization of his golden dreams in the new country, he afterward heard of an immortal fountain toward the setting sun, called Bimini, whose waters not only gave youth and beauty, but a perennial existence. It was before this much-coveted prize the glory of all earthly honors faded into shadows. The traditions of these wonderful rejuvenating waters had lived among the Carib Indians for many years, and from the fact that those who journeyed thither had never returned, the conclusion was inferred that they were roaming through the newly-found Elysian Fields, so delighted they did not wish to leave their new home, never imagining they could have perished by the hand of violence. Ponce de Leon had no difficulty in obtaining companions for this visionary voyage. He fitted out three vessels for the expedition, which sailed from the port of St. Germain, March, 1512, when, steering westward, they landed a little to the north of St. Augustine, March 27, 1512, on Palm·Sunday, naming the country *Pascua Floridas*, which it still retains. Ponce was much charmed with the general appearance of every thing he saw. The number of streams which he drank from is unknown, but as none of the fabled waters imparted fresh vigor to his worn, battered body, made thus from age and toil, he returned home, if no younger, wiser on the subject of adventurous enterprise. After his arrival in Cuba he reported his discovery to Ferdinand, who conferred on him the title of *Adelantado*, which would immortalize him on the records of history after death, if no rejuvenating waters could affect him while living. Hardly had he returned and recovered from the toils of his discovery before information was received that the Caribs were encroaching upon the island of Porto Rico, capturing the Spaniards and carrying them away, and, as they were never seen afterward, it was inferred they had been eaten by these cannibals. An expedition was soon sent out to conquer them, commanded by Ponce de Leon. He landed first on the island of Guadalupe, when he sent his men on shore for wood, and the women to wash their clothes. The hostile Indians made a descent on them, killing the men, and carrying off the women prisoners to the mountains. This movement was a heavy blow to the ambitious Ponce, whose health and spirits both commenced declining. The squadron, on his return from Porto Rico, was taken charge of by one of his captains. After remaining on the island for several years, still retaining the office of governor, he was told the land he had discovered was not an island, but portion of a large unknown country. The fame of Cortez, who was then winning laurels in the conquest of Mexico, reached the ears of Ponce de Leon, who, not wishing to be considered the least among the conquerors, fitted out another expedition of two ships at his own expense, which sailed from Porto Rico, 1521, for the purpose of making farther explorations in the new continent. A bird of ill omen appeared to perch on his pennons from the time he left port. Heavy seas assailed him on every side, tossing his frail bark like a feather on their creamy crests, threatening destruction at every moment. He finally landed at the nearest point on the coast of Florida, being in the vicinity of St. Augustine, where he proclaimed himself governor and possessor of the soil. The Caribs, thinking themselves unauthorized in the recognition of any power outside of their own race, met him with fierce opposition, showering their arrows upon the astonished Spaniards, killing several of them, and mortally wounding Ponce de Leon. He was carried to the ship in a helpless condition, and from thence to Cuba. A Spanish writer makes the following remark upon the visionary scheme in which this unfortunate adventurer had embarked: "Thus fate delights to reverse the schemes of men. The discovery that Juan Ponce flattered himself was to be the means of perpetuating his life, had the ultimate effect of hastening his death." The last undertaking closed his earthly career, and found for him a grave on the island of Cuba. The following is a correct copy of the epitaph placed upon his tomb, translated into Spanish by Castellano:

> Aequeste lugar estrecho
> Es sepulchro del varon
> Que en el nombre fue Leon,
> Y mucho mas en el hecho.

When rendered into English, means, In this sepulcher rest the bones of a man who was a lion by name, and still more by nature.

The failure of Ponce de Leon did not deter other explorers, thirsting for glory and gain, from trying their fortunes in this unexplored paradise.

These, like many settlers in a new country the present day, had miscalculated the toils and privations to be endured, the dangers to be faced, the labors performed, the foes, whose cunning in the use of death-dealing missiles would take their lives with the same freedom they did the snake that sung the siren song of death to the thoughtless victim that crossed his pathway. The names of De Ayllon, Miruello, Cordova, Alaminos, Verazzano, Pamfilo de Narvaez, and Cabeca de Vaca, all come to us covered with defeat and loss of life while attempting to inhabit a country so uncivilized that they had never been able to imagine even its real condition. Mountains of gold, mines of silver, and rivers of pearls, was the Aladdin's dream that lured them from home, and left them to perish on the sands of an inhospitable shore. Nearly twenty years had elapsed since the demise of Ponce de Leon, when Hernando de Soto, an officer second in rank to Pizarro the Conqueror, having accompanied him during his Peruvian conquests, had entered the temples of the Incas, whose brightness was only eclipsed by the great luminary of day, while the Aztecs rendered him the honor that belonged to their gods. De Soto still thirsted for conquest, and Florida was a new field for the gratification of his adventurous schemes and visionary enterprises. He consumed much time on the island of Cuba in recruiting soldiers and sailors who were willing to serve under him, and follow where he would lead. Finally, after his preparations were completed, he sailed, on the 15th of May, 1539, under the ensign, "Possunt quia posse videntur" (They are able, because they seem to be able), arriving at Espiritu Santo Bay on Whitsunday, May 25, with a larger fleet than had ever landed on the shores of Florida before. De Soto was certain he had found "the richest country in the world," where the cupidity of his companions could be gratified to satiety; where precious metals lined the temples, and more precious gems sparkled from their high altars, before which the priests, clad in robes of royal purple, chanted their orisons in the presence of worshiping crowds who, free from solicitude for all worldly possessions, poured their surplus riches from their well-filled coffers into the store-house of the Great Spirit, as an expiatory offering for their misdeeds. It cannot but be conceded that a more industrious, ubiquitous traveler than De Soto ever entered Florida. We are certain, if the courage of his men was unfailing, that their fine, costly apparel, becoming the knighthood of a chivalric age and people, was much shorn of its distinguished ensigns; also, the richly-caparisoned horses of their gaudy trappings, while exploring the wilds of Florida. Each day their hopes were renewed by something they saw, or heard from the Indians, who, being anxious to get rid of their troublesome intruders, entertained them with tales of unexplored territory containing vast treasures just beyond them. Thus they traveled from Tampa to Ocala, thence to Tallahassee, Rome, Georgia, the Cumberland, in Tennessee, finally crossing the Mississippi River near Memphis. Worn out with wandering, disappointed in not finding the El Dorado

of his ambition, he calmly met and faced his last
foe on the banks of the great Father of Waters, as
one writer has remarked, "finding nothing so wonderful as his own grave." Thus ended the career
of a man, representing himself to be a child of
the sun, in search of the fairest land in the world,
and himself the greatest lord that ruled this unexplored region.

The Indians had become wearied with these children of the sun, whose presence had given them
neither peace nor plenty, as they had killed all who
opposed them; besides, these celestial visitants ap-
propriated all their stores for the sustenance of themselves, thus leaving them only the prospect of extra
exertion, to which their heretofore easy, idle habits
of living had rendered them averse. With the rec-
ollection of these events, the natives, fresh from
their former experience, could hardly be expected,
when the messengers of peace came to Florida, as
they saw no difference in their external appearance
and that of their predecessors, besides being goaded
with the memory of their wrongs, that they would
be prepared to give them any thing but a cruel reception. For this reason the beautiful bay of Espiritu Santo, which years before had witnessed the pageant of a far-famed conquering general among
peaceful people, now saw the war-clubs descend with
fearful force upon the defenseless heralds of the
cross, who had come in good faith to convert them.
Afterward appeared Señor Don Tristan de Luna,
from Mexico, landing at Santa Maria, or Pensacola
Bay. The only remaining record of his exploits is

the fact of a Spanish settlement having been established on the shores of Pensacola Bay, in 1561, and that numerous explorations were made through the country at the same time, as they remained four years, but became discouraged and left the country, which had been to them only a scene of reverses, and returned to more friendly climes, leaving the glory of establishing the first permanent settlement on the shores of America to another.

During the religious differences which harassed the Huguenots in the reign of Charles the IX. of France, Coligny, a convert, conceived the project of seeking an asylum in the New World, where God could be worshiped in accordance with their received opinions of his attributes. King Charles required no importuning for the furtherance of this plan, it being a matter of indifference to him whether they succeeded or failed, as he would be rid of these troublesome Protestant subjects, whom he both feared and hated. Jean Ribaut sailed from France in February, 1562, landing first on the south side of Anastasia Island, near the present site of St. Augustine, naming the inlet River of Dolphins, which they could not cross with their large ships because of the bar at its mouth. The river is now called Matanzas. They then sailed in a northerly direction from this point, naming the present St. John's May River, from the month in which they first discovered it. The French historian thus glowingly describes their impressions of the country: "The weather being fair, we viewed the lands as we passed, sparkling with flowers and verdure, the vast forests, the unknown birds, the game which appeared at the entrance of the glades and stood fearlessly gazing at the apparition of man." They entered a large inlet, ninety leagues north from Dolphin River, which Ribaut named Port Royal. On a small island they built a fort, and named it Charles, or Carolus, in honor of the French king. For three years this colony existed through hardships, but without persecution. However, unfortunately, the material they had enlisted to found a Reformed Church on foreign shores was mixed with dross—men without character or principle, whose vices were not improved by transplanting. Thus, the first endeavors made by persecuted men to seek an asylum in the New World, were attended with events too true to be disputed, and almost too tragical to receive credence. They present a striking instance of the chivalrous spirit which animated the reformers of that day, also the sanguinary disposition with which they were harassed by religious bigotry. After Ribaut had settled this colony, consisting of twenty-five men, in charge of Captain Albert, he sailed for France, to relate his discoveries and receive assistance. The captain, being on friendly terms with the Indians, went on expeditions through the country, one of which was to Onade, or Savannah River, where the Indians gave him pearls, gold, and crystals in which the ore was found. They also informed him that it was ten days' journey distant to these treasures, which were no doubt the mountains of Georgia now, then a portion of Florida. Ribaut was detained on his voyage to France by alternate storms and calms, until his ship-stores became exhausted, when they resorted to leather as a means of subsistence, and finally sacrificed one of their number to sustain life in the surviving ones. When he arrived in France, a civil war being in progress between the Catholics and Huguenots, no opportunity presented itself for fitting out an expedition, or sending relief to the little band at Port Royal. In consequence of this neglect they built themselves a mere shallop, in which they started for home. On the voyage they mutinied, killing their commander, and were finally, in a starving, sinking condition, taken on board an English vessel. A portion of them were landed in France, and the remainder on the shores of England. Those in the English dominions were brought before the king, where they related their adventures in the New World, which narration first turned the attention of the English to this country.

The command of the second expedition was given to one of Ribaut's companions, Laudonnière. They again landed south of the River May; but having received the news that Port Royal was abandoned, and being saddened from old associations, they determined to settle near the mouth of May River, it having presented the most attractions to them on a former visit, as here they had been supplied with more corn and grain, besides gold and silver, than at any other place. In the month of June, 1564, they commenced building a fort, felling trees, clearing away undergrowth, hewing timbers, and throwing up intrenchments. The form of this palisade was triangular, on two sides of which were a trench and walls of earth, with retreating angles and platforms for admitting four cannons; the other side was constructed of heavy timbers locked together. This structure was built on the present site of St. John's Bluff, the land being claimed by an Indian chief who rendered them good service in its construction, also in erecting their store-houses and buildings. The Indians were easily remunerated for their labor, being satisfied with a few trinkets, toys, or hatchets. The roofs were of palm-leaves, ingeniously woven together after the Indian method. The French took possession of the country in the name of King Charles, their sovereign, calling their new fort Caroline also. The Indians entertained their visitors with marvelous tales of "a nation who covered their bodies with gold and silver plates when they fought, which protected them from the arrows of their enemies, shot from the largest bows." This information inflamed the ambition of the Frenchmen so much that, as soon as the fort furnished a defense for them, the ships departed for France, leaving supplies with the colony for nine months. The new settlers again became restless, not hearing from those who had sailed, receiving no assistance from France, and as provisions were failing also, they commenced building a vessel for their return. In this extremity they were visited by Captain Hawkins, who had sailed from the West Indies — his object in entering the river being to obtain a supply of fresh water. Seeing what would be the result of their undertaking, he dissuaded them from going to sea in their dangerous craft; he also sold them a vessel and provisions, which produced a reconciliation in their ranks. A fleet of seven vessels sailed from the port of Dieppe, May 22, 1565, landing, three months from that date, on the coast of Florida. Laudonnière, at first, thought them his enemies, who had mutinied and left for France, where they had been circulating evil reports in regard to his judicial character, but was much pleased to find Ribaut had returned, who then took command of Fort Caroline, and Laudonnière commenced making preparations for sailing to France, where he had been ordered. In the meantime information had been received by the Spanish monarch of a Huguenot settlement on the coast of Florida. It was the religious, and not the political, zeal of the Spaniards, as circumstances go to prove, that moved them to plan the destruction of this infant colony. Pedro Melendez de Avilez, a marine officer in the time of Philip II. of Spain, importuned the king, on account of his desire for worldly honors, to be sent to the then wilds of Florida. For the furtherance of his plans he made the following plea as the philanthropic design of his unselfish motives: "Such grief seizes me when I behold this multitude of wretched Indians, that I should choose the conquest and settling of Florida above all commands, or offices and dignities which your majesty might see proper to bestow." His commission was received without difficulty, when he adopted the motto, "Plunder from heretics is good for the soul as well as the purse." On the 4th of September, 1565, six vessels were seen coming from the sea, which dropped anchor near the four large vessels of Ribaut. They were recognized as Spanish galleons, and the French were hailed to know "what they were doing in the dominions of King Philip." No other demonstrations were then made, except that he was their enemy. The enterprise of Melendez had now assumed an appearance of more dignity; it became a crusade, and the eager impulse of ambition was stimulated by all the usual arguments in favor of a religious war. The extirpation of heresy was an object equally grateful to the legitimates both of France and Spain, Charles IX. cheerfully yielding up his Protestant subjects in Florida to the tender mercies of Spanish propagandists. Melendez came to Florida as a conqueror, and to convert the Indians. In consideration of his bearing a greater portion of the expense, he was styled the Adelantado of the Floridas. During the voyage they encountered storms which decreased their numbers nearly one-third. Having heard of the colony being reënforced, doubts were entertained of their strength to attack it, and Melendez appealed to them in the following manner: "The Almighty has thus reduced our force, that his own right arm might achieve the work." The French were unprepared for the rapidity of the progress made by the Spaniards, and when the galleons anchored Ribaut was at La Caroline. Fortunately, they did not reach May River until near night, when darkness prevented an attack, which was the occasion of their civility. They lowered sail, cast anchor, and forbore all offensive demonstrations. But one circumstance confirmed the apprehensions of the Frenchmen: in the brief conversation which ensued between the parties on the arrival of the Spaniards, was their inquiries after the chief captains and leaders of the French fleet, calling them by their names and surnames, thus betraying an intimate knowledge of matters which had been judiciously kept secret as possible in France, showing conclusively that before Melendez left Spain he was thoroughly informed, by those who knew, of the condition, movements, and strength of Ribaut's armament. Why this information, unless there were some designs for acting upon it? The French officers compared notes that night, in respect to these communications, concurring in the belief that they stood in danger of an assault. They accordingly made preparations to leave with the dawn. At an early hour the Spaniards begun to draw near the French, but the sails of these were already hoisted to the breeze. Their cables severed at the first sign of hostility, when the chase begun with the greatest animation. If the Huguenots were deficient in force, they had the advantage in swift sailing. They suffered nothing from the distant cannonading, although the chase lasted all day. At the approach of night the Spaniards tacked ship and stood for the River Selooe, named by the French Dolphin, a distance overland of but eight or ten leagues from La Caroline. Finding they had the advantage of their enemies in fleetness, the French vessels came about also, following at a respectful distance. After having made all the discoveries possible, they returned to May River, when Ribaut came aboard. They reported to him that the great ship of the Spaniards, called "The Trinity," still kept the sea—that two ships had entered Dolphin River, and three remained at its mouth, while the Spaniards had evidently employed themselves in putting soldiers, with arms, munitions, and provisions, upon shore. Emoloa, one of the Indian kings in amity with the French, sent them word "that the Spaniards had gone on shore in great numbers, and that they had deprived the natives of their houses at that village." Generals Patino and Vicente had taken control of a huge barn-like structure, formerly occupied by the Indian Cazique, which was constructed from the trunks of large trees, and thatched over with palmetto. They begun work on this newly-captured fortification by intrenching with sand, employing the negroes they had brought with them, this being the first introduction of slave-labor into the United States. This Indian council-house, used as a fortification by Melendez, was destroyed by fire. Twenty years afterward another structure of logs was reared on the same spot, in the form of an octagon. It was finished in 1722, the design being to impress strangers and frighten savages. It was christened San Juan de Pinas. After some preliminaries, preparatory to a formal reception, the Spaniards took possession of the country amid the firing of cannons, flourishing of trumpets, and flinging of banners to the breeze. The priest Mendoza, with his acolytes, met Melendez with all the pomp of a conquering prince, chanting the "*Te Deum Laudamus*," when the Adelantado and his companions kneeled, kissing the crucifix, while the Indians assembled, gazing in silent wonder, as the solemn mass of "Our Lady" was performed, and the foundation of St. Augustine laid. Thus was planted by Pedro Melendez the broad banner of Spain, with its castellated towers, in the lonely Indian village of Selooe, beside the river which the Huguenots had previously dignified with the title of "La Riviere des Dolphins." It was on the 28th of August, 1565, the day on which the Spaniards celebrate the Feast of St. Augustine, that the Adelantado entered the mouth of the Selooe River, being attracted by the general appearance of the country, and resolved to establish a town and fortress. Having previously come on shore with a portion of his forces, he found himself welcomed by the savages, whom he treated kindly, and who requited him with the assurances of friendship. Mendoza, the priest who accompanied the Adelantado, kept a journal of their movements both on the voyage and after landing in America. If he had been a man of more intelligence, posterity would now be greatly benefited by his records, as they are so closely connected with the birth of our great republic. Ribaut, concluding that the Spaniards designed to assail the settlement of La Caroline from this point, with a view of exterminating the colonists from the country, boldly conceived a move for taking the initiative in the war. He first assembled his chief captains in the chamber of Laudonnière, that official being ill. He compared the relative condition of their own and the enemy's strength, concluding that he could embark with all his forces and seek the fleet of the Spaniards, particularly at a moment when it was somewhat scattered—with only one great ship at sea, and the rest not conditioned to support each other in the event of a sudden attack, as the troops of the Adelantado, with a portion on shore and the remainder on board their vessels, would not be ready for immediate action. Laudonnière was entirely opposed to the scheme of Ribaut, representing the defenseless condition of the fortress and the dangers of a fleet at sea, particularly during a season distinguished for storms and hurricanes. Ribaut, being an old soldier and sea-captain, was too eager for an engagement to heed any arguments that partook of cowardice. He ordered all the soldiers subject to his command to board their vessels. Not satisfied with this force, he lessened the strength of the garrison by taking a detachment of its best men, leaving few to keep the post but invalids. On the 8th of September, 1565, he left in pursuit of the Spaniards, and Laudonnière never saw him again. Nature put on her wildest moods, and the skies were swallowed up in tempests. The storm continued so long that Laudonnière mustered his command and proceeded to put the fortress in the best possible condition for defense. Work advanced slowly in consequence of the continued bad weather. The whole force left in the garrison consisted of but eighty-six men capable of bearing arms. Ribaut, relying upon the impression that he should find his enemy at sea in full force, stripped the garrison of its strength. His vessels being swifter than those of the Spaniards, he was certain that if any demonstration should be made against La Caroline, he could interpose. He made no calculation for the caprices of the weather and cool prudence of Pedro Melendez. He intended first to destroy the fleet of the enemy, and then make a descent upon the troops on land before they could fortify their camps, thus overcoming them with his superior and unembarrassed forces. The condition of things at La Caroline when Ribaut took his departure was deplorable enough, but rendered still more so by a scanty supply of food for the helpless who remained. Laudonnière proceeded to assume the defensive attitude in the event of an attack; but at the recurrence of stormy weather they ceased work, supposing the Spaniards would not expose themselves during the severity of an equinoctial gale.

While Melendez was busy with the preliminaries incident to founding a new settlement, having celebrated the divine mysteries in a manner both solemn and ostentatious, the fleet of Ribaut made its appearance at the mouth of the inlet. His extreme caution in sounding the bar to which his vessels were approaching lost him two precious hours, but for which his conquest must have been certain. Had the two remaining vessels been captured, and Melendez made prisoner, then a descent upon the dismayed troops on shore, not yet intrenched, when the annihilation of the settlement must have ensued: thus the whole destiny of Florida would have been changed, the Huguenot colonies established upon the soil, a firm possession of the land given to the French, that might have kept the *fleur-de-lis* waving from its summit to this day. At the very instant when the hands of Ribaut were stretched to seize

his prize, the sudden force of the hurricane parted
them—the trembling ships gradually disappearing
with their white wings in the distance and darkness,
like feeble birds borne onward in the wild fury of
the tempest. Meanwhile the mind of Melendez was
not idle; a bright thought had flashed across his
pathway which opened daring exploits. His officers
were summoned to a council of solemn debate and
deliberate action in regard to their future movements. It was midnight when the assemblage of
the Spanish captains took place in the great council-
house of the savages of Selooe. Rude logs strewn
about the building, even as they had been employed
by the Indians, furnished seats for the Spanish officers. They surrounded a great fire of resinous
pine, which now blazed brightly in the apartment.
Silently the Castilian noblemen took their seats.
Melendez encouraged an immediate attack on Fort
Caroline while weakened by the absence of Ribaut
and his forces. His arguments and inflexible will
silenced opposition, when all the council gradually
became of his mind—the whole scene closing with
a benediction from Father Salvandi. Every preparation being completed, Melendez, with five hundred picked men, commenced an overland march to
Fort Caroline. It was on the night of the 19th of
September, 1565, Monsieur de La Vigne, being appointed to keep guard, with his company, and having a tender heart for the men in bad weather, pit-
ied the guards so much he permitted them to retire
to their lodgings, and also went himself. Foul
weather appeared to agree with the Spaniards, who

enjoyed the showers from which the French retired so willingly, and that night found them in readiness for an attack on the Huguenot colony. The surprise being complete, all show of resistance was useless. "Slay! smite! and spare not!" was the dreadful command of Melendez. "The groans of the heretic make music in the ears of Heaven!" Laudonnière, with eighteen of his companions, succeeded in escaping. Among this number was the celebrated painter Le Moyne, to whom we owe much for illustrations of Floridian scenery, lineaments, and costumes, preserved in De Bry and other collections. These sailed out the River May, and, after numerous adventures and detentions, arrived on the coast of England. The most cruel portion of this drama is the last act in regard to the fate of the wretched Huguenots taken at the capture of La Caroline, and the dark deed by which the Spanish chief tarnished the record which might have immortalized his name. All resistance having ceased on the part of the Huguenots at Caroline, the standard of Castile was unrolled from its battlements, instead of the white folds and the smiling lilies of France. The name of the fortress was solemnly changed to San Matheo—the day on which they found themselves in its possession being dedicated to the honor of that saint. The arms of France, and also of Coligny, which surmounted the gateways of the fort, were erased, and those of Spain graven instead. The keeping of the fortress was assigned to a garrison of three hundred men, under the command of Gonzalo de Villaroel. These services occupied but little time, not interfering with other performances of the Adelantado, which he thought not the less conspicuous among the duties required at his hands. The surviving prisoners were brought before him, among whom were many women and children. Besides those rescued by Laudonnèire, several had fled to the forests, taking shelter with the tribes of neighboring Indians, who in some instances were protected by them with fidelity, but in the greater number of cases, terrified by the sudden appearance and strength of the Spaniards, they yielded up the fugitives at the fierce demand of the Adelantado. Others of the unfortunate Huguenots, warned by the Indians that they could no longer harbor them, were shot down by their pursuers as they fled through the forests. The sight of weeping and trembling women and children, of naked captives, worn, exhausted, enfeebled by years, by disease, and cruel wounds, all pleading for his mercy, only seemed to strengthen him in his most cruel resolutions. "Separate these women from the other prisoners!" This was done. "Now, detach from these last all children under fifteen years." His command was obeyed. The women and children thus set apart were consigned to slavery: the younger ones were more readily persuaded to the Catholic altars, and thus finally achieved their deliverance. The more stubborn perished in their bonds, passing through various grades of degradation. With reference to the remainder history is terribly definite. Fixing his cold, dark eye upon the male captives, of whose fate he had said nothing, he demanded: "Is

there any among ye who profess the faith of the
Roman Catholic Church?" Two of the prisoners
replied in the affirmative. "Take these Christians
away, and let their bonds be removed. The holy
Father Salvandi will examine them in the faith of
the Mother Church. For the rest, are there any
among ye, seeing the error of your faith, will re-
nounce the heresy of Luther, and seek once more
communion with the only true Church?" A dread
calm ensued, the captives looking mournfully at
each other and the Adelantado, in whose face there
was no encouragement, and nothing but despair in
the appearance of their companions. "Be warned!"
continued the Adelantado. "To those who seek
the blessings of the true Church, she generously
openeth her arms; to those who turn away indiffer-
ently, or in scorn, are decreed death, both temporal
and eternal. Hear ye, and now say!" The silence
was unbroken. "Are ye obdurate? or do ye not
comprehend that your lives rest upon your speech?
Either ye embrace the safety which the Church of-
fers, by an instant renunciation of that of the foul
heretic, Luther, or ye die by the halter!" One
sturdy soldier advanced from the group—a bold,
high-souled fellow—his brows lifted proudly with
the conscious impulse which worked within his soul.
"Pedro Melendez, we are in your power. You are
master of our mortal bodies; but with the death
before us that you threaten, know that we are members of the Reformed Church of Christ, which ye
name to be of Luther, and, holding it good to live
in this faith, we deem it not amiss to die in it."

Then the speaker looked around him into the face of his fellows, as they lightened up with a glow of cheerfulness and pride, though no word was spoken. "Speak this man for the rest of ye?" demanded Melendez. For a moment there was silence. Finally a *matelot* advanced—a common sailor—a man before the mast. "Aye, aye, captain! What he says we say, and there's no use for more palaver. Let there be an end of it. We are of the Church of Monsieur Luther, and no other. If death's the word, we're not the men at the end of the reckoning to belie the whole voyage!" "Be it even as ye say!" answered Melendez, coldly but sternly, and without change of action or show of passion. "Take them forth, and let them be hung to yonder tree!"

The air was rent with the shrieks of women and cries of children—women endeavoring to save their husbands, and children clinging to the knees of their doomed sires, all of which produced no relentings—the parties being separated by a strong hand, and the doomed men hurried to the fatal tree, the priest standing ready to receive their recantations. Exhortations were not spared—soldier and sailor had equally spoken for the martyrdom of the whole —the reverend father preaching and promising all in vain. Amid cries and shrieks, the victims were run up to the wide-spreading branches of a mighty oak, disgraced in its employment for such a purpose, where they perished with fidelity to the faith which they professed. Their bodies were left hanging in the sun and wind, destined equally as trophies of the victor and warnings to the heretic. Melendez caused a monument to be raised beneath the tree, upon which was printed, in large characters, "These do not suffer thus as Frenchmen, but as heretics and enemies to God." Melendez thus became master of Fort Caroline, wresting a country from the Huguenots which they had acquired through so many vicissitudes. Before leaving he lingered to review the garrison, and founded with his own bloody hands a church dedicated to the God of mercy. He then departed with a small body of troops, arriving at his camp in safety. He was received as the vanquisher of heretics. After this slaughter the victors entered St. Augustine in solemn procession, with four priests in front, chanting the *Te Deum* in triumph. However, his victory was not without its disquietude, having heard of Ribaut somewhere on the coast, and his own shipping destroyed. The unfortunate Ribaut, driven before the hurricane, had been wrecked with all his squadron upon the bleak, unfriendly shores of Cape Cannaveral, his troops being saved, but the crew drowned.

On the 28th of September, when the weary Adelantado was taking his *siesta* under the sylvan roof of a Seloy, a band of Indians came in with news that quickly roused him from his slumbers: "A French vessel had been wrecked on the coast toward the south. Those who escaped from her were some four leagues off, on the banks of a river, or arm of the sea, which they could not cross. Melendez immediately sent a detachment of men to reconnoiter. They rowed along the channel between Anastasia Island and the main shore. After landing they struck across the island on foot, traversing plains and marshes, reaching the sea toward night. Craftily concealing his troops on the opposite shore, he climbed a tree for the purpose of reconnoitering. From this point he saw the dismayed band of Frenchmen grouped together, about two hundred strong, and, on account of rough waters, were unable to cross in a raft they had constructed."

We have now seen how, when Jean Ribaut was making an attack on the Spaniards, his plans were thwarted by a storm of strange fury. One of the ships was wrecked at a point farther northward than the rest, and it was her company whose camp-fires were seen by the Spaniards at their bivouac among the sands of Anastasia Island. They were attempting to reach Fort Caroline, in regard to whose fate they knew nothing, while Ribaut, with the remainder, was farther southward, struggling through the wilderness toward the same goal. Of the fate of the former party there is no French record. Solis, the priest and brother-in-law to Melendez, was eye-witness to the following scenes, a report of which was sent to Spain:

When the Adelantado saw the French fires at a distance, he dressed in the garb of a common sailor, and rowed toward the shipwrecked men, the better to learn their condition. A bold Gascon succeeded in making the passage by swimming, when Melendez demanded, "Who are you?" The Frenchman replied, "We are the people of Ribaut, Captain-general of Florida." "Are you Lutherans?" "We are Lutherans." "Gentlemen," continued Melendez, "your fort is taken, and all in it put to the sword, save the women and children under fifteen years of age." In proof of which he caused articles of plunder from Fort Caroline to be shown to the unhappy Frenchmen.

He then left and went to breakfast with his officers, first ordering food to be set before his petitioners. Having eaten, he returned to them. "Are you convinced, now, that what I have told you is true?" The French captain assented. "But assist us to leave—that is, in truth, what we demand." "Demand nothing of me, for I tell you, as a gentleman and an officer, holding a high commission from the Court of Spain, that, if the heavens were to mingle before my eyes, the resolution I once make I never change. If you were Catholics, and I had ships, I would help you, but I have none."

The supplicants expressed a hope that they would be allowed to remain with the Spaniards till ships could be sent to their relief, since there was peace between the two nations, whose kings were friends and brothers. "We are men made equally in the image of Deity, and serve the same God, if not at the same altars." "If you will give up your arms and banners, and place yourselves at my mercy, you may do so, and I will act toward you as God shall give me grace. Do as you will, for other than this you can have neither truce nor friendship with me."

One of the Frenchmen recrossed to consult with his companions. After two hours he returned, offering a large amount for their lives, which was not accepted. Privations had demoralized these starving

Frenchmen, who then gave credence to vain hopes which they would not have entertained from an enemy at any other time. They had no other resource but to yield themselves to his mercy. The boat was again sent across the river, and returned laden with their banners and weapons of warfare. The Adelantado ordered twenty of his men to bring over ten Frenchmen at a time. He then took the French officers aside, and, with a semblance of courtesy on his lips and murder in his heart, he said: "Gentlemen, I have but few men, and you are so many, that, if you were free, it would be easy for you to take your satisfaction on us for the people we killed when we took your fort; therefore it is necessary that you should go to my camp, four leagues distant from this place, with your hands tied." Accordingly, as each party advanced, they were led out of sight behind the sand-hills, and their hands tied behind them with the match-cord of the arquebuses, though not before they had been supplied with food. Twelve Breton sailors professed themselves Catholics, together with four carpenters and calkers, "of whom," writes Melendez, "I was in great need," who were put on a boat and sent to St. Augustine. The remainder were ordered to march thither by land. The Adelantado walked in advance until he came to a lonely spot not far distant among the bush-covered hills. Here he stopped and drew a line in the sand with his cane. Not one of this wretched company, not being Catholics, was allowed to cross, and the whole two hundred perished.

Again Melendez returned to St. Augustine, gloating over his success. Great as had been his victory, he still had cause for anxiety, as Ribaut could not be far off. On the next day Indians came with the tidings that on the spot where the first party of the shipwrecked Frenchmen had been found was now another still larger party. The murder-loving race looked with great respect on Melendez, for his wholesale butchery of the night before was an exploit rarely equaled in their own annals of massacre. Melendez doubted not that Ribaut was at hand. He started on a march thither immediately with one hundred and fifty men, reaching the inlet at midnight, when, like a skulking savage, he intrenched himself on the bank. After daybreak flags of truce were displayed on both sides, when La Caille, Ribaut's sergeant-major, informed Melendez that the French were three hundred and fifty in number, on their way to Fort Caroline, and, like the former party, begged for boats to aid them in crossing the river. Melendez gave them assurances of safety, and sent for Ribaut and six of his companions. On their arrival he met them courteously, caused wine and preserved fruits to be placed before them, and next led Ribaut to the reeking Golgotha, where, in heaps upon the sand, lay the corpses of his slaughtered followers; but he would not believe Fort Caroline had been taken until part of the plunder was shown him. Ribaut then urged that the kings of Spain and France were brothers and close friends, and begged that the Spaniards would aid him in carrying his followers home. Melendez gave the same unequivocal answer as before to the other party. Ribaut, after three hours' absence, came back in the canoe, and told the Adelantado that some of his people were willing to surrender, at discretion, but many refused. "They can do as they please," was the reply of Melendez. Ribaut offered large rewards for those who had surrendered. Melendez replied, "I have great need of the money," which gave the French encouragement, when they asked permission to cross the river. In the morning he returned, and reported that two hundred of his men had retreated from the spot, but the remaining one hundred and fifty would surrender. At the same time he gave into the hands of Melendez the royal standard and other flags, his sword, dagger, helmet, and the official seal given him by Coligny.

Melendez entered the boat and directed his officers to bring over the French by tens. He next led Ribaut among the bushes behind the neighboring sand-hills, when he ordered his hands to be bound fast. Then the scales fell from his eyes, and face to face his fate rose up before him. The day wore on, and, as band after band of prisoners were brought over, they were conducted behind the sand-hills, out of sight from the farther shore, like their general. "Are you Catholics or Lutherans? and are there any among you who will go to confession?" asked Melendez. Ribaut answered, "I and all here are of the Reformed faith," at the same time intoning the psalm, "*Memento, Domine.*" A few were spared. "I saved," writes Melendez, "the lives of two young gentlemen about eighteen years of age, besides the fifer, the drummer, and trumpeter; but I caused Jean Ribaut, with all the rest, to be put to the sword—judging this to be expedient for the service of God our Lord and your majesty."

As each successive party landed, their hands were bound fast behind their backs, when they were driven, like cattle, toward the fort. At a signal from drums and trumpets the Spaniards fell upon them, striking them down with swords, pikes, and halberds. Ribaut vainly called on the Adelantado to remember his oath. By his order, a soldier plunged a dagger into the French commander's heart, when Ottigny, who stood near, met a similar fate. The head of Ribaut was then hewn into four pieces, one part of which was displayed on the point of a lance at each corner of the fort in St. Augustine. Great fires were kindled, and the bodies of the murdered burned to ashes. At night, when the Adelantado again entered St. Augustine, there were some who blamed his cruelty, but many applauded. A few days after, the remainder of the shipwrecked Frenchmen were discovered by the Indians, who again informed Melendez. In all haste he dispatched messengers for a reënforcement of one hundred and fifty men from Fort Caroline. On the 2d of November he set forth with such merciless energy that some of his men dropped dead with fatigue. When, from their frail defenses, the French saw the Spanish pikes, they fled, panic-stricken, taking refuge among the sand-hills. Melendez sent a trumpeter, summoning them, also pledging his honor for their safety. Some of them sent word they "would rather be eaten by savages than trust themselves to Spaniards," and, escaping, fled to the Indian towns. The rest surrendered, and Melendéz kept his word. Those of high birth ate at the Adelantado's table. The captives' fate may be learned from a reply to one of Melendez's dispatches. "Say to him," writes Philip the Second, "that, as to those he has killed, he has done well, and, as to those he has saved, they shall be sent to the galleys." Melendez, although victorious over the unfortunate Frenchmen, had other troubles to contend with at St. Augustine and San Mateo. The Spaniards became restless, mutinied, and deserted, leaving his forces much weakened. In addition to this, a hostile cazique lived between the two forts — thus cutting off all communication by land between them. Melendez made an attack on this chief, in which he was repulsed—thus compelling him to act on the defensive. As these improvident Spaniards consumed every thing, and raised nothing, the Indians became weary feeding them without any reward: for this cause Melendez was forced to sail for Cuba to obtain supplies. During his absence a Spanish fleet arrived, bringing both men and provisions, which gave them much encouragement. The missionaries heretofore meeting with such rough treatment, some time had elapsed since any new arrivals. However, three Jesuit priests were discovered off the coast, near the mouth of San Mateo River,

making inquiries for the fort. These were the first
of that Order that had ever come to America, the
others being Franciscans. One party of Indians directed them, while afterward they were murdered
by another on St. George's Island, at the entrance
of San Mateo River. Melendez now sailed for
Spain, to interest the crown in behalf of his colony.
After a prosperous voyage across the sea, he landed
on the shores of Spain, where he was received with
a great display of empty honors, which did not satisfy the cravings of his ambition. It was money he
wanted, to strengthen his newly-acquired territory,
build up his dominions, and with them a great name
for himself. He was also impatient and apprehen-
sive in regard to a threatened revenge which the
French had proposed taking into their own hands.
In vain had petitions been sent by the relatives of
the slain, but never, until a new Cavalier entered
the field, as contestant, in the person of the daring
Chevalier de Gourgues, did injured humanity find
an avenger, or outraged France a champion. De
Gourgues, being of gentle birth, according to the
chivalrous custom in those days, was educated to
the profession of arms. He entered upon his duties as a private, but was soon promoted on account
of laurels won in battle, being afterward commissioned to an office of distinction, as captain in the
regular army. He was given the command of a
fortress, which, being attacked by a greatly superior
number of Spaniards, compelled him to surrender;
his men were all killed, and himself made prisoner
and condemned to servitude on the galleys. Fortu-

nately for himself, the vessel on which he worked was shortly afterward captured by the Turks, which enabled him to obtain his liberty. Activity being his motto, he sailed on an expedition to Brazil, from which enterprise he realized a considerable fortune. On the return of De Gourgues to France, and hearing of the cruelties committed against his countrymen, the iron of revenge was driven deep into his soul, not only for their mistreatment, but the indignity he had suffered from the Spaniards himself. He accordingly fitted out two vessels and a tender, obtaining a charter without difficulty, under the pretext of going to Africa and bringing back slaves. He communicated his plans to no person, but secured the services of one of Laudonnière's men, who had remained in Florida long enough to have some knowledge of the country and the language of the natives. He also enlisted the services of one hundred and fifty picked men, and set sail from Bordeaux August 2, 1567. In order to better conceal his plans, he first landed on the coast of Africa, where he encountered some of the natives, whom he repulsed—afterward, sailing westward, he came in port for repairs and supplies at Santo Domingo. When he reached this point he revealed to his crew the design of his long and perilous voyage. He depicted, in glowing colors, the wrongs sustained by their countrymen, which yet remained unavenged. The crew, with one voice, replied that they would sustain him in the undertaking. The voyage was soon completed, and so entirely unsuspecting were the Spaniards of an attack that, on passing Fort Caroline—now Fort San Mateo—De Gourgues was honored with a salute of two cannon, supposing them to be of their own nation. He entered the mouth of the Altamaha, and, as his galleys drew but little water, and were provided with oars, he had no difficulty in ascending that river. The natives received them kindly, and the soldiers of Laudonnière being recognized, their mission was not regarded as a friendly one.

Immediate preparations were made to attack the fort, as one of the officers had reconnoitered its strength. These works had been much improved by the Spaniards, to which were added two other forts, the whole garrison consisting of four hundred men. Its present condition was their boast. The priest, Mendoza, said, "Not half of France could take it." De Gourgues formed an encampment twelve miles north of the mouth of a small river. The whole affair was conducted in a most skillful and secret manner, he using the Indians as valuable accessions in the enterprise, they being no friends to the Spaniards. The French approached the fort at dawn, but remained concealed until the tide receded, that they might reach the island on which it stood. They made the attack at midday, when the two small forts were carried by direct assault, killing nearly all the men, about sixty in number, while the avenues of escape leading from Fort Mateo were guarded by the Indians. Fort San Mateo alone remained, which was three miles above. Among the prisoners saved was a sergeant, who knew the heights of the ramparts, and could draw a plan of

the fort. While ladders were being prepared to
scale the works, the garrison precipitated its fate
by a sally, afterward making an attempt to gain the
woods. The thickets were filled with exasperated
Indians, and not one Spaniard escaped. A few
prisoners were taken, which De Gourgues suspended
on the same tree that had borne his countrymen;
and for the monument and inscription of Melendez
was substituted a pine plank with this inscription:
"Not as Spaniards, or mariners, but as traitors, robbers, and murderers." To render this work of destruction more complete, they entirely demolished
the forts. When returning to his ships, he exclaimed, "All that we have done was for the service
of the king, and for the honor of the country!"
His soldiers, flushed with victory, proposed an attack
on St. Augustine, but De Gourgues felt that his resources were insufficient. For some time subsequent to this period the Spaniards retained Florida,
although their forts had been destroyed on San Mateo River. After the arrival of De Gourgues in his
own country the French Government persecuted
him, and the Spanish pursued him until his death.
He died deeply involved from the expense connected
with his expedition. Thus terminated all dispute
in regard to French Florida—the question then to
be decided was between the British and Spaniards.
Melendez, after making other efforts to Christianize
the Indians, having brought over more missionaries,
which they murdered without distinction, regarding
the priests and people as sworn enemies, abandoned
the enterprise, and turned his attention entirely

to arms. However, in the midst of his career, he was cut down by death, at Santander, a town situated on the northern coast of Spain, A.D. 1574, after having received the appointment of Captain-general over a Spanish armada of three hundred vessels.

From the above history it will be seen that Florida remained for many years disputed ground, the scene of numerous conflicts from different sources. Whether the priest with his cross, or the warrior with his sword, they all came to vie with each other in the establishment of creeds and division of spoils. It was in 1564 Sir Walter Raleigh, who, being present when the men from Fort Caroline, or Port Royal, were received by the queen, was thus stimulated with a desire to visit this newly-explored country. This feeling was increased by De Morgues, the companion and artist who came with Laudonnière, and had furnished them with beautiful drawings of his travels in these far-off lands. It was the intention of Sir Walter, besides making discoveries, to capture Spanish galleons, which would satisfy his desire for gain. This plundering policy, which had been pursued so extensively by all the adventurers, was in no way designed to promote the welfare of a new settlement. Under the auspices of the English throne an expedition was sent, commanded by Sir Walter Raleigh, which landed on the coast of Florida, as the division of the country was then recognized. After his arrival he thus mentions the Indians: "These people were most loving and faithful, such as lived after the golden age." He was also much impressed with the land along the shores as they passed. "The fragrance," he says, "was as if they had been in the midst of some delicate garden, with all kinds of odoriferous flowers." Raleigh also visited the Indies, and on his return succeeded in capturing a ship richly laden with Spanish treasures, after which he sailed for England, where a warm welcome awaited him. Contrary to his expectations, on his arrival he became too much occupied with affairs of a different nature to visit America again. However, other expeditions were fitted out, which settled in different parts of the country. It was in 1586 that Sir Francis Drake, the English adventurer, while coming from the West Indies, discovered the lookout at Anastasia Island, which commanded the approach to St. Augustine harbor. He landed, bringing a piece of ordnance, from which, after planting, he fired two shots, one of them damaging the Spanish standard, and the other striking the castle. The next day they renewed the attack, with no return of hostilities from the shore, and on landing found the town deserted. In the fort they discovered the mahogany treasury-chest, containing two thousand pounds sterling, designed for paying the troops, which Sir Francis confiscated. The castle at this time was the foundation of the Selooe defense, repaired by Melendez. It was constructed from the trunks of pine-trees planted upright, similar to our stockades of the present day, without ditches. Trunks of trees were laid across the whole structure, after which it was covered with earth. The works, being unfinished, were incapable of resisting a naval attack. An English officer, while pursuing the Spaniards, was shot, for which act the English sacked and then burned St. Augustine. It is said this town then contained a monastery, church, and hall of justice—certainly very little to tempt the cupidity of a West Indies privateer. Sir Francis made this expedition on the ground that Spain had damaged the English commerce during their troubles. In 1603, more than a hundred years from the discovery of Cabot, and twenty years from the time Raleigh sent out his first expedition, not an Englishman remained in the New World. In 1702, Spain and England not being friendly, Governor Moore, of South Carolina, proposed an expedition against St. Augustine, for the purpose of displaying his military prowess, capturing Indians, or enriching himself with plunder. Colonel Daniel took charge of the land portion of the enterprise, which ascended the St. John's, crossed over the country from Picolata, entered the town without resistance, and sacked it. The inhabitants, being warned of their intentions, had supplied themselves with four months' rations, and taken refuge, with their gold and valuables, in the castle, from which place they could not be dislodged. When Governor Moore landed and saw their position, he sent to Jamaica for cannon and mortars. Before their arrival the Spaniards received assistance by a fleet coming from Havana. On their appearance Governor Moore became panic-stricken, left his vessels, and fled by land to Carolina. On the return of Colonel Daniel, he, not knowing the siege had been raised, narrowly escaped falling into the hands of his enemies. The besieged prisoners now came from the castle, after a stay of three months, to find their pleasant homes destroyed.

During 1715 Florida received a new accession from the Yemassees. These Indians were found in Florida when the Spaniards first landed, but deserted the country on account of efforts being made to convert them to Christianity. They took refuge in Carolina, where, after remaining awhile, they massacred some of the English colonists, and then retreated to St. Augustine for protection. Here they were received with marked demonstrations of kindness, accompanied by the ringing of bells and firing of cannon. The Spaniards in Florida, having had a respite from troublesome invaders for some time, were progressing prosperously, until after the arrival of General Oglethorpe from England. In 1737, hostilities having commenced between Spain and England, Oglethorpe, fearing an attack from the Spaniards, planted a battery on Cumberland Island as a defense. This movement was productive of dissension among the settlers. England claimed as far as the St. John's, on account of discoveries made by Sir Walter Raleigh, while the Spanish sent a commissioner for the English to abandon all the territory south of St. Helena's Sound, which they refused to relinquish. When the Spanish ascertained that Oglethorpe had taken command of the English forces, a party from St. Augustine garrison advanced as far as Amelia Island, killed two Highlanders, and then cut off their heads. The English pursued them to San Mateo, on the St. John's, drove in the

Spanish guards, and then sailed up the river as far as Cavallas. After the return of Oglethorpe he commenced recruiting from the Creek and Cherokee Indians, thus making active preparations for blockading St. Augustine before men and supplies could arrive from Havana. Don Manuel being governor then, he was ready for defense. General Oglethorpe did not succeed in capturing the town, although he invested three fortifications, advancing with his forces to its gates, killing several Spanish troops under the walls of the fort. Fort Diego, twenty-five miles from St. Augustine, Fort Francis de Pupa, seventeen miles, and Fort Moosa, two miles north, commonly called Negro Fort, where the runaway slaves were harbored, all surrendered. In 1748 a treaty of peace was concluded between Spain and England, which left Florida in the quiet possession of the Spaniards for many years.

FLORIDA GAZETTEER OF THE MOST IMPORTANT POINTS IN THE STATE.

ABE'S SPRING.—The county-seat of Calhoun, 104 miles south-west from Tallahassee.

ADAMSVILLE.—A small settlement in Sumter county, 5 miles west of Leesburg, containing a post-office.

ALACHUA COUNTY.—County-seat, Gainesville.

ALAFIA.—A settlement on Alafia River, in Hillsboro county, containing a post-office.

ALIQUA.—Settlement on a river of the same name, in Walton county, West Florida, where, it is said, the houses were forty miles apart.

ALMIRANTE.—Walton county, West Florida, near the Alabama line.

ANCLOTE RIVER.—A tributary of Clear Water Harbor, in Hillsboro county.

ANDERSON.—In Santa Rosa county, West Florida.

APOPKA.—Near Lake Apopka, in Orange county, containing a post-office. The name implies " Potato-eating Town."

APPALACHICOLA.—Contains a post-office, and is situated at the mouth of a river of the same name. It was formerly a prosperous city, but, on account of the cotton being taken by the railroads, has declined.

ARCHER.—Post-offie. A town in Alachua county, 41 miles from Cedar Keys.

ARLINGTON.—In Duval county, opposite Jacksonville.

ARREDONDO.—Post-office. A station 54 miles from Cedar Keys, in Alachua county.

ASPALAGA.—In Gadsden county, on Appalachicola River.

AUCILLA.—Jefferson county, on the Pensacola and Mobile Railroad.

AUGUSTA.—On the hack-line from Gainesville to Tampa.

BAGDAD.—On Pensacola Bay, Santa Rosa county, West Florida.

BAKER COUNTY.—Celebrated for its timber, turpentine, and agricultural productions. In East Florida.

BALDWIN.—Post-office and telegraph-station, 20 miles from Jacksonville, on the Pensacola and Mobile Railroad.

BANANA RIVER.—A branch of the Indian River.

BARRANCAS.—A fort commanding the entrance to Pensacola Bay.

BARRSVILLE.—In Columbia county, south of Lake City. Post-office.

BARTOW.—County-seat of Polk county, South Florida.

BATTON.—A station on the West India Transit Railroad.

BAYPORT.—Post-office. A town in Hernando county.

BEAR CREEK.—Near St. Andrew's Bay.

BEECHER.—A steamboat-landing in Putnam county, on the east bank of the St. John's.

BELLVILLE.—Post-office. A settlement in Hamilton county.

BENELLA.—On the St. John's River, 120 miles above Jacksonville.

BENTON.—Post-office, in Columbia county, on the upper waters of Suwanee River.

BISCAYNE.—County-seat of Dade county, formerly called Miami.

BLACK CREEK.—A tributary of the St. John's River, near Magnolia.

BLACK POINT.—A steamboat-landing, 10 miles above Jacksonville.

BLACKWATER RIVER.—A tributary of Pensacola Bay, in Santa Rosa county, West Florida.

BLOUNT'S FERRY.—On the Suwanee River, in Columbia county. Post-office.

BLUE CREEK.—Liberty county, near Gadsden.

BLUE SPRING.—Jackson county, west of Marianna.

BLUE SPRING.—Post-office, Volusia county.

BLUNT'S TOWN.—Calhoun county, West Florida.

BRADFORD COUNTY.—On the West India Transit Company Railroad. County-seat, Lake Butler.

BREVARD COUNTY.—Lies on both sides of the Indian River. Fort Pierce, the county-seat.

BRISTOL.—County-seat of Liberty county. Post-office.

BRONSON.—County-seat of Levy county. Post-office. On the West India Transit Railroad. 12 miles from here is a bed of iron ore.

BROOKLYN.—A town near Jacksonville. Rather prospective.

BROOKSVILLE.—County-seat of Hernando county. Post-office. On the Tampa stage-line.

BROTHER'S RIVER.—In Calhoun county, West Florida.

BUFFALO BLUFF.—On the west bank of the St. John's, in Putnam county. Post-office.

BULOW'S CREEK.—In Volusia county.

BUNKER HILL.—Near Lake Miccosukee, Leon county.

BURRIN.—Bradford county. On the West India Transit Railroad.

CABBAGE BLUFF.—On the east bank of the St. John's, 162 miles above Jacksonville. Post-office.

CALHOUN COUNTY.—West Florida. County-seat, Abe's Spring Bluff.

CALLAHAN.—On the West India Transit Railroad, 27 miles from Fernandina. Post-office.

CALOOSAHATCHEE RIVER.—A navigable stream which empties into Charlotte Harbor.

CAMPBELLTON.—A settlement in Jackson county.

CAMP IZARD.—In Marion county, on the Withlacoochee River. Post-office.

CEDAR KEYS.—In Levy county. Terminus of the West India Transit Railroad. Post-office.

CEDAR TREE.—In Hernando county, south of Brooksville.

CENTERVILLE.—Near Tallahassee, Leon county. Post-office.

CERRO GORDO.—The county-seat of Holmes county. Post-office.

CHALK SPRING.—Santa Rosa county, West Florida. Post-office.

CHARLES FERRY.—On Suwanee River, in Suwanee county.

CHATTAHOOCHEE.—The terminus of the Jacksonville, Pensacola, and Mobile Railroad. In Gadsden county. Post-office, Penitentiary, Lunatic Asylum.

CHIPOLA RIVER.—A tributary of the Appalachicola River.

CHOCTAWHATCHEE RIVER.—Flows into a bay of the same name, in West Florida.

CIRCLE HILL.—Near Marianna, Jackson county. Post-office.

CLAY COUNTY.—County-seat, Green Cove Spring, on the St. John's.

CLAY LANDING.—In Levy county, on the east bank of the Suwanee, near its mouth.

CLEAR WATER.—Post-office. On the Gulf coast, Hillsboro county.

CLIFTON.—A town in Madison county.

COCOANUT GROVE.—In Dade county.

COLUMBIA COUNTY.—County-seat, Lake City.

COOK'S FERRY.—A landing on Lake Harney, 224 miles above Jacksonville.

CORK.—In Hillsboro county. Post-office.

CORKSCREW RIVER.—Monroe county, South Florida.

COTTON PLANT.—A settlement west of Ocala, Marion county. Post-office.

CRAWFORDSVILLE.—County-seat of Wakulla county. Post-office.

CRESWELL.—In Leon county.

CRYSTAL RIVER.—A clear stream of water flowing through Hernando county, emptying into the Gulf.

DADE COUNTY.—County-seat, Key Biscayne.

DANCEY'S PLACE.—A landing on the St. John's, 65 miles above Jacksonville. Post-office.

DANIEL.—A settlement near the mouth of Suwanee River, in Levy county.

DARBYVILLE.—Near Baldwin, Baker county. Post-office.

DAVIS.—A station on the railroad, near Chattahoochee.

DAYTONIA.—A settlement on Halifax River, in Volusia county. In very flourishing condition.

DEEP CREEK.—A tributary of Lake Harney.

DELK'S BLUFF.—A steamboat-landing on the Ocklawaha River, 100 miles from its mouth.

DRAYTON ISLAND.—On the St. John's, in Lake George, Marion county.

DUMMITT'S GROVE.—A noted orange-grove, in Volusia county, on the northern end of Indian River.

DUNN LAWTON.—A portion of the Turnbull Swamp, in Volusia county.

DUNN'S LAKE.—A small settlement in Volusia county. Post-office.

DURISOE.—A steamboat-landing, 89 miles above the mouth of the Ocklawaha River.

DUTTON.—A station 32 miles from Fernandina, on the West India Transit Railroad.

DUVAL COUNTY.—On the St. John's. County-seat, Jacksonville.

EAU CLAIRE.—A colony from Wisconsin, near Mellonville, Orange county.

EAU GALLIE.—On Indian River, in Brevard county, near Lake Washington. Post-office.

ECONFINA.—In Washington county, West Florida, on a river of the same name. Post-office.

EGMONT ISLAND.—Situated in the Gulf of Mexico, at the entrance of Espiritu Santo Bay.

ELBOW CREEK.—Rises in the swamps near Lake Washington.

Florida Gazetteer. 485

ELLAVILLE.—A station on the Jacksonville, Pensacola, and Mobile Railroad, 95 miles from Jacksonville.

ELLISVILLE.—A place without much celebrity at present, in Columbia county.

EMANUELS.—A landing-place on the St. John's, 184 miles above Jacksonville.

ENTERPRISE.—The county-seat of Volusia county since 1854. Situated 205 miles beyond Jacksonville. Post-office.

ESCAMBIA COUNTY.—Situated in West Florida, bordering on the Gulf. This county was first incorporated by order of General Jackson, July, 1821.

ESCAMBIA RIVER.—A tributary of Escambia Bay, West Florida.

EUREKA.—Two points in Florida bear this popular name. One is on the Ocklawaha, 60 miles above its mouth, in Marion county; the other, on the upper St. John's, in Orange county.

FEDERAL POINT.—Situated on the east bank of the St. John's, 60 miles above Jacksonville, in Putnam county.

FLEMINGTON.—Post-office. A small town on the Gainesville stage-route.

FORT BROOKS.—A steamboat-landing on the Ocklawaha River, near Orange Springs.

FORT GATES.—A steamboat-landing, 110 miles from Jacksonville, on the St. John's River, in Putnam county.

FORT GEORGE ISLAND.—Situated near the mouth of the St. John's River. Contains a good hotel, with accommodations for winter and summer visitors.

FORT MEAD.—On Pease Creek, 80 miles above its mouth. In Polk county. Cattle-sales are its principal commerce.

FORT PIERCE.—Situated on Indian River. County-seat of Brevard county.

FORT REID.—Post-office. An enterprising, growing town, in the neighborhood of Mellonville, on the St. John's.

FORT TAYLOR.—Post-office. In Hernando county.

FRANKLIN COUNTY.—Near the mouth of Appalachicola River. County-seat, Appalachicola.

FREEPORT.—Post-office. Located in Walton county, West Florida.

GADSDEN COUNTY.—County-seat, Quincy.

GAINESVILLE.—A large, flourishing town on the West India Transit Railroad. Post-office, churches, good boarding-houses.

GEORGETOWN.—A steamboat-landing on the east bank of the St.

John's, in Putnam county, 117 miles above Jacksonville. Post-office.

GORDON.—The terminus of the semi-weekly hack-line from Gainesville. In Alachua county.

GORES.—A landing on the Ocklawaha River, 83 miles above its mouth.

GRAHAM.—On the Ocklawaha, 84 miles above its mouth.

GREEN COVE SPRINGS.—A noted resort on the west bank of the St. John's, 30 miles above Jacksonville. County-seat of Clay county. Post-office.

GREENWOOD.—A town in Jackson county, near Marianna. Post-office.

HALIFAX RIVER.—In Volusia county. It is formed by the junction of the Haulover and Bulow Creeks, and the Tomoka River. It is a mile wide, and 30 miles in length, running nearly parallel with the coast.

HATCHEE RIVER.—Rises in Manatee county, and flows into Charlotte Harbor.

HAMBURG.—A town of small note, near Madison, Madison county.

HAMILTON COUNTY.—On the Georgia line. Contains an area of about 400 square acres.

HAMOSASSA.—A settlement in Hernando county, near the Gulf coast.

HANSON TOWN.—Named from the late Surgeon Hanson. Located in the vicinity of Jacksonville.

HATCH'S BEND.—Settlement near the Santa Fe River, in La Fayette county. Post-office.

HAULOVER CREEK.—A branch of Halifax River, in Volusia county.

HAWKINSVILLE.—A landing on the west bank of the St. John's, 160 miles from Jacksonville, in Orange county.

HAW CREEK.—A tributary of Dunn's Lake, Volusia county.

HAYWOOD'S LANDING.—On Chattahoochee River, Jackson county.

HERNANDO COUNTY. County-seat, Brooksville.

HIBERNIA.—A pleasant stopping-place, in Clay county, on the St. John's, 22 miles above Jacksonville. Post-office.

HICKORY HILL.—Near Marianna, Washington county, West Fla.

HILLSBORO COUNTY.—Celebrated for cattle-raising. Tampa is the county-seat.

HILLSBORO RIVER.—A favorite name for rivers in Florida—the first Hillsboro being a tributary of Tampa Bay; the second, Hillsboro

River in Dade county, on the Atlantic coast; the third, a lagoon in Volusia county.

HOGARTH'S LANDING.—On the east bank of the St. John's, 36 miles above Jacksonville. Post-office.

HOLMES COUNTY.—Near the Alabama line. County-seat, Cerro Gordo.

HORSE LANDING.—On the St. John's River, 94 miles above Jacksonville, in Putnam county.

HOUSTON.—On the Jacksonville and Pensacola Railroad, in Suwanee county. Post-office.

IAMONIA.—In Leon county, on a lake of the same name. Post-office.

INDIAN RIVER.—A body of salt-water 100 miles in length—more properly a bay, as it has no current except when agitated by the wind.

IOLA.—The name of two places—one in Calhoun county, containing a post-office—the other, on the Ocklawaha River, 50 miles above its mouth.

ISTEEN HATCHEE RIVER.—In La Fayette county.

JACKSON COUNTY.—Located in West Florida. County-seat, Marianna.

JACKSONVILLE.—The commercial mart, or great *entrepôt*, of Florida. In Duval county, on the St. John's River.

JASPER.—County-seat of Hamilton county. Post-office.

JEFFERSON COUNTY.—County-seat, Monticello.

JENNINGS.—In Hamilton county, near the Georgia line. Post-office.

JUPITER NARROWS.—On the Atlantic coast, near New Smyrna.

KEY LARGO.—The longest on the coast of Florida.

KEY WEST.—County-seat of Monroe county. Post-office.

KEY BISCAYNE.—Small settlement. County-seat of Dade county. Post-office.

KING'S ROAD.—Built by Governor Grant, from New Smyrna to St. Mary's, *via* St. Augustine and Jacksonville.

KISSIME RIVER.—In Brevard county.

KNOX HILL.—A Scotch settlement in West Florida. Post-office.

LA FAYETTE COUNTY.—In South Florida, bounded by the Suwanee River. County-seat, New Troy.

LAKE BUTLER.—County-seat of Bradford county.

LAKE CITY.—A place of resort for asthmatics. County-seat of Columbia county. Post-office.

LAKE EUSTIS.—In Orange county. Post-office.

LAKE GRIFFIN.—Near Leesburg, on Lake Griffin. Rapidly improving. Post-office.

LAKE HARNEY.—A resort in midwinter for excursionists, located partly in Volusia and Orange counties. It is 225 miles above Jacksonville.

LAKE OKEECHOBEE.—The largest lake in Florida, extending over an area of more than 65 square miles.

LAKE VIEW.—On the east bank of Lake George. Post-office.

LAKE WORTH.—Near the Atlantic coast, north of Miami River.

LAWTEY.—Near Trail Bridge. The Chicago Colony has located here, established a hotel, built many residences, planted orange-groves and other fruits.

LA VILLA.—A suburban town near Jacksonville.

LEESBURG.—County-seat of Sumter county. A fine, thrifty, growing place.

LEON COUNTY.—County-seat, Tallahassee.

LEVY COUNTY.—Borders on the Gulf. County-seat, Bronson.

LEVYVILLE.—In Levy county, west of Bronson.

LIBERTY.—In Hamilton county, near the Georgia Line.

LIBERTY COUNTY.—A tract of land known as the Forbes Purchase, bounded west by the Appalachicola River.

LITTLE RIVER.—In Gadsden county.

LIVE OAK.—In Suwanee county, its principal importance being attributable to the junction of railroads. Post-office, telegraph-station.

LOTUS.—In Jackson county, south of Marianna.

LOWER WHITE SPRING.—On the Suwanee River, in Hamilton county. Remarkable for its medicinal properties in curing gout and rheumatism.

MADISON.—County-seat of Madison county. Post-office, telegraph-station, good accommodations.

MADISON COUNTY.—Belongs to the undulating portion of the State. County-seat, Madison.

MAGNOLIA.—A winter-resort on the St. John's, 28 miles above Jacksonville. In Clay county.

MANATEE.—A very nice, flourishing town, on the Gulf coast, in Manatee county. Post-office.

MANATEE COUNTY.—County-seat, Pine Level. Celebrated for its extensive cattle-ranges.

MANATEE RIVER.—A short, navigable stream, in Manatee county.

Florida Gazetteer. 489

MANDARIN.—Located on the east bank of the St. John's, 15 miles above Jacksonville. Post-office.

MARIANNA.—County-seat of Jackson county, 30 miles west of the Chattahoochee River.

MARION COUNTY.—One of the central counties of East Florida. Noted for its fertility of soil and superabundance of hummock-lands.

MAYPORT.—Situated at the mouth of St. John's River. It was named from May River, so called by the French.

MARY ESTHER.—Small settlement in Santa Rosa county, West Florida. Post-office.

MATANZAS INLET.—A body of water separating Anastasia Island from the main-land.

MELLONVILLE.—On the St. John's River (here called Lake Monroe), 200 miles above Jacksonville.

MERRITT'S ISLAND.—In Volusia county, and remarkable for the mildness of its climate.

MIAMI RIVER.—In Dade county. Has its source in the Everglades, and empties into Biscayne Bay.

MICANOPY.—On the hack-line, 15 miles from Gainesville, in Alachua county. Supposed to occupy the site of the ancient village, Cuscowilla.

MICCOSUKEE.—Situated in Leon county, near a lake of the same name.

MIDWAY.—A lumber port in Gadsden county, West Florida. Post-office.

MILLWOOD.—On the Chattahoochee River, in Jackson county.

MILTON.—County-seat of Santa Rosa county. Post-office. Fine facilities for loading ships with lumber.

MITCHELL.—In Escambia county, near the Alabama line.

MOLINA.—Situated on the Escambia River, West Florida. Post-office.

MONROE COUNTY.—County-seat, Key West, Gulf of Mexico.

MONTICELLO.—County-seat of Jefferson county. Post-office, telegraph-station. Near this town was located the old Murat plantation, called "Liponia."

MONTICELLO JUNCTION.—Where a branch road connects with the Jacksonville and Pensacola Railroad.

MOSS BLUFF.—A landing on the Ocklawaha River, 140 miles from its mouth.

Mount Royal.—A landing on the east bank of the St. John's, 109 miles above Jacksonville.

Mount Vernon.—At the confluence of the Flint and Chattahoochee Rivers, in Jackson county.

Mulberry Grove.—In Duval county, 11 miles above Jacksonville, on the St. John's River.

Musquito Inlet.—Near Indian River, in Volusia county.

Myakka.—A small stream of water in Manatee county, South Florida.

Nassau County.—Includes Amelia Island, on which is located Fernandina.

Neal's Landing.—A commercial point on the Chattahoochee River. Post-office.

Newnansville.—An old settled town in Alachua county. Stage-line from Gainesville. Post-office.

Newport.—In former times a trading-point, 3 miles from Wakulla Spring.

New River, or Santa Fe.—Rises in Santa Fe Lake. It forms a natural bridge by sinking into the earth and rising again.

New Smyrna.—On the Halifax River, in Volusia county. Post-office.

New Troy.—A small settlement on the Suwanee River, and county-seat of La Fayette county. Post-office.

North River.—An inlet forming a part of the harbor at St. Augustine.

Oak Bluff.—Near Leesburg, Orange county. Post-office.

Oakfield.—In Escambia county, West Florida, on the Florida and Alabama Railroad.

Ocala.—Near the old Indian settlement of Ocali, mentioned by De Soto. County-seat of Marion county. Post-office.

Ocklawaha River.—A narrow stream formed from springs and lakes, which discharges its waters into the St. John's, 25 miles above Pilatka.

Okahumkee.—The terminus of navigation on the Ocklawaha River, 275 miles above Pilatka. Post-office.

Old Town.—A settlement in La Fayette county, on Suwanee River. Post-office.

Olustee.—In Baker county, on the railroad. Post-office. In 1864 a battle was fought here between the Federals and Confederates, resulting in the defeat and loss of 1,200 Union troops.

ORANGE BLUFF.—A landing on the St. John's, 140 miles above Jacksonville.

ORANGE COUNTY.—County-seat, Orlando. It is situated partly on Lake Monroe.

ORANGE MILLS.—A landing on the east bank of the St. John's, in Putnam county, 64 miles above Jacksonville. Post-office.

ORANGE POINT.—In Putnam county, on the St. John's, 103 miles above Jacksonville.

ORANGE SPRING.—A sulphur spring in Marion county, on the Ocklawaha River, 35 miles above its mouth—formerly a resort for the afflicted. Post-office.

ORLANDO.—County-seat of Orange county. Post-office.

OTTER CREEK.—Station and eating-house on the West India Transit Railroad, 19 miles from Cedar Keys. Post-office.

PALMETTO.—A station on the West India Transit Railroad, Levy county.

PALMETTO LANDING.—On the Ocklawaha River, 78 miles above its mouth.

PEASE CREEK.—A large, navigable stream, flowing into Charlotte Harbor, on the Gulf coast.

PENSACOLA.—County-seat of Escambia county. Post-office.

PERDIDO MILLS.—A new settlement in the pine-woods, which promises to be the finest lumber-mart in the South.

PERDIDO RIVER.—A tributary of Perdido Bay, in West Florida.

PICOLATA.—A landing on the St. John's River, 45 miles above its mouth. Post-office.

PILATKA.—On the west bank of the St. John's River, 75 miles above its month. County-seat of Putnam county. Post-office.

PINE LEVEL.—County-seat of Manatee county. Post-office.

POLK COUNTY.—County-seat, Bartow.

PORT ORANGE.—In Volusia county, between Halifax River and the Atlantic Ocean. Post-office.

PORT WASHINGTON.—In Walton county, on the south side of Choctawhatchee Bay.

POWELLTON.—Station on the Florida Railroad, Escambia county, West Florida. Post-office.

PUNTA RASSA.—On the Gulf coast, in Monroe county. Post-office and submarine-telegraph station.

PUTNAM COUNTY.—County-seat, Pilatka, through which the St. John's River flows.

QUINCY.—County-seat of Gadsden county, where a case of hydrophobia has never been known, nor an instance of sun-stroke occurred. Post-office and telegraph-station.

REMINGTON PARK.—A resort on the east bank of the St. John's, 25 miles above Jacksonville. Post-office.

RIVERSIDE.—A finely-located, prospective city, on the St. John's, near Jacksonville.

ROSE HEAD.—Located in Taylor county. Post-office.

ROSEWOOD.—On the West India Transit Railroad, 10 miles from Cedar Keys. Post-office.

SALLIE'S CAMP.—Landing on the upper St. John's, 229 miles from Jacksonville.

SANDERSON.—County-seat of Baker county. Post-office, telegraph-station.

SANDY BLUFF.—Landing on the Ocklawaha River, 68 miles above its mouth.

SAND POINT.—Seven miles from Salt Lake, on the St. John's, and 30 miles from Canaveral Light-house.

SANFORD.—It is 199 miles from Jacksonville. Contains a sanitarium, besides all necessary comforts for the sick and well. Post-office.

SAN MATEO.—In Putnam county, on the St. John's, 80 miles above Jacksonville. Post-office.

ST. SEBASTIAN RIVER.—An estuary which is crossed in going from the depot to St. Augustine.

SANTA FE.—A settlement in Bradford county, near Starke. Post-office.

SANTA FE RIVER.—A tributary of the Suwanee River.

SANTA ROSA COUNTY.—County-seat, Milton. Contains large milling interests.

SARASOTA.—In Manatee county, on the Gulf coast, 12 miles from Manatee, South Florida.

SHADY GROVE.—A settlement in Taylor county. Post-office.

SHARP'S FERRY.—Landing on the Ocklawaha River, 114 miles above its mouth.

SHELL BANK.—Landing on the St. John's, 193 miles above Jacksonville.

SHOAL RIVER.—A stream of water in Walton county, which empties into Pensacola Bay.

SILVER SPRING.—A most remarkable phenomenon in nature—the

principal source of the Ocklawaha River, 100 miles from its mouth. In Marion county. Post-office.

SOPCHOPPY.—In Wakulla county. Post-office.

SPRING HILL.—In Hernando county, west of Brooksville.

SPRUCE CREEK.—In Volusia county, 8 miles from Smyrna.

STARKE.—In Bradford county, 73 miles from Fernandina, on the West India Transit Railroad. Post-office.

STARK'S LANDING.—On the Ocklawaha River, 155 miles above its mouth, in Sumter county.

ST. AUGUSTINE.—In St. John's county. Remarkable for being the first settled town in the United States. Post-office.

ST. JOHN'S COUNTY.—County-seat, St. Augustine. Bounded on the west by the St. John's River.

ST. JOHN'S RIVER.—A remarkable stream of water, which has its source in the Everglades of South Florida. It is about 350 miles in length, flowing north to Jacksonville, where it makes an abrupt turn to the east, and discharges into the Atlantic Ocean.

ST. JOSEPH'S.—In Calhoun county, West Florida.

ST. LUCIE SOUND.—A name given to a portion of Indian River, in Brevard county.

ST. MARK'S.—Terminus of the Pensacola and Mobile (St. Mark's Branch) Railroad. It is in Wakulla county, at the head of Appalachee Bay. Post-office.

ST. MARK'S RIVER.—Considered by most persons to be the reäppearance of Lake Miccosukee which loses itself in the earth.

ST. MARY'S RIVER.—Rises in the enchanted land of the Yemassee Indians, forming a short boundary-line between Georgia and Florida.

SUWANEE COUNTY.—County-seat, Live Oak. Well timbered with pine. Has marl shell-beds and white clay. In the center of the county is a white stone, soft when dug, but hardening on exposure to the air—used for chimney-backs and furnaces.

SUWANEE RIVER.—Rises in Southern Georgia, and empties into the Gulf, near Cedar Keys; navigable for small steamers as far as Troy.

SUWANEE SHOALS.—In Columbia county. Post-office.

TALLAHASSEE.—Capital of the State. County-seat of Leon county. Located by Governor Walton, and named by his daughter Octavia. The State-house and Court-house were built by the United States Government.

Tampa.—County-seat of Hillsboro county. On Tampa Bay. Terminus of the tri-weekly hack-line from Gainesville.

Taylor County.—On the Gulf coast, south of Madison.

Temple.—Station on the West India Transit Railroad, 78 miles from Fernandina.

Titusville.—A flourishing settlement in Volusia county, on the west bank of Indian River. It contains a fine sanitarium for invalids. Post-office.

Trail Ridge.—The highest point on the West India Railroad, 62 miles from Fernandina.

Tocoi.—Landing on the east bank of the St. John's, 52 miles above Jacksonville. Post-office.

Ucheeanna.—County-seat of Walton county, West Florida. Post-office.

Uchee Valley.—Named from the Uchee tribe of Indians, who formerly occupied it. In Walton county.

Vallombrosa.—Settlement in Washington county, West Florida.

Vernon.—County-seat of Washington county, West Florida. Post-office.

Volusia.—Landing on the east bank of the St. John's, 187 miles above Jacksonville. In Volusia county. Post-office.

Volusia County.—County-seat, Enterprise.

Wacahoola.—A settlement near Flemington, Marion county. Post-office.

Wacassa River.—Meaning "Cow Range River"—a corruption of Indian and Spanish. In Levy county.

Wacassa River.—A stream flowing through Jefferson county, and emptying into the Gulf of Mexico.

Wakulla County.—In this county is the celebrated Wakulla Spring. The principal settlements are St. Mark's, Crawfordsville, and Sopchoppy.

Wakulla River.—Rises in Wakulla Spring, and flows into the Gulf, near St. Mark's.

Waldo.—On the West India Transit Railroad, in Alachua county, 12 miles from Gainesville. Post-office.

Walton County.—County-seat, Ucheeanna, West Florida.

Warrington.—On Escambia Bay, 7 miles from Pensacola. Post-office.

Washington County.—County-seat, Vernon, West Florida.

Waukeenah.—Settlement in Jefferson county.

WEBBVILLE.—A settlement in Jackson county, near Marianna.

WEELAUNEE.—Located in Jefferson county. Post-office.

WEKIVA.—Settlement in the Sanford Grant, on the upper St. John's. Post-office.

WEKIVA RIVER.—A stream in Orange county, flowing into the St. John's.

WELAKA.—Landing on the east bank of the St. John's, 100 miles above Jacksonville, opposite the mouth of the Ocklawaha River. Post-office.

WELLBORN.—On the Jacksonville, Pensacola, and Mobile Railroad, 94 miles from Tallahassee. Post-office.

WITHLACOOCHEE RIVER.—Rises in Sumter county, and empties into the Gulf, near Cedar Keys.

WOODLAND.—In Putnam county, on Dunn's Lake. Post-office.

WOOLSEY.—A settlement on Escambia Bay, in Escambia county.

WYOMING.—A suburb of Jacksonville, Duval county. Unimportant.

YELLOW RIVER.—Rises in Walton county, and empties into Pensacola Bay, near Milton, West Florida.

THE END.

INDEXES.

Index to *Petals Plucked from Sunny Climes.*

Acosta, Domingo, 49
Alachua County, 262–63; incidents of Seminole War, 263–65
Albion, 269
Alligators, 373–74
Amelia Island, 23–24, 478
Amelia River, 28
American Sponge Co., 322
Anastasia Island, 215, 231–32, 447, 463, 476
Appalachicola River, 351
Archer, 269
Arredondo, 269
Arredondo, Antonio de, 184, 187–88
Atlanta, 17, 346, 350
Atlantic & Gulf Central Railroad, 353
Atlantic, Gulf & West India Transit Railroad, 24–25
Auhayca (Tallahassee), 333
Aury, Louis, 24

Bainbridge, 350–51
Barnard, T., 339
Bartram, John, 20–21, 122
Bartram, William, 110, 332
Battons, 269
Big Cypress Swamp, 123, 125, 248, 251; in Seminole War, 123, 131; described, 132–33
Bimini, 441
Black Creek, 338
Boca Grande, 310
Bowlegs, Billy, 264, 287
Bronson, 269
Bryan, Mary E., 343-46
Byrd, J. H., 341

Cabot, Sebastian, 439–40, 477
Call, Richard K., 124

Indexes.

Caloosahatchee River, 125, 255
Campbell, General, 356
Cape Roman, 313, 319
Cape Sable, 314
Cape San Antonio, 385, 388
Carlton House, Jacksonville, 64
Castellos de los Santos Reyes, 424–25, 428
Castle Folly, 343
Castle San Marcos, 158; history and description, 183–89, 476
Cedar Keys, 111, 270–72
Cemetario de Espeda, 435–37
Charleston, 19, 104
Charlotte Harbor, 310
Chattahoochee, 350
Chécho-ter, 104
Chekika, 129, 243
Cherokee Indians, 117, 479
Chitto Island, 247, 249
Christ Church, Pensacola, 377
Chuleotah, 73–74
Cienfuegos, 388–98
Clear Water Harbor, 272
Clinch, General Duncan L., 101–2
Coacoochee, 49, 128, 145–51, 289–95
Cock-fighting, 409–10
Coligny, Gaspard de, 447, 459, 468
Columbia County, 327
Columbus, Christopher, 387, 440
Conchs, 318, 320
Convent of St. Helena, St. Augustine, 374
Cow Ford, 35
Coxetter, Louis, 48
Crackers, 58–66; derivation of term, 62–63, hospitality of, 64–65
Creek Indians, 104, 110, 117, 130, 235, 479
Cruces, 399–400
Cuba, 124, 285, 312, 317, 320, 338, 356, 360, 378, 387–438, 441, 443, 470; sea voyage to, 378–87; historical sketch, 387, 392–93; Cienfuegos described, 388–92, 394–98; revolutionaries, 393–94, 403; travel in, 399–400, 402–4; chicken (cock) fighting, 409; Matanzas described, 410–19; Cavern of El Cueva de Bellamar, 419–22; Havana, 425, 438, history, 425, described, 427–32, cathedral and religion in, 432–35, and Cemetario de Espeda, 435–37
Cumberland Island, 21, 478

Dade, Major F. L., 99–100
Dade Massacre, 89, 99–100

Dalton, Private, 97
de León, Ponce, 210, 440–43
de Soto, Hernando, 82–83, 89, 114, 118, 286–87, 333, 444
Dickens, Charles, 324
Dictator (steamboat), 48
Dixon, John, 325
"Doctor, the," 161
Dolphin River, 447, 448, 453, 454, 455
Drake, Sir Francis, 155, 476
Driggers, Matt, and Great Mastodon Hunt, 84–86
Dummit, Douglass, Plantation, 241
Dungenness, 21
Dunn, John F., 268

Edwards, John, 343
Egmont Key, 305
El Cueva de Bellamer, 419–22
El Moro, 424–25, 428
Emathla, Charlie, 94, 98
Escambia Bay, 360, 373
Espiritu Santo Bay, 333, 445, 446
Eufaula, 350
Everglades, 117, 123, 125, 245, 246, 247, 252, 253, 257, 259; described, 254–55

Ferdinand Del Jauga Bay, 388
Fernandina, 19, 21, 28, 269; historical sketch and description, 23–27
Fernandina Beach, 25–27
Florida, early history of, 439–79
Florida State Fair, 46–47
Florida State Penitentiary, 350
Fort Brooke, 97, 99, 289
Fort Caroline, 34, 448, 449–51, 452, 453, 455, 456, 457, 458–63, 469, 475, 477, 478; renamed San Mateo, 459; as San Mateo, 473–74; massacre at, 459–63
Fort Clinch, 28
Fort Dallas, 246, 253
Fort Diego, 479
Fort Don Carlos de Barrancas, 357–58, 360
Fort Francis de Pupa, 479
Fort George Island, 29
Fort Keas, 126
Fort King, 93–94, 95, 96, 97, 98–99, 100
Fort Lauderdale, 252
Fort Marion, 103, 146–47, 183–89, 192, 198–99, 210, 230–31
Fort Matanzas, 237–39

Fort Mellon, 129
Fort Moosa, 158, 185, 479
Fort Moultrie, 234
Fort Myers (spelled Myres), 311
Fort Peyton, 103
Fort Pickens, 355, 359
Fort Picolata, 52–53
Fort Pierce, 133, 150, 257
Fort San Mateo, 459, 473–74, 478. *See also* Fort Caroline
Fort St. Bernard, 359
Fort St. Michael, 356, 359
Fort Taylor, 323
Franciscan Order, 42, 471
Freedmen's Bank (of Jacksonville), 40–41

Gadsden, James, 93
Gaines, Edmund P., 100, 265
Gaines, Mrs. Myra Clark, 265–66
Gainesville, 265–67, 268, 269, 319
Gálvez, Count, 356, 359
Garcias, J., 141
Gourgues, Dominique de, 471–74
Green Cove Springs, 51
Greene, Nathanael, 21
Groves, H., 140
Gulf House, Bainbridge, 351
Gulf of Mexico, 262, 312, 323, 334, 385, 388

Hadjo, Mico, 100, 264
Harney, William S., 125, 127, 129, 245–55
Harris, E. J., 82
Hart, Hubbard L., 53–54, 88
Hartley, George, 49
Hartley, Nathan, 49
Hartley, William, 49
Hattie Baker (steamboat), 135–38
Havana, 245, 318, 319, 320, 399, 424, 425–38, 477, 479; history, 425; described, 427–32; cathedral and religion in, 432–35; and Cemetario de Espeda, 435–37
Hawkins, Capt. John, 450
Hereda, Don Alonzo Fernando, 187–88
Hernandez, Joseph M., 102–3, 146
Hibernia, 50
Hillsboro Inlet, 253
Houghton, R. B., 345
House, F. A., 82
Huguenots, 155, 447, 449, 453, 457, 459–63

Indexes.

Indian burial mounds, 106–20
Indian Key Massacre, 241–44
Indian Lake, 327
Indian River, 123, 133–34, 246, 257
International Telegraph, 312, 319; building of, 319–20
Isle of Pines, 384

Jackson, Andrew, 35, 93, 96, 265, 280, 319, 359–61
Jacksonville, 34, 57, 58, 64, 121, 141, 330; description of, 35–48; population of, 37; suburbs of, 37; religion and churches, 38–41; journalism in, 41–42; annual state fair at, 46–47
Jamaica, 477
Jefferson County, 330
Jesuits, 470–71
Jesup, Thomas S., 102–3, 124
Jones, Sam, 128–29, 249, 251
Jumper, 94, 99

Kennedy, Pat, 85
Key Biscayne, 246, 259
Key West, 296, 314–15, 356; Indian history, 315; description and general history, 316; conchs and salvagers, 318–19; cigar-making in, 320–22; sponge-industry, 322–23; fortifications, 323–24
Kiowa Indians, 230

Lafitte, Jean, 310
Lake City, 327; described, 328–329; 330
Lake DeSoto, 327
Lake Dunham, 89
Lake Eustace, 87
Lake George, 122
Lake Griffin, 87
Lake Hamburg, 327
Lake Harney, 114, 123, 133
Lake Harris, 87, 88
Lake Isabella, 327
Lake Jessup, 115
Lake Monroe, 123
Lake Okeechobee (spelled Okachobee, Ogeechubee), 126, 150, 256
Lake Santa Fe, 262
Lake Superior, 117
Lake Thompson, 126
Laudonnière, René, 29–30, 34, 449, 451, 455, 456, 457, 459, 460, 472–73, 475
LeConte, Prof. John, 75; describes Silver Springs, 76–81
Lee, Light Horse Harry, 22

Lee, Robert E., 22
Leesburg, 88
Le Moyne de Morgues, Jacques, 459, 475
Leon County, 343
Levy County, 269
Lindsley, George W., 374
Little River, 246
Live Oak Camp, 41
Loada, Don Quiroga, 198
Luna, Tristán de, 355
Lundy, Archibald, 158

McBride, Julia, 345
McGregor, Gregor, 23
McIntosh, Capt. Rory, 157
Macomb, Alexander, 124
Macon, Ga., 17
McRae, Rev., 264
McWhir, Dr., 158
Magnolia, 50
Manatee, 110, 271, 272; described, 273–80; historical sketch, 280–81; paleontological sketch, 281–84; 285, 287
Manatee Spring, 349
Mandarin, 48; described, 49; historical sketch, 49–50; 158
March, Dr. Daniel F., 201–2
Marion County, 76, 82; as "backbone of Florida," 84; 268
Mastodons, 78; and legend of Matt Driggers, 84–86; at Manatee, 281–84
Matanzas (Cuba), 399, 410–19, 424
Matanzas Bay, 413–16, 423
Matanzas River, 237, 240, 447
Mather, Solomon, 340
Mayflower (steamboat), 215–16, 219
Mayport, 29
Mellonville, 122, 123
Menéndez de Avilés, Pedro (spelled Melendez), 155, 451–52, 454, 455, 457, 458–71, 474–75, 476
Miami, 319
Micanopy, 99, 102, 264–65
Micasukee Indians, 93, 130, 150
Ming, Fred L., 95
Mitchell House, Bainbridge, 351
Mobile & Pensacola Railroad, 350
Molpus, William, 49
Montgomery (Ala.), 350
Montiano, Don Manuel, 184

Monticello, 330–31
Morgues, Jacques Le Moyne de, 459, 475
Moro Castle, 424–25, 428
Mound-builders, 106–20
Murat, Achilles, 341–43
Murat, Joachin, 341–42

Narváez, Pánfilo de, 272, 285, 444
Negroes, in Pensacola government, 372; in Pensacola schools, 374–76; in Cuba, 407–9
Negro Fort, 479
New Orleans, 151, 266
New River, 252–53
New Smyrna, 110, 239–41
New York, 82, 151, 160, 237, 287, 350
New York Herald, 80
Nichols, Colonel, 359
North Beach, 214–19

Ocala, 82, 83–84, 268, 445
Ochusa (Pensacola), 356
Ocklawaha (Oklawaha) River, 54, 58, 66–68, 70, 76, 84, 89, 121, 338; described, 55–57
Oglethorpe, James, 18, 20, 23, 158, 185, 232, 478–79
Okahumkee (Indian chief), 72–73
Okahumkee (steamboat), 54, 57, 69
Okefenokee (Okafinokee) Swamp Expedition, 354
Old Town, 28
Oliveros, B., 191–92, 200
Orange City, 269
Orange Lake, 267–68
Orange Springs, 57
Ortiz, Juan, 285–86
Osceola, 93, 95–96, 98–104, 145, 257
Otter Creek, 269

Palmetto houses described, 303
Pascua Florida, 441
Payne, Chief, 264
Payne's Landing, 89; treaty of, 91–93; 96
Pease Creek, 148
Pelicer Creek, 103
Pensacola, 355, history and fortifications, 356–61; described, 361–69; and yellow fever epidemics, 371–72; churches and schools, 374–77
Pensacola Bay, 447

Perdido (Lost) Bay, 372
Philip II of Spain, 451, 470
Philip, King (Seminole), 114
Picolata, 51–52, 140, 477
Pilatka (Palatka), 30, 52–54, 76, 87
Pilatka Herald, 53
Pine Keys, 249
Planter's Hotel, Tallahassee, 339
Point Blanco, 310
Ponce de León, 210, 440–43
Porpoises, 368
Port Royal, 448, 449, 475
Prophet, the (Creek Indian), 128, 249
Puerto Rico (spelled Porto), 440, 442
Punta Rassa, 311, 314, 329
Putnam County, 52
Putnam House, Palatka, 52

Quincy, 349–50
Quitman, Ga., 353

Raleigh, Sir Walter, 475–76, 477, 478
Ribaut, Jean, 370, 447–49, 451, 452, 453, 455, 456, 457, 464, 468–69
River of Dolphins, 447, 448, 453, 454, 455
Rome, Ga., 445

St. Augustine, 51, 52 53, 102, 103, 139, 140, 141, 142, 143, 214, 231, 234, 235, 237, 238, 255, 263, 357, 441, 443, 447, 469, 470, 474, 476, 477, 478, 479; bishop of, 53–54, 167; and incidents of Seminole War, 142–48; winter in, compared to New York, 151–53; historical sketch, 155–59, 454–55, 457–58; descriptions of, 156–57, 158–61, 166–72, 198–211, 219–23; people of, 162–64, 224; cathedral and religion in, 173–82; atrocities at, 190–92; sea wall, 198, 220
St. Augustine Hotel, 219, 223
St. George's Island, 471
St. Helena, Convent of, St. Augustine, 374
St. Helena's Sound, 478
St. James Hotel, Jacksonville, 64
St. Johns Bluff, 34, 450
St. Johns Railroad, 142
St. Johns River, 28, 29, 30, 34, 48, 76, 105, 110, 121, 133, 327, 439; named River of May, 447; as River of May, 449, 452, 453, 459, 477, 478; conditions at bar, 28
St. Joseph's Academy, St. Augustine, 165

Indexes.

St. Mark's, 51–52, 190, 346
St. Mary's Convent, St. Augustine, 166–67
St. Marys River, 23
St. Sebastian River, 185
St. Simon Island, 20
Sam Jones Island, 248, 252
Sand Key Light, 314
San Juan de Pirias, 454
San Mateo, Fort, 459–63, 470, 473–74. *See also* Fort Caroline
San Mateo River, 470, 471, 474
Santa Maria Bay, 355
Santee (steamboat), 241
Santo Domingo, 399
Sarasota Bay, 392
Savannah, 17–19, 353
Savannah Morning News, 225
Savannah River, 448
Secoffee, 263
Seloue (St. Augustine), 445, 458, 476
Seminole Indians, 117, 130, 150, 234, 264
Seminole War, 90–104, 123–25, 131, 140–41, 142–53, 241–44, 245–56, 289–95, 334–40; and Mandarin massacre, 49–50; and Dade massacre, 89, 99–100; and Treaty of Payne's Landing, 91–93
Semi-Tropical, Jacksonville newspaper, 42
Silver Spring River, 76–77
Silver Springs, 69; described, 70–72, 75–82; Indian legend of, 72–75; 86
Slavery, in Cuba, 407–9
Snake Warrior's Island, 247
Soto, Bernardo del, 385
Soto, Hernando de, 82–83, 89, 114, 118, 286–87, 333, 444
Spinner, General F. E., 47
Starke, 262
Stowe, Dr. Calvin E., 39
Stowe, Harriet Beecher, 39, 48
Sun and Press, Jacksonville newspaper, 42

Tallahassee, 51, 330; founding, 333; location, 333–34; incidents of Seminole War, 334–40; 341–43, 346, 445
Talleyrand, Marquis de, 34
Tampa, 110, 118, 151, 271, 285–95, 296, 445; historical sketch, 286–87, 289; described, 287–89; incidents of Seminole War, 289–95
Tampa Bay, 285, 305, 313
Tapoquoi, Indian village, 199

Indexes.

Taylor, Zachary, 125, 281
Ten Thousand Islands, 298
Terrasilla Island, 298
Thomasville, 351–53
Thompson, Capt. Wiley, 89, 96, 98–99
Thrasher House, Lake City, 327
Tiger Tail, 256–57, 258, 316–17
Tocoi, 139, 142
Tourists described, 135–38, 209, 304–5
Turnbull, Dr. Andrew, 239–40
Tustenuggee's Island, 247

Valdosta, Ga., 353–54
Valls, Jose, 224
Valls, S. B., 224–25
Verot, Bishop, 167
Villaroel, Gonzalo de, 459

Wahoo Swamp, 98–99
Wakulla River, 347
Wakulla Spring, 346, 349
Waldo, 262
Waldo House, 262
Walton, G. W., 141
Washing Bayou, 369
Washington, George and Martha, 324, 342
Wasp, U.S.S., 18
Weedman, Dr. Philip, Sr., 140–41
Weenonah, 72–75
Welaka, 121
Wesley, John, 20
Western, or Plains Indians, 194–97
West Florida, 31
West India Transfer Railroad, 270
West Indies, 320, 476–77
White Horse, Chief, 230
Whitney, J. F., 216
Wild Cat (Coacoochee), 49, 128, 145–51, 289–95
Wilson, J. L., 204
Withlacoochee, Battle of, 102
Withlacoochee River, 89
Worth, Col. W. J., 50, 150, 271, 289–93

Yamacraw Indians, 18
Yellow Fever, 371–72
Yemassee Indians, 23, 110, 478

Indexes.

Index to the Introduction.

Amelia Island, *xiv*
Archives of the Indies, Seville, *xxvii, xxviii, xxix, xxx*
Atlanta, *xxv*
Averette, Mrs. Annie, *xxviii, xxix*

Bosque de Segovia, *xxx*
Brooks, Abbie M., *xiii–xxxii*; love of anonymity, *xii, xxv–xxvi, xxix, xxxi–xxxii*; as journalist and writer, *xiv–xvi, xxv*; travels abroad, *xiv, xxvi, xxvii*; as historiographer, *xiii, xx–xxi, xxiii, xxv, xxvi, xxvii, xxviii–xxxi*; in Florida, *xiv, xvi–xx, xv, xxvi*; attitude towards tourists, *xix*; life and work, *xxiv–xxix*; health, *xv*; as Silvia Sunshine, *xiii, xv*

Chapel Hill, N.C., *xxvi*
Chuleotah, *xv*
Cienfuegos, *xviii*
Coacoochee, *xxii*
Cuba, *xiv, xviii, xxvi, xxx*

Driggers, Matt, *xv*

Egypt, *xvi*

Ferdinand of Spain, *xxiv*
Fernandina, *xiv, xxx*
Florida, *xiii, xiv, xx, xxi, xxv, xxvi, xxx, xxxi, xxxii*
Florida history, historiography, *xiii, xiv, xviii, xx, xxi, xxii, xxiv–xxv, xxvii, xxviii, xxxii*
Florida Times-Union, Jacksonville, *xxix*
Fort Caroline, *xxi, xxx*
Fort Marion, *xxi*
France, French Florida, *xxi, xxx*

"Great Mastodon Hunt," *xv*
Grenier, Nicholas, *xxx*

Havana, *xviii*

Indian Key, *xxiii*
Indians, *xxi, xxii, xxiii*
Isabella of Spain, *xxiv*

Jacksonville, *xvi, xxx*
José, Santiago, Bishop of Cuba, *xxx*

Indexes.

Key West, *xvii*
King of Spain, *xxix*

Library of Congress, *xxvi, xxviii, xxxii*
Lowery, Woodbury, *xxvii, xxviii, xxix, xxxi*

Madrid, *xxvii, xxx*
Menéndez de Avilés, Pedro, *xxix, xxx*
Mormons, *xvi*

Nashville, *xxvi*
News, The, St. Augustine, *xxix*
North Beach, St. Augustine, *xviii*
North Carolina Historical Collection, *xxvi*

Oklawaha River, *xviii*
Osceola, *xxii*

Payne's Landing, Treaty of, *xxii*
Petals Plucked from Sunny Climes, xiii, xx, xxiv, xxv–xxvi, xxvii, xxviii, xxix, xxxi, xxxii
Philip II, King of Spain, *xxx*

St. Augustine, *xviii, xix, xx, xxi, xxiii–xxiv, xxviii, xxix, xxx, xxxi*
St. Augustine Institute of Science and Historical Society, *xxviii*
St. James Hotel, Jacksonville, *xvi*
Salt Lake City, *xvi*
Seminole Indians, *xxi, xxii, xxiii*
Seminole War, *xxi, xxii*
Seville, Spain, *xxvii, xxviii*
Silver Springs, *xv*
Smith, Buckingham, *xxvii, xxxi*
Southern Historical Collection, *xxvi*
Southern Methodist Publishing House, *xxvi*
Spain, Spanish Florida, *xx, xxi, xxiii–xxiv, xxvii, xxviii, xxix, xxx, xxxi*
Stowe, Dr. Calvin, *xviii*
Stowe, Harriet Beecher, *xviii*
Suárez, Sr. Don Antonio, *xxvii*
Sunshine, Silvia, *xiii, xv*

Tennessee, *xxvi*

University of North Carolina, *xxvi*
Unwritten History of St. Augustine, The, xxviii–xxxi

Weenonah, *xv*
Wild Cat, *xxii*

www.ingramcontent.com/pod-product-compliance
Lightning Source LLC
Chambersburg PA
CBHW031747220426
43662CB00007B/312